CONTENTS

continued

ACKNOWLEDGEMENTS

We are very grateful to the Department of Sociology, the Office of the Provost and the President and the Sponsored Programs Office of John Jay College of Criminal Justice for sponsoring the conference that resulted in this book. The organization of the conference and editorial work on the book was also partly supported by a grant from the National Institute on Drug Abuse (1K21DA00242-05), and partly by South Bank University, London. The chapters in this book were subject to an anonymous peer review process, and we would like to thank our reviewers for their helpful and constructive suggestions.

The viewpoints in this book do not necessarily represent the official positions of the U.S. Government, the National Institute on Drug Abuse, John Jay College of Criminal Justice or South Bank University.

Mangai Natarajan
Mike Hough

INTRODUCTION:
ILLEGAL DRUG MARKETS, RESEARCH AND POLICY

by

Mike Hough
South Bank University, London

and

Mangai Natarajan
John Jay College of Criminal Justice, New York

INTRODUCTION

Illicit drug use is widespread across most industrialised countries. The prevalence of illicit use is probably measured best in the United States: at least 14 million people, or 6% of the population, use illicit drugs every month (Office of National Drug Control Policy [ONDCP], 1999). Nor is this pattern of use confined to the U.S. In Britain, for example, around 2 million people use illicit drugs each month, representing 6% of the population aged 16 to 59 (Ramsay and Partridge, 1999).

Only the brave would try to make a precise count of global annual production of illicit drugs. There are some "order of magnitude" figures, however. For example the annual global production of heroin has been put at 550 tonnes (metric tons) per year in the 1990s; the corresponding figure for cocaine in 1996 was 1,000 tonnes (United Nations Drug Control Programme [UNDCP], 1997). Some countries have estimated levels of consumption, though these estimates will also be subject to wide margins of error. In the U.S., the figure for expenditure on illicit drugs in 1995 was put at $57 billion (ONDCP, 1997a). The corresponding figure for the U.K. is £3.9 billion to £8.5 million (Office of National Statistics [ONS], 1999). Even allowing for very substantial imprecision, these figures suggest that the illicit drugs industry accounts for a sizable slice of the gross national product in industrialised countries.

Despite the size of the illicit drugs market, little is known about the structure of the distribution process in different countries, the way in which markets respond to changes in supply and demand, and the impact of enforcement. Expenditure on research has been limited, whether measured against the scale of the business or against public expenditure designed to curtail illicit drug use. Much of the research that *has* been done has been conducted with the primary aim of developing academic theory, with limited attention to the policy implications; some research has positively distanced itself from the concerns of drug control policy. For whatever reason, public and political debate about drugs has remained largely insulated from the body of research that has actually been carried out to date.

We have put this book together in the hope that it may play a part in drawing researchers a little closer to policy and in encouraging politicians and their advisors to engage more willingly with the research community. We do not wish to see a situation in which research is simply the servant of policy. Policy perspectives and priorities should not dominate the research agenda. However research in the field can and should "speak to" policy concerns more explicitly, without necessarily losing any critical edge to its voice.

The book has its origins in a conference that we organised at John Jay College, New York in April 1999. We invited leading academics and policy advisors in the U.S. and Europe to prepare papers that described their most recent research in this field and drew out the implications for drug control policies. The papers are collected together in this book. The purpose of this introduction is to orient the reader to the various themes that emerge from their work.

Varieties of User

While a large number of people engage in illicit drug use in industrialised Western countries, most do so in a relatively controlled way. Their use is restricted largely to cannabis (cf. ONDCP, 1999; Ramsay and Partridge, 1999; European Monitoring Centre for Drugs and Drug Addiction [EMCDDA], 1999; Johnston et al., 1999). A minority engages in heavier use of a wider variety of drugs and a proportion of this minority are chaotic users with serious problems of dependency. Difficulties both of definition and measurement make it hard to estimate what proportion of illicit drug users show dependent or chaotic patterns of use. ONDCP (1997) estimated that in the U.S. in 1995 there were 4 million "hardcore" users of cocaine and 810,000 "hardcore" users of heroin. According to the data by the National

Household Survey of Drug Abuse and DUF (Drug Use Forecasting, now known as ADAM Program for the Arrestees Drug Abuse Monitoring System), the majority of heroin users are hardcore users (ONDCP, 1997a). This estimate defined hardcore users as those who use either drug at least once a week; a significant proportion of these, of course, would maintain nondependent patterns of use. In Britain it has been estimated that between 100,000 and 200,000 people — around 3% of all those who use illicit drugs annually — might be defined as drug-dependent or as having other serious drug-related problems. Problem users may represent a minority of the total, but the sheer quantity of their use means that they will account for a large portion, at least, of expenditures on illicit drugs.

There are wide variations in patterns of drug use both within and among countries. Among drugs of dependence, cocaine (especially as crack) has predominated in the U.S. since the early 1980s even if its use has been declining. In Britain, by contrast, and in most other European countries heroin use easily outstrips that of cocaine (Ramsay and Partridge, 1999; EMCDDA, 1999). However, its use in the U.S. is now increasing. MDMA (methylenedioxymethamphetamine or ecstasy) has become well-embedded in youth culture in many European countries, but less so in the U.S. until recently. At the time of writing, the use of methamphetamine (ice) was well established on the West Coast of the U.S., but less so on the East coast (ONDCP, 1997a). Despite predictions over a period of years that methamphetamine use would sweep across Europe, it remains comparatively rare there.

As might be expected, different types of users typically use different types of retail markets, and these are supported by different types of distribution or supply systems. Howard Parker's research (this volume) discusses how, for recreational users in Britain, the process of acquiring drugs is rarely seen as a retail transaction. He found that networks of friends and acquaintances help each other out, give and receive drugs without payment, and buy drugs in a consortium. By contrast, regular dependent users are more likely to engage in explicit commercial transactions. For example, Murphy and Arroya's study of women users on the West Coast of the U.S. (this volume) paints a picture of an unequivocal retail market, albeit one characterised by high levels of mistrust between buyers and sellers.

Varieties of Retail Market

As with any other type of commodity, illicit drugs are traded within a market through which buyer and seller have to locate one another in order to conduct a transaction. Previous research has described various forms of the retail market system. Curtis and Wendel's chapter in this volume sets out a two-dimensional typology that differentiates forms of retail distribution according to:

- Social organisation — freelancers vs. socially-bonded businesses vs. corporation
- Technical organisation — street-level vs. indoor vs. delivery.

Several studies have documented place-specific markets, such as street-level or indoor markets in Curtis and Wendel's typology. These usually involve the sale of cannabis, heroin, crack or other drugs to anyone who looks like a plausible buyer (e.g., Curtis and Wendel, this volume; Edmunds et al., 1996; Lee, 1996; Johnson et al., 1990). Rengert et al. (this volume) describe how retail markets in Delaware were spatially concentrated in ways that facilitated access both to local users and those users using interstate highways.

It is helpful to refer to these as *open markets*; they are open to any buyer, with no need for any prior introduction to the seller, or other similar barriers to access. For licit transactions, an open market has advantages for both buyers and sellers. Buyers know where to go in order to find the goods they want and can trade quality against price. Sellers are able to maximise customer access. In an illicit market, there are complications including the need to balance access with security. Not only must buyer and seller be cautious of police activity — both overt and undercover — they must also be aware of their own personal safety (Eck, 1995).

The main advantage of an illicit open street market — ease of locating buyers and sellers — is also its major drawback for participants: it renders them vulnerable to policing (Eck, 1995). In response to the risks of enforcement, open markets tend to be transformed into *closed markets*. These are ones in which sellers will only do business with buyers whom they know, or for whom another trusted person will vouch. The degree to which markets are closed — the barriers to access put in the way of new buyers — will depend largely on the level of threat posed by the police. Intensive policing can quickly transform open markets into closed ones. Johnson and colleagues (this volume) describe the evolution of New York City crack markets, which moved from open systems to closed ones in response to enforcement. Throughout the decade covered by his research, the distribution system serving the retail market remained fairly structured, with clear task differentiation. Similar patterns of adaptation have been described by Hamid, 1998; Edmunds et al., 1998; and May et al., 1999.

If retail drug markets have always been responsive to policing, their capacity to adapt has been greatly extended by the emergence of mobile phones. The pace of change has been so rapid that ethnographic work conducted before the mid-1990s is only a very partial guide to the way in which retail drug markets now function. Until the mid-1990s, street sellers tended to operate in specific, well-defined places. This was to allow buyers to locate them with ease. Increasingly, contact is now made by the buyer ringing the seller's mobile and making an appointment to meet at an agreed (or prespecified) place (Hamid, 1998, Curtis and Wendel, this volume; Edmunds et al., 1996; Chatterton et al., 1995). A variant on this is for delivery systems where drugs are delivered to the buyer's home or other specified locations. Mobile phones thus minimise the risks associated with illicit transactions by making police surveillance largely impractical (Natarajan et al., 1996; Natarajan et al., 1995).

Other developments in communications technology, both licit and illicit, are likely to pose increasing challenges to enforcement. For example, there is a proliferation in the ways in which telephone air time can be bought, or stolen, in ways that render the buyer untraceable. For example, smart cards can be bought that provide a set amount of phone time, which can be accessed from any phone; there are 1-800 companies that pre-sell airtime for cash, and "pay-as-you-go" cell-phones that cannot be linked to the user's name and address. These systems all make it increasingly difficult to maintain effective surveillance. The "cloning" of stolen cell-phones can make surveillance virtually impossible (cf. Natarajan et al., 1995); stolen credit cards can also readily be used to make local and international calls from payphones with little prospect of interception.

The role of the Internet is also likely to develop. Already there are documented cases of sales of ecstasy and other illicit drugs being arranged through Internet chat-rooms (*New York Times*, 17 November 1999). Cannabis seeds can be bought over the Internet — legally in some jurisdictions — from suppliers based in the Netherlands. E-mail, especially when sent from Internet cafes, may prove useful to traffickers as a discreet way of communicating. One can foresee a game of cyber-leapfrog between distributors and enforcement agencies, as the former adapt to the preventive measures of the latter. The likelihood is that exploitation of advanced communications technology will be restricted to trafficking, where the number of people involved is relatively small and the risks high. At the retail level the need for sophisticated methods of communication is less pressing and is likely to mirror those used by legitimate businesses (Eck and Gersh, this volume).

It is unclear what proportion of illicit drugs are bought in open street markets and what proportion are bought in phone-based closed markets and delivery systems that are replacing the open street markets. It is even harder to assess the degree of drug distribution that occurs through social networks. Given the choice, most users would buy from friends, or from sellers whom they know and trust, in a private rather than a public space. For example, according to a ONDCP report (1997b) in Trenton/Newark, some suppliers of heroin are most often older students or recent graduates who are users and are familiar faces among the students. Most users do have a degree of choice, as their wish to buy drugs is not fuelled by dependency. As mentioned above, Parker's studies in the North West of England (this volume) found that very few young users had direct face-to-face contact with people whom they regarded as dealers. Rather, they were "sorted" by a friend of a friend, or the brother of a mate, for example, buying in circumstances where they felt that they could invest some trust in the source of supply. These supply networks can be thought of as another form of closed retail market.

Pub- and club-based retail markets are likely to form another significant part of drug distribution systems, in particular for ecstasy and other drugs used by clubbers. These should probably be thought of as semi-open, in that sellers will generally do business in the absence of any prior introduction, provided the buyer looks the part. Ruggiero and South (1995) reckoned that most illicit drug buying in Britain takes place in private or semi-public places such as pubs and clubs. This may well be true in the sense that a majority of buyers use such systems. It is more questionable whether the majority of drug *expenditure* takes place in dealing networks of this sort. While problem users comprise a minority of the total, they consume drugs at such a rate that they account for a significant slice of illicit drug sales. It may well be that problem users' needs for very regular and dependable supplies of drugs locks them into street markets or phone-based markets serviced by sellers who operate on a full-time basis.

Varieties of Distribution System

Behind any system of retailing must lie a distribution system, which imports or manufactures and then distributes drugs. Traditionally, the structure of drug-distribution systems has been viewed as pyramidical, with large-scale importers and traffickers operating at the apex, filtering down to street dealers who operate on the lowest tier (Gilman and Pearson, 1991). Many popular films have portrayed drug-trafficking organisations as large, highly disciplined, hierarchical organisations. Research has suggested a more complex picture.

Certainly some studies, such as Natarajan's (this volume) have uncovered organisations with clear hierarchies and well-defined job functions. However, distribution systems can take widely differing forms. Building on Johnson et al.'s (1992) typology and that of Curtis (1996), Natarajan and Belanger (1998) derived a two-dimensional typology from their analysis of 39 American drug-trafficking organisations, classifying them according to drug-dealing task and organisational structure. The latter dimension comprised:

- Freelancers — small, non-hierarchical entrepreneurial groups
- Family businesses — cohesive groups with clear structure and authority derived from family ties
- Communal businesses — flexible groups bound by a common tie such as ethnicity
- Corporations — large, formal hierarchies with well-defined divisions of labour

Natarajan and Belanger (1998) found that organisational structure varied according to function or task (manufacturing, import/smuggling, wholesale distribution/regional distribution). Freelance groups tended to restrict themselves to one or at most two stages in the trafficking process and were rarely involved in regional distribution. Corporations, on the other hand, tended to operate at several levels. Not all were concerned with importation or manufacture; however, most tended to get involved in retail as well as wholesale operations. Eck and Gersh (this volume), examining the structure of domestic trafficking organisations within the Washington/Baltimore area, found that the system predominately took the form of a cottage industry.

In Britain, Dorn et al. (1992) found that in the late 1980s at least, *domestic* supply systems (as opposed to importers) were not organised as neat, top-down hierarchies controlled by a "Mr Big." This is not quite the same as saying that British supply systems are disorganised. Rather, Dorn and his colleagues painted a picture of a fragmented and fluid system populated by a range of opportunistic entrepreneurs from a variety of backgrounds — licit businesses with an illicit sideline. These entrepreneurs are career criminals who turn from other "project crimes" such as bank robbery or major fraud to trafficking. They are people who may, to some extent, believe in their product; users buying for each other. Akhtar and South (this volume) describe a lower level supply network in which kinship and friendship play a significant role. However, in more recent research on importation into Britain, Dorn and other colleagues (1998) paint a rather different picture, one more in keeping with media images of "organised crime." Perhaps arrangements vary over time and at different levels of the market.

Little research to date has succeeded in mapping the interrelationships between distribution systems above low-level street and retail markets. Nor have any studies shed much light on the intersection between distribution systems and the closed supply networks through which most young people get drugs. It is clear that the typologies of upper level distribution and of retail markets are similar and compatible. However, very little research has been done on whether, for example, freelance or family-based traffickers have links with corporate distributors at the domestic distribution and retail levels.

Supply, Demand and Enforcement

The relationships between the supply of illicit drugs, the demand for them and enforcement activities are poorly conceptualised by politicians and policy officials and are seriously under-researched. Popular debate about drugs tends to take for granted that illicit drug use is supply-led, and that illicit drug use is best controlled by stopping drugs getting into the country and onto the streets. In reality there is a buoyant demand for a commodity whose value is well embedded in youth culture and that simultaneously meets the need for excitement, risk taking, and novelty (cf. Parker et al., 1998a and 1998b). This may suggest that the market for illicit drugs is demand-led — that supply follows demand, and is a response to it. In reality, of course, there is a dynamic and interactive relationship between supply and demand. With no supply of illicit drugs, no demand would ever evolve and, unless drugs offered users some immediate attractions, there would never be enough demand to consolidate sources of supply.

Policy initiatives often make distinctions between supply reduction strategies and demand reduction strategies. The former involve enforcement activity designed to disrupt supply, while the latter may deploy enforcement or other means to reduce demand. The distinction becomes hard to maintain when one recognises that changes in levels of supply are likely to affect prices, and that changes in prices are likely to affect demand. Except in those rare situations where it is genuinely possible to stifle the supply of illicit drugs, the impact of supply-reduction strategies is likely to be mediated through changes in price.

We know very little about the ways in which supply reduction strategies impact prices, and the ways in which prices are related to demand. Economic theory would lead us to think of interdiction and enforcement strategies as methods of increasing prices. There are two ways this could happen. First, the simple process of removing drugs from the distribution system should increase scarcity and thus increase price. Secondly, the increased risks imposed by the police on participants should be translated into higher prices. Either way, the higher prices should encourage consumers to depress their consumption in much the same way that they would respond to added taxation of alcohol and tobacco.

In reality, the prices of most illicit drugs in most developed countries have been stable or falling (ONDCP, 1997a; Institute for the Study of Drug Dependence [ISDD], 1999; EMCDDA, 1999) For example, cannabis prices in the U.S. peaked in the early 1990s and have been falling since. Heroin prices have also been falling (Hamid et al., 1997). Cocaine prices have been fairly stable (Johnson et al., this volume) and quality has fallen. In real terms, therefore, prices may actually have risen. In Britain cannabis prices have been fairly stable in cash terms for many years, representing a fall in real terms. The cash price per gram of both heroin and cocaine has fallen quite steeply in recent years, even if the unit of purchase remains the same — a £10 wrap of heroin and a £20 rock of crack.[1]

It remains obscure precisely how closely these patterns in price relate to enforcement activity. Is the maintenance (or rise) of cocaine prices in the U.S. a function of enforcement? And can this price maintenance account for the reductions in U.S. cocaine use? Has there been a switch from (crack) cocaine use to cannabis? Does the fall in U.S. heroin prices account for the rise in use or the abundant supply? The short answer is that we do not know. However, it is a reasonable conjecture that other factors, such as changes in youth culture, and the collective learning from experience, may be equally important explanatory factors. It is certainly plausible that young people who directly witness the destructive consequences of high-risk drug use, such as smoking crack or injecting heroin, will themselves be "inoculated" against such forms of drug use (cf. Johnson, this volume; Parker et al., 1998a; Inciardi and Harrison, 1998).

There are several reasons for expecting very complex relationships between enforcement, supply and demand. Some writers (e.g., Rasmussen and Benson, 1994; Kleiman, 1992; Reuter, 1992; Reuter et al., 1990) have focused on the adaptations that distribution systems make to enforcement, and to the perverse effects that apparently effective enforcement may bring. Possibly the main adaptation is the replacement of personnel, where others take over the roles and functions of those who have been arrested. Where there is a buyer's market, it is obvious how this process could undercut the impact of enforcement: removing a few sellers from an oversupplied market will not increase scarcity at all; at best it will stop prices from sliding.

The most likely perverse effect of supply reduction strategies is a complex one. The very act of sustaining prices may actually stimulate the market by drawing new "players" into the system. According to this argument, enforcement can be successful in sustaining or increasing risks of criminal sanctions. These risks are translated into maintained or increased prices, but the result is to attract more people into the highly lucrative — if risky — drug business. If this argument holds up, successful enforcement strategies contain the seeds of their own failure.

Dependency and Elasticity of Demand

Assuming that drug control strategies can have at least a degree of impact on drug prices, it is important to consider how such changes will affect levels of consumption. As we have discussed, most illicit drug use is controlled and involves sales in small amounts. Purchases are often opportunistic, and if a specific drug is in short supply, there is a range of licit and illicit alternatives. There should therefore be considerable elasticity of demand in response to price changes. In principle at least, it should be possible to price controlled drug users out of specific drug markets.

Problem drug users will demonstrate much greater inelasticity (cf. Thomas, 1992; Wagstaff and Maynard, 1988). The extent to which dependency locks people into a state of irresistible demand is open to question (cf. Ditton and Hammersley, 1995; Rasmussen and Benson, 1994). The more it does so, however, the more that levels of demand will be insensitive to changes in price. Dependent users with access to large amounts of money will simply spend more. Criminally involved dependent users will spend more of other people's money.

The implications of this are twofold. First, if it proves possible to maintain or increase prices through supply reduction strategies, the impact will be greater on the large number of moderate users than on the small number of heavy users. Secondly, it is clearly important to find strategies which reduce problem users' demand in additional to any of those which rely directly or indirectly on price control.

Inconvenience Policing

Low-level policing methods strive to disrupt markets, making them less predictable for both buyer and seller (Murji 1998; Lee, 1995; Kleiman, 1992). This strategy is seen to be most effective when combined with attempts to divert drug offenders away from the criminal justice system and into treatment services (cf. Edmunds et al., 1998), and has been abetted by the introduction of arrest referral schemes (South, 1998). Selective policing aims to target dependent users in an attempt to reduce demand within a market. The argument is that by removing regular customers from the market, consumption will decrease, resulting in a reduction in price, which in turn would lead to a decline in drug related crime (Kleiman and Smith, 1990).

A second principle of low-level enforcement is inconvenience policing that aims to increase the drug search time or to otherwise place obstacles in the way of the buying process. Although such measures will probably do little to deter problematic users, the idea is that casual and novice users will be discouraged from buying, therefore constricting the market (Murji, 1998). Knutsson (this volume) describes how Swedish retail markets appear to have been very responsive to intensive policing.

It is clear that whatever strategies are employed to tackle the distribution of illicit drugs, those responsible for drug policy must be aware of the intended consequences such strategies often bring. The relative inelasticity of demand among dependent users means that the markets will be very lucrative and will adapt and transform rather than disappear.

Demand Reduction and Treatment

Traditionally most jurisdictions have envisaged strategies of both supply reduction and demand reduction in terms of enforcement. In other words, the main levers for reducing supply and demand have been thought of as deterrent threat, incapacitation of offenders, and the seizure of drugs. For supply reduction this is largely correct, although there may be some room for source-country strategies such as crop substitution programmes. For demand reduction, treatment of dependent users represents an increasingly promising avenue. Killias and Aebi (this volume) describe the results of an effective experiment in the maintenance prescription of heroin for long-term dependent users, which not only achieved marked reductions in crime and health benefits for those involved, but also substantially disrupted the illicit heroin market.

The logic of demand reduction through treatment is that dependent users, though a small proportion of the total number of illicit users, actually accounts for a large degree of consumption (cf. Edmunds et al., 1999; ONDCP, 1997a). Thus, effective treatment services targeted on heavily dependent users may have an impact on overall levels of demand disproportionate to the numbers of people involved. The harder services to put in place are those that effectively encourage typically young, casual or novice users to contain or reduce their use.

Ethnic Minorities and Distribution of Drugs

A consistent feature of drug distribution systems in industrialised countries has been the involvement of ethnic minority groups in some stages of the process (Natarajan, 1998; Akhtar and South, this volume; Hamid, 1998; Pearson and Patel, 1998; ONDCP, 1997b). In part this can be seen as a consequence of the international nature of much drug trafficking: those from source countries will by definition be minorities in the country of import. Ruggiero's discussion (this volume) of Albanian trafficking of cannabis is a case in point. Akhtar and South (this volume) describe a South Asian distribution network whose viability depended to a significant degree on privileged access to suppliers. However, there is also a tendency for minority groups to play a part as dispensable "foot soldiers" both as mules in importing drugs and as runners at retail level. The extent to which ethnic minority involvement is a reflection of social exclusion, and the extent to which it is a function of access and opportunity is clearly a question in need of further research. The likelihood is that those involved in street-level retail markets are drawn into the process mainly because of their disadvantaged social and economic status. By contrast those at higher levels of the distribution system are more likely to have links with the source country even when they occupy fairly dispensable roles in the process.

Drug Markets: From Research to Policy

The final chapter in this book, by Peter Reuter, considers how more policy-relevant research can be motivated, and discusses the sort of research agenda that would make a more significant contribution to policy. Perhaps his most important point is that policy questions have to be built into the design of research studies, not simply grafted on the end. This will require some changes in the way that research on drug markets is funded. To date, there has been an uneasy collusion between government funding agencies anxious to get research off the ground and academic researchers anxious to find money for their studies. They have both proceeded on the questionable assumption that improved academic understanding of problems will lead inevitably to improved policy. The result has been that funding agencies often do not get what they need in terms of policy relevance and the blame tends to fall on the researchers. In fact, as

Reuter points out, policy-oriented research must be attentive to policy questions from the outset. We would not suggest that researchers must accept in an unquestioning way the assumptions that underpin policy thinking. But policy research has to *engage* with the preoccupations of policy, however distorted these may be by the highly politicised nature of discourse on drugs. Dorn (this volume) provides an excellent example of the intelligent deployment of research to help policy address the arcane — even Byzantine — problems of performance measure in an environment in which simple "single figure" measures are at a premium.

Reuter's chapter goes a long way to framing a policing research agenda for the future. At a lower level of specificity we would identify four thematic priorities of our own. First, we believe that the imbalance between research on retail markets and on upper-level trafficking needs to be corrected and in the process more needs to be discovered about the links between traffickers and retailers. Because of the considerable difficulties of undertaking research on trafficking noted by Natarajan in this volume, this will require researchers to develop new methodologies for obtaining the required information. One promising approach involves much more systematic analysis of various kinds of data collected by law enforcement agencies in their efforts to identify and prosecute traffickers. Gaining access to these data has proved difficult to date because of trust and privacy concerns, but this could change if studies were more explicitly tailored to address policy perspectives. As well as new methodologies, perhaps some new disciplinary perspectives would enhance the study of trafficking. In particular, a business perspective on the ways that traffickers identify, supply and exploit new markets could be very illuminating.

Second, the crucial interaction between supply and demand needs to be better understood. This topic seems to have fallen between the cracks in the boundaries between funding agencies. In the United States, for example, speaking very generally, research on supply is the responsibility of the National Institute of Justice, while research on demand is the province of the National Institute of Drug Abuse (NIDA). Neither agency has been very willing to fund work that may seem to impinge on the territory of the other and researchers may not know how to negotiate the difficult terrain at the boundary. NIDA's support of this book, which goes beyond its traditional research remit, may be one sign that solutions to this funding impasse are being sought.

Third, the growing recognition that prevention is as relevant to drug dealing as to drug use will spur new research agendas. The preventive approaches relevant to dealing and trafficking rely more upon reducing opportunities for these activities than upon attempting to change the attitudes or beliefs of those involved in these activities. They depend upon detailed studies of the modus operandi of dealers and traffickers, and less upon their personal backgrounds. Consequently, these preventive approaches have more in common with the situational methods that are the subject matter of *Crime Prevention Studies*, than the rehabilitative and therapeutic approaches in the probation, counselling and psychiatric literatures.

Our final conclusion is that, just as dealing and trafficking span international boundaries, so research needs to be international in character. This does not mean that every research study should have an international dimension. It means only that the findings of studies conducted in different countries need to be constantly interpreted in the light of knowledge gained from similar studies conducted elsewhere. This volume, consisting of papers by a distinguished group of international scholars, is intended to contribute to this endeavour.

Address correspondence to: Mike Hough, Director, Criminal Policy Research Unit, Technopark, South Bank University, 103 Borough Road, London SE1 OAA, UK. E-mail: mike.hough@sbu.ac.uk
Mangai Natarajan, Associate Professor, Department of Sociology, John Jay College of Criminal Justice, 899 Tenth Avenue, New York, NY 10019. E-mail: mnjjj@ cunyvm.cuny.edu

REFERENCES

Chatterton, M., G. Gibson, M. Gilman, C. Godfrey, M. Sutton and A. Wright (1995). *Performance Indicators for Local Anti-Drugs Strategies: a Preliminary Analysis.* (Crime Detection and Prevention Series, Paper #62.) London, UK: Home Office Police Research Group.

Curtis, R. (1996). "War on Drugs in Brooklyn: Street-level Drug Markets and the Tactical Narcotic Teams." Doctoral dissertation, Teachers College, Columbia University, New York, NY.

Ditton, J. and R. Hammersley (1995). "The Typical Cocaine User: How Our Blinkered Vision of the Cocaine User Has Created the Myth of Cocaine's Irresistability." *Druglink* 9(6):11-14.

Dorn, N., L. Oette and S. White (1998). "Drugs Importation and the Bifurcation of Risk: Capitalization, Cut Outs and Organised Crime." *British Journal of Criminology* 38(4):537-560.

—— K. Murji and N. South (1992). *Traffickers: Drug Markets and Law Enforcement.* London, UK: Routledge.

Eck, J. (1995). "A General Model of the Geography of Illicit Retail Markets." In: J.E. Eck and D. Weisburd (eds.), *Crime and Place.* (Crime Prevention Studies vol. 4.) Monsey, NY: Criminal Justice Press.

European Monitoring Centre for Drugs and Drug Addiction [EMCDDA} (1999). *Annual Report on the State of Drugs Problems in the European Union 1999.* Lisbon, PORT.

Edmunds, M., M. Hough, P.J. Turnbull and T. May (1999). *Doing Justice to Treatment: Referring Offenders to Drug Services* (Drugs Prevention Advisory Service Paper #2.) London, UK: Home Office, Drugs Prevention Advisory Service.

—— T. May, I. Hearden and M. Hough (1998). *Arrest Referral: Emerging Lessons from Research.* (Drugs Prevention Initiative Paper #23.) London, UK: Home Office, Central Drugs Prevention Unit.

—— M. Hough and N. Urquia (1996). *Tackling Local Drug Markets.* (Crime Prevention Initiative Paper #80.) London, UK: Home Office, Police Research Group.

Gilman, M. and G. Pearson (1991). "Lifestyles and Law Enforcement." In: D. Whynes and P. Beans (eds.), *Policing and Prescribing.* Basingstoke, UK: Macmillan.

Hamid, A. (1998). *Drugs in America.* Gaithersburg, MD: Aspen.

—— R. Curtis, K. McCoy, J. McGuire, A. Conde, W. Bushell, R. Lindenmayer, K. Brimberg, S. Maia, S. Abdur-Rashid and J. Settembrino (1997). "The Heroin Epidemic in New York City: Current Status and Prognoses." *Journal of Psychoactive Drugs* 29(4):375-391.

Inciardi, J.A. and L.D. Harrison (eds.) (1998). *Heroin in the Age of Crack Cocaine.* Beverly Hills, CA: Sage.

Institute for the Study of Drug Dependence (ISDD) (1999). *UK Trends and Updates.* London, UK. [www.isdd.co.uk/trends].

Johnson, B.D., A. Hamid and H. Sanabria (1992). "Emerging Models of Crack Distribution." In: T. Meiczkowski (ed.), *Drugs, Crime, and Social Policy.* Boston, MA: Allyn and Bacon.

—— T. Williams, K. Dei, and H. Sanabria (1990). "Drug Abuse and the Inner City: Impact on Hard Drug Users and the Community." In: M. Tonry and J.Q. Wilson (eds.), *Drugs and Crime.* (Crime and Justice Series, vol. 13.) Chicago, IL: University of Chicago Press.

Johnston, L.D., P.M. O'Malley and J.G. Bachman (1999). *National Survey Results on Drug Use from the Monitoring the Future Study, 1975-1998.* Rockville, MD: National Institute on Drug Abuse.

Kleiman, M. (1992). *Against Excess: Drug Policy for Results*. New York, NY: Basic Books.

—— and K. Smith (1990). "State and Local Drug Enforcement." In: M. Tonry and J.Q. Wilson (eds.), *Drugs and Crime*. Chicago, IL: University of Chicago Press.

Lee, M. (1996). "London: 'Community Damage Limitation' Through Policing?" In: N. Dorn, J. Jepsen, and E. Savona (eds.), *European Drug Policy and Enforcement*. Basingstoke: Macmillan.

May, T., M. Edmunds and M. Hough (1999). *Street Business: The Links between Sex and Drug Markets*. (Police Research Series Paper #118.) London, UK: Home Office, Policing and Reducing Crime Unit.

Murji, K. (1998). *Policing Drugs*. Hampshire, UK: Ashgate.

Natarajan, M. (1998). "Drug Trafficking in New York City." In: A. Karmen (ed.), *Crime and Justice in New York City*. New York, NY: McGraw Hill.

—— and M. Belanger (1998). "Varieties of Upper-level Drug Dealing Organisations: A Typology of Cases Prosecuted in New York City." *Journal of Drug Issues* 28(4):1005-1026.

—— R. Clarke and M. Belanger (1996). "Drug Dealing and Payphones: The Scope for Intervention." *Security Journal* 7:245-251.

—— R. Clarke and B.D. Johnson (1995). "Telephones as Facilitators of Drug Dealing: a Research Agenda." *European Journal of Criminal Policy and Research* 3(3):137-154.

New York Times (1999). "13 on Staten Island Accused in Internet Sales of Illicit Drugs." 17 November, p.B5.

Office of National Drug Control Policy (1999). *National Drug Control Strategy: 1999*. Washington, DC.

—— (1997a). *What America's Users Spend on Illegal Drugs, 1988-1995*. Washington DC.

—— (1997b). *Pulse Check National Trends in Drug Abuse*. Washington DC.

Office of National Statistics (ONS) (1998). *Economic Trends No. 536*. London, UK.

Parker, H., C. Bury and R. Eggington (1998a). *New Heroin Outbreaks among Young People*. (Crime Detection and Prevention Paper #92.) London, UK: Home Office.

—— J. Aldridge and F. Measham (1998b). *Illegal Leisure: The Normalisation of Adolescent Recreational Drug Use*. London, UK: Routledge.

Ramsay, M. and S. Partridge (1999). *Drug Misuse Declared in 1998: Results from the British Crime Survey*. (Home Office Research Study #197.) London, UK: Home Office.

Rasmussen, D. and B. Benson (1994). *The Economic Anatomy of the Drug War: Criminal Justice in the Commons.* Lanham, MD: Rowman and Littlefield Publishers, Inc.

Reuter, P. (1992). "The Limits and Consequences of US Foreign Drug Control Efforts." *The Annals of the American Academy of Political and Social Science* 521:151-162.

—— R. MacCoun and P. Murphy (1990). *Money from Crime: A Study of the Economics of Drug Dealing in Washington D.C.* RAND.

Ruggiero, V. and N. South (1995). *Eurodrugs, Drug Use, Markets and Trafficking in Europe.* London, UK: UCL Press.

Sarno, C., M. Hough and M. Bulos (1999). *Developing A Picture of CCTV in Southwark Town Centres.* London, UK: Report for London Borough of Southwark [www.sbu.ac.uk/cpra].

South, N. (1998). "Tackling Drug Control in Britain: From Sir Malcolm Delevingne to the New Drugs Strategy." In: R. Coomber (ed.), *The Control of Drug Users, Reason or Reaction.* Harwood, UK: Academic Press.

Thomas, J.J. (1992). *Informal Economic Activity.* London, UK: Harvester Wheatsheaf.

United Nations Drug Control Program (UNDCP) (1997). *Global Illicit Drug Trends.* Vienna, AUS: United Nations, Office for Drug Control and Crime Prevention.

Wagstaff, A and A. Maynard (1988). *Economic Aspects of the Illicit Drug Market and Drug Enforcement Policies in the United Kingdom.* (Home Office Research Study #95.) London, UK: Home Office.

NOTES

1. The other variable to take into account is purity. If the quality of street drugs has declined, then there are no grounds for arguing that real prices have actually fallen.

CRACK DISTRIBUTION AND ABUSE IN NEW YORK

by

Bruce D. Johnson

Eloise Dunlap

Sylvie C. Tourigny

National Development and Research Institutes Inc., New York

Abstract: *A major ethnographic project, conducted from 1989-1997, greatly improved the scientific understanding of crack and illicit drug distribution and markets in New York City. Staff developed procedures and outreach methodologies to access and safely conduct research among active sellers, dealers, and low-level distributors of crack, cocaine, and heroin. Nearly 300 subjects were studied on different occasions. The crack distribution business involved specific roles classified into four major groups: low-level distributors, sellers, dealers, and high-level distributors. Role proliferation helped evade police and the most serious penalties, as well as to protect sellers from competitors. The relative effectiveness of police tactics in "gaining control" of the streets in the mid-1990s, had modest impacts on the crack and drug markets. Prices of retail and wholesale units of crack and cocaine remained relatively stable for a dozen years. Inner-city youths born in the 1970s (and reaching young adulthood in the 1990s) had avoided crack smoking and injection of heroin or cocaine. However, having been reared in severely distressed households, their social capital (e.g., their family and social backgrounds plus acquired skills) was very low as they reached adulthood in the 1990s. They had low probabilities of gaining steady legal employment or welfare payments during adulthood.*

Crime Prevention Studies, volume 11, pp. 19-57

INTRODUCTION

Although the federal funding process severely inhibited and delayed systematic research about crack abuse and sales during the 1980s (Holden, 1989), later research documented that the crack era exploded in 1984-86 in New York and around the United States. Extensive ethnographic and quantitative research enables us to describe and document continuity and shifts in the natural history of crack sellers/distributors and abusers. This chapter[1] focuses on the structure of drug markets, gendered differences in participation in drug dealing, and related factors. Existing policies regarding cocaine and crack distribution and users are addressed in the concluding section.

THEORY AND BACKGROUND: UNDERSTANDING "STRUCTURE" IN THE CONTEXT OF DRUG MARKETS

This research outlines the adaptability and fluidity of crack sellers and distribution systems by drawing from ethnographies lasting several years, which allowed us to document iterative changes in drug markets operating in various contexts. Drug sellers responded to changes in the drug economy as the drug of choice changed among the clientele and the pressures exerted through intensified policing (Johnson et al., 1990). Some factors involved alterations within the communities where most of these markets operate (Dunlap and Johnson 1992; Johnson et al., 1992). Other factors reflect the decreased availability of General Assistance and welfare supports, particularly in the face of spiraling demands confronting AIDS-afflicted households (Tourigny, 1998; Des Jarlais et al., 1998, 1994; Friedman et al., 1997).

Few doubt that crack markets and other drug markets have remained successful in spite of the challenges of efficient policing and lengthy sentences for crack sellers. Yet, research has paid little attention to the internal structure and functioning of drug markets in response to the range of exogenous pressures they have faced in recent years. Because the drug economy is illicit and its participants are seen as violent and (often as intentionally) deviant, analysis of its structure is difficult. This lacuna leaves us uninformed about the lifestyles and internal dynamics of those most involved in these markets; it also leaves us bereft of novel strategies that seek to minimize crack and drug use, particularly in inner cities.

Because crack sellers operate outside the law and undercover officers continually seek them out, drug selling operations must include high levels of risk. But they must also be predictable. The sellers must know where to find cocaine or crack supplies; the clients must know where to find the sellers and also how to avoid police. The suppliers must locate street-level sellers and the clients must be able to buy somewhere. What may superficially appear to be chaos is seller response to remain flexible enough to respond quickly to threats to their market share or to their personal freedom from incarceration. Drug sellers must sustain both this predictability and this flexibility without any support from those structures — social, legal, or corporate — customarily available to legal enterprises. Drug dealers as well as social scientists can draw the analogy between corporate and drug market structures:

> If you can sell cocaine or any other type of drug, you can start your own business. It's that easy...When you're selling drugs, you learn how to do your books, you learn how to save your money, you know how to invest it, and with a business, it's the same thing. The brothers out here that have seven or eight people working for them, they are managers and businessmen, they're already entrepreneurs [Jah & Shah'Keyah, 1995:83].

Our major theoretical approach is borrowed from a more general model of disease epidemics.[2] Our analyses suggest that "crack era," rather than a "crack epidemic," most appropriately describes the historical progressions documented during this research. A *drug era* is conceptualized as a time-delimited, sociohistorical period in which a new drug or "innovative" mode of use is introduced and adopted by large numbers and proportions of persons and its use becomes institutionalized within certain segments of the population. Drug eras move through several major components: (1) Each involves a specific drug or new mode of use. (2) Each era has its own phases including *expansion, plateau, decline,* and *persistence.* (3) Mass initiation and development of regular use or abuse patterns primarily occurs among adolescents and high-risk subpopulations. (4) Drug-era "cohorts" are important because their persistent use of substances may continue throughout their lives. Several publications elaborate this model (Golub and Johnson, 1999a, 1999b, 1997, 1996, 1994a, 1994b, 1994c; Johnson and Muffler, 1997; Johnson, 1991; Johnson and Manwar, 1991; Johnson et al., 1990; also see Brunswick and Titus 1998; Inciardi and Harrison, 1998).

In the past 30 years, New York City experienced at least four major "drug eras" (Johnson and Muffler, 1997; Johnson et al., 1990), each persisting in the 1990s: (1) marijuana and psychedelic era (1960-79); (2) heroin era (1965-73); (3) cocaine powder era (1975-84); and (4) crack era (1985-88). "After-hours" cocaine-snorting settings were common in the 1970s and were transformed into "freebase parlors" and "base houses" during 1980-83 (Hamid, 1992a, 1992b). The popularity of crack (freebase cocaine prepared for retail sales) around 1983 spawned a very swift expansion phase (1984-86), which gave way to the plateau phase (1987-89) (see Golub and Johnson, 1999b, 1997, 1996; Johnson et al., 1992; Johnson et al., 1990, 1985; also see a summary of these drug eras in Johnson and Muffler, 1997; and Johnson et al., 1995). In Manhattan, the crack era then persisted or declined very slowly. A definite negative stigma against smoking crack emerged among street drug users. Inner-city, high-risk youths born in the 1970s (the "post-crack cohort") appear to be avoiding crack smoking and heroin injection in particular (Johnson and Golub, 2000; Johnson et al., 1998; National Institute of Justice 1999, 1997). No street youth wants to be called a "crackhead" (Furst et al., 1999, 1998; Dunlap et al., 1995; Furst and Johnson, 1995). Whatever the reasons for youthful avoidance or irregular use of co-caine/crack and heroin, current norms are so powerful that despite intensive searches, several major AIDS projects located in New York City have major difficulty locating persons under age 25 who snort heroin, and finds virtually no drug-injecting inner-city African-American youths (Friedman et al., 1998; Sifaneck, 1998; Friedman, 1997; Furst et al., 1996; Neaigus et al., 1994; Parker et al., 1988; Pearson, 1987). A major ethnographic study of heroin use (Curtis and Spunt, 1999; Hamid et al., 1999) has found almost no heroin use or injection among minority youths and young adults in New York City.

Johnson and colleagues first explicated these phases of drug markets in New York City in 1990, and documented the structural similarities evident in the mid- to late 1980s between these markets and legal businesses (Johnson et al., 1990). These, of course, have changed somewhat, as a response to intensified policing, but also to the changing profile of those available to work reliably within drug markets, and to the routinization of illegal sales work as a career. This chapter explains the current structure, which essentially reflects a great deal of continuity during the 1990s. It also documents an ad-aptation to some of the changing realities of drug markets operating as structured entities in the New York City of the 1990s.

METHODOLOGY

When this project began in 1989, very little was known about crack use/abuse, and even less about crack selling and distribution. Staff successfully implemented an ethnography of crack sellers and their distribution behaviors, including their use of crack and other drugs. The primary assumption underlying this qualitative methodology holds that the best and most important source of information about phenomena involves asking those who are most intimately involved in it. Thus, persons who routinely engage in crack use and sales are anticipated to have unique points of view and perspectives. Indeed, the illegality of their behavior implies the need to hide or conceal it from others, especially from police and public officials and from those — including family members — in alliance with conventional society.

Ethnography is a primary approach in several social sciences (see Miles and Huberman, 1994; Fetterman, 1989; Emerson, 1988; Clifford and Marcus, 1986; among others for the rationale and purpose of ethnographic research). The method relies upon three major data collection emphases: (1) locating and establishing good rapport with key informants or participants, who discuss in their own words their ways of thinking about the phenomena of interest; (2) directly observing the person, setting, and phenomena of interest, and recording impressions in written field notes; and (3) conducting in-depth, usually tape-recorded, interviews, raising topics and asking questions that leave respondents free to formulate their own answers. Transcribed interviews constitute the primary documents for data analysis. While difficult to code quantitatively,[3] the resulting respondent narratives and field notes offer descriptions containing participants' words and their meaning systems, contextualized by the researcher's direct observations and impressions.

The project staff successfully developed procedures and outreach methodologies to access and safely conduct research (Pequegnat et al., 1995; Williams et al., 1992; Dunlap et al., 1990) among active sellers, dealers, and low-level distributors of crack, cocaine, and heroin. Because of the severe criminal penalties involved with selling crack, ethnographic staff needed to locate, gain introductions to, and, most importantly, establish trust and build rapport among street selling networks. They needed to obtain informed consent from persons in various distribution roles. Respondents often introduced other sellers and higher-level dealers (Dunlap and Johnson, 1999), and field workers identified and established relationships with potential subjects. Despite some interest in the financial reward given for completed interviews, that the project would result in "a book" was a powerful inducement. Many, especially street-level crack sellers and low-level distributors, were eager to talk about themselves, their accomplishments, and travails.

Gaining access to crack dealers and higher level operatives proved much more difficult. The higher these individuals are in the drug distribution hierarchy, the more progressively reclusive they become, carefully shielding themselves behind a hierarchy of operatives. Once a research relationship is successfully established and an initial interview is completed (Dunlap and Johnson, 1999), however, many adopt mentor-like attitudes toward the naive academic or ethnographer. Eager to explain dramatic events or drug procedure, they sometimes bristled if spoken details were inadequately noted or explored. Some urged researchers to turn on the tape recorder or to write something down. At other times, aware of the sensitivity of their responses, they asked that the tape recorder be turned off or that specific remarks be omitted from the transcript.

Ethics of Ethnographic Research

In establishing their presence as bona fide researchers, ethnographers must build substantial rapport, carefully explain the purpose of the research, provide assurances of protection and safety, and obtain informed consent from participants. Ethnographers also need to establish a zone of personal safety (Williams et al., 1992; Williams, 1991, 1989, 1978) early on, and to maintain neutrality.

Key Subjects

Crack distributors recruited for this study [Table 1] probably reflect the larger population distributing crack. Over a third are women, over two-thirds are African American and West Indian, and only a small proportion is white. Most are in their 30s or 40s, and have sold drugs for many years.

By the completion of data collection in September 1996, project staff had documented over 1,500 persons at various crack and drug dealing scenes across New York City. Staff had interviewed 296 persons in depth; over 100 were interviewed repeatedly over several years. Approximately 800 transcripts for the 296 focal subjects and for staff meetings and roughly 1,050 separate ethnographer and paraprofessional field notes, total 75,000 pages of text. Representing about 135 million words, this constitutes one of the largest qualitative data sets ever compiled in this field. Many variations in distribution roles and activities were systematically recorded. Participant classifications reflect their level in the drug dealing hierarchy as: (1) dealer (n=36), (2) retail seller (n=65), (3) low level distributor (n=108), (4) distribution role difficult to classify (n=36), and (5) abuser, not distributor (n=41).

Table 1: Demographic Characteristics of Crack Seller Subjects With One or More Ethnographic Interviews

	N	Percent
All subjects with one in-depth interview	296	
Gender	296	
Male	187	63.2
Female	109	36.6
Ethnicity	296	
African American	230	77.7
Hispanic	49	16.6
White	17	5.7
Age at first interview	268	
Under 25	47	17.5
25-39	54	20.1
30-40	109	40.7
Over 40	58	21.6
Year of initial interview	296	
1989-90	68	23.0
1991-92	79	26.7
1993	5	1.7
1994	48	16.2
1995	59	19.9
1996	37	12.5
Borough of primary activity	296	
Manhattan	219	74.0
Bronx	17	5.7
Brooklyn	55	18.6
Queens/Staten Island	5	1.7

All ethnographic data are compiled into a powerful hypertext program, Folio VIEWS, which contains textual data organized for instant retrieval. Many categories of concern, such as addiction, dyads, reciprocity, support, and so on, are concepts that are not used often by crack-selling subjects. However, "in textual data, the search is ... for meaning of the text that involves the choice of analytic perspectives" (Manwar et al., 1994:288). The hypertext program supports the systematic matching of the requirement of scientific abstractions (the researcher's perspective) with participants' descriptions of behavior and purpose.

This chapter's first author also directs the Drug Use Forecasting (DUF) program in Manhattan. The National Institute of Justice funds the data collection to document trends in patterns of illicit drug use among arrestees in 24 cities.[4] DUF-Manhattan[5] datasets provide a major *quantitative* database with very large samples quite representative of Manhattan arrestees. About 1,400 subjects a year provide trend data across years and birth cohorts, and considerable precision about rates of drug use, both self-reported and detected via urinalysis (Golub and Johnson, 1997; Chaiken and Chaiken, 1993; Lewis et al., 1992). Primary analyses of trends (1987-1997) and cohort changes in drug use patterns allowed us supplementary contextualization of ethnographic data obtained in this study.[6]

THE CRACK DISTRIBUTION BUSINESS

The major focus of this research project was to improve scientific understanding of how persons sell crack, interact with others to maintain their business, deal with police and competition, and to understand crack markets. Staff have extensively documented that the vast majority of respondents engaged in crack selling were raised in severely distressed households of the inner city (Johnson et al., 1998; Maher, 1997; Dunlap et al., 1997; Dunlap et al., 1996; Maher et al., 1996; Dunlap, 1995, 1993, 1992). Similar findings characterized inner-city Detroit (Tourigny, 1998). Their career "choices" and their major life changes largely result from, and are coextensive with, their background and the disturbed family systems in which they were raised and/or currently reside.[7] Persons who grew up in severely distressed households learned strategies that leave them ill-equipped for conventional society. Children who were reared in settings where they often observed adults engaging in fights and occasionally injuring each other, were also systematically trained to fight and defend themselves (Baskin and Sommers, 1998; Johnson et al., 1998; Dunlap et al., 1996; Maher et al., 1996). Most learned to curse, be loud, aggressive and defensive in interpersonal situations.

Participation in such violence is normative and expected by everyone in the drug markets (Dunlap et al., 1996). Moreover, the self- and social-selection processes in crack distribution effectively recruit and retain the most violent drug-involved youths into distribution groups employing violence to control street sellers (Johnson et al., 1995; Waterston, 1993). Indeed, transcripts with most of the crack distribution participants extensively document high levels of violence both to themselves (e.g., multiple victimization episodes over their lifetime) and admittedly committed against others (e.g., multiple perpetration). In the absence of role models engaged in predominately conventional economic activities, they were socialized into drug market activities. This influence was exacerbated by the macro-social forces (Dunlap and Johnson, 1995; 1992) that developed and combined between the 1960s and the 1990s to *effectively exclude* very sizable proportions (possibly a majority) of inner-city minorities from having any steady legal job or obtaining even a modest (especially above-poverty) income (Waterston, 1993).

While the careers of individual crack/drug abusers and sellers vary substantially, crack is seldom their first drug of use or sale (Johnson et al., 1995). Commonalities in pre-crack drug use and sales abound, usually including pre-crack use of alcohol, marijuana, cocaine powder, and sometimes heroin injection, as well as routine sales of marijuana and/or cocaine powder. Most crack sellers report modest to extensive experience in nondrug criminality, persist in it when not selling crack, and obtain some portion of income from such crimes, although crack sales or low-level distribution activities are much more important to their livelihood (Johnson and Muffler, 1997; Johnson et al., 1994, 1990). During the past 40 years, the illicit drug economy expanded so dramatically that it became a major occupational activity for many low-income persons, especially in inner-city neighborhoods. In the mid-1980s, because of crack sales and marketing, the drug economy underwent a further dramatic expansion. Virtually all persons who sold hard drugs (which includes a very significant proportion of all hard-drug users) engaged in selling crack (Johnson and Muffler, 1997; Johnson et al., 1994, 1990; Manwar and Johnson, 1993; Fagan, 1992). Crack selling is a highly amorphous, structurally fluid undertaking (Rouse and Johnson, 1991). While its aims are to maximize profits for dealers and distributors and to ensure access for users, its methods vary over time and across settings in response to the strategies of law enforcement and competition.

ROLE STRUCTURE IN CRACK DISTRIBUTION

Several functions or roles effectively regulate the labor inputs of crack business participants, structure their interactions, and influence the returns from engaging in illegal crack transactions. Crack distributors frequently lack a terminology to distinguish these levels, and the terminology that is used varies considerably by neighborhood and distribution group. Even without categories, however, suppliers make very clear intuitive decisions about someone's competence to successfully manage money and drugs before entrusting them with crack to sell at any level of distribution. Table 2 identifies and describes some typical functions and roles in crack distribution.

Organized according to their primary functions, we categorize specific roles into four primary groupings: (1) *low-level distributors,* (2) *sellers,* (3) *dealers,* and (4) *high-level distributors.* This loose hierarchy involves increasingly greater rewards for successful performance, as

Table 2: Roles and Functions at Various Levels of the Drug Distribution Business

Approximate Role Equivalents in Legal Markets	Roles by Common Names at Various Stages of the Drug Distribution Business	Major Functions Accomplished at this Level
Grower/producer	Coca farmer, opium farmer, marijuana grower	Grow coca, opium, marijuana; the raw materials
Manufacturer	Collector, transporter, elaborator, chemist, drug lord	All stages for preparation of heroin, cocaine, marijuana as commonly sold
Traffickers		
Importer	Multikilo importer, mule, airplane pilot, smuggler, trafficker, money launderer	Smuggling of large quantities of substances into the United States
Wholesale distributor	Major distributor, investor, "kilo connection"	Transportation and redistribution of multikilograms and single kilograms
Dealers		
Regional distributor	"Pound and ounce men," "weight dealers"	Adulteration and sale of moderately expensive products
Retail store owner	House connections, suppliers, crack-house supplier	Adulteration and production of retail level dosage units ("bags," "vials," "grams") in very large numbers
Assistant manager, security chief, or accountant	"Lieutenant," "muscle men," transporter, crew boss, crack-house manager/proprietor	Supervises three or more sellers, enforces informal contracts, collects money, distributes multiple dosage units to actual sellers
Sellers		
Store clerk, salesmen (door to door and phone)	Street drug seller, "runner," juggler, private seller	Makes actual direct sales to consumer; responsible for both money and drugs
Low-Level Distributors		
Advertiser, security guards, leaflet distributor	Steerer, tout, cop man, lookout, holder, runner, help friend, guard, go-between	Assists in making sales, adver-tises, protects seller from police and criminals, solicits cus-tomers; handles drugs or money, but not both
Servant, temporary employee	Run shooting gallery, injec-tor (of drugs), freebaser, taster, apartment cleaner, drug bagger, fence, launder money	Provides short-term services to drug users or sellers for money or drugs; not responsible for money or drugs.

Source: Johnson et al., 1990:19.

well as increasingly greater risk of incarceration if arrested and convicted. In current legal statutes, a "sale" generally involves the exchange of money for an illegal drug. In response, sellers and dealers created various roles separating transactions of money from exchanges of drugs, to reduce their legal vulnerability to a "sale" arrest (Jacobs, 1999; Johnson and Natarajan, 1995; Johnson et al., 1991). This strategy sought to make it harder for police to detect — and especially to prove — that two geographically and temporally distinct transactions involving different persons were somehow related to the same sales transaction event. Legal statutes were then redefined so that persons performing these low-level distribution roles could be charged with sales transactions as a part of a continuing criminal enterprise. This change in the law triggered countermoves from distributors attempting to elude police attention while promoting their product. The role proliferation we describe below is thus specifically intended to evade police and to avoid the most serious penalties.

- *Low-level distributors* engage in a loose assortment of roles in which an actor is responsible for either, but never for both, drugs or money. This function populates the bottom of the crack distribution market. "Holders," "transporters," or "deliverers" handle someone else's drugs without receiving money from the receiver/buyer to whom they hand the product. Handling money only, "counters" or "guards" neither possess nor stand near illegal drugs. "Lookouts," "backups" or "muscle" handle neither money nor drugs, but help or safeguard the actual sale process. Many low-level distributors also promote ("tout") another seller's drug, help "steer" potential buyers to a seller, or "cop" drugs for buyers.

- *Retail sellers* are responsible for both money and drugs (at least temporarily). This role is the functional — if illegal — equivalent of retail clerks in stores, in that they collect money from someone (usually the final retail consumer) purchasing a commodity. Trying as best they can to hide their activities, they routinely engage in several illegal transactions a day to obtain their income. In the New York City crack markets, sellers usually purchase "bundles" of 10-25 vials (containing crack) from a dealer. The retail units are typically sold for $2-$25 (at various times and places), with the modal retail price being $5, to the crack buyer/consumer (Randolph 1995, 1996). Wide variations in styles of selling were noted.

- *Dealers* routinely purchase large "wholesale" level units of crack (e.g. ounces, grams, eight-balls, pounds), by weight or, especially, by dollar amounts. A dealer typically buys several "eight-balls" (supposedly an eighth of an ounce of prepared crack), up to quantities totaling a couple of kilograms of cocaine. Generally, a minimum purchase (or consignment) involves several hundred dollars' worth of cocaine or crack to prepare for resale in smaller retail units sold in multiunit lots. Dealers oversee the repackaging, often after adulteration, into retail or near-retail level sales units.

- *Upper-level distributors:* Such persons, who often import cocaine from South America, purchase and/or sell multiple kilograms of cocaine. They oversee the financing, smuggling, and transport of these drugs, rarely "handling," "possessing" or "transacting in" the drugs they own. Others, who do the actual work, take on the risks of lengthy incarceration. (While this project had major difficulty gaining access to or obtaining the cooperation of such upper-level distributors, staff interviewed several persons who had worked for them in various roles (e.g., as "mules," "transporters" of wholesale amounts of cocaine, or who had "baby sat" [guarded] wholesale quantities of cocaine, etc.) (Dunlap et al., 1997).

Virtually all crack distribution participants routinely switch among the various roles, often within minutes. Across distribution careers, downward mobility is the more common trajectory. When interviewed in their late 20s or later, most crack distributors had sustained arrests or incarcerations. They also report having made "good money" as regular sellers or dealers in their adolescence or early 20s. Having since acquired a large crack habit in the 1990s and, with it, a reputation as untrustworthy with money or drugs, cocaine/crack suppliers would no longer give them crack on consignment. They were no longer able to raise funds to make wholesale purchases. Thus, most could only function as low-level distributors (Furst et al., 1998; Dunlap et al., 1997; Dunlap, 1992; Hamid, 1992a, 1992b; Johnson et al., 1992). As an aggregate result of this pat tern, the consignment system became relatively uncommon; most crack dealers would only sell wholesale amount of cocaine or crack to persons who wished to sell crack for cash purchases. Many persons who were active as crack sellers in the late 1980s became crack heads and cannot obtain funds or advances of crack to sell; while willing to sell, they are effectively excluded from such sales roles by their reputation for unreliability.

Crack Selling Organizations

Four major organized styles of crack selling emerged in New York during the decade 1986-97.

- *Freelancing:* Virtually all crack distributors preferred freelance work (where they sold alone and were responsible for both money and drugs). "Lone freelancers," although common, did not predominate in New York City.[8] The more organized competitors drove most freelance crack sellers out of the more lucrative public selling locations; police arrested and removed others. The primary long-term hindrance, however, was crack dependence among freelancers. Most heavy crack abusers failed to "keep the money straight," eventually consuming supplies they were supposed to sell. Without enough cash to buy multiple sales units from a supplier, they generally find themselves in day-laborer roles for someone else. As detailed below, some of the most effective "freelancers" are female crack sellers who sell from houses. Freelancers also made substantially better returns than did the day laborers (Caulkins et al., 1999).

- *Freelance Cooperatives:* This arrangement involves several freelance sellers collaborating in a loose cooperative in a particular location, relying on informal agreements to help each other. Each of two to 10 freelance sellers working on the same block claimed their own "spot" from which to sell drugs. Each seller became a lookout for police and a source of referral of customers to the others. Freelance sellers might lend each other money or drugs or help out in emergencies (e.g., provide bail money, pay for funerals, etc.) or jointly sponsor community block parties in order to co-opt support from nonusing citizens who might otherwise complain to police. Collectively, they discourage new distributors from establishing other selling locations on the block. But sellers individually obtain their own suppliers of crack, their own regular customers, and responsibility for both money and drugs. The number of freelance sellers can vary substantially at different times of the day. Collectives often organize their hours in "shifts" so they are not in directly competition for customers. Such freelance cooperatives were more common in the late 1980s than in the mid-1990s (Johnson et al., 1991).

- *Day laborers:* Crack distributors unable to purchase supplies of crack to sell often seek work from other crack sellers and buyers. Usually hired for a day, they may hand out drugs ("pitch") after someone else obtains the money, or serve as a lookout. Effectively, the day laborer is paid to do as directed in a quasi-employee role. Typically, the day laborer is paid in drugs rather than cash; the rapid consumption of such returns ensures a steady and cheap labor supply.

- *Business-like crack sellers:* These individuals constitute a minority of crack distributors. They hire and pay regular salaries to a few key employees, often providing various other benefits as well. Most workers are hired as day laborers to sell crack in public and private locations, without guarantee of work on any given day, and without benefits. The project located a variety of crack-distribution crews, which tended to be organized around two distinct management practices (Curtis, 1996, 1995; Curtis and Svirdoff, 1994).

Localized crack distribution groups primarily comprise persons related to each other as family members or kin, or else they emerge out of cliques of childhood/adolescent friends. Almost all members have many years of association, trust each other, and generally work together effectively as a team of sellers. But police buy-bust tactics would often remove many or all such distributors at one time. Likewise, personal fights and jealousies often undermined group cohesion and sales work.

Businesslike crews of crack sellers were more common. Usually, one dealer hires and manages several unrelated persons paid for performing various roles, hiring the most trustworthy and effective low-level distributors from among a very large pool of persons with untrustworthy reputations. Such organized crews of crack sellers are among the few offering monetary wages to low-level distributors (the "day laborers") for performing various crack distribution roles. The dealer provides all crack sold by the crew boss and street sellers, and gains almost all the monetary returns accruing from their sales. The street manager/crew boss does not sell drugs, does not hold them when they are being sold, and is not holding money just derived from sales, making it more difficult for police to "prove" that he is the manager and part of the team.

Typically, a successful dealer hires one or more "street manager(s)" each of whom, as a "crew boss," assumes responsibility for hiring and supervising street selling groups of two to five persons. While the employer/dealer pays the crew boss regular wages or commissions, street sellers are usually hired as day laborers and given a choice of payment in money or drugs. The crew boss provides workers with instructions "not to sell to police or undercover" and to "never take shorts" (sell at a discount). Street sellers who are arrested receive no legal representation, and are in fact often expected, after release from jail, to repay the drugs seized during their arrest. The turnover of crack sellers, who need the constant supervision of a crew boss, is substantial. Some dealers employ unrelated teams of sellers in different locations throughout the city.

Cocaine/crack distribution organizations and crack-use/sale institutions underwent considerable change during the 1980s and 1990s. Crack sales and markets have clearly dominated illegal drug markets in New York City since 1985. The predominant tactics used by crack distributors changed along with the history of the crack era, however (Lipton and Johnson, 1998; Hamid, 1992b; Johnson et al., 1992; Mieczkowski et al., 1992). During the 1970s and early 1980s, informal after-hours locations (serving alcohol after liquor stores and bars closed) drew cocaine users congregating to snort cocaine (Williams, 1978). During the period of 1981-83, many cocaine after-hours locales became freebase parlors where one could purchase and "cook up" cocaine into freebase, which was then smoked (Williams, 1989). These indoor locales were converted to crack houses and apartments in 1984-86 (Williams, 1991). During 1987-90, freelance crack sellers conducted most crack distribution in public curbside locations, and crack supermarkets abounded throughout the city (Hamid, 1992b). Since 1990, aggressive policing has reduced curbside distribution. By the mid-1990s, many sellers moved inside into *bodegas,* pool halls, laundromats, video arcades and other seemingly legitimate storefronts and apartments (Curry and Dunlap, 1996; Curtis, 1996, 1995; Curtis et al., 1995; Goldsmith, 1995). More crack sales probably occur indoors than outdoors, a change accompanied by an equally fundamental shift in the roles of sellers and low-level distributors.

With increased police pressure, fewer young crack users, and declining crack markets, many freelance sellers have not fared well. Likewise, vertically organized, relatively large crack distribution groups controlled by one or two dealers who benefit from the labor of 15 or more people are disappearing. They are specifically targeted and broken up by police. Many organized business groups, while maintaining an active street outreach to buyers, function from indoor locations. Many freelance sellers in the late 1980s, unable to maintain their freelance status in the 1990s, have joined the large pool of low-level distributors and function primarily as "middlemen" between buyers and sellers who never meet.

Due to well-grounded fears of police buy-bust tactics, however, crack sellers (those responsible for both money and drugs) grew unwilling to sell to any person who was not a "regular" (or at least previously known) customer. They established new tactics (Furst et al., 1996; Goldsmith, 1996; Johnson, 1996; Johnson and Natarajan, 1995), significantly reducing the number of visible police targets (Curtis, 1996, 1995; Furst et al., 1996; Maher 1996). Sellers are rarely on the street "hawking" crack or attempting sales to any new prospective buyer. Many use cloned cellular phones to maintain contact with customers and fill orders (Natarajan et al., 1995). Steerers and touts direct buyers to apartments while middlemen complete transactions for many buyers. These alternative strategies mean that virtually all drug purchasers can make buys within a half-hour, even when they need to evade police to do so (Riley, 1998). While policing has had little measurable impact upon the availability of crack or upon crack markets, or upon consumers' ability to purchase drugs, the police strategies and tactics did effectively end the city's drug supermarkets and has substantially affected the style and social organization of distribution (Curtis and Sviridoff, 1994; Sviridoff et al., 1992).

Increased Importance of the Middleman Distribution Role

In the mid-1990s, largely as a result of policing, an important transition also occurred in the role of the "middleman." During 1994-96, intensified policing in New York increased the importance of the middleman for both sellers (concealing their identity and reducing their risk of arrest) and buyers (to complete drug purchases) in avoiding contact with the police (Furst et al., 1998). Because long-time crack abusers/buyers from the community generally "know" who, where, and how to contact regular neighborhood crack sellers, and are known to be trustworthy — and not to be undercover police — they can usually avoid middlemen. Persons seeking to purchase crack or cocaine in a new community, however, are unlikely to find anyone willing to sell them crack directly, as was the case in the late 1980s. In addition, potential buyers (often correctly suspected of being undercover police officers) will likely encounter a "middleman" often called a "cop man" or "go-between." The middleman, who has no drugs to sell directly but "knows" where to obtain crack for a fee, offers to transport money and drugs between buyers and sellers who never meet. The buyer can either give this intermediary the money in the hope that he will return with the crack or look elsewhere.

From the vantage points of the buyer and the police, the intermediary appears to be the seller. Any marked or recorded money given by an undercover officer will typically have been used to pay the drug seller. When the middleman turns over the crack, which is usually less than ordered and paid for, the undercover officer could arrest him, but typically only for a lesser charge. In short, the middleman has been able to earn a profit from both the crack seller (whom he or she protects against an undercover buy and arrest) and the buyer (who obtains the drug). The middleman thus earns money and/or drugs from both (Johnson et al., 1985).

Such intensified policing resulted in greater caution among those engaging in drug distribution in public places. Street level sellers knew the high probability of being "stopped" by police during a typical week in 1996. Thus, they carried accurate identification, had no outstanding warrants, had no illicit drugs in their possession, kept supplies well hidden, and avoided direct sales to any "new" buyer.

FEMALE CRACK DISTRIBUTION AND SEX WORK

Earlier research (Fagan, 1994a, 1994b; Inciardi et al., 1993) documented crack selling and prostitution as the primary career choices for inner-city crack-using women. This project had a substantial opportunity to carefully examine the living standards and lifestyles of crack-abusing women in New York City, including their involvement in crack and other drug sales, nondrug criminality, and sex work. During periods when they sold crack or other drugs, their involvement in prostitution was substantially lessened; conversely, when women crack users were unable to sell/help sell drugs, their reliance on sex work increased substantially.

An important disagreement existing within the literature was mirrored among project staff regarding the extent of gender equality in crack distribution business. Staff conducting fieldwork mainly in Harlem and the South Bronx focused upon women actively engaged in various crack and drug distribution roles (Dunlap et al., 1997; Dunlap and Johnson, 1996; Maher and Daly, 1996; Maher et al., 1996), but neither on their sex work activity, nor upon crack-using women who were primarily sex workers. Crack-using women studied in Harlem claimed, and were observed, to be relatively equal to male counterparts in their performance of street-level distribution roles (as sellers or low-level distributors).[9] Ethnographers conducting fieldwork among crack-abusing women in the Bushwick section of Brooklyn, where many women engaged in sex work, reported more gender and ethnic biases directed against women as distributors. Crack-using women were left with virtually no option other than sex work, primarily because they would not be hired as day laborers by crack-selling crews (Maher, 1997; Maher et al., 1996). While the most successful female crack sellers managed house connections, the majority had intermittent involvement in crack selling and usually performed low-level distribution roles.

A few women operated "house connections" from which they sold crack to a selected clientele. These women, who usually came from relatively more stable family backgrounds (Dunlap and Johnson, 1996) were able to pay the rent, or have welfare pay the landlord directly, as well as manage a household. One female crack seller, Rachel, was using and selling crack from her apartment in the early 1990s (Dunlap and Johnson, 1996; Dunlap et al., 1994). Yet, she raised a daughter, sent her through college, and paid for the daughter's expensive wedding. Rachel avoided both arrest and dereliction. Her career evolved around shifts in drug markets from marijuana to cocaine to crack. A female in a male-dominated profession, she was a deviant among deviants. She used sales techniques common to middle-class female dealers, rather than those more typical of her inner-city location. She succeeded in these efforts primarily by avoiding collaboration with and control by male suppliers, although she usually purchased wholesale supplies from them.

Rachel catered to the "hidden" and employed crack user, avoiding the stereotypical street crack abuser (also see Hamid 1992a, for men). Her apartment was one of few places where buyers could both purchase and consume crack. Her clientele illuminates an unknown side of the crack economy — the older, better-educated, working/middle-class drug user. Rachel provided discretion and confidentiality, in an appropriate setting. She helped customers manage the effects of crack and oversee their finances so they did not spend all their money on the drug. She controlled unruly customers and avoided unwanted sexual attention. She maintained good relations with neighbors so they would not call the police. Above all else, she controlled her personal consumption, always setting aside rent money, and eating and sleeping regularly. Seemingly a middle-class woman in the inner city, she avoided arrest, even when stopped by police.

This project encountered two other female house connections, who managed but did not pay the rent for a separate apartment from which crack was sold. Project staff were not able to identify male crack sellers operating "house connections" (like Rachel's) from their own apartment. That is, males were less successful at managing an apartment-cum-crackhouse where crack is both sold and used. Several male sellers, however, either operated out of, or sold crack in households maintained — or where the rent was paid by — a girl friend, a female relative, or the welfare system. Male sellers would frequently offer to pay female crack users for the use of their apartment for storing, cutting, or selling crack and other drugs but rarely paid in cash for that privilege, preferring to provide crack instead.

Unlike Rachel, the vast majority of female crack distributors primarily function in the lowest roles in drug distribution networks. The project carefully documented the lifestyles of female crack distributors. The vast majority of women (like a majority of men) occupied distribution roles at the bottom of the distribution hierarchy where, as "touts," "steerers," "go-betweens," "middlemen," "holders," "cooks," "lookouts," they do not simultaneously handle both money and drugs (Dunlap et al., 1997). While women distributors sometimes function as freelance sellers, they more frequently work for male dealers in street sales roles (making direct sales to retail customers), or in other low-level distribution roles.

Female crack users observed in Brooklyn experienced the discrimination against female users in sales roles shared by virtually all the crack suppliers, who are male (Maher, 1997). Least likely of the day laborer pool of crack users to be "hired" as pitchers and sales helpers by male "crew bosses" and distribution organizations, women were the first to be laid off or not subsequently rehired. While almost all women claim past "higher-level sales jobs" and "more responsible" positions in the drug sales workforce, virtually all report holding these positions when they were younger (ages 16 to 25), and before they began using crack. With few exceptions (like Rachel), however, female crack users/distributors in Brooklyn only had infrequent and/or marginal work as crack sellers/distributors. When engaged in sales, males closely supervise their activities. Often women are dominated and cheated by male bosses and exposed to high levels of violence from other male sellers or managers.

Most crack-abusing/selling women experienced a variety of alternative living arrangements; very few had a stable conventional residence (Maher et al., 1996). Crack-abusing women are effectively "de-homed": they do not have a regular place to live, sleep, relax, bathe, eliminate, or store possessions. Because they usually found alternative, though temporary, living arrangements, however, most are not street persons. They demonstrate considerable effort and ingenuity, spending little or no money on rent, yet finding places to stay for relatively limited time periods. Almost all women came from very poor, precariously housed families, and lost the support of family or friends as a result of their crack use. Few could remain on welfare and most had no legal income during the study. The women avoided Single Room Occupancy (SRO) or "welfare" hotels and public shelters, viewing them as criminogenic and dangerous. A few "slept rough" or squatted curbside, usually with a man. By far the most common alternative living arrangement was for women to reside for a limited period in the household of an older male who had a dependable income. Women typically provided these men with sex and drugs, and, less often, with cash, domestic service, or companionship. They also stole from or exploited the older men in various ways. A number of women lived in "freakhouses" — apartments or homes where several women entertain sexual customers and share crack or other drugs. These women avoid crack houses or shooting galleries as residential locations. These alternative living arrangements reflect the women's powerlessness and document the high levels of sexual exploitation and degradation of women in the inner-city crack culture. Among crack abusers/sellers, males were at least as likely as females to be without permanent residence. It is important to note that proportionately more males than women were clearly homeless, and slept on the streets, in abandoned buildings, and public places (Clatts and Davis, 1993). The preferred housing situation for male crack abusers/sellers was to live with, and usually have a sexual relationship with, a women who had an apartment that was often paid for by welfare. Such arrangements were typically short-term; the male was often put out or left the woman and her household within a few weeks or months. Relatively few women in the Brooklyn study area regularly generated income through theft and shoplifting, although virtually all women had done so at some time. Low-risk theft and shoplifting by female crack-abuser/distributors was infrequent, mainly because there were so few goods to steal from local establishments that local residents would then purchase from crack-using women (Maher, 1997).

Crack-abusing women are very near the bottom of the status hierarchy within the mainstream economy as well as the street-level economy. Virtually no female crack distributor held a legal job of any kind. For the most part, they are effectively excluded from the legal, mainstream economy. Many factors effectively exclude crack-abuser/distributors from the legal economy, from informal kin network supports, and even from most positions in the street-level and drug economy (Maher, 1997; Maher et al., 1996; Fagan, 1994a; Johnson and Dunlap, 1992; Johnson et al., 1990). They rarely apply for legal jobs, seldom get jobs they apply for, and hardly ever keep the rare job they get for more than a few days. Indeed, legal employment was many years in the past for most of them. Likewise, most crack-abuser/distributor women are unable to remain on welfare and/or maintain a household. Therefore, few had legal income from any source. Moreover, their situation is little better in the street-level economy. While crack-using women in Brooklyn alternate between drug distribution roles and sex work, sex work predominates because male sexual partners frequently pressure women into it, and because of customer preferences.

The contributions of female crack abuser/distributors to the drug economy (via commercial sex work, drug distribution, and thefts) are confined to the margins by male sellers and substantially structured by customers' racial/ethnic preferences (Maher, 1997; Bourgois, 1995; Inciardi et al., 1993; Bourgois and Dunlap, 1992; Ratner, 1992). While many of the Brooklyn females occasionally engage in crack distribution when male crew bosses hired them as day laborers, the strictures and structures of street life effectively relegate most of them to the "oldest profession." The Brooklyn research shows that women's sex work effectively results from — or reflects their systematic exclusions by — the structures of the formal economy, the informal sector, and illicit drug markets. In all sectors, crack-using women have few alternatives to prostitution for generating income and/or for obtaining drugs.

Much social science research, many police accounts, male seller's accounts, and journalistic reports apply an "hypersexuality hypothesis" that effectively demonizes these women crack abusers. This convenient explanation blames the drug (e.g., crack) for women's extensive engagements in sexuality. The research (Maher, 1997) found that crack did not produce a cohort of hypersexual women primarily accepting payment in crack. Rather, they followed occupational norms for prostitution governing price, sexual acts, physical safety and bartering practices, and emphasizing sex work for money. While on occasion most women exchange in sex-for-crack or for other drugs, this is clearly against their usual practices. Yet a variety of discriminatory practices (based upon ethnicity, gender stereotypes, and family linkages) by male "dates" and by drug sellers effectively force women to accept crack/drugs or very low monetary payments for their sexual services. Indeed, women competed strenuously for "dates" paying relatively high prices. Moreover, many male crack sellers exploit crack-using women sexually and dominate them with violence when and if they complain.

Likewise, Maher's (1997) study found no evidence that these women became more liberated, more violent, or behaved "more like" their male counterparts. While many exhibit a "violent" or "crazy" public persona when distributing crack or drugs, as part of street drug culture, they are physically victimized much more often than they actually harm anyone else. Women resist male domination and exploitation as best they can. A primary form of resistance is what they call "viccing" [victimizing someone] that is, stealing money or possessions from dates, or not providing services [sex or drugs] after receiving payments. While "getting over" on dates or drug buyers [who almost never report them to police] is a crude cultural adaptation to their own victimization, women's "viccing" is only a short-term solution raising short-term money. "Viccing" does not lead women away from the street life and continues to bind women to the oppressive structures that control their street-level sex work or occasional involvement in drug distribution (Maher, 1997).

Few female crack abusers/distributors are able to rear (or even maintain an on-going relationship) with their children. The vast majority of crack abuser/distributor women never married; most do not have a long-term, common-law relationship. Yet most have borne children. These women generally "gave" their babies to relatives in their kin networks or had their children taken by foster care/adoption (Johnson et al., 1998; Maher, 1997; Dunlap, 1995, 1992). Direct observations of crack-abusing women living with their children in household settings indicate that most lack many critical child-rearing skills (time and household management, psychological nurturing, emotional warmth and intimacy, appropriate discipline, etc.). If and when they assume responsibility for their children, they often neglect and sometimes physically punish them (Johnson et al., 1998).

Even the kin networks and female relatives who rear these children follow conduct norms likely to result in children having serious behavioral problems in adolescence and adulthood (Johnson et al., 1998; Maher, 1997). Moreover, child-rearing problems worsened across generations. In the 1990s, primary caregivers consist mainly of women born before 1945, rearing many of the children born in the 1980s and 1990s to street-involved, crack-abusing women. These kin networks will almost certainly disintegrate during the early 2000s as the older women who maintain the households and care for children die or become incapacitated (Johnson et al., 1998). Almost none of their crack and drug-abusing daughters (usually under age 50 in the 1990s) will successfully overcome their addictions in their late adulthood; fewer still will gain enough legal income to pay the rent and maintain a household in which infants and children can be raised. The results are already evident in the next generation, even as they initiate their own participation in the drug economy.

YOUNG RELUCTANTLY ENGAGE IN DRUG SALES, BUT WITH LIMITED SUCCESS

Inner-city youths and young adults in the 1990s see both sides of crack selling; the (rarely actualized) promise of 'easy money' sharply contrasts with the downward spiral of those caught by the criminal justice system or by their own addiction. They also observe violence and death in the drug trade, witness cheating by sellers, experience stiff competition among sellers, and recognize the high probability of crack and heroin addiction. Distribution roles in crack and other drug markets are well known and easy-to-access by inner-city youths. For many, drug distribution roles appear to be the only available economic option. Yet, these youths are apprehensive. Selling requires a wide range of skills they lack, including the "heart" and the "street smarts" to recognize undercover police (Jacobs, 1999, 1996a, 1996b,), manage to possess and use guns (Taylor et al., 1999), and to deal with competition.

Although research staff located some persons who function as mentors to younger sellers, few youths have someone to show them how to sell effectively while avoiding police. Youths who begin engaging in drug sales often are quickly arrested. Additionally, drug markets may be crowded with older, experienced crack users who undercut retail prices for a "hit." Partly as a result, sales roles are less open to newcomers, and youths find financial success in drug selling increasingly improbable. Higher-level managers perceived the few youths who themselves used crack as extremely unreliable. Thus, many high-risk youths currently appear reluctant to sell crack or other hard drugs, and to fare poorly if they do so (Furst et al., 1999).

With the probabilities of arrest and incarceration high, many young adults in the younger generations have made a reasoned choice to not sell crack (Golub and Johnson 1999b; Johnson, 1997). They choose not to sell drugs they do not use. Youths do not want to sell to "crack heads" or "junkies" whom they despise, for dealers and crew bosses eager to exploit them, while having to dodge police trying to arrest them. Yet without available jobs or welfare support, many young adults who would prefer to avoid drug sales find that such illicit distribution is the only economic activity available to them. Their participation in crack distribution is typically a sporadic and intermittent way to earn some limited income. Women of this generation often engage in prostitution for the same reasons.

CONCLUSIONS AND IMPLICATIONS

This research project sought to increase scientific understanding of the phenomena of crack selling and distribution. The significance of the findings permeates the more than 40 existing and the many forthcoming publications from this research project. The authors offer only a brief overview of the most important public policy implications flowing from this research. The main conclusions emerging from this project remain fundamentally negative. Extensive investment in crime control has not had — and probably never will have — important measurable impacts upon drug use patterns, drug selling patterns, or prices of illicit drugs in the nation's inner cities. It remains an open question whether, in fact, intensified policing has had any significant impact on drug use, or whether the greater influence has been to shift the locations of illegal drug transactions. Fewer drug supermarkets may reduce street violence (Johnson et al., 2000) and in other ways alter the negative impact of drug dealing upon inner cities. This is not the same, however, as arguing that policing is directly effective in stopping the distribution and consumption of crack and illegal drugs.

Markets for heroin, cocaine, and crack will be very extensive and enforcement costs will continue to increase as distributors adapt their strategies in response to those of police. Ethnographic and governmental evidence (Caulkins et al., 1999; Caulkins, 1997; Drug Enforcement Administration [DEA], 1996) show that retail prices of these drugs have declined or remained consistent over a decade. Moreover, cocaine purities are as high as they were a decade ago, at the height of the crack era. Indeed, all of the extensive ethnographic observations and quantitative evidence (Riley, 1998) suggest that regular customers and occasional buyers alike have little difficulty obtaining heroin, crack, or cocaine whenever they have the funds. The variety of crack sellers, the diversity of sellers' marketing strategies, the purchasing pattern of their clientele, and user/seller tactics effectively conceal illegal drug sales from police (Jacobs, 1999; Maher, 1996; Johnson and Natarajan, 1995; Johnson et al., 1993).

The overwhelming majority of all illegal transactions thus occur without detection by law enforcement, much less arrest and/or incarceration. Yet the federal government remains committed to spending several billion additional dollars each year to support drug interdiction, crop eradication, arrests of and expansion of prison cells for retail drug sellers (Bureau of Justice Statistics 1999). These efforts will continue despite excellent evidence (Caulkins, 1997; DEA, 1996) that such investments have not substantially influenced the quantity, quality or prices of illicit drugs in America, and are unlikely to do so in future decades.

In response to intensified police enforcement efforts, crack distributors have moved their activities indoors, making it more difficult for police to observe transactions, identify and document specifically which persons were involved in what distribution roles, or make buy-bust arrests that stand up in court. Improvements in police suppression of illicit drug sales in public places will undoubtedly continue, as will the much larger number of transactions occurring in private. In short, illicit sales and distribution of crack, cocaine, heroin, and marijuana (Sifaneck, 1997, 1996; Sifaneck and Kaplan, 1997, 1995; Sifaneck and Small, 1997) will remain a major occupational activity for a few hundred thousand New Yorkers for years to come, despite the improved efficiency of the police department and continued efforts of political leaders to suppress the business.

Several major public policy initiatives have contributed to, and are likely to further destabilize, the already dismal prospects for the crack-using and selling generation. Major policy changes in the nation's social welfare system are being implemented at about the same time under different legislation, administered by a variety of federal, state and local agencies. These policies are certain to have important negative impacts upon crack distributors/users and the members of the youth generations in the next dozen years.

Several key provisions in the welfare legislation of 1996 are designed to specifically preclude users of illicit drugs from various types of income transfer payments. Title I legislatively mandates that persons convicted of a drug felony be specifically excluded from receiving welfare support during their lifetime. Probably a million low-income Americans have been convicted of a drug-related felony, and could be denied welfare benefits. Exclusion of drug felons from welfare benefits could become as automatic as police "field checks" of persons stopped in the community. Although this legislation gives each state the opportunity to "opt out" of some preclusions, few states have done so to date; indeed, states may and do, impose more stringent conditions upon drug users. Another, separate, piece of legislation removes "addiction" as an eligible disability category for receiving Social Security Insurance (SSI) and food stamps. SSI has been the steadiest and largest cash amount of transfer income available to the small minority of drug abusers who have received it.

The welfare legislation passed in 1996 will likely remove the primary (and often only) legal income supporting the households in which the children of, and crack abuser/sellers themselves, reside for varied periods. The advent of the 1996 welfare legislation, limiting welfare payments to an individual person to a maximum of five years, will further aggravate the already dismal situation confronting drug abusers and those with whom they live. Women who occasionally used crack or illicit drugs in the mid-1990s, and who receive welfare and maintain low-income households, are very likely to lose their welfare benefits and households after the turn of the century. Lacking the required skills for legal jobs, a sizable number may enter the street-level economy, as potential competitors in the already competitive street-level sex work and low-level drug distribution markets.

While few members of the post-crack generation have ever married or established a modestly long-term (over one-year), common-law relationship, most men have sired, and most women have borne, one or more children before their mid-twenties. Even when the identity of a child's biological father is known, he rarely provides — nor is he able to provide — economic support and is seldom involved in that child's rearing. Yet, the long-term future may also involve the loss of welfare payments that directly pays for housing units where most members of the youth generation now live. The older women (now generally in their 50s, 60s or 70s) who maintain the households, and where the welfare system directly pays rent to the landlord, may be removed from the welfare rolls within the next five years. Moreover, these older women are likely to die or become incapacitated or otherwise unable to meet the complex demands of raising young children with meager resources, in the next decade.[10] Few of their daughters and younger relatives — many with adult careers as drug abusers and sellers — can maintain rental payments, manage what welfare/foster care support may be available, or as they become older, rear their own grandchildren.

The correctional system is the primary government "service" being systematically expanded to *include* crack and drug abusers and the post-crack generation. Various public policies and dramatic expansion in funding have been designed to "get tough" on criminals, especially sellers of crack cocaine (Johnson and Muffler, 1997; Johnson et al., 1990), including mandatory minimum sentences for the sale or possession of small amounts of crack cocaine, repeat offender sentencing, "three strikes" legislation with lifetime incarceration, elimination of early parole, and continued increases in funding for police, prosecution, and courts. Additionally, the expansion in the number of jails and prisons and the total capacity to incarcerate offenders is well documented. The growth in correctional populations has averaged 4 to 9 percent annually, so the number of jail and prison inmates has about doubled during each of the past two decades (BJS 1999). Projections of current increases suggest that approximately two million persons will be incarcerated at the end of 1999, three million by 2005 and four million persons will be in jails and prisons by year end 2010.

For every incarcerated person, approximately three others are at liberty but on parole or probation or under criminal justice supervision. The projections suggest that the total number under criminal justice supervision will increase from about 6 million in 2000 to over 10 million in 2010. The proportion of African-American males under criminal justice supervision, which increased from 25% in 1990 to 33% in 1995 (Mauer, 1995, 1990), will probably reach 50% by 2010. Although the data are not as specific, a sizable minority (about a third) of persons incarcerated and/or under criminal justice supervi-

sion will have been convicted of the possession or sale of crack, cocaine, or heroin. Likewise, an additional proportion of those convicted of other offenses (e.g., robbery, burglary, thefts) will also have
sold crack or other drugs.

The beliefs and practices towards crack and cocaine among the
"post-crack" cohort (those born in the 1970s) will likely change, although in unanticipated (and thus far unforeseeable) directions.
Further shifts towards more use or away from crack or heroin remain
critically important for policy makers. The emergent behaviors of
youths reaching adulthood in the 1990s ("post-crack era" cohort)
shows that cocaine use was detected in fewer than 30% of arrestees.
Crack use could "bottom up" or undergo an "upswing" or "upsurge."
Future research must document the long- and short-term trends in
drug use and abuse.

The prognosis for the future lives of the crack and post-crack generation is exceedingly bleak. Most inner-city youths born in the
1970s and reared in severely distressed households have dismal fu-
tures. Overall, the generation born in the 1970s have generally been
severely deprived during their childhood and have gained minimal
conventional skills. Ethnographic evidence makes clear that sizable
numbers of youths from severely distressed household may engage in
crack selling. Some of those avoiding crack in late adolescence may
eventually become cocaine/crack users (Golub et al., 1996). Furthermore, the very large pool of unemployed, out-of-labor force, minority youth has few options: many if not most will *never have any
significant legal employment during their entire adulthood*. Except for
their relatively vigorous participation in the street culture and drug
economy, a sizable proportion of post-crack generation members has
failed to achieve any of the key roles which American society expects
of persons during their early adult years. They are thus at high risk
for involvement in use and sale of heroin, marijuana, heavy alcohol
intake, violent crimes, and various illegal activities. Were cocaine and
crack prices to drop substantially, such youths might move into
dealing roles, sell other drugs (like heroin), or become active in nondrug criminality and violence. But with heavy police enforcement efforts, virtually every high-risk youth can expected to be stopped on
suspicion of something, and be arrested and booked for relatively
minor charges.

Now in early adulthood, the post-crack generation is effectively
excluded by their upbringing and lack of conventional skills from the
legal economic system, from welfare support, and even from many
illegal occupations. Their failure to obtain legal employment, much
less above-poverty wages, contributes directly to another ominous
condition: the near collapse of, or failure to establish, new families

and households. The only bright aspect the research found in their lives of the post-crack generation is the absence of crack smoking, and avoidance of heroin abuse and injection. Nothing else provides much hope or promise for a better future for most members of this cohort.

Moreover, the conditions existing in the families and households settings of the very poor and among drug users have steadily worsened. These persons will remain excluded from legitimate jobs, have declining or no access to welfare and income supports, and few options other than drug sales and prostitution. The recent past (1980s and 1990s) was very hard upon those living in the inner city. The future looks equally bleak for the next generation, and probably for their children and descendants in the first quarter of this new century. No magic bullet or policy has yet been discovered that prevents drug use nor criminal behavior.

Address correspondence to: Bruce D Johnson, National Development and Research Institutes, Two World Trade Center, 16th Floor, New York, New York 10047.

Acknowledgments: This research was supported by the National Institute on Drug Abuse (NIDA) (1R01 DA 05126-08, 5R01 DA09056-02, 5 T32 DA07233-17) and NIDA Minority Research Supplemental Award (1 R03 DA 06413-01). The opinions expressed in this report do not represent the official position of the U.S. Government, National Institute on Drug Abuse, or National Development and Research Institutes, Inc. (NDRI).

REFERENCES

Note: An asterisk (*) identifies a reference as a publication or presentation from the Crack Distribution/Abuse Project. Reprints can be requested from the senior author.

Baskin, D.R. and I.B. Sommers (1998). *Casualties of Community Disorder: Women's Careers in Violent Crime.* Boulder, CO: Westview Press.

Bourgois, P. (1995). *In Search of Respect: Selling Crack in El Barrio.* New York, NY: Cambridge University Press.

*—— and E. Dunlap (1992). "Exorcising Sex-for-Crack: An Ethnographic Perspective from Harlem." In: M.S. Ratner (ed.), *Crack Pipe as Pimp: An Ethnographic Investigation of Sex-for-Crack Exchanges.* New York, NY: Lexington Books/Macmillan.

Brunswick, A.F. and S.P. Titus (1998). "Heroin Patterns and Trajectories in an African American Cohort (1969-1990)." In: J.A. Inciardi and L. D. Harrison (eds.), *Heroin in the Age of Crack Cocaine.* Beverly Hills, CA: Sage.

Bureau of Justice Statistics (1999). *Prison and Jail Inmates at Midyear 1998.* Washington, DC.

Clatts, M. and W.R. Davis (1993). "A Demographic and Behavioral Profile of Homeless Youth in New York City: Implications for AIDS Outreach and Prevention." Paper presented at the American Public Health Association Meeting, San Francisco.

Caulkins, J.P. (1997). "Is Crack Cheaper Than (Powder) Cocaine?" *Addiction* 92(11):1437-1443.

*—— B.D. Johnson, A. Taylor and L. Taylor (1999). "What Drug Dealers Tell Us About Their Costs of Doing Business." *Journal of Drug Issues* 29(2):323-340.

Chaiken, J.M. and M.R. Chaiken (1993.) *Understanding the Drug Use Forecasting (DUF) Sample of Adult Arrestees.* Report to the National Institute of Justice. Lincoln, MA: LINC.

Clifford, J. and G.E. Marcus (1986). *Writing Culture: The Poetics and Politics of Ethnography.* Berkeley, CA: University of California Press.

Curtis, R.S. and B. Spunt (1999). Personal Communication. Direct Major Ethnographic Study of Heroin Use and Selling in New York City, NY. John Jay College of Criminal Justice.

*—— R. Friedman, A. Neaigus, B. Jose, M. Goldstein and G. Ildefonso (1995). "Street-level Drug Market Structure and HIV Risk." *Social Networks* 17:229-249.

—— and M. Svirdoff. (1994). "The Social Organization of Street-level Drug Markets and its Impact on the Displacement Effect." In: R.P. McNamara (ed.), *Crime Displacement: The Other Side of Prevention.* East Rockaway, NY: Cummings and Hathaway.

Des Jarlais, D.C., T. Perlis, S.R. Friedman, S. Deren, J.L. Sotheran, S. Tortu, M. Beardsley, D. Paone, V.L. Torian, S.T. Beatrice, E. Dunlap, E. Bernardo, E. Monterroso and M. Marmor (1998). "Declining Seroprevalence in a Very Large HIV Epidemic: Injecting Drug Users in New York City, 1991-1996." *American Journal of Public Health* 88(12):1801-1806.

—— S.R. Friedman, J.L. Sotheran, J. Wenston, J. Marmor, S.R. Yank-ovitz, B. Frank, S.T. Beatrice and D. Mildvan (1994). "Continuity and Change within an HIV Epidemic: Injection Drug Users in New York City, 1984 Through 1992." *Journal of the American Medical Association* 27(2):121-127.

Drug Enforcement Administration (1996). *The Supply of Illicit Drugs to the United States.* Washington, DC: National Narcotics Intelligence Consumers Committee.

*Dunlap, E. (1995). "Inner-city Crisis and Drug Dealing: Portrait of a Drug Dealer and His Household." In: S. MacGregor and A. Lipow (eds.), *The Other City: People and Politics in New York and London.* New Jersey: Humanities Press.

*—— and B.D. Johnson (1999). "Gaining Access to Hidden Populations: Strategies for Gaining Cooperation of Sellers/Dealers in Ethnographic Research." *Drugs and Society* 14(1/2):127-149.

*—— B.D. Johnson and L. Maher (1997). "Female Crack Dealers in New York City: Who they Are and What They Do." *Women and Criminal Justice* 8(4):25-55.

*—— and B.D. Johnson (1996). "Family and Human Resources in the Development of a Female Crack Seller Career: Case Study of a Hidden Population." *Journal of Drug Issues* 26(1):177-200.

*—— B.D. Johnson and J.W. Rath (1996). "Aggression and Violence in Households of Crack Sellers/Abusers." *Applied Behavioral Science Review* 4(2):191-217.

*—— B.D., T. Johnson and T. Furst (1995). *Crack Use: Towards Self-regulation and Stabilization: Challenges of Crime and Social Control.* Paper presented at the American Society of Criminology, Boston, November.

*—— B.D. Johnson and A. Manwar (1994). "A Successful Female Crack Dealer: Case Study of a Deviant Career." *Deviant Behavior* 15:1-25.

*—— (1992). "Impact of Drugs on Family Life and Kin Networks in the Inner-city African-American Single Parent Household." In: A. Harrell and G. Peterson (eds.), *Drugs, Crime, and Social Isolation: Barriers to Urban Opportunity.* Washington, DC: Urban Institute Press.

*—— and B.D. Johnson (1992). "The Setting for the Crack Era: Macro Forces, Micro Consequences (1960-92)." *Journal of Psychoactive Drugs* 24(3):307-321.

—— B.D. Johnson, H. Sanabria, E. Holliday, V. Lipsey, M. Barnett, W. Hopkins, I. Sobel, D. Randolph, and K. Chin (1990). "Studying Crack Users and Their Criminal Careers: Scientific and Artistic Aspects of Locating Hard-to-Reach Subjects and Interviewing Them About Sensitive Topics." *Contemporary Drug Problems* 17(1):121-144.

Emerson, R.M. (ed.) (1988). *Contemporary Field Research: A Collection of Readings.* Prospect Heights, IL.: Waveland.

Fagan, J. (1994a). "Women and Drugs Revisited: Female Participation in the Cocaine Economy." *Journal of Drug Issues* 24(2):179-226.

—— (1994b). "Do Criminal Sanctions Deter Drug Crimes?" In: D.L. MacKenzie and C. Uchida (eds.), *Drugs and the Criminal Justice System: Evaluating Public Policy Alternatives.* Newbury Park, CA: Sage.

—— (1992). "Drug Selling and Licit Income in Distressed Neighborhoods: The Economic Lives of Street-level Drug Users and Dealers." In: A. Harrell and G. Peterson (eds.), *Drugs, Crime, and Social Isolation: Barriers to Urban Opportunity.* Washington, DC: Urban Institute Press.

Fetterman, D.M. (1989). *Ethnography: Step by Step.* Newbury Park, CA: Sage.

Friedman, S.R. (1997). Personal communication.

—— T. Furst, B. Jose, R. Curtis, A. Neaigus, D.C. Des Jarlais, M.F. Goldstein and G. Ildefonso (1998). "Drug Scene Roles and HIV Risk." *Addictions* 93(9):1403-1416.

—— B. Jose, R. Curtis, G.A. McGrady, M. Vera, R. Lovely, J. Zenilman, V. Johnson, H.R. White, D. Paone, D.C. Des Jarlais (1997). "Adolescents and HIV Risk Due to Drug Injection or Sex with Drug Injectors in the United States." In: L. Sherr (ed.), *AIDS Among Adolescents.* Chur, SWITZ: Harwood Press.

Furst, R.T., B.D. Johnson, E. Dunlap, and R. Curtis (1999). "The Stigmatized Image of the Crack Head: A Sociocultural Exploration of a Barrier to Cocaine Smoking Among a Cohort of Youth in New York City." *Deviant Behavior* 20:153-181.

—— R. Curtis, B.D. Johnson and D. Goldsmith (1998). "The Rise of the Street Middleman/Woman in a Declining Drug Market." *Addiction Research* 5(4):1-26.

*—— R. Curtis and B.D. Johnson (1996). "The Police Crackdown in Bushwick, New York Against IDUs and 'Quality of Life' Crimes." Paper presented at the American Criminological Association, Chicago, November.

*—— R. Nettey, W. Wiebel, C. Richmond, and P. Capers (1996). "The 'Jelling-up of Dope': Implications for Transmission of HIV Among IDUs." *Addiction Research* 4(4):309-320.

*—— and B.D. Johnson (1995). "Sociocultural Barriers to Cocaine Abuse: Some Notes on an Emerging Trend." Paper presented at the American Society of Criminology, Boston, November.

*Goldsmith, D.S. (1996). "Running a Crack Cocaine Operation: A Manager's Perspective." Paper presented at the Society for the Study of Social Problems, New York, August.

*—— (1995). "The Neighborhood Context of a Crack Cocaine Operation." Paper presented at the Society for the Study of Social Problems, Washington, DC, August.

*Golub, A. and B.D. Johnson (1999a). "Coerced Treatment for Drug Abusing Offenders: A Referral Device for Use in New York City." *International Journal of Public Administration* 22(2):187-215.

*—— and B.D. Johnson (1999b). "From the Heroin Injection Generation to the Blunted Generation: Cohort Changes in Illegal Drug Use Among Arrestees in Manhattan." *Substance Use and Misuse* 34(13):1733-1763.

*—— and B.D. Johnson (1997). *Crack's Decline: Some Surprises Across U.S. Cities.* (Research in Brief.) Washington, DC: National Institute of Justice.

*—— and B.D. Johnson (1996). "The Crack Epidemic: Empirical Findings Support a Hypothesized Diffusion of Innovation Process." *Socio-Economic Planning Sciences* 30(3):221-231.

*—— F. Hakeem and B.D. Johnson (1996). *Monitoring the Decline in the Crack Epidemic with Data from the Drug Use Forecasting Program.* (Final Report to National Institute of Justice.) New York, NY: John Jay College of Criminal Justice. [Available from National Criminal Justice Reference Service, NCJ 164659.]

*—— and B.D. Johnson (1994a). "The Shifting Importance of Alcohol and Marijuana as Gateway Substances Among Serious Dug Abusers." *Journal of Alcohol Studies* 55(5):607-614.

*—— and B.D. Johnson (1994b). "Cohort Differences in Drug Use Pathways to Crack among Current Crack Abusers in New York City." *Criminal Justice and Behavior* 21(4):403-422.

*—— and B.D. Johnson (1994c). "A Recent Decline in Cocaine Use Among Youthful Arrestees in Manhattan (1987-1993)." *American Journal of Public Health* 84(8):1250-1254.

*Hamid, A. (1992a). "Drugs and Patterns of Opportunity in the Inner-city: The Case of Middle Aged, Middle Income Cocaine Smokers." In: A. Harrell and G. Peterson (eds.), *Drugs, Crime, and Social Isolation: Barriers to Urban Opportunity.* Washington, DC: Urban Institute Press.

*—— (1992b). "The Developmental Cycle of a Drug Epidemic: The Cocaine Smoking Epidemic of 1981-1991." *Journal of Psychoactive Drugs* 24(3):337-348.

—— R. Curtis, K. McCoy, J. McGuire, A. Conde, W. Bushell, R. Lindenmayer, K. Brimberg, S. Maia, S. Abdur-Rashid and J. Settembrino (1997). "The Heroin Epidemic in New York City: Current Status and Prognoses." *Journal of Psychoactive Drugs* 29(4):375-391.

Holden, C. (1989). "Street-wise Crack Research." *Science* 246:1376-1381.

Inciardi, J.A. and L.D. Harrison (eds.) (1998). *Heroin in the Age of Crack Cocaine.* Beverly Hills, CA: Sage.

—— D. Lockwood and A. Pottieger (1993). *Women and Crack Cocaine.* New York, NY: Macmillian.

Jacobs, B.A. (1996a). "Crack Dealer's Apprehension Avoidance Techniques: A Case of Restrictive Deterrence." *Justice Quarterly* 13:359-381.

—— (1996b). "Crack Dealers and Restrictive Deterrence: Identifying Narcs." *Criminology* 34:409-431.

—— (1999). *Dealing Crack: The Social World of Streetcorner Selling.* Boston, MA: Northeastern University Press.

—— V. Topalli and R. Wright (1999). "Drug Robbery, Deterrence, and Informal Social Control." Paper presented at American Society of Criminology, Toronto, November.

Jah, Y. and S. Keyah (1995). *Uprising: Crips and Bloods Tell the Story of America's Youth in the Crossfire.* New York, NY: Scribner.

*Johnson, B.D. (1997). *DUF-Manhattan 1996.* (Drug Use Forecasting 1996 Annual Report). Washington, DC: National Institute of Justice.

*—— (1996). "Drug Use Patterns Among 'Quality of Life' Arrestees in Manhattan." Paper presented at the American Criminological Association, Chicago, November.

*—— (1991). "Crack in New York City." *Addiction and Recovery* (May/June):24-27.

*—— E. Dunlap and A. Hamid (1992). "Changes in New York's Crack Distribution Scene." In: P. Vamos and P. Corriveau (eds.), *Drugs and Society to the Year 2000.* Montreal, CAN: Portage Program for Drug Dependencies, Inc.

*—— E. Dunlap and L. Maher (1998). "Nurturing for Careers in Drug Abuse and Crime: Conduct Norms for Children and Juveniles in Crack-abusing Households." *Substance Use and Misuse* 33(7):1515-1550.

—— P.J. Goldstein, E. Preble, J. Schmeidler, D.S. Lipton, B. Spunt and T. Miller (1985). *Taking Care of Business: The Economics of Crime by Heroin Abusers.* Lexington, MA: Lexington Books.

—— and A.L. Golub (2000). "Generational Trends in Heroin Use and Injection in New York City." In: D. Musto (ed.), *One Hundred Years of Heroin.* Westport, CT: Greenwood Publishing Corp.

*—— A.L. Golub and E. Dunlap (2000). "The Rise and Decline of Drugs, Drug Markets, and Violence in New York City." In: A. Blumstein and J. Wallman (eds.), *The Crime Drop in America.* New York, NY: Cambridge University Press.

*—— A. Golub and J. Fagan (1995). "Careers in Crack, Drug Use, Drug Distribution, and Nondrug Criminality." *Crime & Delinquency* 41(3):275-295.

*—— A. Hamid and H. Sanabria (1992). "Emerging Models of Crack Distribution." In: T. Mieczkowksi (ed.), *Drugs and Crime: A Reader.* Boston, MA: Allyn-Bacon.

*—— C. Lewis and A. Golub (1992). "Crack Onset in the 1980s in New York City." In: P. Vamos and P. Corriveau (eds.), *Drugs and Society to the Year 2000.* Montreal, CAN: Portage Program for Drug Dependencies, Inc.

—— and A. Manwar (1991). "Towards a Paradigm of Drug Eras: Previous Drug Eras Help to Model the Crack Epidemic in New York City During the 1990s." Paper presented at American Society of Criminology, San Francisco, November.

*—— and J. Muffler (1997). "Sociocultural Aspects of Drug Use and Abuse in the 1990s." In: J. Lowinson, P. Ruiz and R. Millman (eds.), *Substance Abuse Treatment: A Comprehensive Textbook* (3rd ed.). Baltimore, MD: Wilkins and Wilkins.

*—— and M. Natarajan (1995). "Strategies to Avoid Arrest: Crack Sellers' Response to Intensified Policing." *American Journal of Police* 23(3/4):49-70.

—— M. Natarajan, E. Dunlap and E. Elmoghazy (1994). "Crack Abusers and Noncrack Abusers: Profiles of Drug Use, Drug Sales, and Nondrug Criminality." *Journal of Drug Issues* 24(1&2):117-141.

*—— M. Natarajan and H. Sanabria (1993). "'Successful' Criminal Careers: Towards an Ethnography Within the Rational Choice Perspective." In: R. Clarke and M. Felson (eds.)m *Rational Choice and Routine Activity Theory.* (Advances in Criminological Theory.) New Brunswick, NJ: Transaction Books.

*—— G. Thomas and A. Golub (1998). "Trends in Heroin Use Among Manhattan Arrestees from the Heroin and Crack Eras." In: J.A. Inciardi and L.D. Harrison (eds.), *Heroin in the Age of Crack Cocaine.* Beverly Hills, CA: Sage.

*—— T. Williams, K. Dei and H. Sanabria (1990). "Drug Abuse and the Inner City: Impact on Hard Drug Users and the Community." In: M. Tonry and J.Q. Wilson (eds.), *Drugs and Crime.* (Crime and Justice Series, vol. 13.) Chicago, IL: University of Chicago Press.

Johnston, L.D., P.M. O'Malley and J.G. Bachman (1999). *National Survey Results on Drug Use from the Monitoring the Future Study, 1975-1998.* Rockville, MD: National Institute on Drug Abuse.

*Lewis, C., A. Golub and B.D. Johnson (1992). "Studying Crack Abusers: Strategies for Recruiting the Right Tail of an Ill-defined Population." *Journal of Psychoactive Drugs* 24(3):323-336.

*Lipton, D.S. and B.D. Johnson (1998). "Smack, Crack, Score: Two Decades of NIDA-funded Drugs and Crime Research at NDRI, 1974-1994." *Substance Use and Misuse* 33(9):1779-1815.

Lowinson, J., P. Ruiz, R. Millman and J.G. Langrod (eds.) (1997). *Substance Abuse Treatment: A Comprehensive Textbook* (3rd ed.). Baltimore, MD: Wilkins and Wilkins..

*Maher, L. (1997). *Sexed Work: Gender, Race and Resistance in a Brooklyn Drug Market*. New York, NY: Oxford University Press.

*—— (1996). "Law Enforcement Crack Downs and Harm Minimization Policies: Upping the Ante in a Street Level Heroin Market." Paper presented at the American Criminological Association, Chicago, November.

*—— E. Dunlap, B.D. Johnson and A. Hamid (1996). "Gender, Power, and Alternative Living Arrangements in the Inner-city Crack Culture." *Journal of Research on Crime and Delinquency* 33(2):181-205.

*Manwar, A., E. Dunlap and B.D. Johnson (1994). "Qualitative Data Analysis with HyperText: A Case Study of New York City Crack Dealers." *Qualitative Sociology* 17(3):283-292.

*—— and B.D. Johnson (1993). "Street Level Drug Dealing as Informal Sector Activity: An Ethnographic Study of New York City Crack Dealers." In: L. Harris (ed.), *Problems of Drug Dependence*. (Research Monograph 132.) Rockville, MD: National Institute on Drug Abuse.

Mauer, M. (1990). *Young Black Men and the Criminal Justice System: A Growing National Problem*. Washington, DC: The Sentencing Project.

—— (1995). *Young Black Americans and the Criminal Justice System: Five Years Later*. Washington, DC: The Sentencing Project.

McKeganey, N. and M. Bernard (1992). *AIDS, Drugs, and Sexual Risks*. Buckingham, UK: Open University Press.

*Mieczkowski, T. , M.D. Anglin, S. Coletti, B.D. Johnson, E.A. Nadelman and E.D. Wish (1992). "Responding to America's Drug Problems: Strategies for the '90s." *Journal of Urban Affairs* 14(3-4):337-357.

Miles, M.B. and A.M. Huberman (1994). *Qualitative Data Analysis* (2nd ed.). Newbury Park, CA: Sage.

*Natarajan, M., R.V. Clarke and B.D. Johnson (1995). "Telephones as Facilitators of Drug Dealing: A Research Agenda." *European Journal on Crime Policy and Research* 3(3):137-153.

National Household Survey on Drug Abuse (1996). *Main Findings 1995*. Rockville, MD: National Institute on Drug Abuse.

National Institute of Justice (1997). *Drug Use Forecasting 1996*. (Annual report.) Washington, DC.

—— (1999). *1998 Annual Report on Drug Use Among Adult and Juvenile Arrestees*. (Research Report.) Washington, DC.

Neaigus, A., S.R. Friedman, R. Curtis, D.C. Des Jarlais, T. Furst, B. Jose, P. Mota, B. Stepherson and M. Sufian (1994). "The Relevance of Drug Injectors' Social and Risk Networks for an Understanding and Preventing HIV Infection." *Social Science Medicine* 38(1):67-78.

Parker, H., K. Bakx and R. Newcombe (1988). *Living with Heroin: The Impact of a Drug Epidemic on an English Community.* Philadelphia, PA: Open University Press.

Pearson, G. (1987). *The New Heroin Users.* New York, NY: Basil Blackwell.

Preble, E. and J. Casey (1969). "Taking Care of Business — The Heroin Addict's Life on the Streets." *International Journal of the Addictions* 4:145-169.

*Randolph, D. (1996). "Changes in Crack Packaging: 1985-1995." Paper presented at the Society for the Study of Social Problems, New York, August.

*—— (1995). "Illegal Packaging: Past and Present." Paper presented at the Society for the Study of Social Problems, Washington, DC, August.

Ratner, M.S. (ed.) (1992). *Crack Pipe as Pimp: An Ethnographic Investigation of Sex-for-Crack Exchanges.* New York, NY: Lexington Books/ Macmillan.

Rittenhouse, J. (ed.) (1977). *The Epidemiology of Heroin and Other Narcotics.* (Research monograph.) Rockville, MD: National Institute on Drug Abuse.

Riley, J. (1998). *Crack, Powder Cocaine, and Heroin: Drug Purchase and Use Patterns in Six U.S. Cities.* Washington, DC: National Institute of Justice and Office of National Drug Control Policy.

*Rouse, J.J. and B.D. Johnson (1991). "Hidden Paradigms of Morality in Debates About Drugs: Historical and Policy Shifts in British and American Drug Policies." In: J.A. Inciardi (ed.), *American Drug Policy and the Legalization Debate.* Beverly Hills, CA: Sage.

Sifaneck, S.J (1998). Personal communication.

*—— (1997). "Retail Marijuana Markets in New York City." (Working manuscript.) New York, NY: National Development and Research Institutes.

*—— (1996). "An Ethnographic Analysis of the Sale and Use of Cannabis in New York City and Rotterdam." Doctoral Dissertation, Graduate Center of the City University of New York, New York, NY.

*—— and C.D. Kaplan (1995). "Keeping off, Stepping on and Stepping Off: The Stepping Stone Theory Reevaluated in the Context of the Dutch Cannabis Experience." *Contemporary Drug Problems* 22:483-512.

Sommers, I., D. Baskin and J. Fagan (1996). "The Structural Relationship Between Dug Use, Drug Dealing, and Other Income Support Activities Among Women Drug Dealers." *Journal of Drug Issues* 26:975-1006.

Sviridoff, M., S. Sadd, R. Curtis and R. Grinc (1992). *The Neighborhood Effects of New York City's Tactical Narcotics Team on Three Brooklyn Precincts*. New York, NY: Vera Institute of Justice.

Taylor, A., B.D. Johnson, E. Dunlap and J. Caulkins (1999). "Drug Sellers' Accounts Regarding Gun Possession Nonuse During Episodes Involving Conflict or Violence." Paper presented at American Society of Criminology, Toronto, Canada.

Tourigny, S.C. (1998). "Some New Dying Trick: African-American Youths "Choosing" HIV/AIDS." *Qualitative Health Research* 8(2):149-167.

Waterston, A. (1993). *Street Addiction: The Political Economy*. Philadelphia, PA: Temple University Press.

Wasserheit, J.N., S.O. Aral and K.K. Holmes (eds.) (1991). *Research Issues in Human Behavior and Sexually Transmitted Diseases*. Washington, DC: American Society of Microbiology.

*Williams, T. (1991). *Crack House*. Reading, MA: Addison-Wesley Publishing Co.

*——— (1989). *The Cocaine Kids*. Reading, MA: Addison-Wesley Publishing Co.

——— (1978). "The Cocaine Culture in After Hours Clubs." Doctoral dissertation, Graduate Center of the City University of New York, New York, NY.

*——— E. Dunlap, B.D. Johnson and A. Hamid (1992). "Personal Safety in Dangerous Places." *Journal of Contemporary Ethnography* 21(3):343-374.

NOTES

1. This chapter summarizes central findings from information presented in a much more extensive ethnographic research project funded by the National Institute on Drug Abuse and conducted from 1989 to 1997. The project's numerous publications (see citations*) address a variety of focal analytic issues, review the relevant literature, summarize the methodology, provide qualitative analysis of data, typically incorporate extensive quotations from subjects, and provide relevant policy implications.

2. We acknowledge the complexity of epidemiology as a discipline (Wasserheit et al., 1991; Lowinson et al., 1997; McKeganey and Bernard,

1992). An extensive literature exists specifically about the epidemiology of drug use and abuse (Johnston et al., 1999; National Household Survey on Drug Abuse, 1999; Inciardi and Harrison, 1998; Preble and Casey, 1969; Rittenhouse, 1977). Few epidemiological studies, however, apply the epidemic model to the study of crack cocaine, and almost none apply it to crack selling.

3. In particular, the analyst must first determine how to best identify the concept of interest across narratives, and then develop and operationalize a meaningful coding scheme (Manwar et al., 1994). Project staff assembled a semi-quantifiable data set, coding subject demographics (gender, age, ethnicity, education), and classifying participants' levels of involvement in drug selling and violence, although this resulted in much missing data. An additional secondary analysis (Caulkins et al., 1999; Taylor et al., 1999) involves careful identification and coding of sections of transcripts conveying the pricing of retail amounts of cocaine or heroin powder by time and by place into a semi-quantitative format.

4. Chaiken and Chaiken (1993) document that the completed DUF sample is similar to the distribution of arrestees in several jurisdictions, including Manhattan. Also see NIJ (1997).

5. The DUF program was renamed the "Arrestee Drug Abuse Monitoring" (ADAM) program in May 1997. NIJ plans to expand this data collection effort to 75 cities by the year 2001, and to include juvenile arrestees at all sites. ADAM staff regularly compile the entire DUF data set for Manhattan (1987-1999) and make it available for statistical analysis about two months after data collection.

6. DUF-Manhattan arrestees are primarily under age 35. Over half are African-American, about 30% are Hispanic, and 14% are white. That 30% are female is a function of interviewing quotas set by the DUF program. Only about a quarter graduate from high school, while a third are high school dropouts. The most serious arrest charges are possession (13%) and sale (about 6%) of crack, cocaine, or heroin. About two thirds of DUF-Manhattan arrestees are positive for cocaine and 20% positive for opiates (most also reporting drug injection). Marijuana use increased modestly from about a sixth in 1990-91 to 30% in 1996-97. Analysis of data from all participating cities shows Manhattan arrestees as having the highest proportions positive for cocaine and heroin (Golub and Johnson 1997; Golub et al., 1996; Golub and Johnson 1999b).

7. A fundamental problem facing New York City and American society is how to develop appropriate social responses and supports for a whole generation of inner-city youths from severely distressed households and communities who have "said no" to heroin injection and crack smoking but still find integration into mainstream society impossible. From their

vantage point, they have no opportunities or supports to gain access to decent jobs or conventional roles.

8 They did so in St. Louis (Jacobs, 1999).

9. Sommers et al. (1996) and Baskin and Sommers (1998) studied incarcerated female drug sellers, many of whom claimed to have had relatively lucrative careers as dealers and sellers prior to their arrest. Crack distribution project staff could not locate a female dealer routinely purchasing as much as a kilogram of cocaine for distribution to other sellers.

10. Some of these older women may have previously worked, and/or had husbands with employment income, and may thus qualify for social security. These non-welfare sources of income, however, may not be sufficient to support multigenerational households in which some members experience the loss of welfare eligibility.

HOW YOUNG BRITONS OBTAIN THEIR DRUGS: DRUGS TRANSACTIONS AT THE POINT OF CONSUMPTION

by

Howard Parker
Manchester University, UK

Abstract: *The enormous expansion in recreational drug use (cannabis, amphetamines, LSD, ecstasy) amongst young Britons during the 1990s has had a normative effect whereby gender and social class differences are now negligible and consequently most young drug users are otherwise law abiding and conventional. Based on five contemporary studies of adolescents' drug use, nightclubbers and new young heroin users, this paper explains how while young "hard" drug users utilise "real" dealers, the vast majority of young drug users do not. Instead they rely on friendship and acquaintance chains and networks to "sort" each other out and thereby put physical and social distance between themselves and "real" dealers from criminal worlds. While de jure this means a significant minority of young Britons are drug suppliers, in practice few are apprehended because these transactions take place in their own semiprivate social space where they are largely condoned. Thus far these informal transactions at the point of consumption have kept the recreational- and heavy-end drugs arenas apart. However there are worrying signs that purposeful heroin distribution and marketing is penetrating recreational-drugs settings and recruiting a new generation of "susceptible" heroin users.*

THE BRITISH DRUG SCENE ACROSS THE 1990S

While far from the highest international per capita alcohol consumption rates (Harkin et al., 1995), the U.K. has the most drug involved population of all the European Union States. This status is not primarily generated by problematic use, although heroin, crack and poly drug dependency are at significant rates, but by the "recreational" drugs consumption of young Britons (ages 12 to 30). It is the use of cannabis, followed by amphetamines, LSD, ecstasy and increasingly cocaine (powder), that generates the U.K.'s top slot across Europe both per capita (European Monitoring Centre for Drugs and Drug Addiction [EMCDDA], 1999) and specifically among comparative youth populations (European School Survey Project on Alcohol and Other Drugs [ESPAD], 1997).

While household surveys suggest that 51% of males and 38% of females between 18 and 21 years old have ever tried an illicit drug (Ramsay and Spiller, 1997), this is almost certainly an underestimate given that young people in State care, students away from home and homeless youth are missed in such surveys. School- and college-based confidential self-report surveys in some regions, especially in the north of Britain, report that six in 10 young people have tried an illicit drug by the age of 18; and around 25% to 30% are recreational users in late adolescence and early adulthood, primarily of cannabis, followed by the dance drugs (Aldridge and Parker, 1999; Parker et al., 1998a; Barnard et al., 1996). While we should be clear that most youthful recreational use remains occasional and primarily weekend-based, the prevalence of these rates generate estimates that 1.2 to 1.8 million 15 to 19-year-olds alone have some experience of drugs in the U.K. (Parliamentary Office of Science and Technology [POST], 1996). This is an enormous expansion compared with the 1980s that, inevitably, has in turn had a normative effect. Most surveys now find that as many young women as men are involved and that all social groups are affected. Drug takers are found as often in both higher and lower social groups (Leitner et al., 1993), in private education as much as in State provision (The Guardian, 1999), and with university students leading the way (Webb et al., 1996).

Moreover, while drug use is endemic among the delinquent minority of recent generations (Graham and Bowling, 1995) the corollary is not found. The vast majority of today's young recreational users have either no or only light criminal antecedents and virtually no significant differences exist between young people who eschew recreational drug use and those who indulge (Aldridge and Parker, 1999). In short, most adolescent, recreational drug users in the U.K. are otherwise largely conforming, law abiding, young citizens. Delinquency rates seem independent of these particular changes in the drugs landscape.

A similar process has been underway among young adults. The rise of the dance-rave party "culture" and the consequent rejuvenation of the U.K.'s 4,000 nightclubs during the decade has been at the heart of the expansion. With those under 30 years of age dominating the age profile of Britain's 16 million club visitors (Finch, 1999), and leisure forecasters *Mintel* claiming one in two 18 to 24 year olds are regular nightclubbers, this scene captures (and largely contains) the most serious end of the U.K.'s recreational scene. The handful of studies of this dance-club scene suggest that between a half and 90% of clubbers dance to stimulant drugs. They are also very drug experienced: almost all have used cannabis, around 90% have tried ecstasy and over three quarters have used LSD and amphetamines (Release, 1997; Forsyth, 1996).

This environment clearly requires an elaborate drug supply system. One estimate is that a million ecstasy pills were consumed each week in Britain in the mid 1990s (POST, 1996). However, since these "party goers" are dedicated combination drug users, their drug usage typically involves amphetamines and, most recently, GHB[1] and cocaine in addition to ecstasy. Clubbers routinely spend £50 a night on their drugs of choice.

Turning to problematic drugs and drugs careers, there are now clear signs that the U.K. is seeing a major reemergence of heroin use among a minority of young people (Parker et al., 1998). This will eventually generate a steeper increase in the numbers of young people dependent on illicit drugs. Using a particularly broad definition, it is estimated that there are around 400,000 youths ages 16 to 24 England and Wales using drugs (Advisory Council on the Misuse of Drugs [ACMD], 1998); "official" counts report the overall problem use population to be between 100,000 and 150,000 users. Unlike the recreational scene, we must expect to find a direct drugs-crime relationship among these young hard-drug users because of both the cultural and socioeconomic milieu from which they come and the size of their weekly or daily drugs bills.

This overview of the 1990s British drug landscape clearly identifies a major increase in drugs consumption. Since the prices of nearly all street drugs have remained stable or fallen (e.g., ecstasy) during this decade of expansion, we can also be sure, backed by convincing international intelligence, that supplies are strong and have coped easily with (and perhaps stimulated) increased demand.

This paper attempts to explore how a new generation of youth with these unprecedented drugs appetites have, given their unlikely social profile, actually obtained their illegal drugs. If most adolescent and young adult recreational users are largely conforming, nondelinquent citizens who are in school, in college, in training or employed, how do they comfortably and "safely" procure drugs from an illegal and constantly demonised drugs market? What is occurring close to the point of consumption that accounts for the millions of young people who have breached the Misuse of Drugs Act 1971 by possessing controlled substances? How have hundreds of thousands of otherwise law abiding young citizens become engaged in illegally supplying Class A drugs, such as ecstasy, which carry the potential penalty of five years imprisonment? The discussion additionally considers how and why heroin use is also rising steeply, and assesses the risks this poses for an overlap between the recreational and hard drug scenes.

METHODS

This paper is based on recent and on-going research undertaken by the author and colleagues at Social Problems Applied Research Centre (SPARC). All five studies used to glean data describe the contemporary situation in England.

(1) **The North West Longitudinal Study** was a five-year investigation (1991 to 1996) into the role of alcohol and illicit drugs among 700 14 to 18 year olds (inc.) in two regions of urban-suburban northwest. England. The data collection involved five annual, confidential self-report questionnaires and interviews with 86 of the cohort in Year 4, when they were 17 years old, plus several "critical incidents" case studies (e.g., of a panel member being caught by the police in a drug dealer's house). The data used here are derived from the interviews (Parker et al., 1998a).[2]

(2) **The Integrated Prevention Programme Evaluation** is a four-year investigation in which more than 3,000 young people 13 to16 and 15 to 18 years of age are being tracked by annual, confidential self-report questionnaires exploring their use of alcohol and drugs in the context of their lifestyles. A small cohort (n=19) of initially 15-year-olds from the panel were interviewed in-depth three times between 1996 and 1998 by the same interviewers. The data from these structured conversations are utilised in this paper (see also Measham et al., 1998).[3]

(3) **The Dance Drugs, Nightclubs Study** is a two-year study of the health and safety of clubbers and involved 21 nights of

fieldwork in three nightclubs in northwest. England. Brief interviews, using a team of eight interviewers, were undertaken with over 2,000 customers and nearly 300 in-depth interviews (including voluntary urine samples, temperature and pulse measurements, and intoxication monitoring over several hours) were conducted as well as extensive observational work and conversations with club security and bar staff. The data used in this paper are extracted from the in-depth interviews that were coded and "quantified" using the Statistical Package for the Social Sciences (SPSS) and the observational work (see Measham et al., 2000).[4]

(4) **The New Young Heroin Users in England and Wales** study was basically a rapid audit of the spread patterns and profiles of a new cycle of heroin outbreaks affecting numerous small cities and towns. A survey of all Drug Action Teams (interprofessional local networks) and police forces, generating over 200 returns, was supplemented by visits to new heroin "hotspots" where local professionals and young heroin users were interviewed. This study informs part of the main discussion about dealing patterns (see Parker et al., 1998). [5]

(5) **Profiles of New Young Heroin Users in England** was undertaken during 1999 and involved interviewing 100 young, "recently initiated" heroin users in a small city, and a large and a small town in England all experiencing heroin outbreaks. Those interviewed spoke in detail about how they obtained their drugs, and some accounts are included here (Egginton and Parker, 1999).[6]

All the interviews were conducted directly by SPARC staff and the methodologies employed are discussed in detail in the sources given. Because very few British studies have been undertaken that focus directly on drugs transactions at the point of consumption (but see Edmunds et al., 1996) one of the few feasible ways of, at least, outlining the situation is to collate accounts and descriptions from studies that indirectly or incidentally explore the final transaction. Each of the five investigations above all purposely collected drug dealing data which are brought together for the first time in this paper.

ADOLESCENT RECREATIONAL DRUG USERS

The longitudinal studies, particularly the qualitative components, confirm that most young people's (ages 13 to 17 years) drugs initiations are in social settings where their friends or acquaintances offer free drugs to try. Passing round the spliff (marijuana joint) is the archetypal example of this. For many drug triers and occasional users this remains their modus operandi: take drugs only when they're offered to you and are being used in "safe" social settings.

That was pot...I think I was about 13...with my sister and my mates. These lads who had it, we got in with them, they'd been smoking it for a while but it was our first time. [Female, 17, recreational user]

I don't buy some so that I can smoke it (by) myself). It's normally just when it's being passed around people that I end up smoking it. So I'm not going out and buying some because I think 'oh I need some. It's just if somebody's got some then I'll have a bit, but I don't feel the need to have to go out and buy some. [Female, 16, moderate recreational user]

Beyond these experimenters and opportunistic occasional users we found young people who rely on drugs provided from within their social worlds. This can be at school.

I know some guy at school who can get it (cannabis), although he's not a dealer he knows someone who's not a dealer who can get it. [Reliable quality?] The quality's not bad, but getting it's a pain in the arse quite frankly...I never think I'll be able to get it in time and if I do I think it'll be rubbish, until I'm stoned, then I realise it's not actually that bad. [Male, 17, cannabis-only user]

More often it is within "time out" friendship networks where one or more (usually males), become the drug hunters who sort things out by taking "orders" from others. An 18-year-old female single parent, who was able to go out "dancing" only once a week, saw cannabis as a regular relaxant while "stuck in the 'ouse.'"

Just my close friends and my sister, usual crew. Before we go out...My mate's got her own house and everyone sits in there...The speed we used to get it off my other sister's mate. But my mate's boyfriend he deals the pot so we get the pot off him and he can also get hold of speed so we mostly get it off him and if he can't get hold of it we try and get it off my sister's mate. [Female, 17, recreational user]

Not Real Dealers?

Not being in direct contact with "real" dealers is a key factor utilised by many young people in the social construction of the responsible, respectable, recreational drug user. When asked where he got his cannabis and amphetamines, one young man was adamant:

Depends, friends normally if I can, if not I'll send a friend to a dealer.
[Ever go to the dealers yourself?] No. I've *never* been to a dealer. [Male, 18, recreational user]

Somehow in this discourse friends, and friends of friends who supply drugs are also recast positively because they're "OK." They sometimes also supply free drugs. In addition, they have to take risks and so deserve the little bonus of either an 1/8 of cannabis, a wrap of amphetamines, or an ecstasy PM, for their endeavours. There is also a very blurred line between who is a dealer and who is a customer. In the northwest study the majority of regular recreational users in the interview sample, when asked if they'd ever "sorted" other people requiring drugs, agreed they'd been on both sides of the transaction.

Yes for friends. [For profit?] No probably just they give me enough for a few spliffs for getting it for them. [How often?] Once in a while. Just when they can't get it themselves say once in every one month or two months or something. [Male, 17, occasional recreational user]

Like being the middle man you mean? Yes. [Which drugs?] Trips, pot, speed, tablets. [For profit?] No, just for my mates. [Cost price?] No, the lad who I got them off he'll have made a profit. [But you didn't?] No. [Who were you selling to?] My mates and my cousin. [Strangers?] No. [How often?] Someone might phone me up and say can you get us something, one week it might be 3 to 4 times a week, then it mightn't be for a month or something. (Male, 18, regular, recreational user)

These networks or chains in the procuring of drugs near the point of consumption overtly protect the majority of young drug takers from direct negotiations with people they regard as real drug dealers. Distance is put between supplier and user and, because the intermediaries are friends of friends, the deliverer is considered to be "OK" and part of the straight world and not a "scally" or "radgy."[7]

However, because there are so many real low-level dealers and user-dealers at the local community level who live ordinary lives and can be approached relatively safely, the supply chain is sustained. One female sixth former in a small suburban town met her supplier simply by being in the local pub with her boyfriend.

> It's a dealer we know in the pub round the corner...Any day, any time he's in the pub waiting for you. If he's ill like he was ill last week, so his brother was there, you just go in and nod to him and he comes out. [Female, 18, cannabis-only user]

With normalisation we find abstainers and cautious drug experimenters, because they are friends with using peers, might also become involved in these transactions. One young man from the same town went off in a car with friends "who were buying for their friends."

> Ecstasy, cannabis. Just the most frequent ones. That's all they go in for, it's the two cheapest to be honest. E you only have a tablet a night and cannabis for a fiver (£5). [Male, 17, abstainer]

Another who'd given up cannabis but kept the same friends continued to sort his friends in a fairly risky way.

> I was the one who usually got it for all of them...I still go down for them all. They just give me two quid [each] to go and get it and bring it back. It's about a five minute walk...just around the area...If he hasn't got none, I know someone else. [Male, 16, former cannabis user]

In both of the longitudinal studies it was possible to see how, with experience and increasing drug wisdom, the chain of intermediaries near the point of sale created opportunities to make a profit.

> Once I knew a lad that was selling Es and this girl came up to me and said 'do you know anyone who's selling Es?' So I said yes, how many do you want and she said "oh two." So I went and got two and took the money off her £30. I charged her £15 and they were only supposed to be £10. That's about it really. [Female, 18, problem drug user]

Several experienced drug users became involved in more clear cut dealing for profit but invariably as a second job. One young man who left school at sixteen worked away from home returning each week-end. He, in fact, informally bridged two recreational drug-using networks some hundreds of miles apart. He occasionally profited from distributing cannabis and LSD "trips."

> [Who for?] Friends up there and I've got it for friends down here as well. [Ever sold for profit?] Yes...I bought a quarter and paid £30 for it and I made £15 on it...but that was cutting it up and selling it on to different people. [Male, 18, recreational user]

None of these respondents considered themselves real drugs dealers. They saw their role as facilitative, as sorting or helping out friends and acquaintances.

Becoming Real Dealers?

A handful of drug users in the longitudinal studies became involved in more purposeful dealing for profit. They were certainly, to their customers, real dealers. One young man whose family lived and survived on a tough estate grew up in a drug-using and a drug-dealing environment. Upon leaving school he took a night job working behind the bar of a local nightclub. The doorman dealt (mainly amphetamines and ecstasy) and also had an arrangement to let in a few other dealers. Our respondent and his friend, who worked in the club, began to sell ecstasy, amphetamines and cannabis with the agreement of the doorman. They quickly built up a good trade and for over a year had numerous repeat customers. To avoid tensions the doorman then limited dealing to himself and these two.

> So we cleaned up with the doorman and said right fine we'll just stick with this [current arrangement] and we'll also send people to you...but as part of the deal you back us up if any shit comes off, so like he backed us up and we basically cut everyone out and there was just two sets of dealers me and my friend and the doorman.

> The only complaints was if we'd had something [amphetamines] for too long, you know we didn't realise it was off and we'd say OK, fair enough and give them a free bag, keep them happy. We weren't going to be out of pocket, if you kept them happy they kept coming back and if you got the really good stuff instead of going to other normal dealers they'd come back to you and then...their friends would come and if it was like a first timer we'd go "oh, there's half free" and they'd be happy.

However operating in the real world of dealing for profit led them into serious problems both with the police (CID) and a local gang unimpressed by "trespassers."

> I think the worse one was about 12 black guys try dragging you out of the car, that's got to be the worst. I was at college and apparently I'm meant to have sold something to this lad, forced him to buy it then I'm meant to have mugged him with a gun and a couple of other things which I didn't know shit-all about...and all these guys surrounded the car I was in...Get out the car otherwise we're gonna shoot you through the window. The police turned up and everything got sorted....[Male, 17]

A combination of dangerous situations and the Criminal Investigation Department (CID) detectives in the club watching the numerous transactions led the pair to stop dealing. They had made several thousand pounds but could see that their activities were going to be stopped by either the police or local organised criminals with stakes in the drugs market.

While at least half of all young Britons will, by consuming illegal drugs, have broken the possession law, only a minority, perhaps around 20% of late adolescents/young adults, will have been in situations where they were technically actually supplying drugs. The vast majority of these transactions will go undetected and, as we have seen will, not be personally or socially defined as supplying or dealing.

However a minority do and will get caught either at school or college, or by the police. Here the two very different perspectives or social constructions of drug use and dealing clash, as adult authority and drugwise youth clash. Two young women who had taken LSD trips at school regarded the punishment of a week's suspension (with no police involvement) and a ceremonial dressing down as excessive.

> We have the head master shouting and screaming at us saying that we're no good dirty druggies, whatever. I was glad I was suspended for a week, I saw it as a week's holiday. I had to sit in here, I had to cry to get back into the school, I had to put on all the acting. "Oh I'll never do any drugs again, I'm sorry that I've put you through this, I know it's all wrong." One of the governors was sat there saying, "You're dicing with death." I was sat there thinking to myself, shit, I only had a trip. I was "dicing with death" and I only had a bit of acid. [Female, 15, problem drug user]

Their sense of injustice would have been far greater if, as is usually the case, the police were also called in and cautions issued.

A lass in our school...was caught selling a deal, like a fiver deal [of cannabis] to one of her pals. But what had happened was her boyfriend deals and she had found a deal in her bag and one of the lasses had said "Well let me buy it off you." And that's all it was. She wasn't coming in to the school and going "Oh, do you want to buy a fiver deal?" and all this. And somebody found out or somebody grassed her up and there were just complete hell. The headmaster, the police, the parents, everything was totally bang on to her. It was totally bad. [Female, 16, recreational user]

Functions of Recreational Drug Users' Networks

In adolescence most recreational drug taking is a social event. The effects of the drug usually interact with the social setting to enhance the enjoyment of the episode. Such networks of experimenters and users also tend to provide a relatively safe environment for trying drugs and also, through conversation and the swapping of drugs stories, to upgrade the drug wisdom of each young person. This helps them apply a cost-benefit assessment as to what drugs to take/avoid and what strategies should be utilised to stay safe. These networks also allow conventional young people to acquire illegal drugs with little risk of apprehension, except for the chance discoveries of illegal drugs transactions at home, school or in everyday public space. Not having to meet real dealers or take risks in alien environments is another key function of these drugwise friendship networks.

However, there are also weaknesses in these apparently drugwise networks. They are being exploited by those wishing to entice young, recreational drug users to take up more addictive and expensive substances — cocaine and heroin.

THE DANCE CLUB — DANCE DRUG SCENE

Moving beyond adolescents into the mainly young adult nightclub — dance club scene we find a particularly outgoing sector of serious recreational drug users. In the SPARC study drugs bills for the main sample (n=330) were routinely between £20-£100 for a psychoactive night out. These recreational users are very drug-experienced clubbers whom one would expect to use drug dealers.

During the 1990s public sentiment about ecstasy deaths, all night raves and dangerous nightclubs have focussed on nightclub dealers, particularly bouncers and security/door staff, who are believed to be the main suppliers to clubbers. Undoubtedly they have real involvement (Morris, 1998) but the reality is that most recreational drug users, including clubbers, are wary of buying drugs from strangers and getting too close to heavy duty characters. In the SPARC study around 20% of clubbers interviewed were freely provided with their drugs by friends, partners and relatives. Moreover, of the 70% or so who paid for their drugs, only a minority — around 10% — obtained their drugs from unknown dealers and security/bar staff.

Some 60% of those in the main sample regularly procured their drugs via friends and friends of friends and, where dealers were used, they were nearly always known, regular sources. With 92% disclosing they have received drugs from friends and 77% agreeing they've sold drugs to friends, the basic relationships and strategies described for the adolescent recreational scene are repeated.

The public and political discourses about the post-modern nightclub have also influenced policing priorities. Clubs and clubbers suddenly become targets for drugs raids, queue searches and elaborate inspections, as the local media or city hall politics demand action. This forces clubbers to take safety precautions. They consume their drugs before queuing or hide them in (usually female) body orifices in addition to obtaining them ahead of time from "safe" sources. Even so, members of this group, because they have been out and about since mid-adolescence, are netted by routine policing of the pub, club, car and street. One in five were cautioned or were convicted under the Misuse of Drugs Act (mainly for cannabis possession).

In conclusion, young adult recreational drug users play the key role in drugs distribution near the point of consumption. The desire to maintain safety in a potentially hazardous environment and to minimize the likelihood of receiving "dodgy" drugs from "dodgy" characters continues to shape drugs transactions. The informal friends of friends chain continues to dominate. This type of committed dance-drug user clearly comes closer to real dealers and being downtown at the weekend patently increases the risk of being caught up in both the drugs economy of criminal dealers on the one hand, and reactive "symbolic" policing on the other. Thus, the trick, for them, is to obtain quality drugs and enjoy the night out without contact with either side of the war on drugs.

MARKETING HEROIN TO YOUTH POPULATIONS

A Second Heroin Epidemic

During the 1980s the U.K. experienced its first real heroin epidemic with outbreaks affecting several cities and satellite towns. Estimates suggest that by the late 1980s around 150,000 problem heroin users were identifiable. These outbreaks, as in the U.S., affected unemployed, unqualified young men and women from the inner areas and the poor estates of these cities (e.g., Liverpool, Manchester, Glasgow and Edinburgh). Through macro diffusion (Parker et al., 1998; Hunt and Chamber, 1975) the poorer parts of nearby towns saw their own outbreaks. Heroin was, from this time on, associated with social exclusion.

After a quieter epidemic period (1990-95), signs of a second epidemic have begun to appear. With heroin seizures climbing steeply and international intelligence confirming expanding heroin production globally, heroin has become more widely available than ever before and in the U.K. is now being sold at £10 per deal (about 30% pure, 0.1 to 0.08 gms.).[8] Availability has this time spread far beyond the cities and is now found in towns right across Scotland, England and parts of Wales (but not Northern Ireland). A rapid assessment/national audit (Parker et al., 1998) commissioned by the U.K. government confirmed the picture. Heroin outbreaks are unfolding in literally hundreds of towns and at least three small cities have reported major outbreaks with thousands of new young users. It has become clear that these outbreaks are supply led. The kilos of heroin are warehoused in the old heroin cities. They are then, through criminal associations, moved in smaller consignments to new markets. Local town level dealers cut ounces into grams or bags and in turn trade with other local dealers and user-dealers. The heroin is primarily moved along the motorway networks by car.

Penetrating the Recreational Scene

The numerous positive functions of drugwise peer networks for young recreational drug users have been described. However, these same networks of drugs distribution near the point of consumption also have weaknesses. They exchange illegal drugs that are obtained from subcultural worlds and international organised crime. They can be manipulated unless young drug experimenters and users can protect themselves.

This second heroin epidemic is supply led. Through new availability and shrewd marketing, heroin is being offered through the local dealerships selling recreational drugs. Heroin is penetrating local youth networks. One measure of this is that heroin "offers" or opportunities are now being reported in the more sensitive regional school surveys. Around 20% of 13 to 16-year-olds in affected areas are currently reporting access to heroin — a tripling of rates found in the early 1990s (Aldridge and Parker, 1999).

In the profiling study, while the traditional picture of social exclusion continues to match the majority of the new young heroin users, we must now extend the susceptibility spectrum to include young people who have taken up heroin primarily because of its clever marketing via the local recreational drugs scene. There is an increase in new users who come from conventional homes and report few damaging childhood experiences. While those who move beyond trying episodes to become problem users appear to have lower self esteem and do less well at school, they share many characteristics with the recreational users: being early risk takers, smokers, frequent drinkers and experimenting widely with drugs (Egginton and Parker, 1999).

Almost all in the profiling study first tried heroin in a social setting that was normally taken up with drinking or cannabis use — the very same scenarios that are found in the recreational scene. One 20-year-old who used to hang out with a group of friends who started heroin use by accepting a "blowback" into his mouth from one of the group. He then had "a line or two":

> I puked up badly, a minute or two later had a pain in my stomach, then afterwards felt really nice, really warm inside.

The setting was a friend's big bedroom with a personal computer, playstation "everything, a right big house" — not a dealer's den.

These journeys to dependent use routinely took one to three years and initially many months often elapsed between early experiments and the period when they began to search out and buy heroin. However, once daily use sets in, these new young heroin users become estranged from straight friends and no longer keep the buffers between themselves and the real dealers. Instead they have their own dealers who:

> You phone them up and they'll come and meet you where they say. [Female, 18, heroin users]

They start to see the geography of their town as determined by heroin dealerships:

> ...within 500 yards (of here) there's about 15 dealers I know of. [Male, 18, heroin user-dealer]

The quality and value of the heroin is keenly talked about:

> it changes everyday, all the time, one minute it's three bags for £25.... [Male, 20, heroin user]

> ...It were shit it were really bashed up. [Male, 19, heroin user]

To support growing habits many have become user-dealers, often working for their older dealer with whom they often become friends and heroin partners. One interviewee who had built up a considerable debt because his dealer continued to give him credit or "lay-ons," was selling £1,500 to £2,000 worth of bags a week to pay off his debt.

While in this brief overview the range of these heroin pathways and journeys cannot be described, the key point is that the mechanisms that were described earlier and that support and sustain the recreational drugs supply have, in some areas, been utilised to make heroin available to a new generation of young people with no heroin "respect" or knowledge. While the uptake[9] even for trying is far smaller than the opportunities or offers now occurring in these settings, this penetration is unprecedented outside the big cities.

At the age of 15 one middle-class young woman talked enthusiastically about her drug use, particularly her enjoyment of cannabis and LSD. She was already in the club scene through older boyfriends and claiming to be drugwise and sensible:

> Because I was with my boyfriend and he was upstairs (in a nightclub)...One of the lasses comes up to me and she said "Do you want some smack?" It makes you feel beautiful, it makes you feel mint, it makes you feel proper high up'. But I didn't want to try it because it's sure bad for you. I've always thought steer well clear of E and stay well clear of heroin and stay well clear of crack. They're just too bad for you. I know the risks with cannabis and LSD...but they are accepted.

A year later, and after many nights of ecstasy, this young woman was also becoming a regular heroin user. Her fascination with the club scene and her associations with older men provided too many opportunities to try heroin. At age 16 she felt she could take it or leave it:

Once you've done heroin you don't see it as such a big thing. People who haven't done it they see it as a big...wow heroin! But after you've done it it's like well, it's just a smoke.

At age 17 she had built up numerous heroin contacts and while she remained located in a middle-class world of home, Saturday job, and sixth form education, her other subcultural world was always calling from the housing estate at the wrong end of town.

The people at the flats, I wouldn't say that they were my friends to be honest. They're associates who I take drugs with. There's one guy down there, who I do really get on with. We always take...well most of the time we take drugs when we're with each other. I mean we are best friends, anyone who ever looks at me funny, he's like in their face. We get on really well, but at the end of the day if I didn't take drugs, then I wouldn't go down there as much and I wouldn't...I mean there's that close-ness when you take heroin with someone but only while the heroin lasts. Just heroin partners.

Within this world she has met and become associated with well or-ganised local level dealers.

I bought some brown (heroin) on Thursday and the guy I bought it off, after me moaning "No, I want more brown than that, I want more than that and by the way I'm doing it at your house." He got out these tablets, he was showing me these methadone tablets and I just said "give me one." So he just gave me a couple of these methadone tablets.

[So when did you have them, before or after the heroin?] No I didn't have them that day. I had them on Sunday.

[What were they like?] It just killed off my rattle. I took it about eleven, and I was alright until about nine, and then I was down at the flats having a couple of bags.

Her inclusion in drug dealers' worlds went further:

Actually there was one guy, I used to hang around with him when we were younger. I started to hang round with him again, and he was dealing small time. Then he started dealing big time for the main guy, and I didn't get on with him after that. But the main guy, he was supposed to come to Alton Towers with me on Sunday, but he didn't because he didn't wake up, the lazy bastard. But it's like I get on with the main guy better than the guys who deal for him. He doesn't do it himself, the main guy, he doesn't smoke it. If you saw him you'd just think "ordinary guy" but he is actually pretty big in the druggy and gangster world. (Female, now 18, problem drug user)

In short, while probably most of these new heroin users still come from the social exclusion zones they are being joined by a small group who, without heroin availability and marketing, would have probably maintained largely unproblematic, recreational drug careers. Yet because heroin has arrived in their town or village and become attached to the recreational distribution processes, we now have clusters of young heroin takers who do not fully fit the classic socially excluded profile. For those who move beyond experimenting into dependency, the way they procure their drugs slowly changes as the neutralising buffers between users and real dealers crumble. These new users, like their predecessors, now have their own dealers, determined strategies to obtain their brown, an argot and business discourse and contact with criminal worlds. They often, in turn, become fully fledged user-dealers or resort to acquisitive crime and misusing State benefits to fund growing drugs bills.

CONCLUSIONS

During the 1990s there has been an unprecedented expansion of recreational drug experimentation and use among British youth. We now have a normative population balanced by gender, social class and urban-rural location. Leaving aside the complex decision making processes that drug takers utilise (but see Parker et al., 1998a) this whole environment could not have developed without the strong availability of a wide range of street drugs and mechanisms for these drugs to become accessible and acceptable to what is, by and large, a conventional, conforming population of young citizens. If over half of adolescent and young-adult Britons have breached the Misuse of Drugs Act, and a significant minority have done so in a way that, if detected, could lead to what are very serious changes of supplying Class A drugs, then some substantive social processes have been underway within youth culture(s).

These processes have been described as a range or spectrum of attitudes and behaviour vis-à-vis procuring drugs (see Figure 1). For the vast majority of recreational experimenters and users, uncomfortable with obtaining drugs from real dealers, informal but complex social arrangements have developed where drugs are obtained for free, from shared purchases and, most of all from relatives, friends and friends of friends. It is only when we explore the serious end of recreational drug use (the dance drug/stimulant scene) and profile the new, young heroin and problem users that we find customer and dealer routinely meeting and, indeed, users becoming real dealers.

Figure 1: Users' Rules of Engagement with the Drugs Market

Have nothing to do with drugs. Keep away from people who do, if at all possible.

Remain an "abstainer" but accommodate drug taking and "sorting" and sharing among friends and acquaintances.

Take certain drugs, mostly cannabis, but only when they are being used, offered and shared in a safe social setting. Never ask for or attempt to obtain controlled drugs yourself.

Never make a transaction (money for drugs) yourself. Always rely on a partner, friend or "friend of a friends" of a drugs dealer. Ideally "club" your financial contribution with others.

Only buy drugs from a friend or acquaintance, never a stranger. Only buy certain drugs and never heroin or crack cocaine.

Only buy drugs from a drug dealer you know. Do this because you're drugwise and streetwise and are acting as an intermediary providing a service for friends and acquaintances. As reward your own drugs bill is usually covered.

Only buy drugs from a real dealer in exceptional circumstances and only ones you know.

Be realistic buying drugs for your regular personal use and/or friends by negotiating with one or more established dealers in order to get best value or credit (lay-ons).

Buy drugs to divide up and sell to cover your own significant drugs bill or to make a profit.

Buy drugs, despite the risks, if necessary from any dealer or from whomever you can because you need them.

The number of police cautions, for instance, for cannabis possession have risen from 4,000 in 1986 to 40,000 in 1996 (England and

Wales), and continue a sharp ascent; the number of young people convicted of drugs possession and supply offences has risen sharply. These increases in apprehension merely illustrate the scale of recreational drug use since, as we have shown, the ways drugs' transactions are undertaken make enforcement and detection, except for by chance via routine policing, highly unlikely. These processes have facilitated the growing normalisation of recreational drug use, since so many young people become de jure surrogate, low level drug dealers. On the other hand, these processes put distance between "conventional" young users and the more subterranean, subcultural and criminal worlds of those operating the local drugs markets for profit. They have tended to keep the recreational and hard drug arenas separate.

The unwelcome challenge to this bifurcation is coming from a supply-led heroin epidemic based on the well organised supply and distribution to new markets of brown heroin. At the ground level this has meant heroin has been introduced and initially marketed through the recreational drugs-distribution system. While the vast majority of young Britons, whether abstainers or recreational "soft" drug users, will eschew heroin this sinister development has combined with a lack of respect for heroin, produced a new heroin population among some susceptible adolescents. Heroin naïvity is in part a consequence of a quiet, endemic period where today's adolescents have few recollections of the heroin addiction during the 1980s, particularly if they live in towns and small cities with no heroin history. This attitude is also related to primary prevention programmes, underpinned with the war on drugs discourse, that view all street drugs together as bad and dangerous. While demonising ecstasy, this has caused both confusion and contempt not among abstainers but among young and very young recreational drug users, the very group now containing the minority susceptible to heroin experimentation. The growth of cocaine availability and use will further complicate and confuse drug using youth. Unfortunately, by refusing to provide impartial public health/harm reduction messages to recreational users, a parallel opportunity to reinforce or extend their condemnation of heroin and cocaine has thus far been lost.

The millions of young Britons who occasionally use certain drugs would probably side with decriminalising cannabis possession. However, few would support any broader legalisation. They would instead wish to see far greater distinctions of "dangerousness" made between drugs like cannabis and amphetamines as compared to heroin and crack cocaine. From their perspective, law enforcement would concentrate on the suppliers and dealers of these dangerous drugs and also all dealers who sell impure drugs, classically the "dodgy E." On the other hand, those who "sort out" friends with softer drugs would be treated fairly leniently. Redefining what is an offence and revising seriousness thresholds is one way of reducing crime.

There are no solutions to the drugs problem, just different ways of managing the consequences of widespread use. In the U.K., fighting the war on drugs at the point of consumption implies battle with one's own offspring. While there are clear signs that the current government is moving away from such a position by focussing on heroin and cocaine and revising expenditure priorities by moving towards treatment options, these changes are primarily about crime reduction. Apprehended problem or dependent drug users are treated as they pass through the criminal justice system. Politicians have no intention of reviewing the current drugs legislation or providing a public health/harm reduction service for young drug users. Moreover, the new strategy continues to support and fund abstentionist primary prevention drugs education programmes, which appear to be not only ineffective but also, sometimes unintentionally, to undermine young people's informal drugs wisdom. Most recreational drug users try to keep away from criminal worlds and real drug dealers, while routinely breaking drugs laws. The dilemma is real enough — either there's something wrong with today's youth or there's something wrong with the State's approach to controlling what psychoactive substances they consume.

Address correspondence to: Professor Howard Parker, SPARC, Department of Social Policy and Social Work University of Manchester, 4th Floor, Williamson Building, Manchester, U.K. M13 9PL.

Acknowledgments: I would like to thank my colleagues, in and connected with, SPARC especially Judith Aldridge, Roy Egginton, Fiona Measham and Dianne Moss.

REFERENCES

Advisory Council on the Misuse of Drugs (1998). *Drug Misuse and the Environment*. London, UK: Home Office.

Aldridge, J. and H. Parker (1999). *Drug Trying and Drug Use Across Adolescence*. (Drugs Prevention Initiative Green Series Paper #24.) London, UK: Home Office.

Barnard, M., A. Forsyth and N. McKeganey (1996). "Levels of Drug Use among a Sample of Scottish Schoolchildren."' *Drugs: Education, Prevention and Policy* 3(1):81-96.

Edmunds, M., M. Hough and N. Urquia (1996). *Tackling Drug Markets*. (Police Research Group Paper #80.) London, UK: Home Office.

Egginton, R. and H. Parker (1999). *Hidden Heroin Users: Young People's Unchallenged Journeys to Problematic Drug Use.*. London, UK: Drugscope.

European Monitoring Centre for Drugs and Drug Addiction (1999). *Drugs Problems in the European Union: Annual Report*. Lisbon, PORT.

(The) European School Survey Project on Alcohol and Other Drugs (ESPAD) (1997). *Alcohol and Other Drug Use Among Students in 26 European Countries*. Stockholm, SWE: Swedish Council on Alcohol and Other Drugs,.

Finch, J. (1999). "Death Dance of the Disco." *The Guardian* January 23.

Forsyth, A. (1996). "Places and Patterns of Drug Use in the Scottish Dance Scene." *Addiction* 91(4):511-521.

Graham, J. and B. Bowling (1995). *Young People and Crime*. (Home Office Research Study #145.) London, UK: Home Office.

The Guardian (1999). "Survey Results Published by the Headmasters' and Headmistresses' Conference." January 21.

Harkin, A., P. Anderson and J. Lehto (1995). *Alcohol in Europe — A Health Perspective*. Copenhagen, DK: World Health Organization, Regional Office for Europe.

Leitner, N., J. Shapland and P. Wiles (1993). *Drug Usage and Prevention*. London, UK: Home Office.

Measham, F., H. Parker and J. Aldridge (1998). *Starting, Switching, Slowing, Stopping.* (Drugs Prevention Initiative, Green Series Paper #21.) London, UK: Home Office.

—— J. Aldridge and H. Parker (forthcoming). *Dancing on Drugs: Risk Health and Hedonism in the British Club Scene.* London, UK: Free Association Press..

Morris, S. (1998). *Clubs, Drugs* and *Doormen.* (Police Research Group Paper #86.) London, UK: Home Office.

Parker, H., J. Aldridge and F. Measham (1998a). *Illegal Leisure: The Normalisation of Adolescent Recreational Drug Use.* London, UK: Routledge.

—— C. Bury and R. Egginton (1998b). *New Heroin Outbreaks Amongst Young People in England and Wales.* London, UK: Home Office Police Research Group.

Parliamentary Office of Science and Technology (1996). *Common Illegal Drugs and Their Effects: Cannabis, Ecstasy, Amphetamines and LSD.* London, UK.

Ramsay, M. and J. Spiller (1997). *Drug Misuse Declared in 1996: Latest Results from the British Crime Survey.* London, UK: Home Office.

Release (1997). *Release Drugs and Dance Survey* London, UK.

Webb, E., C. Ashton, D. Kelly and F. Kamali (1996). "Alcohol and Drug Use in U.K. University Students." *Lancet* 348:922-925.

NOTES

1. GHB is the common name for gamma-hydroxy-butyric acid.

2. See Parker et al. (1998a) for a full discussion of the methodology. Funded by the Alcohol Education and Research Council and the Economic and Social Research Council.

3. Funded by the Home Office Drugs Prevention Initiative.

4. Funded by the Economic and Social Research Council.

5. Funded by the Home Office Police Research Group.

6. Funded by the Department of Health/Standing Conference on Drug Abuse.

7. "Scally" and "radgy" are both local terms for a street-wise criminal.

8. Gms. refers to grammes metric.

9. Uptake is the proportion of people who are offered or can obtain a drug who actually use the opportunity to consume it.

THE IMPACT OF HEROIN PRESCRIPTION ON HEROIN MARKETS IN SWITZERLAND

by

Martin Killias

and

Marcelo F. Aebi
University of Lausanne, Switzerland

Abstract: *A program of heroin prescription was introduced in Switzerland in 1994. This initially targeted 1,000 heavily dependent heroin users, most of whom were also involved in drug dealing and other forms of crime. It has recently been extended to cover 3,000 users. Evaluation of its impact on users shows large reductions in use of illicit drugs and in drug-related crime. The evaluations were not designed to assess the program's impact on drug markets, but some data can shed light on this. It seems likely that users who were admitted to the program accounted for a substantial proportion of consumption of illicit heroin, and that removing them from the illicit market has damaged the market's viability. Before involvement in the program, a large proportion of users sold drugs to finance their own use, since the illicit drug market in Switzerland relies heavily on users for retail drug selling. It is likely, therefore, that the program additionally disrupted the function of the market by removing retail workers. The workers no longer sold drugs to existing users, and equally important, no longer recruited new users into the market. The heroin prescription market may thus have had a significant impact on heroin markets in Switzerland.*

SWISS DRUG POLICY: FROM NEEDLE PARKS TO DRUG SUBSTITUTION

Until the late 1980s, Switzerland followed a conventional drug policy, with heavy police pressure on addicts and dealers. Until around 1985 and after, it was standard practice to confiscate injecting materials. The sudden appearance of AIDS, and — in an international perspective — the unusually high prevalence rate of HIV infection led to a rethinking of conventional practice. It was recognized that the drug problem played a substantial role in this context. Nearly one half of the regular heroin users were found to be HIV positive at that time.

The immediate response was the establishment of medical care for drug addicts. Among other measures, sterile injection materials were made available to addicts on a large scale, and certain cities opened injection rooms where addicts could also get various forms of social and medical assistance. This policy was very successful in the sense that those who started injecting heroin after its implementation, i.e. after around 1985, were found to test positive for HIV at a rate of less than 5% (Grob, 1993). An unanticipated side effect of offering social and medical assistance to addicts and, concomitantly, reducing police pressure on drug markets, was the extension of needle parks in major Swiss cities to dimensions never seen before. This stage of Swiss drug policy produced particularly ugly images of drug misuse that attracted international coverage as an example of the dangers of liberal drug policies.

Within Switzerland, public drug-using sites led to major public order problems in certain urban areas (Eisner, 1993). The feeling that "something" should be done about these sites was shared by all significant political forces. However, vigorous steps to "close" the Zurich needle park failed to eradicate the problem; such initiatives only shifted addicts to adjacent residential and commercial areas. After a few weeks, a new needle park emerged less than a mile away from its predecessor.

Thus, a wide political consensus to close all needle parks emerged in the country, as well as the wish to try new drug policies that might allow the maintenance of medical and social assistance to addicts without producing new public using sites. In this context, drug substitution became an essential part of Switzerland's national drug policy (Killias, 1999). Despite strong opposition to its introduction in late 1993, several referendums have confirmed that drug substitution is supported by a large majority of voters. In October 1998, the Parliament voted a law allowing extension of heroin prescription to 3,000 (instead of fewer than 1,000) subjects. On June 13, 1999, this law was accepted in a national referendum with 55% of the votes approving the measure.

HOW DOES DRUG SUBSTITUTION WORK?

Late in 1993, the Swiss government decided to allow, on an experimental basis, trials with prescription of heroin (and a few other opiates). After an initial pilot period, this program was extended to about 1,000 recipients, of which 800 received heroin. In addition to this project, methadone was made available to about 15,000 users. Thus, a significant part of Switzerland's opiate users became engaged in substitution programs.[1] In this paper, we are only concerned with heroin prescription.[2]

The main features of heroin prescription are (Uchtenhagen, 1997a; Rihs-Middel, 1994):

- In order to qualify, users have to (1) be at least 20 years of age; (2) have been addicted to heroin — daily use — for at least two years; (3) present signs of deterioration of health and/or social relations as a result of drug use; and (4) be engaged in conventional treatment without success despite two or more attempts.

- Those prescribed heroin are assigned to special clinics that offer also a wide array of medical and social assistance. No clinic has more than 150 patients.

- Heroin can be obtained solely at the clinic, and it has to be injected on the spot. No heroin can be taken away. If the patient is unable to attend the clinic, he/she will be aided by receiving methadone.

The population enrolled on this program presented a wide range of medical[3] and social problems (Uchtenhagen, 1997b); they also displayed an unusually high involvement in drug use and crime:

- Overall, the average age of participants was just over 30, with an average career of heroin use of 10 years.

- The prevalence of criminal backgrounds was unusually high: 87% had a criminal record, with an average of eight previous convictions. More than half had been imprisoned at least once. For the general (male) Swiss population of that age, the lifetime prevalence of convictions is about 25%, and the lifetime prevalence of custodial sentences is about 6%.

- According to self-reports (Killias and Rabasa, 1998), around 70% were engaged in offending during the six months before admission to the program, more than 50% were involved in drug trafficking, around 40% in minor thefts (e.g., shoplifting, receiving or selling stolen property) and more than 10% in serious thefts (e.g., mugging, robbery, burglary).

Given the profile of the treated population, occasional criticisms that the Swiss program included many low-level and occasional users seem absolutely unfounded.

It has been estimated that the number of seriously dependent heroin users meeting the program's criteria of eligibility is likely to be about 3,000. Thus, the new extension voted by the Parliament will make heroin substitution available to a significant proportion, if not the most current "problematic" users.

EVALUATIONS OF THE PROGRAM

As an essential part of the project, all trials had to be evaluated by independent research institutes. The main findings can be summarized as follows:

(1) Medical and social psychiatric research (Uchtenhagen, 1997a; 1997b) has shown a substantial improvement in health and social conditions among those prescribed heroin. The same is true in relation to employment and social rehabilitation.

(2) The criminological evaluation (Killias and Rabasa, 1998; Killias et al., 1998) has established a substantial fall in criminal involvement (whether measured by rates of prevalence or incidence). This fall was greatest (50% to 90%) for the most serious offenses, such as burglary, muggings, robbery and drug trafficking. It was observed with all indicators used, i.e. self-reports, victimization, police records, and conviction records. Thus, it is hard to think of any validity problem that could have affected these various and independent crime measures so consistently and to such an extent. Moreover, a comparative study of these measures has shown the validity of self-reported delinquency in this particular context (Aebi, 1999).

(3) The program's impact on national and city crime levels was not evaluated. It was felt that the number of subjects eligible for heroin substitution was too low to affect aggregate crime levels. Data on muggings from Zurich suggest, however, that some effect might have occurred in this respect (Killias and Rabasa, 1998). Another visible outcome was the substantial reduction of open, drug-using sites in Swiss cities.

(4) For the most part, the evaluations were based on "before and after" comparisons. Only a few randomized trials could be conducted comparing heroin and methadone. The tentative conclusions are that: (1) heroin is more effective in the recruitment of addicts, particularly among those who have failed treatment in the past; (2) those prescribed heroin are complying better with treatment conditions (i.e., less additional drug use); and (3) the drop-out rates tend to be lower for this group (Dobler-Mikola et al., 1998; Uchtenhagen, 1997a).

THE IMPACT OF HEROIN SUBSTITUTION ON DRUG MARKETS

In all its public statements about drug policy and heroin substitution, Swiss government officials consistently denied that this program could produce any effect on drug markets. Of course, the purpose was not to overstate the case of drug substitution, and to gain public support by pointing to positive effects of the program in areas where its success was less debatable (such as, for example, improving health conditions and reducing criminal involvement among addicts).

Since disrupting the heroin market was not included in the program's goals, evaluations have, so far, largely neglected outcomes in this domain, and few data have been collected that might be helpful in analyzing this issue. The following sections of this paper assemble what limited empirical results there are on drug dealing and describe, to a large extent hypothetically, longer-term effects of drug substitution on the heroin market.

Reduction of Demand Through Heroin Substitution

The main reason why Swiss policy makers did not anticipate effects of the current program on drug markets was the small number of addicts treated with heroin. At best, three to five percent of the estimated number of regular heroin users are currently prescribed heroin. Some might argue, therefore, that by taking out this small a share of actual buyers, no significant reduction in demand might be obtained on the market. The same argument might, implicitly, apply even with program's future extension to 3,000 regular users.

The problem with this view is that, within a given population of users, the distribution of actual consumption may be heavily skewed. As with alcohol — where 5% of the drinkers might account for 50% or more of the actual demand — a minority of heavy, regular heroin users might absorb a disproportionate quantity. Since heroin substitution tends to reach especially problematic users, i.e., heavy consumers, and assuming that 3,000 addicts represent 10% to 15% of Switzerland's heroin users, it does not seem not unrealistic to speculate that they may account for 30% to 60% of the demand for heroin on illegal markets.

The Outlook for Potential Market Responses

The question arises as to how the market will react to a drop in demand of such proportions. One possible strategy might be to promote new drugs, or those which are currently less popular in Switzerland, such as cocaine. It is difficult to assess whether such strategies will be successful, as displacement effects are always hard to study, whatever the offense to be prevented and the possible "alternative" crimes might be.

The data collected so far tend to show, however, a decline not only of nonprescribed heroin consumption, but also of other illicit drugs. As the following tables illustrate, police, as well as self-report data, consistently show that use of illicit drugs fell among those prescribed heroin; more significantly, incidence as well as "daily" use — i.e., proxy measures of the actual volume of consumption — decreased more than the number of users.

For example, in Table 1, police records show that the prevalence rate of police contacts (i.e., the percentage of patients contacted by the police) for use or possession of heroin during the first six months of treatment decreased by 68% in comparison to the six months preceding the treatment. When the comparison is extended to periods of 24 months before and after admission to the program, the decrease is 71%. Concerning the incidence rates of police contacts (i.e., the mean number of contacts per person), Table 2 shows that, for the same offense, the decrease is 78% for the six-month period and 88% for the two-year period.[4]

In Table 3 we can see that before admission and according to self-reports, those who did not use cocaine over the previous six months represented only 15% of the sample; but the proportion of noncocaine users increased progressively to 28% six months after admission, 35% after 12 months and, finally, 41% after 18 months. At the same time, Table 4 shows that 18 months after the beginning of the treatment, the daily users of nonprescribed heroin had fallen to 6%, while nonusers increased to 74%.

The reduction in the use of illicit drugs among subjects enrolled in heroin substitution points to a possibly opportunistic character of the use of additional drugs. Cocaine and other drugs were perhaps used whenever heroin was unavailable or available only under unacceptable conditions.

Table 1: Drop in Prevalence Rates of Police Contacts for Use/Possession of Hard Drugs by Matched Periods of Time Before and After Admission to the Program

Substance	Observation Period			
	6 months before vs. 6 months after (N=604)	12 months before vs. 12 months after (N=336)	18 months before vs. 18 months after (N=153)	24 months before vs. 24 months after (N=108)
Heroin	–68%	–68%	–77%	–71%
Cocaine/ecstasy	–47%	–40%	–50%	–48%
Other drugs	–68%	–72%	–43%	–43%

Table 2: Drop in Incidence Rates of Police Contacts for Use/Possession of Hard Drugs by Matched Periods of Time Before and After Admission to the Program

Substance	Observation Period			
	6 months before vs. 6 months after (N=604)	12 months before vs. 12 months after (N=336)	18 months before vs. 18 months after (N=153)	24 months before vs. 24 months after (N=108)
Heroin	–78%	–82%	–87%	–88%
Cocaine/ecstasy	–54%	–47%	–48%	–54%
Other drugs	–85%	–69%	–35%	–36%

Table 3: Prevalence of Self-reported Use of Cocaine Before and After Admission, by Reference Periods of Six Months (N=237)

	6 months before the beginning of the treatment	After 6 months in treatment	After 12 months in treatment	After 18 months in treatment
No use in the last six months	15%	28%	35%	41%
Some use in the last six months	56%	63%	61%	52%
(Almost) daily use	29%	7%	4%	5%
Answer not clear	0%	3%	0%	2%

Sign tests for each line between first and last period: p ≤ .001.
Source: Uchtenhagen (1997b:70).

Table 4: Prevalence of Self-reported Use of Nonprescribed Heroin Before and After Admission, by Reference Periods of Six Months (N=237)

	6 months before the beginning of the treatment	After 6 months in treatment	After 12 months in treatment	After 18 months in treatment
No use in the last six months	4%	61%	72%	74%
Some use in the last six months	14%	30%	20%	19%
(Almost) daily use	81%	6%	5%	6%
Answer not clear	0%	3%	4%	1%

Sign tests for each line between first and last period: p ≤ .001.
Source: Uchtenhagen (1997b: 70).

Another market response might be to maintain demand at current levels by lowering prices. This might help in the recruitment of new consumers, an option we shall look at more carefully in the following section. Demand could also be stimulated by encouraging the remaining black-market customers to increase their consumption. Earlier research has indeed shown demand to be highly elastic in the sense that users of opiates manage to adapt consumption to market conditions, such as availability of preferred drugs, quality, prices, and the availability of cash (Grapendaal et al., 1995; Grapendaal, 1992). Therefore, lower prices could lead existing users to increase the quantities consumed and thereby increase the severity of their dependency. Research conducted in the U.S. has shown that drug use varies consistently according to availability of drugs, prices, and legal restrictions (cf. Hawkins et al., 1995). On the other hand, the results shown in Tables 1 to 4 suggest that a shift to increased consumption, either of heroin or other nonprescribed drugs, did not occur once addicts got their "base rate" through substitution programs.

Lower prices mean reduced profits, at least if costs of production, supply, and distribution cannot be adapted. Thus, such policies might impose some strain on organizations of dealers and increase internal conflict. Recent shifts in distribution networks and the emergence of new distributors (as well as the disappearance of others) may well be related to shrinking margins.

Interestingly, we are not aware of any research available, in Switzerland and other European countries, on the effects of lower prices on users, their habits of use, and networks of dealers. This lack of research is the more surprising as Europe has seen a dramatic drop in street prices of heroin over the last five to eight years. In Switzerland before 1990, one gram used to be sold for at least 500 Swiss francs, i.e., about $300. Since then the price per gram has fallen to about 70 francs, about $45. The reasons for this dramatic drop could be external, i.e., related to the emergence of new supply lines and distribution networks, and totally independent of local substitution programs and the impact they might have had on demand.

However, the prices of heroin, cocaine, and marijuana did not follow the same trend. Marijuana remained fairly stable at about 10 Swiss francs per gram (about $6.5) over the last 10 years. Cocaine prices dropped from less than 200 francs ($130) to about 120 francs ($80) per gram.[5] Thus, the drop of heroin prices was incomparably more dramatic. These different trends support the idea that demand for heroin might have declined. On the other hand, heroin prices started to decrease before 1994, when heroin treatment became an official option. The trend was similar in other countries without heroin prescription programs. The "missing link" may have been methadone prescription. Although somewhat less effective in preventing use of nonprescribed drugs, it certainly reduces the volume of demand among those treated, and it is, as a treatment option (Office Fédéral de la Santé Publique [OFSP], 1996), available to far larger numbers within and outside of Switzerland. Currently, about 15,000 of an estimated number of 30,000 regular opiate users receive methadone as a treatment. It would be surprising if a program of that size had no effect on demand. Research on drug markets in London confirmed, indeed, that markets are vulnerable to demand reduction through drug substitution programs (Edmunds et al., 1996).

With cocaine and marijuana the story may be different. Although the production of marijuana has increased substantially in recent years, especially within Switzerland, the prices may have been stabilized by an increasing demand, as documented by longitudinal data on drug use (OFSP, 1998). In the case of cocaine almost nothing is known concerning supply and demand, but the best guess may be that there were few changes.

Drug Substitution and the Recruitment of New Users

The current evaluation of substitution programs has established that selling heroin to other users had been the most common criminal activity of heroin users admitted to the program. According to self-reports, more than 50% of all subjects admitted to the program turned out to be dealers. This prevalence rate far exceeds the extent of acquisitive crimes, such as burglary or mugging (Killias and Rabasa, 1998). Police records confirm, for this population, the central role of drug dealing in earning illegitimate incomes (Killias et al., 1998).

Under the heroin substitution program, according to both self-report and police data (Tables 5 and 6), the prevalence and, even more so, the extent of drug selling dropped considerably. Interestingly, those who continue to sell illegal drugs, tend to be those who maintain use of nonprescribed illegal drugs (mostly cocaine, Table 7), probably because they do not cut their links to this particular milieu, unlike the majority of those on the program.

For example, in Table 5 we can see that, according to self-reports, the prevalence rate of hard-drugs trafficking (i.e., the percentage who admitted this offense) over the six months preceding treatment was 43%. This dropped to 10% during the first six months of treatment and to 6% during the last twelve months. At the same time, the incidence rate (i.e., the mean number of offenses per person) for the same offense decreased from 22.8 to 0.8.

Table 5: Prevalence and Incidence Rates of Self-reported Drug-trafficking for Periods of Six (A, B-1, B-2) and 12 Months (C-1) Before Each Interview (N=242)

	6 months before the beginning of treatment (A)	After 6 months in treatment (B1)	After 12 months in treatment (B2)	After 24 months in treatment (C1)
Prevalence of soft-drug trafficking	23%	15%	12%	12%
Prevalence of hard-drug trafficking	43%	10%	6%	6%
Incidence of soft-drug trafficking	7.8	1.5	2.5	1.3
Incidence of hard-drug trafficking	22.8	2.8	1.4	0.8

Table 6: Drop in Prevalence and Incidence Rates of Police Contacts Related to Drug-trafficking, by Matched Periods of Time Before and After Admission to the Program

	Observation Period			
	6 months before vs. 6 months after (N=604)	12 months before vs. 12 months after (N=336)	18 months before vs. 18 months after (N=153)	24 months before vs. 24 months after (N=108)
Prevalence	–63%	–51%	–61%	–61%
Incidence	–58%	–50%	–73%	–80%

In Table 6, police records confirm this trend showing the prevalence rate of police contacts for drug trafficking during the first six months of treatment decreased by 63% in comparison to the six months preceding treatment, while the incidence rate decreased by 58%. When the comparisons are extended to periods of 24 months before and after admission to the program, the decrease is 61% for the prevalence rate and 80% for the incidence rate.

Finally, in Table 7 we can see that, according to self-reports and during the first six months of treatment, 10% of the patients who did not use illicit drugs ("nonconsumers") had sold soft drugs, while among those who used illicit drugs ("consumers") this percentage was 18%. At the same time, the average number of soft-drug trafficking offenses was 0.7 for the non-consumers and 2.6 for the consumers.

Table 7: Prevalence and Incidence Rates of Self-reported Drug-trafficking for a Period of Six Months Before Each Interview, by Consumption of Nonprescribed Hard Drugs (Cocaine and/or Heroin; N=305)

	After 6 months in treatment (B1)			After 12 months in treatment (B2)		
	non-consumers	consumers	p*	non-consumers	consumers	p*
Prevalence of soft-drug trafficking	10%	18%	.09	12%	14%	NS
Prevalence of hard-drug trafficking	0%	16%	<.01	1%	15%	<.01
Incidence of soft drug trafficking	0.7	2.6	NS	2.3**	2.2	NS
Incidence of hard drug trafficking	0	4.2	<.01	0.01	4.0	<.03

* T-test between groups (nonconsumers and consumers)
** This rate is heavily increased by a patient who admits selling soft drugs daily (i.e., 180 times in six months)

In sum, the data consistently suggest that selling of heroin can successfully be reduced to a very large extent by drug substitution.

The question is how this might affect the recruitment of new users. According to conventional criminological wisdom, any arrested drug dealer will immediately be replaced by a new one (Blumstein, 1986). Even if this may be true, the question remains of how the "loss" of addicted users as sellers of drugs on the streets and outside urban areas might affect supply lines and, especially, the recruitment of new users.

Over the last 15 years or so, the organization of drug distribution systems in Switzerland and other continental countries has undergone a special kind of differentiation. While gangs from Eastern Europe have taken over import and wholesale, the small retail business on the streets tended to remain in the hands of local addicts who sold the substance to their "friends." They also tended to recruit new users through their friendship networks. This pattern matches the results of American research (Hawkins et al., 1995), suggesting that drug-using peers are among the strongest predictors of substance use among youth. Although no recent information is available on this issue in Switzerland, user-dealers seem to play a significant role in the initiation of teenagers into drug use.

Thus, by losing this special "workforce," foreign and international traffickers may face some problems in maintaining the recruitment of new users at former levels. Although they tend to be highly sophisticated in the importation of large quantities at low prices, to date they have had great difficulty in gaining access to new and occasional users. In fact, the number of regular heroin users (prevalence rates) seems to have remained remarkably stable over the last years in all age groups. This conclusion derives from data of the Swiss Health Survey (OFSP, 1998) that suggest stable rates of heroin users, some increase of cocaine use, and a substantial increase of marijuana smoking. Estimates based on police contacts arrived at very similar conclusions (Estermann, 1998). Nor does the drop in drug-related fatalities from 419 (in 1992) to 209 (in 1998) point to a contrary trend in illicit drug use (Office Fédéral de la Police [OFP], 1999).

Thus, the idea that lower prices may automatically attract new consumers into the market (see Hawkins et al., 1995, concerning American research) may be somewhat simplistic and neglect the crucial role of distribution chains. In fact, such networks are no less crucial in stimulating sales of commodities in legal markets. Simultaneously, the stability of the number of regular heroin users in Switzerland invalidates occasional claims that heroin prescription is "sending the wrong message" to young people, and that it will ultimately increase the number of juvenile drug users (on such claims, see also MacCoun, 1998).

Anecdotal accounts from police officers in Zurich suggest that a few changes in distribution networks might have taken place recently. Dealers are no longer operating in the streets but in apartments. The contacts are being established through addicts, often of Swiss background, who look out for clients in the streets, but who no longer sell drugs themselves.[6] This kind of distribution may work well in urban areas with established users, but it may be less effective in rural areas. These contain significant proportions of the Swiss population, and many users originate from them.

In sum, drugs like heroin might become less easily available to casual or novice users or to those who otherwise might wish to experiment out of curiosity. If this should hold true, heroin substitution might become not only a strategy of harm reduction, but contribute to reducing the extent of the drug problem.

CONCLUSIONS AND NEW PRIORITIES FOR THE RESEARCH AGENDA

The Swiss heroin prescription program was targeted at hard-core drug users with very well established heroin habits. These people were heavily engaged in both drug dealing and other forms of crime. They also served as a link between importers, few of whom were Swiss, and the — primarily Swiss — users. As these hard-core users found a steady, legal means for addressing their addiction, they reduced their illicit drug use. This reduced their need to deal in heroin and engage in other criminal activities. Thus, the program had three effects on the drug market:

- It substantially reduced the consumption among the heaviest users, and this reduction in demand affected the viability of the market.
- It reduced levels of other criminal activity associated with the market.
- By removing local addicts and dealers, Swiss casual users found it difficult to make contact with sellers.

So far, very little is known about habits of consumption, ways of recruitment and initiation, and distribution networks. Therefore, one future research priority should be to look more carefully into these factors in order to anticipate potential effects of substitution programs on drug markets. Another priority should be the study of market responses to reduced drug prices. How has the market absorbed the tremendous drop in drug prices in many Western countries? How did trafficking organizations manage the increased internal strain and conflict? Eventually, did some traditional organizations (such as Italian and Turkish mafias) leave this market to new ones, e.g., from Albania, for reasons related to insufficient profitability? Or, as recent research suggests (Nett, unpublished), did Turks lose their market position because more and more of their local offspring became addicted themselves?

Address correspondence to: Martin Killias, Ph.D., MA (sociology) Professor of Criminology and Criminal Law, School of Forensic Science and Criminology, University of Lausanne, CH-1015 Lausanne, Switzerland. E-mail: Martin.Killias@ipsc.unil.ch

REFERENCES

Aebi, M.F. (1999). "La validité des indicateurs de la criminalité: Les sondages de délinquance autoreportée face aux données de police et du casier judiciaire dans le cadre de l'évaluation des essais suisses de prescription d'héroïne." Doctoral dissertation, School of Forensic Science and Criminology, University of Lausanne. Lausanne, SWITZ.

Blumstein, A. (1986). "Coherence, Coordination, and Integration in the Administration of Criminal Justice." In: van Dijk, J. et al. (eds.), *Criminal Law in Action.* Arnhem NETH: Gouda Quint.

Dobler-Mikola, A., S. Pfeifer, V. Müller and A. Uchtenhagen (1998). *Methadon- und heroingestützte Behandlung Opiatabhängiger im Vergleich* (Methadon and Heroin-Based Treatment of Addicts Compared). (Report No. 62.) Zurich, SWITZ: Addiction Research Institute.

Edmunds, M., M. Hough and N. Urquia (1996). *Tackling Local Drug Markets.* London, UK: Home Office.

Eisner, M. (1993). "Policies Towards Open Drug Scenes and Street Crime: The Case of the City of Zurich." *European Journal on Criminal Policy and Research* 1(2):61-75.

Estermann, J. (1998). "Doch kein zunehmender Heroin- und Kokainkonsum in der Schweiz?" *Sozial- und Präventivmedizin* 43:173-174.

Grapendaal, M. (1992). "Cutting Their Coat According to their Cloth: Economic Behavior of Amsterdam Opiate Users." *The International Journal of the Addictions* 27(4):487-501.

—— E. Leuw and H. Nelen (1995). *A World of Opportunities: Life-Style and Economic Behavior of Heroin Addicts in Amsterdam.* Albany, NY: State University of New York Press.

Grob, P. J. (1993). "The Needle Park in Zurich: The Story and the Lessons to be Learned." *European Journal on Criminal Policy and Research* 1(2):48-60.

Hawkins, J.D., M.W. Arthur and R.F. Catalano (1995). "Preventing Substance Abuse." *Crime & Justice* 19:343-427.

Killias, M. (1999). "Fighting Evils or Preventing Harm: Switzerland's Drug Policy as a Test of Situational Crime Policies?" In: R. Hood and N.E. Courakis (eds.), *The Changing Face of Crime and Criminal Policy in Europe.* Oxford, UK: University of Oxford, Centre for Criminological Research.

—— M.F. Aebi and D. Ribeaud (1998). "Effects of Heroin Prescription on Police Contacts among Drug-Addicts." *European Journal on Criminal Policy and Research* 6(3):433-438.

—— and J. Rabasa (1998). "Does Heroin Prescription Reduce Crime? Results from the Evaluation of the Swiss Heroin Prescription Projects." *Studies on Crime and Crime Prevention* 7(1):127-133.

—— and A. Uchtenhagen (1996). "Does Medical Heroin Prescription Reduce Delinquency among Drug-Addicts? On the Evaluation of the Swiss Heroin Prescription Projects and its Methodology." *Studies on Crime and Crime Prevention* 5(2):245-256.

MacCoun, R.J. (1998). "Toward a Psychology of Harm Reduction." *American Psychologist* 53(11):1199-1208.

Nett. J.C. (unpublished). "Austausch and Kooperation in lokalen Drogenmärkten."

Office Fédéral de la Police (1999). *Statistique suisse des stupéfiants 1998.* Berne, SWITZ.

Office Fédéral de la Santé Publique (1998). "Nette augmentation de la consommation de cannabis." *Spectra: Prévention et Promotion de la Santé* 14(Dec.):8.

—— (1997). *Politique de la Confédération Suisse en matière de drogue: Des chiffres et des faits.* Berne, SWITZ.

—— (1996). *Swiss Methadone Report* (3rd ed.). Berne, SWITZ: author/Addiction Research Foundation.

Reuband, K.-H. (1998). "Drug Policies and Drug Prevalence: The Role of Demand and Supply." *European Journal on Criminal Policy and Research* 6(3):321-336.

Rihs-Middel, M. (1994). "Medical Prescription of Narcotics in Switzerland: Basic Issues and Research Plan." *European Journal on Criminal Policy and Research* 2(4):69-83.

Uchtenhagen, A. (1997a). *Programme for a Medical Prescription of Narcotics: Summary of the Synthesis Report.* Zürich, SWITZ: Institut für Suchtforschung, University of Zurich. [Available on internet:http://www.admin.ch/bag/sucht/forschev/e/forschg/provebe.pdf]

—— (1997b). *Essais de prescription médicale de stupéfiants: Rapport de synthèse.* Zürich, SWITZ: Institut für Suchtforschung, University of Zurich.

—— A. Dobler-Mikola, T. Steffen, F. Gutzwiller, R. Blättler and S. Pfeifer (1999). *Prescription of Narcotics for Heroin Addicts: Main Results of the Swiss National Cohort Study.* Basel, SWITZ: Karger.

NOTES

1. Estimates of the number of regular hard-drug users oscillate around 30,000 (Reuband 1998; OFSP 1997).

2. The details of heroin substitution programs in Switzerland have been reported in a number of publications available in English (Uchtenhagen et al., 1999; Killias and Rabasa 1998; Uchtenhagen 1997a; Killias and Uchtenhagen 1996); therefore, only a few essential characteristics of this project are given here.

3. A medical evaluation at the start of the program established that around 20% of the patients were in a bad physical condition and around 40% in bad psychological condition. 16% were found to test positive for HIV, 70% suffered hepatitis A infections, 74% suffered hepatitis B infections and 83% suffered hepatitis C infections (Uchtenhagen 1997b: 54-57).

4. At the time of data collection in the different police forces, 604 patients had been treated for at least six months, but only 108 of them had been treated for at least 24 months (see Ns in Tables 1 and 2).

5. The authors are much indebted to Lt. N. Klossner of the Zurich City police for having provided information on recent changes in drug market.

6. This "job" is certainly less rewarding than selling drugs. This trend illustrates how dealers' organizations try to straighten supply lines (and control costs of distribution) by eliminating addicts as dealers in the streets.

WOMEN AS JUDICIOUS CONSUMERS OF DRUG MARKETS

by

Sheigla Murphy

and

Karina Arroyo
Institute for Scientific Analysis, San Francisco, USA

Abstract: Drawing on analyses of qualitative data gathered from National Institute on Drug Abuse (NIDA)-funded projects beginning in 1989 to April 1999, we examine the role of women as illegal drug consumers. Specifically, we depict how their attempts to manage finances, drug procurement and use resulted in a dialectic of control. Inherent in many of the women's strategies to manage drug markets, as well as to control their own drug use and life circumstances were the sources of constraints on control. Exerting control in a changing marketplace required being an informed consumer. This, in turn, called for ongoing involvement in drug-using worlds to maintain up-to-date knowledge. Despite a male dominated underground marketplace where force, or potential retaliation, were the basis for settling disputes, women enacted strategies to increase their control. To maintain up-to-date knowledge concerning the people and places where drugs were sold, women had to be inundated in drug-using social worlds. Women who were good negotiators and communicators wielded more control in their dealings with drug sellers. Dealers settled conflicts through the use of threats or actual violence. A woman buyer was at a decided disadvantage due to her unequal ability to retaliate. Nonetheless, women employed tactics and strategies that minimized their risks and increased their control.

INTRODUCTION

Drawing on selected analyses of qualitative data gathered from three National Institute on Drug Abuse (NIDA)-funded projects beginning in 1989 to April 1999, we examine women's roles in drug markets as drug consumers. Unlike other research that has looked at women's roles in powder-cocaine sales (Waldorf et al., 1991; Murphy et al., 1990) and in crack and heroin markets (Sterk and Elifson, 2000; Jacobs and Miller, 1998; Fagan, 1994; Curtis and Maher, 1993; Bourgois and Dunlap, 1992) we focus primarily on their roles as *buyers* of marijuana, crack/cocaine and heroin. Specifically, we examine the ways in which their attempts to manage finances, drug procurement, use and intoxication resulted in what we conceptualize as a dialectic of control or the interaction of gendered contextual strategies and constraints. Inherent in strategies used by many of those interviewed to manage drug markets, their drug use and other life circumstances were the sources of constraints on their control.

Like buyers in any other marketplace, women attempted to get the best bargain for their money in terms of both pricing and quality. Being a judicious customer in a dynamic marketplace required being an informed consumer. Maintaining up-to-date information called for ongoing and time-absorbing involvement in drug-using social worlds. Women's personal qualities were also important. Especially effective were networking and negotiating skills appropriate to the social contexts of the underground economies in which the women interacted. In this paper we address the following two topics: (1) Women's gendered relationships within drug markets; and (2) Pregnancy as a real liability for women trying to negotiate drug buys.

DESCRIPTION OF DATA SETS AND METHODS

We must begin this section with a caveat. None of the three studies we analyzed for this paper were focused on women's drug buying. Since all three data sets were based on a qualitative theoretical and methodological perspective, specifically, the discovery process known as grounded theory (Glaser and Strauss, 1967), information about women's relationships to drug-markets emerged from the interviews to the extent that the interviewees saw their drug market experiences as important to our understanding of the various study topics described below.

"Women and Cocaine" was conducted from 1988 to 1991 with a sample of 100 women crack users from the San Francisco Bay area.[1]

Women's crack experiences were analyzed as a struggle to control potential loss of self. The primary focus of the theoretical framework developed was an explication of the interaction between the emerging self and the political economy. African Americans comprised 67% (n=67) of the sample; 26% were white, 5% Latina (representing Central and South America), and the remaining 2% were Asian. Women ranged in age from 18 to 58 years old with the majority in their early thirties. The mean age was 32.8 years (s.d. = 8.5 years), and the modal age was 32 years.

"An Ethnographic Study of Pregnancy and Drugs," conducted in the San Francisco Bay area between 1991 and 1994, was an ethnographic-type study of drug use during pregnancy.[2] We employed in-depth-interviewing, fieldwork and closed-ended questions as the primary data-gathering tools. We interviewed a total of 120 pregnant or postpartum adult women who were using heroin, methamphetamine or cocaine singly or in combination and who were not in treatment. The study population used drugs for a minimum of 25 days during the time of interview or most recent pregnancy. Women who were enrolled in drug treatment more than five days within a five-week period were not included in the study. Those women who were in treatment for fewer than five days had to have returned to drug use for five or more days since their last day of treatment. These criteria allowed us to interview women who had brief encounters with drug treatment and had subsequently returned to drug use. Therefore, we were able to explore women's reasons for leaving treatment.

In order to fully explore AIDS risks, attitudes and behaviors, half (20) of the women interviewed in each stage were intravenous drug users (IDUs). IDUs were defined as those women who had injected heroin, cocaine, or methamphetamine at least once a week during the six months prior to discovering their pregnancy. These inclusion criteria permitted us to examine the changes in drug administration before and after the onset of pregnancy. "Noninjection drug users" were defined as any woman who had not injected drugs in the previous two years. Each of our subgroups, consisting of 20 subjects, were IDU and non-IDU in each of the three stages of pregnancy: (1) discovery, (2) five months to delivery and (3) six months postpartum. Our previous research had demonstrated that a minimum of 20 interviews was necessary to discover meaningful patterns and to produce a robust theoretical framework.

In the course of the life history interviews, the interviewer and study participant explored the introduction and initiation to each drug used, social environments of use, pressures to use or not to use, the relationship of pregnancy to patterns of use, and barriers to treatment. The other areas investigated included methods of ingesting drugs, violence, involvement in criminal activities, high-risk AIDS behavior (including needle sharing and sexual practices) and attendance at prenatal care.

This sample comprised primarily African-American (53%, n=64) and white (34%, n=41) women who relied on public assistance (88%) to support themselves and their children. Approximately 40% were homeless at the time of interview and another 20% lived in publicly subsidized housing projects in neighborhoods characterized by high levels of drug sales, drug use and violent crime.

We also used selected findings from "An Ethnography of Victimization Pregnancy and Drug Use," (1996-2001).[3] The Pregnancy and Violence Study, as we came to call it, is an exploratory in-depth interview study of pregnant drug users who experienced one or more victimizations (physical, sexual and/or emotional) while pregnant. We began this project by using ethnographic field work methods to locate and recruit women who were pregnant or recently pregnant and had used marijuana, crack/cocaine, heroin/opiates and/or methamphetamine singly or in combination (including alcohol with one or more of the above). We then collected information concerning demographics, family, drug use, relationship and reproductive histories employing a structured questionnaire. This instrument was designed to measure levels of drug use and incidence of victimization. Originally we estimated that we would have to screen approximately 300 women in order to enroll 100 who would qualify for and agree to participate in the second session, a qualitative depth interview focusing on their drug use and victimization histories with an emphasis on victimizations experienced during pregnancy. As it turned out, we only had to screen 126 women. Sadly, 79% of the interviewees experienced physical and emotional abuse while pregnant.

The mean age for this sample was 29. Only 9% were married, 63% were in a relationship and 28% were single. Fifty-two percent were African Americans, 27% white, 15% Latina and 6% Native American or Asian/Pacific Islanders. The type of drug used affected the women's risk of experiencing violence. Of those women in our study reporting physical abuse, 46% were crack users, 26% were marijuana users, 17% were heroin users and 11% used other drugs. More than one third (35.8%) had no permanent home; 23 (18.3%) were homeless and living on the streets or in temporary shelters, 15 (11.9%) were in single occupancy hotels and seven (5.6%) were in treatment centers or group homes. More than two fifths of them (42.9%) reported that they had been homeless for three or more days in the prior six months. All three of these study samples were made up of drug using women who for the most part lived below the poverty line.

Throughout this paper when we quote directly from interview transcripts we will indicate in which of the three studies the person interviewed participated. With few exceptions, which will be noted where appropriate, women were from communities of color (African Americans, Latinas, Asians, Pacific Islanders), were unemployed and living close to, if not below, the poverty level.

WOMEN'S RELATIONSHIPS WITHIN DRUG MARKETS

Women were at a decided disadvantage when they interacted in drug markets. What Theidon (1995) called "ambient violence," or emotional, verbal and/or physical abuse resulting from exchanges with people in the environment outside the home, i.e., drug dealers, johns, pimps, etc., was unfortunately a far too common occurrence in the lives of those interviewed. Just like other social worlds in our patriarchal society, women were more likely to occupy these lower rungs of the social world of drug use (Inciardi et al., 1993; Ratner, 1993) in part because they were willing to trade sex for drugs, and also because they were thought to have little access to drug supplies (Williams, 1992). Women were at higher risk of exposure to ambient violence than men, especially when a significant part of their lives involved the acquisition of drugs. The urgency and desperation to obtain drugs cast many of our interviewees along the dangerous paths of dealing drugs or becoming prostitutes. Amaro and Hardy-Fanta (1995) stated that "women who exchange sex for drugs or sex for money are typically subjected to constant violence from customers and generally from men on the street who rob, beat, and rape them" (Amaro and Hardy-Fanta, 1995:333). Sterk's work reveals that as women were pushed out of conventional social circles, their lives became more and more enmeshed in drug users' deviant subcultures. The women she interviewed also reported feeling pressured to resort to illegal work to fund their drug use (Sterk, 1998). In the subculture of addiction, masculine values relegate women to secondary roles, making them dependent on the dominant males (Amaro and Hardy-Fanta, 1995; Millstein, 1993). As both drug users and women, they were vulnerable to physical and emotional abuse. The repeated humiliation, abuse, and rape that women suffered at the hands of their partners, customers, and men on the street were a direct result of women's lower position of power in society (Miller et al., 1989). Women may also see prostitution as less dangerous than drug dealing, although the risks of victimization from customers and pimps are considerable

(Mayer and Curtis, 1993; Williams, 1992; Cohen, 1980; Goldstein, 1979). A 20-year-old interviewed for the Pregnancy and Violence study shared her experiences as a prostitute:

> Well, I got raped on the streets about four times. Twice while I was pregnant... I thought being raped, I didn't know whether it was okay. I didn't know whether I was in the wrong. I, I blame myself sometimes, like how could I be stupid? And you know, I could have done something, but I really couldn't've done anything, 'cause I can't overpower a man. I've been tied up. I've been burnt with cigarettes while I was pregnant. I've been, I've been humiliated, talked about...I been through a lot.

Nonetheless, like buyers in any marketplace, women attempted to exert some control over the quality and price of the drugs they were buying and using. Exerting control in a changing marketplace required being an informed consumer. This, in turn, called for ongoing involvement in drug-using worlds to maintain up-to-date knowledge. Involvement in prostitution and removal from other crime partnerships with males often narrowed their social contacts, support systems and linkage to drug sellers/buying knowledge (Fagan, 1994). Personal qualities were also important, specifically, effective negotiating skills in a black market economy.

Women operated under gendered disadvantages when they bought drugs. For example, for the women in the 1989-1991 Women and Cocaine study, buying crack was problematic because dealers sometimes sold "gaffle" or "bunk," i.e., fake crack. Often when women bought bunk or gaffle, they were forced to absorb the loss. Most were not physically strong enough to confront predominately male dealers. Some, however, employed specific strategies to get drugs or money refunded. A few women sold gaffle to other users themselves.

A 30-year-old African-American woman explained the importance of knowing the actors in the scene as protection against buying defective merchandise:

> Q: Was it difficult to find it (crack)?

> A: No. No, it's all over. But when I was using, I never did deal with any and everybody. There was just certain people that I always dealt with 'cause you never know what you was buying. It could be soap or macadamia nuts. They sell all kinds of stuff.

Another 41-year-old, African-American woman related how she decided whether or not the proffered product was genuine crack, and she also describes the price people paid for not following the dealers' rules:

The feeling, what you feel. The gaffle that they're selling now is wax and flour. It has a smooth edge. Cocaine is rough. Cocaine is hard. You can throw a rock of cocaine against the wall and it will not break. Gaffle will crumble. It's slick. And you can't go by taste any more because they [dealers] don't want [you] to put it in your mouth. No, anything — because they say you're biting their dope and your going to pay for it, gaffle or whatever. That's why so many people are coming up dead or hurt or beat up. People are being forced to buy something they don't want. No matter, really, whatever.

A 32-year-old African-American woman reiterated that "knowing people" helped protect buyers from bad purchases:

Q: What do you do, when somebody burns you?

A: If you got more money, you don't care. You just go on.

Q: Don't you go back and beat the shit out of them though?

A: Well, there ain't nothing you can do, besides — by that time they done split.

Q: Yeah. So how often does that happen? What percentage of the time?

A: It used to happen, 30% — but now, you know, once you get into an area where you know people, you know, like you can go to OC [a group of African-American drug dealers called the Out of Control gang] in Laguna and Turk and you won't get gaffle.

Q: Because you know them?

A: Uh-huh (yes).

Many crack-smoking women let their male friends and partners do the buying. Smokers rationalized that dealers were less likely to sell men fraudulent drugs. Dealers were expected to be less fearful of women's than men's retaliatory capacities. This, however, was not always the case. Some women were better buyers for reasons outlined by a 41-year-old African-American woman included in the Pregnancy and Drug Use Study:

A: I wouldn't allow him to, because, like I say, he come from a totally different background than me. He can't deal with the niggers out there. In this crack thing, okay? He can't deal with them like I can. I was brung [sic] up dealing with these stupid niggers, okay? So, I'm not going to send him out there to deal with them because...

Q: He just doesn't, what? Talk right? Act right? What?

A: Yeah! [exactly] There's my old man, he go out there, he spend $20 and they're [dealers] giving him ten, you know. And I end up going back out there, `What we supposed to do with this (small amount of crack)? I have to be stupid behind, he took it. I had enough. That's my man. Don't do him like that.'

The timing of crack purchases was important, as was the seller's perception of the buyer's intoxication level. Women reported that the later in the day, the more likely it was that the crack would be "cut," or adulterated. They claimed the best time to buy was around noon when dealers began sales. Intoxicated buyers risked getting "burned" or sold gaffle. A 35-year-old African-American woman who participated in the Woman and Cocaine study illustrated how this happened:

Friends don't burn friends. Just when they know you burned up [high on crack], that's when you get burned...Yeah. If a person is burned out they going to fiend [be desperate] for anything, right? And you [dealer] going to give it to them...Some (other users) brought something and it wasn't melting. I said, "All you do. Well, maybe it's too much cutting [adulterant] in it. Heat up some water and drop it in the water.'" They heated up some water, dropped it in and it sizzled like Alka Seltzer. "Oh no.'" I said, "You through. You shot to the curb [lost your money]. They sold you $20 worth of Alka Seltzer." And I was rolling [laughing]. They were mad as hell. They lost, honey. I was rolling.

Timing was also critical to avoid the street violence often engendered by fraudulent sales. This 30-year-old, African-American woman described a possible outcome of bad timing:

Down there on [Oakland streets]. I really don't have problems with it. It's not really that rough out here, but I know they sell drugs and whatever. I mean, I just don't want to happen to be out there at the wrong time, 'cause they shoot out here. They haven't shot in a while, but almost practically every night. I guess they just shooting up in the air, but you know, those bullets don't have no name, and so I just don't want to be mixed up in nothing like that.

The expression "bullets have no name" was an "in vivo" (participant's words) code for women in all three studies. The taken-for-granted fatalistic perspectives of never knowing which bullet might in fact "have her name on it" was a theme repeated by many women we interviewed.

Despite a male-dominated, underground marketplace where force, or potential retaliation, was the basis for settling disputes, women enacted strategies to increase their control. A 30-year-old Latina employed ingenious public-relations techniques:

> I don't know. Maybe I don't like the way I am when I do it. Because if somebody tries to burn me, I would go off...I go back, "You give me my fucking money, you know, or else." I know like usually I'm really, you know, "Okay, V____ that's cool." You know, I'll go back to that son of a bitch, "That is not real. I want my money back." You know? And if they don't, then I'll start getting really loud, you know, or I'll stay out there and when they try to sell people stuff, I'll say, "It's bunk, ...it's gaffled. It's not real." And people, they won't buy it, you know. They end up getting pissed and giving me something or giving me my money and get out of there.

A few, like the 28-year-old African-American woman quoted below, sold "bunk" and used the profits to buy real crack:

> A: Cause I would sell B-12. B-12 melts. It smokes. And I wouldn't sell nothing else that didn't do those things — just like crack cocaine did. But I couldn't sell them little — these little bits of gaffle — I mean I want to buy — six foot five come [angry male customer] that's who you talking about. [Customer will say] "I want my money back or you're going to take..." So I would sell B-12.
>
> Q: So did you have somebody helping you sell so that you were okay and safe?
>
> A: Yeah, just — well, we used to always — the girls we used to get together and gaffle people.
>
> Q: Oh yeah, girls? Goddamn! You are a brave woman.
>
> A: That was drugs — that wasn't brave. That was stupidity. I was just drugged up.

Social constraints refer to the way in which other people, and/or the problematic aspects of relationships with others, activated women's drug cravings and/or use. On those days when a woman received her welfare check, her control could be compromised by pressure from significant others. Difficult relationships with partners and children also induced drug use. Dealers who sold drugs-on-credit weakened women's resolve, friends who used, and even strangers on the streets who sold and/or used drugs, weakened women's resolve and added to their difficulty in sustaining controlled use or abstinence.

Their male companions played influential roles in starting them using drugs on welfare check days. On the first and the fifteenth of the month, the brothers of a 31-year-old African American woman would "get her good" while her mother tried to help her:

A: I have some [money]. If my brother wants some, I give him about twenty or thirty dollars to get out of my face. They knew how to get me good, once I am high. That's why my mama say, my mama used to say, "Well, you should just cash your check and hand it over to them."

Q: So your mom knows what is going on?

A: Uh-huh. Because she'll tell me, when I get paid, she'll say, she'll send me down to my auntie's house where my brothers aren't around.

A 28-year-old, African-American woman recalled how she and her husband made promises to each other not to "...waste our money no more." But when his pay day came around they both "...know what's gonna happen."

The day before, he [husband] get paid. For no reason, I start snapping, and I say "God, what is it? What's wrong with me? Is it because I want the stuff?" And I've tried to say, "I'm not going to buy it. I'm not gonna buy it." You know, when he get paid, we go do shopping. We pay the rent and everything, and he'll have like a hundred, or two hundred dollars left or maybe even three hundred. And we go "Oh, no!" And we like try to avoid coming home, 'cause we know what's gonna happen. We go out to a movie or we go to dinner sometime. We get home, I rush the kids to go to bed and I'll be saying 'Now slow down. Don't do this, don't do this.' But I can see myself rushing to go to bed when they [children] go to bed and he'll sit there. He'll get up and go out the house, and I'll know what he gonna do and waiting, anxious for him to come back, and he come back and we be up [smoking crack] all night, no matter how we try.

For some women, a constraint on control was emotional pain stemming from problematic relationships with significant others. A 32-year-old African-American woman realized in the course of her interview that she really only used crack when her husband was around, to help her cope with his verbal abuse:

I basically used it because my husband uses it. And at the time, when I first met my husband in '78, he was like — he was an alcoholic. And he was real abusive with it. I mean, he never jumped on me or beat me, but it was abusive, verbally abusive. You know, he'd come home late at night and throw stuff all over the house. You know, and then in the morning I'd wake up and got to go to work, and I've got this mess to clean up. And it kind of like — like I said, equalizes the high. It made the alcohol less terrorizing.

One 32-year-old, African-American woman talked about her recent relapse caused by the pain of separation from her son and her sister's continued crack use:

And I've had a relapse just this last month because I got so discouraged about this place that they have my son at. And it's so hard for me to get up that hill to go and see him. I have asthma and it's hard for me to walk up the hill. And so I really felt like I've lost the responsibility of being a mother, because they -- they make these changes in your child's life and they'll tell you after... It made me angry and so I went to go visit my sister just to have someone to talk to. When I walked in, they were getting high. And I almost turned and walked out the door. But then I said, "What the hell?" I might as well just get one — just get high this one time.'

A 44-year-old, African-American woman's account illustrated more generally the role of women's emotional pain:

It's something that's going to happen, where they've triggered something. Or ticked in their head, or anger. Feeling sorry for yourself or death happened in your family, or something went wrong. And then you find -- here comes the devil or a goblin. Or anybody. Here comes anybody. "Ah, come on, let me get you a hit to cheer you up." Or "come on, let's go have a drink."

Sometimes friends or family members who were users offered to buy women their drugs to help them cope with emotional problems. The same woman described this incident:

This happened to me, it must have been Monday. I smoked maybe, took my hit Sunday and didn't smoke it as much. "Come on girl, let's go get us a hit." So I don't have no money to get no hit. "Well, come on and go with me, I'm going over here to pick up this money. And then we're going to get a hit, and I'm going to turn you on [give her some for free]. I'm going to serve [put rocks on the pipe and light] you half of what I get."...I don't know why she didn't — but mostly people don't want to smoke alone.

Other women had difficulty controlling their drug use because dealers of both heroin and crack either took food stamps, or offered them drugs on credit. A 38-year-old, African-American woman discussed the drugs-on-credit plan:

It wasn't a money problem. The people was around — I mean, you got some dealers that would give you credit, or you'd have food stamps and some would take food stamps. I mean, because that's one, you start giving in, I mean, everything, if you know what I mean?

Detailing the difficulties of tapering off use, a 23-year-old African American woman talked about her heroin-smoking friends' anger because of her decreased usage. She related the way just being around heroin-using people is like "...smelling the scent":

A: You don't want to go. And lately I've been getting a lot of people that get mad at me, because I don't want to go with them no more. And it's kind of —

Q: Oh, so you're trying to stay away from those friends, too?

A: That's what it is. If I can stay, if you can stay away from the people or situations that happen to be convenient, it makes tapering off and getting away from it a whole lot easier. It really does...Because it's like being around those type of people, smelling the scent — it actually like, like of a tree root, going and look out for a bird. It's like the smell is in the air that there's a bird around somewhere. You're going to go looking for it till you get it. And the same with the dope. You know, ...the knowledge that it's somewhere around, that it can be had, you go looking for it. Or if you don't even look, it's going to come looking for you.

Women lived in neighborhoods where drugs were sold and used in public, where they knew "that it's somewhere around." Being around people who used stimulated continued use. So in order to reduce or quit use, women tried to stay away from the people and places where drugs were sold or used. This was problematic since the "places" were often their homes and/or neighborhoods, and the "people" their partners, relatives and friends.

Women's social and economic conditions of poverty placed them in neighborhoods where both environmental and social constraints on controlled drug use predominated. Family, friends, and partners contributed to continued drug use by facilitating use and/or precipitating emotional and physical pain. In these settings, the struggle to control drug use was difficult. The same people and places which pulled them into using initially, often kept them using.

STRATEGIES FOR CONTROL

Family, friends, partners were also supportive of women's strategies to control their drug use. Some relied on relatives and friends to teach them effective techniques. Several of those interviewed asked relatives to manage their money. A 22-year-old African-American crack smoker from the Women and Cocaine sample recollected how her sister, a heroin user, taught her how to budget her money:

> Which is all she told me. She said, "I'm going to show you how to do it. You go get your check." She took my check, right. And I said, "What are you doing? You know, give me my money, you know." And she said, "No, uh-uh." She said, "You want this check to come in my name or do you want to still have it, or do you want to have your kids taken away from you and put in somebody else's custody?" So she took my check. She got $175 money order. She got some big deal, $60 money order, for the food you know. And I paid my wash bill and everything. And she said "now look." ... And then she said, "and now the babies need this, the babies need that." We went shopping and she told me. And she said, "And now you have a little sum to get you a little piece of rock with." And the next day she come up, she said, "Now look — your kids have diapers. They have milk and food. And you have food. Now you can go in that refrigerator and eat any time you want, and you have clean clothes. Now, you see, she said, now you wouldn't have had all that if you would have spent the rest of that money on cocaine." So ever since then I got accustomed to doing that.

Other women employed similar strategies, but they found themselves cashing the money orders and/or selling the food from their refrigerators after they had spent the "little sum" on drugs.

Another 33-year-old, African-American woman, who felt she was in control, held family meetings and prioritized expenditures:

A: The way I always did it on welfare with my boys is that the rent's paid and then what's ever left over after the rent and the food, we decided on who needs what and what needs to be done. Three times a month we'd have that meeting.

Q: This woman told me, she gets her check, and it's gone. She doesn't pay the rent. She doesn't feed her kids.

A: I would do that, not paying the rent. But not feeding my kids, uh-uh [no]! One good feeling outdoes the other, and I couldn't go through not seeing my kids happy.

A 34-year-old, African-American woman gave her brother power of attorney:

Everything I did had to go through my brother, 'cause he was my power of attorney. He put me on like a $10 a day expense. So he felt like, "If you have to have some dope, P___, you're gonna go out and get it any other way."

This strategy had its inherent difficulties, however, as this 33-year-old, African American woman's account demonstrated:

I would have to give my mother my money to hold and beg her "don't give it back to me when I come back and ask you for it. Please don't give it back." I mean that's losing a lot... Yeah, your self respect for not managing your money.

Some women enlisted their significant others help to exert control over their drug expenditures. Sometimes these strategies worked and sometimes they did not. Relinquishing financial control had the unintended consequence of making women feel childish and diminished their self-respect.

Another strategy for control was "not to get with the dope man" in order to avoid increasing their drug use. Living with a drug dealer was an impediment to controlling drug use. In the following passage, a pregnant heroin user, who eventually stopped selling drugs altogether, described why she chose not to leave a retail dealer and "get with" a wholesaler:

I was selling drugs for this other guy and this was when we stopped selling. Me and my old man was selling for this other guy. He was a friend of mine. The man had been in jail for like ten years and he got out and everything was different and he got all this assets and stuff. So, I showed him how to start rolling and selling drugs. And so, he was giving me quantities of drugs. And my old man was messing them up. [Using the drugs instead of selling them.] And I would have to face this man. This man liked me. I could have got with him and had everything, but that's not what I wanted anymore. I was tired of drugs and all I could do was drugs.

THE DIALECTIC OF CONTROL

Women's attempts to manage finances and drug use resulted in a dialectic of control. Inherent in many of the women's strategies to control were the seeds of potential constraints. Staying home to avoid using drugs only worked if the woman did not live in a dope house or in a hotel inhabited primarily by drug users. For some women, such as the couple who tried to stay away from home on their pay day, or the woman whose brothers encouraged her use, avoiding home was the more appropriate strategy. Moving from one environment in an attempt to control use sometimes put women "out of the frying pan and into the skillet." Home could mean people who would support women's continued crack use, condemn it, or both.

The budgeting strategies of purchasing money orders, food and then using leftover monies for drugs sometimes backfired. For example, crack smokers, after buying small amounts of crack, either on the same day or in the ensuing two weeks sold the money orders and even the food to purchase more crack.

Women tried to maintain food and shelter for their children. As the woman quoted previously said, "...one good feeling outdoes the other." Although crack use feels good, not taking care of children overtook the crack-induced good feelings. However, failure to meet those responsibilities was also a source of emotional pain and a consequent constraint on control.

Successfully implementing control strategies made women feel good about themselves because they were meeting their adult responsibilities. Some of these same strategies, however, made women lose respect for themselves; and because they were not living as self-actualizing adults, these strategies contributed to already damaged self-images.

BEING PREGNANT AND BUYING DRUGS

In the two studies of pregnant drug users, we found that this dialectic of constraints and controls was operating for pregnant women as well. Pregnancy, however, increased difficulties and constraints and was detrimental in drug-market negotiations. Drug dealers would not sell to them. If they had partners, the fathers-to-be would bring home drugs and then berate the pregnant woman for harming "their baby." Purchasers of heroin, crack, cocaine and marijuana all made clear that having someone else buy drugs for you increased the costs. The purchaser paid more money if unable to buy directly from the seller, or the go-between would come back with lesser amounts of drugs by "shorting the bag" or by taking some of the drugs for their own use.

In the following interview, a woman from the Pregnancy and Drug Use project described the public humiliation likely felt by visibly pregnant women who tried to buy drugs:

> Oh, people are really strong against being pregnant, especially big pregnant, and they see them out there using. A lot of dope dealers will not sell to pregnant women... Yeah, they treat you like shit, too. They tell you off right there. They'll say, "What's the matter with you? Don't be so stupid! You're hurting the baby. We don't care about you. Look at that baby." But yeah, a lot of people are totally against pregnant women getting high, which I don't I don't blame them. I get like that, too. I don't like to see anybody get messed up because I know what can happen. And especially using coke while you're pregnant, too, 'cause I know a few girls that are out there working the streets, using a lot of coke and heroin, but they don't care about even thinking about trying to clean up or thinking about getting on methadone.

Both men and women sellers refused to sell to pregnant users. In the following a woman from the Pregnancy and Drug Use Study who was a primary heroin user and who continued to use while pregnant, reflected on why dealers should not sell coke to pregnant users. She believed her heroin use was much less deleterious to her forming fetus. She knew, since she had injected cocaine a few times while pregnant.

> That's why I told them I wouldn't sell it to them, and I'd tell my husband, "Don't sell it to them." And I was pregnant, too, at the time myself, and I used to tell him, "Don't give it to them." Because then they knew not to come to us, too, 'cause we wouldn't give it to them being pregnant... It's hard. It's hard. And there's a lot of people, too, that won't sell to pregnant women, because I remember one time this girl, she was using a lot of coke. And I used to know a few of the guys that used to sell it, and they go, `Here comes that girl. Tell her, "Don't come over here and buy nothing any more," because she's...' Coke is, I think, a hell of a

lot worse than heroin, because I have used coke before being pregnant, but it wasn't a steady thing. But just the feeling of using the coke, you can feel it as soon as you inject it. I mean, the baby will get into like a big ball and cramp up and stuff and then you start feeling the baby moving a lot inside your stomach. So I don't know how they can keep shooting it one right after another all night long. Once I'd feel it I'd go, "Oh, God, how could you do that?" and just stop.

Women in all three samples agreed that having to rely on others to buy drugs usually meant you paid more and got less. The women with abusive and controlling partners suffered physical and emotional abuse as well. A white 43 year old, who was a participant in the Pregnancy and Drug Use study, talked about her struggle with her controlling partner. Not only did he control her money, but tortured her by withholding from her the drugs she had obtained from prostitution:

He would buy the drugs, right? He'd buy the crack. And he would control it. He'd sit there and take his couple a hits. And I'd sit there. And I, I'd have to like patiently wait for mine, right? And then I'd get mad. I'd say, "Goddamn it, gimme a hit!" You know? "Gimme the pipe!" And he'd, he'd like ignore me. And, uh, it was like this big control issue. To where he says [emphatic] when and how much. He would break me off a little piece and...My money paid for it, but it's sitting' out there and he's controlling it...If we were fighting? And I wanted to leave sometimes, he wouldn't let me out a the room. And he would like restrain me on the bed and stuff. And I would just freak out. And I really would make things worse because of my reaction. If I would have, um, been calm and just let him have his little power play...everything would be fine.

Women were at a decided disadvantage when they interacted in drug markets. Ambient violence permeated women's drug market exchanges. If they were pregnant, if they could get someone to sell to drugs to them, they were scorned and humiliated. Women, assigned to a lower rank in drug using social worlds, were at higher risk of exposure to ambient violence than men. The urgency and desperation to obtain heroin, coke or crack cast many of our interviewees along the dangerous paths of dealing drugs or prostituting. Inundation in deviant subcultures was requisite for women in order to get the best deal they could for money earned at great personal risk.

CONCLUSION

As other research shows (Johnson et al, this volume), we also found that if women participated in drug sales they occupied the lowest rungs of distribution networks. Most of those interviewed for these three studies had participated in drug sales at some point in their lives. For all the reasons outlined in this paper — drug use, ambient violence, gender roles and inadequate retaliatory capacities — most women did not sell for very long periods of time. When they did sell, they usually only sold for personal use. Those few women who told us they were regular drug sellers usually had a male partner or associate, to whom they were subordinate, working with them. We make this last statement with a caveat; we did not focus on drug sales or drug sellers in any of the three studies. Other researchers studying drug dealing specifically have found that women's roles in drug distribution were changing (Fagan, 1994).

In this paper we focused on women as consumers, since we could find little in the literature that described that role in detail. In our work we have found that the role of user and seller are often interchangeable and that understanding women's roles as buyers informs our understanding of selling practices as well.

What sorts of policies might effectively intervene in women's lives? Our findings leads us to recommend community-based programs that include basic education, life-skills training, job training and employment opportunities. Low-threshold and gender-specific drug treatment programs would allow interventionists to help women with their specific needs wherever they are in their drug-using careers. Programs need to provide psychological services to help women talk about and deal with past experiences of abuse and violence. On-site child care, particularly in drug treatment programs, would allow women to bring their children with them and thereby increase their chances of staying with the program. We believe these kinds of interventions would go a long way in reducing both problematic drug use and drug sales.

Address correspondence to: Sheigla Murphy and Karina Arroyo, Institute for Scientific Analysis, 2595 Mission Street, Suite 200, San Francisco, California 94110.

Acknowledgments: We would like to acknowledge the women who shared with us so many deeply personal and often painful parts of their everyday lives. The Institute for Scientific Analysis supported all three projects and we owe a great debt to our outstanding and understanding program officer Coryl Jones, Ph.D.

REFERENCES

Amaro, H. and C. Hardy-Fanta (1995). "Gender Relations in Addiction and Recovery." *Journal of Psychoactive Drugs* 27(4):325-337.

Bourgois, P. and E. Dunlap (1992). "Exorcising Sex-For-Crack Prostitution: An Ethnographic Perspective from Harlem." In: M. Ratner (ed.), *Crack Pipe as a Pimp: An Eight City Ethnographic Study of the Sex-for-Crack Phenomenon*. Lexington, MA: Lexington Books.

Cohen, B. (1980). *Deviant Street Networks: Prostitutes in New York*. Lexington, MA: Lexington Books.

Curtis, R.A. and L. Mayer (1993). "Highly Structured Crack Markets in the Southside of Williamsburg, Brooklyn." In: J. Fagan (ed.), *The Ecology of Crime and Drug Use in the Inner Cities*. New York, NY: Social Science Research Council.

Fagan, J. (1994). "Women and Drugs Revisited: Female Participation in the Cocaine Economy." *Journal of Drug Issues* 24(2):179-225.

Glaser, B. and A. Strauss (1967). *The Discovery of Grounded Theory*. Chicago, IL: Aldine.

Goldstein, P. (1979). *Prostitution and Drugs*. Lexington, MA: Lexington Books.

Inciardi, J.A., D. Lockwood and A.E. Pottieger (1993). *Women and Crack Cocaine*. New York, NY: MacMillan.

Jacobs, B.A. and J. Miller (1998). "Crack Dealing, Gender, and Arrest Avoidance." *Social Problems* 45(4):550-569.

Maher, L. and R. Curtis (1993). "Women on the Edge of Crime: Crack Cocaine and the Changing Contexts of Street Level Sex Work in New York City." *Crime, Law and Social Change* 18(1):221-258.

Miller, B.A., W.R. Downs and D.M. Gondoli (1989). "Spousal Violence Among Alcoholic Women as Compared to a Random Household Sample of Women." *Journal of Studies on Alcohol* 50(6):533-539.

Millstein, R.A. (1993). *Focus on the Future: A Steadfast Commitment to Research.* (NIDA Research Monograph 132, Problems of Drug Dependence.). Rockville, MD: National Institute on Drug Abuse.

Murphy, S., D. Waldorf and C. Reinarman (1990). "Drifting into Dealing: Becoming a Cocaine Seller." *Qualitative Sociology* 13(4):321-343.

Ratner, M.S. (1993). *Crack Pipe as Pimp: An Ethnographic Investigation of Sex-for-Crack Exchanges.* New York, NY: Lexington Books.

Sterk, C.E. (1998). *FAST LIVES: Women Who Use Crack Cocaine.* Atlanta, GA: Emory University.

—— and K.W. Elifson (2000). "Fluctuating Drug Markets and Consequences for HIV Risk-Taking: Findings from an Ethnographic Study Among Female Drug Users." *Medical Anthropology.*

Theidon, K. (1995). "Taking a Hit: Pregnant Drug Users and Violence." *Contemporary Drug Issues* 22(4)(Winter): 663-686.

Waldorf, D., C. Reinerman and S. Murphy (1991). *Cocaine Changes: The Experience of Using and Quitting.* Philadelphia, PA: Temple University Press.

Williams, T. (1992). *Crackhouse.* Reading, MA: Addison-Wesley.

NOTES

1. Funded by NIDA-DA05332.

2. Funded by NIDA-DA06832.

3. Funded by NIDA-DA09827.

TOWARD THE DEVELOPMENT OF A TYPOLOGY OF ILLEGAL DRUG MARKETS

by

Ric Curtis

and

Travis Wendel
John Jay College of Criminal Justice
New York, USA

Abstract: *Ethnographic research is particularly well suited to investigate emergent phenomena and to access and describe populations and social environments which are obscured from normal observation. Ongoing ethnographic research on Manhattan's Lower East Side combines direct observation and qualitative interviews to describe the wide variety of local retail drug markets, the social contexts in which they evolve, and how the interactions between the various markets affect drug availability, styles of distribution, patterns of use, and types of crime and violence associated with particular types of markets. By drawing a multifaceted sample, the study offers a moving picture of how trends in drug use and distribution emerge, mature, encounter difficulties, and metamorphose. The research compares and contrasts distributors who participate in markets that are differentiated according to the social and technical organization of distribution. It also documents the differential and changing sociodemographic composition of consumer groups associated with the variety of illegal drug markets and describes transformations over time in the behaviors, beliefs and norms of each category of users with regard to drug distribution and use.*

Crime Prevention Studies, volume 11, pp. 121-152

INTRODUCTION

Drug distributors, users, and the markets they form, have been the subject of a considerable amount of research in the last 30 years, but most work in this area (see e.g., Ouellet et al., 1993; Waterston, 1993; Johnson et al., 1992; Buerger, 1991; Mieczkowski, 1990; Bourgois, 1989; Fagan, 1989; Williams, 1989; Kleiman, 1988; Goldstein et al., 1984) has been largely descriptive and limited by static approaches that ignore both change in drug markets over time and variation from market to market. One prime reason has been the lack of a theoretical perspective that would enable comparisons between different markets, advance our understanding of how markets may influence each other, appreciate how drug markets are integrated into neighborhoods, or plumb the connections between types of drug markets and other social phenomena such as patterns of crime and violence. This paper addresses these shortcomings by defining a model that will allow for the comparative analysis of drug markets and suggest where the analysis of drug markets may intersect with and benefit from existing bodies of social theory.

The need for more detailed and focused information about drug markets[1] has been noted by many researchers, particularly in the last decade (Riley, 1997, Hagedorn, 1994; Kleiman and Smith, 1990; Fagan, 1989; Hayeslip, 1989; Moore, 1977), but those who call for more information are often interested in a very specific type of knowledge that is related to the narrow goals of their funding agencies or their political and/or ideological biases. For example, Kleiman and Smith (1990:71) evaluate the effects of law enforcement crackdowns on street-level drug sales, but note that the "effects [of interventions] have to be traced through the drug markets before any conclusion can be drawn about whether those effects are, on balance, beneficial." The authors acknowledge that current information about drug markets is rudimentary, at best, but like much research on illegal drugs, their primary concern is not understanding the roles that illegal drugs play in everyday life or the structure of illegal markets, but rather eliminating the "problem." By focusing their inquiry on the relative success of law enforcement (or other types of) interventions that aim to eliminate illegal drugs, many drug researchers often employ units of analysis or methods of inquiry that make it difficult to understand how illegal drugs and their markets fit in the larger social contexts in which they exist. By neglecting these wider issues, however, they ensure that drug research, however well funded, will remain isolated from the main body of social science theory and research.

In a similar vein, a recent report by the Arrestee Drug Abuse Monitoring (ADAM) program found that powder cocaine, crack and heroin markets "differ substantially from one another in a variety of ways, including purchase and use practices" (Riley, 1997:26). The report goes on to state that "detailed information about local drug habits and patterns would be a valuable tool for law enforcement authorities, service providers, and policy makers" (Riley, 1997:26). While the insight that drug markets vary considerably and are not monolithic entities controlled by a single criminal enterprise is not groundbreaking news, it only confirms what a plethora of ethnographic studies have documented over the past 25 years (see e.g., Maher, 1995; Waterston, 1993; Hamid, 1992; Sviridoff et al., 1992; Williams, 1989; Agar, 1973; Preble and Casey, 1969). Clearly, research that seeks to assist in the elimination of social phenomena is different from most social science that strives for greater understanding and insight. Even those who seek to eliminate the problem, however, like the ADAM researchers, have begun to acknowledge that the behavior of distributors and consumers may exhibit considerable variation depending on the types of markets in which they participate, and a better understanding of those differences may be necessary to devise effective interventions. A more comprehensive view of the phenomena is also sorely needed.

A major problem with the largely atheoretical, ahistorical and descriptive accounts, which have characterized drug research, is that comparative analysis has been virtually impossible. Researchers tend to fall into two camps in this regard: one side tends to present their actors as unique in some way, often using categories native to specific markets to describe distributors and consumers, thereby further hindering comparison with the work of others (see, e.g., Buerger, 1991; Mieczkowski, 1990). Buerger (1991:7-18) outlines several different "organizational strategies" for selling drugs, including the "Club," the "Drive-in," the "Speakeasy," the "Dealership," the "Bazaar," the "Cuckoo's Nest" and the "Rotation System." Though he gives detailed descriptions of how each of these selling strategies works, it is not clear what dimensions differentiate them from one another or whether they actually constitute qualitatively different markets, are simply variations on a theme, or are different phases of development of one market.

At the other end of the spectrum are those researchers who see all distributors and/or consumers as essentially similar, as if there were no differences between them (Johnson et al., 1992; Stephens, 1991; Preble and Casey, 1969). Without a theoretical grounding to understand which differences are important and which are simply superficial, and without addressing the characteristics of both of the sets of actors who constitute a market — distributors and consumers — it becomes extremely difficult to understand what a particular market is really like, how it works, and how it and the actors within it might be similar to or different from others, let alone compare markets in different times, places and/or circumstances.

Descriptions of drug markets have often concentrated on either distributors or users, but seldom both. Other researchers do not focus on people at all (e.g., Rengert, 1996; Eck, 1994; Weisburd et al., 1994), but rather, use aggregate data from law enforcement sources to identify "hot spots" of drug activity to define markets. Such analyses, however, entirely discount some of the important features that differentiate drug markets, and often find that they cannot disaggregate the data in ways that permit an analysis of how markets differ from site to site.

Typically, an examination of drug markets is reduced to a discussion of the characteristics of distributors or to the more obvious or superficial aspects of their business such as whether drugs are sold inside or outdoors. While the location of sales, as will be explained below, forms a significant part of our typology, this is far from the most fundamental distinction that can be made. With the emergence of crack markets in the mid-1980s, some researchers began to focus on the relationships between distributors and consumers, and how both actors change over time. Hamid (1992) postulated that markets were the arenas where these actors and their relationships should be analyzed rather than examining the actions of disconnected distributors and consumers. By focusing on markets as locales where distinctive types of distributors and consumers meet to exchange goods, money, and create identities, the unit of analysis was shifted from individuals to relationships and socially constructed entities that clearly change over time. Focusing initially on "freelance" crack markets, Johnson and his colleagues (Johnson et al., 1992) began to identify other types of crack markets. They posited that there were two basic types of illegal drug markets: "freelance" and "business" models. While this broad division recognized that there was indeed variation in drug markets, by focusing almost exclusively on crack markets in a limited number of field sites they overlooked other market forms and markets for other drugs. Furthermore, there was yet no sense of process in these models that described how one form might evolve into another.

Several researchers have suggested that distribution inevitably evolves in complexity over time (Dorn et al., 1992; Hamid, 1992; Johnson et al., 1992; Reuter, 1985) and that a progressively more complex sequence of styles is discernible. Some have even postulated a "developmental cycle" of drug eras (Hamid, 1992; Johnson et al.,

1992) suggesting that the drugs themselves have agency and that the human beings who move them from place to place are mere automatons at the service at the service of a "higher power." Rengert (1996:73-85), for example, employs a unidimensional categorization — four "phases" in the evolution of distribution "locations" — "mutual societies," "periodic markets," "fixed site neighborhood sales," and "drug marts" — to describe the evolution of markets. Reuter (1985) compared illegal enterprises with their counterparts in the noncriminalized economy and noted a number of important differences, including the structural constraints that limited the growth potential of illegal enterprises. His description of illegal businesses suggested, but did not explicitly describe, a developmental sequence of increasing organizational complexity. The researchers who came closest to accurately describing an entire range of drug distribution styles, from the least to the most complex, were Dorn et al. (1992), who described the evolution of drug distribution in England since the 1960s. Although the authors acknowledged complexity by noting that distribution styles can vary from simple "trading charities" to large corporate-like structures, their presentation of the data was somewhat confusing in that they made little effort to distinguish markets for different types of drugs nor to discuss how markets for various drugs may interact. Thus, though the various distributors and/or consumers they describe may share some important characteristics, the markets to which they belong may be quite dissimilar. More troubling yet is the implicit assumption that the progression of distribution styles is inherently unidirectional: in their view, the 1960s were a time when distribution styles were simple (and, by implication, nicer), but since then everything has gotten more sophisticated (and rougher). Despite this nostalgic perspective, which somewhat detracts from their argument, the authors made a significant contribution to the development of a typology of distribution styles.

Using ethnographic data collected in several neighborhoods, the analysis presented in this paper will describe the structure of illegal retail drug markets that exist in New York City, and will discuss the evolution of drug markets in neighborhood settings. By comparing data from different neighborhoods and markets found within them, we have described and analyzed the evolution of various styles, types, levels and methods of drug distribution. While we realize that markets are formed by at least two parties[2] — distributors and consumers — this paper will focus primarily on distributors and the structure of distribution.

METHODS

This ethnographic research combines direct observation and qualitative interviews in order to describe the range of retail drug markets in New York City, and the social and neighborhood contexts in which they evolve. The research was conducted under the auspices of two Federal grants: "Heroin in the 21st Century," funded by the National Institute on Drug Abuse; and the "Lower East Side Trafficking Project," funded by the National Institute of Justice. Fieldwork involving heroin users and distributors began in June 1996, as a five-year ethnographic investigation into heroin markets in New York City. At the end of the third year of research, the project staff had interviewed and conducted extensive field observation of 227 heroin users and 146 heroin distributors. Of the total sample of 373 research subjects, 151 were white, 138 were Latino, 75 were African American,[3] 2 were Asian, and 7 of unknown ethnicity. Research concentrated in major heroin markets located on the Lower East Side, Harlem and the Washington Heights sections of Manhattan, and the Bushwick and Williamsburg neighborhoods of Brooklyn, although other areas of New York City have also been included. The Lower East Side Trafficking Project began as an outcome of observing so many poly-drug users and distributors, especially on Manhattan's Lower East Side. The authors applied for and received a grant from the National Institute of Justice for an ethnographic study which began in March 1999 of drug markets and their interactions. All quotations not otherwise attributed are drawn from these two research projects and, unless otherwise noted, were chosen as typical or representative of the attitudes and opinions of our sample. By drawing a multifaceted inter- and intra-market sample, the research offers a moving picture of how trends in drug distribution and use emerge, mature, encounter difficulties, and metamorphose.

Study participants were recruited in the "natural settings" of use and distribution. The researchers also relied heavily on persons they knew from previous research projects, and employed "chains of referral" and "snowball" sampling techniques (Biernacki and Waldorf, 1981) to expand the sample of more than 400 drug distributors and users.

In addition to background information, which recorded age, gender, race/ethnicity, and state and/or country of origin, the researchers probed at length, repeatedly and in varied settings, such topical areas as: the reasons for initiating distribution, the distributors' ambitions and outlooks, attitudes and relations towards others in the trade or towards drug users, methods and beliefs about avoiding arrest, harm, losses or violence, accounting methods, actual records of the individual drug business, expenditures, assets and reinvestments. A life history of each distributor and user was obtained, in which such issues as early childhood upbringing, marriage and family life, educational and employment achievements, and the career in criminality and drug distribution were pursued.

Ethnography is often employed to describe populations and social environments that are hidden from normal observation (see, e.g., Lambert, 1990; Weppner, 1977), and it is indispensable when exploring emergent phenomena, such as innovations in distribution or new drug use trends. Ethnographic fieldwork requires extended work in the naturalistic settings in which topics are investigated; a principal strength of ethnography rests on the physical presence of researchers who use their privileged positions at activities and events to "test" the accuracy and truthfulness of what they hear and see. In this study, investigations were made in places of drug use and distribution, the homes of study participants, their kin and others, in the neighborhood, at school, in clubs, near clinics and treatment centers, and many other locales.

General observations by researchers gauged the extent and diversity of drugs found in the neighborhoods through key informants and participant observation in such locales as homes, raves, nightclubs, drug-selling bodegas, and other "copping" (buying) areas, shooting galleries, places selling paraphernalia, coffee bars, abandoned buildings, empty lots, needle exchange programs and drug treatment programs. General observations were also attentive to the daily routines of drug distributors and users and included such items as how they earned and spent money (both legally and illegally), their participation in criminal pursuits, violent disputes, sports and leisure, family-centered tasks and enjoyments, child care, medical treatment, social services contacts, courting and sexual relations, intergenerational contacts, education and training.

Ethnographic methodologies are uniquely capable of addressing the complex dynamics of drug markets and permit the constant refinement of theory through field-based observations. To learn about how drug users and distributors perceive their social world, wherever possible, conversations and interviews were tape-recorded and afterwards transcribed (Spradley, 1979). In fieldnotes and logs, the ethnographers continuously compiled interview summaries and developed incrementally more comprehensive descriptions of the various drug markets and their participants. The combination of direct observation and ethnographic interviews served as a built in cross-check of information and helped synthesize multiple viewpoints, heavily contextualizing each phenomenon to facilitate arrival at an holistic and accurate rendering of reality (Bernard, 1994).

THE MODEL

While recognizing that markets are social arenas where a wide variety of activities and dramas may be played out, describing the entire range of these activities is beyond the scope of this paper. In the space remaining, we will primarily focus on describing the distinguishing characteristics of a nine-part typology of drug-distribution style[4] that emerged from an examination of the data, and explore the reasons why and manner by which these ideal types change over time. Our typology emerges from asking two basic questions: how do you sell and with whom do you sell? The data clearly indicated that there was variation in drug distribution activities from neighborhood to neighborhood, over time in the same neighborhood, and from drug to drug in the same neighborhood. Two primary axes of differentiation were indicated by the data: the *technical organization* and the *social organization* of distribution. The technical organization of distribution refers to issues such as the physical location, policies, procedures, technology and equipment employed by distributors. The social organization of distribution refers to issues of cooperation, differential responsibility, and power and authority among distributors. These two main axes are refined and described in greater detail below.

The Technical Organization of Drug Distribution

The technical organization of distribution has traditionally commanded the most attention from drug researchers, law enforcement agencies, and the general public, perhaps because of its graphic visibility as compared with the social-organizational aspects of distribution[5]. Included as part of the technical organization of distribution are such items as the timing and sites of distribution activities, the types of materials and equipment used by distributors, and the policies and procedures adopted to ensure that distribution activities function smoothly. For the purpose of constructing different typologies of distribution, some aspects of the technical organization of distribution are more important than others. For example, distributors may vary greatly by the type of equipment they use to effect retail sales. This equipment may have law enforcement implications, but for analytic purposes, such distinctions are often of relatively little value. For this paper, the "location of sales" has been selected as the critical variable to focus on in constructing distribution typologies because it offers greater analytic power than other measures of technical organization. There are many examples in the data of different types of selling locales, but we have grouped them into three categories: (1) street-level sales; (2) indoor sales; and (3) delivery services. These are described in greater detail below.

(1) Street-level Sales

By definition, street-level sales occur outdoors, but beyond that, they may vary greatly. Street-level markets may be characterized by blatant transactions between anonymous buyers and sellers that may engender complaints from community residents, or sales may occur between buyers and sellers who know each other intimately and who are scarcely visible to those who are not party to the transaction. The volume of these markets may be high or low. They may be dominated by buyers or sellers. They may involve a single drug or may be conducted in a one-stop-shopping style with more than one drug available. If more than one drug is available, it is significant whether one individual sells more than one drug or if different drugs are sold by different individuals.

(2) Indoor Sales

Indoor sales may take place in a wide variety of locales, including apartment or "house" connections, sales from indoor public spaces (e.g., the lobbies, stairwells or basements of residential buildings, and in abandoned buildings), sales from storefronts, bodegas (small, neighborhood grocery stores), nightclubs, after-hours clubs, bars, and raves. In addition to variations in locale, indoor sales also differ along many of the same axes that serve to further differentiate street-level markets.

(3) Delivery Sales

Delivery of drugs removes drug transactions from the streets and risky indoor venues and offers consumers the opportunity to have drugs delivered directly to home, office or other safe locations. This form of distribution, which scarcely existed ten years ago, represents a growth area of the market and, in some neighborhoods, has rapidly become the predominant form of distribution for marijuana and heroin. There are number of forms that delivery sales may take. Two common models are delivery services and beeper dealers. Delivery services employ "runners" who may travel on foot, by bicycle, car, taxi or public transportation. The deliveries are typically made to the homes or workplaces of the customer. The customer pays a premium price reflecting insulation from the risks of a street transaction, as well as for the convenience represented by home delivery. By contrast, beeper dealers wait for customers to call them on a pager. The beeper digitally transmits a phone number enabling the dealer to return the customer's call in order to plan a meeting location, rather than lingering on street corners or in the lobbies of buildings. This practice offers a much greater degree of security for the dealer, since he/she is not forced to wait at a particular location (which may have become known to law enforcement) to meet customers. The dealer knows in advance to whom he or she will be selling and how much is wanted. Beeper dealers can avoid areas known to be "hot" (under police surveillance), and instead transact business in areas not known for narcotics activity.

Other Aspects of the Technical Organization of Drug Markets

Aside from noting the increased sophistication in weaponry that accompanied the crack boom of the 1980s, researchers have largely ignored the importance of changes in the equipment and technology used in retail drug distribution and the significance of those innovations in drug markets. For example, street-level drug markets have evolved from the use of lookouts, who shout out warnings of police presence, to the use of such sophisticated technology as cell phones and two-way radios for the same purpose: "In the summer, we had shit locked down on bikes with walkie-talkies. Wherever the cops would go, we would know, every move they made. I'm telling you, we had those niggas confused, yo" (interview, Destroyer). The rise of delivery services is a direct outcome of the widespread diffusion of sophisticated telecommunications technology such as pagers and cell phones. Delivery services also typically use computers to keep track of their often extensive lists of clients. Some forward-looking entrepreneurs have even distributed illegal drugs through the use of e-mail.

The type of drug that is sold seems, at first glance, to be an obvious criteria by which different types of markets may be distinguished. But while it is easy to differentiate between, for example, marijuana versus cocaine markets, some researchers might not differentiate between markets for different forms of cocaine. In this study, two basic forms of cocaine were identified: powdered cocaine and precooked cocaine, usually sold in the form of crack. Powdered cocaine was sold in markets that targeted three distinct types of consumers: sniffers, "freebasers," and injectors. Though it may be difficult to discern what consumers might do with powdered cocaine once they buy it, some markets were clearly organized with particular consumers and/or modes of consumption in mind. For example, those markets that existed in bars and that offered highly adulterated powdered cocaine in twenty-dollar foil packets were clearly targeting occasional sniffers. It was extremely unlikely that freebasers or injectors would have been interested in purchasing that type of cocaine (given the amount of adulterant in it) or that distributors in that environment would have been interested in servicing nonsniffers since they would likely have attracted unwanted attention. In some neighborhoods, powdered cocaine markets existed along side heroin markets and targeted injectors almost exclusively.

In smokable cocaine markets, "freebase" distributors and consumers took pains to distinguish themselves from crack-market participants. Freebase markets tended to be slightly more discreet than other street-level crack or cocaine markets. The point of this apparent splitting of hairs is that, what might appear to be the same drug to researchers, may be quite different to those who participate in those markets. Distributors and consumers often perceived these items to be different substances (for example, freebasers often said that crack was not really cocaine) and they formed distinct markets based on those understandings.

Indeed, some of the most heated arguments that the researchers had were with cocaine smokers who defined themselves as "freebasers" and who denigrated "crackheads" as people beneath contempt. When the researchers suggested that they were, in fact, smoking exactly the same substance, freebasers usually became quite animated and vigorously argued their point. Freebasers were so adamant about differences between what they smoked (which they prepare — "cook" — themselves) and what was sold as crack (which they suggested was adulterated with a wide variety of substances), that in the absence of any definitive information which attested to their essential similarity, they convinced several ethnographers that there was truth to their claim (personal communication, ethnographic team from the Natural History of Crack Distribution Project at the National Development and Research Institutes, Inc.). While pharmacologically there may be no difference between the two substances, the fact that they are perceived as being different and acted upon as such, does indeed make them different (Zinberg, 1984).

The standardization of unit sales (or lack of them) reveals much about markets for particular drugs. The manner in which drugs are packaged, including whether they are adulterated before being sold to consumers, may have a profound impact on the character of a market. For example, for the last 20 years, heroin has been uniformly sold in $10 bags, but recent changes in market conditions have seen the appearance of $50 bags and weight in amounts measured in grams and half grams. These sales portend a qualitative change in the once-distant relationship between sellers and buyers. Marijuana also is packaged in several ways that vary between different types of markets. On the street or in storefronts, it tends to be sold in small plastic bags that retail for $10 apiece. By contrast, delivery services, which tend to sell marijuana at the more expensive end of the scale, typically demand a minimum purchase of $50.

The manner in which various drugs are adulterated may hold implications for the type of market in which distributors and users participate. For example, freelance distributors who sell powdered cocaine from bars often find that they can adulterate their product heavily with any number of diluents without incurring complaints from their clients. Users who smoke or inject cocaine know that they should avoid buying supplies in these types of markets. Heroin, methamphetamine, PCP and "rave" drugs[6] are also susceptible to adulteration.

The Social Organization of Distribution

Three ideal types of social organization among drug distributors are presented below, that represent a conceptual sequence of increasing complexity: (1) freelance distributors; (2) socially bonded businesses; and (3) corporate-style distributors.

(1) Freelance Distributors

The defining characteristics of freelance distributors are: (1) a lack of formal hierarchy; and (2) the absence of a division of labor. Relationships between distributors are, ideally, egalitarian — no one owes anything to anyone else and every person is his own boss. For example, Red was a 19-year-old, African-American crack distributor (and user) who lived and worked a block in Flatbush, Brooklyn. As he proudly noted, his operation was strictly freelance.

> My relationship with other dealers is "fuck that." Fuck them all. 'Cause I'm tryin' to get mine. You know what I'm sayin'? Let me tell you something about dealing drugs. See, when you [are] selling drugs, rule number one is to be independent. See, if you a true drug seller, you don't want to owe nobody nothing. What ever you fuck up is yours.

Alliances in street-level freelance markets, the most fluid and ephemeral of the nine market-types we discuss, are made strictly on an ad hoc basis and are typically short-lived. Freelancers tend to perceive the business world in Hobbesian terms: "every man for himself." Altruism is for suckers, and good deeds are done only when there is a payoff in the immediate future. For this reason, relationships between distributors are often fragile, and undoubtedly the source of some of the violence associated with such markets (Curtis and Sviridoff, 1994; Sviridoff et al., 1992). Street markets, potentially the most competitive (anyone can set up shop), are also the most highly policed and therefore riskiest market form. They are most likely to generate violence and have other undesirable effects on the neighborhoods where they operate. Given the often blatant and cavalier manner in which they operate, street-level freelance distributors tend to be despised by neighborhood residents, even those who are intimately involved in street-level drug markets (Curtis, 1996; Sviridoff et al., 1992). By contrast, freelance indoor and freelance delivery distributors depend for their very existence on invisibility.

Freelance distributors typically dominate drug markets that are formed whenever a new product (or innovation) is introduced to a population. Because of the need to promote the new product, freelancers are most often users as well. To avoid consuming all of their supplies, they often establish a frantic pace of distribution and aggressively hawk their product. During the cocaine-smoking era of the 1980s, because of the rate at which they smoked the substance, freelance distributors typically had difficulty accumulating money, and every day was a struggle to raise enough capital to make a purchase from a wholesaler (Hamid, 1992; Sviridoff et al., 1992). As proselytizers for new drugs, freelance distributors are particularly adept at building a client base, but they tend to be incompetent entrepreneurs. Instead of continuing to build and maintain a client base, they often pave the way for more organized distributors to move in (Hamid, 1992).

(2) Socially Bonded Businesses

The next level of organizational complexity is what is described here as a socially bonded business. These are drug-distribution enterprises that have evolved in complexity beyond the "every-man-for-himself" style characteristic of freelance distribution. They do not involve the complexity of organization and division of labor of the corporate style of distribution described below. As the name implies, organizations of this type are usually based upon extra-economic social ties — typically kinship, race, ethnicity, nationality, and/or neighborhood. Those who make up the group share some common feature (or set of features), beyond simply making money, that binds members of the group together. Charles, a crack distributor in Brooklyn, described an example of this loose-knit type of organization: "There's a posse of about eight [Jamaicans]. They don't have a name, they just get together and do business. They sell drugs together. Nobody's the head, they all have a share in the business.

They do it by shift, every week a next man gets to work." Another type would be businesses based on ideological or cultural commitments, such as Rastafarian marijuana distributors, the network of distribution of so-called "designer drugs" by "ravers," and, according to the Drug Enforcement Agency (DEA), the upper echelons of LSD markets (Intelligence Division, 1995) which are dominated by these types of distributors.

While freelance and corporate-style distributors are very specific and easily recognizable forms of distribution, socially bonded businesses exhibit wide variation. Some are quite egalitarian in their structure and functioning and resemble collectives of freelancers (like the Jamaicans mentioned above) while others are hierarchical and appear almost corporate-like in the way they operate. Such businesses may vary along many axes, such as degree of hierarchy, division of labor, and "bondedness"/profit orientation.

Special cases are those businesses that are based upon blood ties (see Curtis and Maher, 1992). Though often limited in size, such organizations frequently exhibit some type of division of labor by age and gender. In businesses based on kinship, young adult and juvenile members of the family will often be assigned the riskier tasks (usually, those that involve working on the street), whereas older members will be in charge of positions that require more responsibility (e.g., making purchases of product, handling money, etc.). Female members will often be assigned tasks that are tangential (though not unimportant) to the business (e.g., packaging and/or "cutting" drugs, house-sitting, etc.). Leadership of such organizations often falls to the family patriarch, though this can obviously change very quickly in the drug business. Kinship-based organizations often operate upon the principle of redistribution. Money generated by sales is often funneled to the head of the family, who in turn, pays the various members accordingly.

Family businesses, almost by definition, are interested in improving the condition of the family before catering to individual interests. A family's parochial interests may or may not benefit the larger community in which they are embedded, but given their ability and occasional need to expand to include fictive kin as members of the business, as well as their obligations to family members who may not be directly involved in the business, there may be many points at which family and community interests intersect.

Other types of socially bonded businesses may also be quite sensitive to the larger needs of their "people," and this style of distribution may be less noxious to the surrounding community. For example, Rastafarian marijuana distributors in central Brooklyn were widely known for spreading their considerable wealth around neighborhoods and allowing many people to make a living through economic opportunities that would not have otherwise come their way (Hamid, 1992).

In Bushwick, corporate distributors generated considerable resentment from community residents. When they began to experience difficulties from law enforcement interventions, the socially bonded businesses that were more "integrated" into the neighborhood and whose profits circulated locally, were able to thrive while the corporate-style organizations were dismantled (Curtis, 1996). Bolo, a Puerto Rican distributor who had once worked for corporate street sellers of heroin and crack in his native Bushwick, set up a network of several streetcorner "spots" selling crack. Unlike corporate owners, Bolo ran a tight-knit organization, and he cared about his workers and the neighborhood. He hired only people who lived in the area with their families and carefully scrutinized their motives for wanting to join his organization. Bolo made a conscious effort to stay away from young drug sellers who publicly announced their intention to buy fancy clothes, jewelry or expensive cars with drug profits:

> Most of the fellows who work for me need the money. I mean, I'll be honest with you, I'm not going to bring a kid who just needs money to buy a pair of sneakers. I will bring a guy with me that has to support his family in one way or another. I mean, I told everybody, "nobody is here getting rich. All we are doing is surviving. If you know how to save and cut corners, you can have all the money to save."

In interviews with his street-level workers, they all voiced similar motivations for working — none sported flashing clothing, jewelry or other consumer display items that many people thought were characteristic of drug dealers. Bolo was prideful of the fact that his business "supported 25 families in the neighborhood" and he enjoyed being seen as a "godfather" by community residents who often sought his assistance, protection, or advice.

By grounding a business in family or other types of extra-economic ties, a business can often gain a competitive edge over freelancers or other organizational forms that do not enjoy such high levels of trust and cohesiveness. Law enforcement initiatives that rely on "turning" arrestees to provide information about their bosses are likely to be less successful in market places dominated by socially bound businesses, especially those based on kinship ties. At the same time, such businesses can become vehicles where labor can be deeply exploited. As drug distributors have largely moved off the streets in the 1990s, the increasing reliance of the police on "snitches" (who are routinely threatened with lengthy prison sentences under the draconian Rockefeller laws) to manufacture drug arrests has had a profound impact on neighborhoods, disrupting families and pitting neighbors against each other.

(3) Corporate-style Distributors

Corporate-style distributors are the most complexly organized of our three ideal types. They are the most hierarchic and exhibit the highest degree of division of labor, and the associations between persons involved are primarily based on making money. The line distinguishing corporate-style from socially bonded businesses is often blurry because members of corporations, particularly those in positions of power and/or authority, often share similar characteristics such as ethnicity, subcultural style (hip-hop, punk, etc.) or neighborhood affiliation. They tend to share common characteristics because, like socially-bonded businesses, corporate-style distributors also risk prosecution under conspiracy and racketeering statutes (such as the Racketeer Influenced and Corrupt Organizations [RICO]. Thus, employees must be greatly trusted[7] by the organization (and employ people who share a common background represents an attempt to ensure trustworthiness) or be kept completely in the dark about the details of the business.

Variations in the technical organization of distribution are significant here. For example, corporate street-level distributors typically deal with this problem by keeping low-level workers in the dark about the operations of the organization or who is involved, and closely supervising sellers, who are provided with very limited supplies of drugs thus limiting the amount they can steal. In such instances, low-level workers in high-risk positions are often deliberately selected from groups who are unlike those who own or run the corporation. For example, several Dominican-owned businesses in Brooklyn regularly hired Puerto Ricans, African Americans and whites, but virtually no Dominicans were placed in risky, street-selling locales. One crack dealer who operated a socially bonded business contrasted his operation with the corporate sellers who dominated street-level sales several blocks away:

> Troutman [Street] is the only international spot where they have Blacks, Puerto Ricans and whites, where everybody's working. Other areas they do not. The guys who run Troutman are good, but they're sloppy. So many of those guys are in prison from Troutman. Nobody with a mind [works there]. All they care is "hey, fuck the workers. As long as my money comes..." That kind of attitude.

Street-level corporations also may deal with the issue of trust and loyalty by instilling terror through the routine use of public "beat-downs," humiliations and killings, and many "enforcers" are hired expressly for this purpose. By contrast, indoor corporate distributors, such as the marijuana-selling "doors" (Lower East Side) and "herb-gates" (Brooklyn) relied more on a high degree of social cohesion based on long-standing neighborhood friendships and ethnicity (Puerto Rican on the Lower East Side and West Indian in Brooklyn).[8] Corporate delivery services are characterized by the highest degree of trust of employees, since they are routinely "fronted" (advanced on credit) drug supplies of a thousand dollars retail value. They tend to employ only close friends of existing employees and attempt to generate camaraderie and espirit de corps among members of the organization through paying employees well, providing perks (e.g., free or discounted drug supplies for personal use), and sponsoring social functions such as Christmas parties.

Drug dealing corporations are predicated on many of the same principles as those in the legal economy. In corporate structures, sharp divisions between ownership, management and labor are common. Indeed, many junior-level managers in some drug corporations never know who "owns" the company (Curtis, 1996). This distancing of ownership from management and labor often gives rise to tremendous tensions within the organization over their competing interests. In theory, membership in the organization is defined according to seemingly "objective" criteria, and advancement is attained through merit rather than membership in a favored group. In practice, however, like corporations in the formal economy, the upper echelons of management are often reserved for family members or members of the "in" group, and there is a ceiling beyond which some employees can never expect to pass. Below, Bruce identifies the limitations to advancement within local corporate street-level distribution organizations experienced by drug-using employees.

> The street workers, the guys that actually pitch the stuff, those could be all kinds of different guys. But it's highly unlikely that a guy like myself could become a manager. They have something against anyone who uses drugs even though they sell it. It's very illogical; but that's the way they are.

> They have people that work Blue Bag [cocaine] that they don't even know where the hell they come from. They don't really care whose hand they put their product in as long as they can stand over them and watch them and...you know, a lot of times, guys are getting cheated. The managers charge them 5% off a bundle. Guys are workin' out there for like, you know,

$10 off every hundred when they're supposed to get $20. It's dog eat dog. If it was up to some of the managers, they wouldn't hire anybody because of their greed. 'Till he sees two or three cops and then he says, "hey Bruce, come here. You want to work?"

When street-level enforcement activities increased, the estrangement between ownership, management and labor was clearly seen in the increased incidence of street-level violence, as "disloyal" employees attempted to compensate for their high level of risk and meager earnings by stealing from the company and incurring violent retaliation from management in response (Curtis, 1996). Below, "G-Man" discusses why he feels justified in periodically running off with unsold product.

Though at times I feel it wrong to step off or what have you, a lot of times it really is the manager's fault for not taking better care of the workers because the ten dollars per bundle [$100 worth of drugs] is nothing when you're taking the big risk of getting held up, which I've done; getting shot at, which I've done; getting run over by cars; getting beaten up by cops; getting your drugs taken away by the cops and not getting arrested. They feel if you don't get arrested, then you're always responsible. What do you do when a cop just comes and takes your drugs from you and just tells you to take a walk? You know, the percentage that's given — ten dollars — is really nothing. When you go to jail they don't come and bail you out! I feel bad because at times you put your life at a risk, but I don't feel bad about stepping off with their product.

Like street-level freelancers, street-level corporate-style distributors tend to care little about the particular community in which they might be located. Corporations are about making money for the owners, not about the welfare or enrichment of employees, their families or neighborhoods. Employees and neighborhoods are interchangeable for such corporations, and most of them have several outlets where they can shift their business should one neighborhood become too "hot." This lack of commitment to the people or places where they are located often earns corporate drug businesses considerable resentment from residents of those communities. The owners of such businesses are wise to conceal their identities from all but a few trusted employees. While corporations enrich a few people at the top, their workers remain economically stagnant and the majority of dollars flow out of communities where they are generated. This pattern of not contributing to community development and/or enrichment is often also true of corporations in the formal economy and those in the informal sector, and suggests that there are may be many lines of similarity which may be drawn between the two.

The Dynamics of Change in Drug Markets

The three ideal types of social organizations briefly described above in many ways violate the complexities that are observed in the field. While recognizing the shortcomings of typologizing, nevertheless, it is necessary to begin to lay out a set of principles — a structure — by which drug researchers can compare and contrast their findings rather than continuing to talk past each other, focusing on superficial characteristics that often serve to confuse rather than clarify.

One disadvantage to constructing typologies is that they are not conducive to describing change. Clearly though, drug markets evolve over time, and they can become more or less complex as they metamorphose. New distributors also enter the market with regularity; some use well-worn methods of selling drugs while others introduce new wrinkles to the drug business. Distributors also learn of new techniques of distribution and evasion of law enforcement from acquaintances or friends active in other drug markets: "But it only lasts for a little while, you always got to think of something new. You always got to change up. I hadda change up already. It was time. I look around, talk to different people, and I look for the next thing, how they doing it, cause I know mad people, different spots" (interview, "Destroyer").

While acknowledging that change is inevitable and that it is not unidirectional — it may lead to more or less complex forms of organization — our data led us to develop the model presented in the section that identifies a conceptual sequence of increasingly complex styles of distribution. This does not mean that styles of distribution must necessarily develop along a linear path. In fact, while many different variations are possible and have been noted in the data, several themes have been recurrent.

When a drug is newly introduced, markets are typically disorganized and dominated by freelance distributors who initiate new consumers. Freelancers are usually users of the substances they sell and they typically act as ambassadors by touting the virtues of their products. Unlike other forms of drug distribution, freelancers have the flexibility to give free samples, demonstrate how the drug is consumed, take time to explore new places and situations that enhance the drug's effect, and in general, do things that seem to contradict the notion of "organization" and violate the precepts of capital accumulation.

Once freelancers successfully build a steady and visible consumer base, corporate distributors often begin to enter the picture. Because of the resources at their disposal, corporations find it easy to force freelancers out of the picture. By this point, freelancers have often been weakened by their poor management skills, their own use of a substance and their inability to generate enough capital to stay competitive in the market. Unlike freelancers, corporations can more easily adapt to unfavorable local conditions (especially increased scrutiny by law enforcement) by shifting personnel and resources from neighborhood to neighborhood.

As consumer demand for a drug begins to level off or recede and profits begin to stagnate, corporations find it increasingly difficult to maintain themselves. In addition, corporations that operate on the street often have the additional burden of having to respond to community opposition as a result of the disrespectful ways in which they sometimes conduct business. And, of course, because of their large size, they become the primary targets of law enforcement efforts. When street-level markets begin to recede, socially bonded businesses, which are much more discreet and generally less driven by sheer profit margins, begin to assert themselves as the dominant forces among distributors in a market place.

Socially bonded business also evolve in complexity over time. For example, family businesses are often begun by groups of siblings and/or cousins who are all approximately the same age. At first, their organization may exhibit many features that are characteristic of freelancers, i.e., egalitarianism, no division of labor, etc. Over time, however, a division of labor will likely emerge as the strengths and weaknesses of different family members become apparent. With a division of labor will also likely develop a sense of hierarchy since some jobs will be more important than others. At the other end of the organizational spectrum, some family businesses become too large to include just family members and the inclusion of fictive kin will begin to stretch the concept of family business to its limit.

Clearly, the technical and social organization of distribution change over time, but what explains such change? Conventional wisdom asserts that variation in the intensity and style of policing are a primary force that shapes drug markets. Given the New York City Police Department's assault on drug distribution in minority neighborhoods and the casualties generated in the "war on drugs," it would be surprising indeed if there were not a substantial effect. However, a number of other factors are significant as well. Consumer preferences shape markets as decisively as policing. Drug distributors are also victims of predatory crime both by rivals and those who realize dealers are unlikely to report robberies. Capital and labor market flows in the noncriminalized economy also affect drug markets, both directly and by shaping the neighborhood settings in which distribution takes place. Finally, all the other factors that shape neighborhoods also affect drug markets: class, ethnicity, residential and other land use patterns, etc. Of course, none of these factors exists in isolation; they are all constantly interacting in complex and multifarious ways. Drug markets affect neighborhoods, which, in turn, affects policing, which affects drug markets.

THE MODEL APPLIED: CHANGES IN MARIJUANA MARKETS ON THE LOWER EAST SIDE, 1983-99

In the remaining space, we will present a truncated version of the model as it is applied to marijuana markets on the Lower East Side of Manhattan between 1983 and 1999 (See Table 1). A "thick description" of the model would describe the various examples in far greater detail and would more fully explore the impact of the range of external factors (e.g., population change, gentrification, policing, etc.) on the evolution of markets.

The Lower East Side is compact, centrally located in Manhattan and characterized by great cultural and economic diversity. It is densely populated with aging Eastern European immigrants, yuppie stockbrokers, dreadlocked squatter punks and Latino families. Since the late 1970s, the area has been subject to considerable gentrification; it was one of the few remaining areas in Manhattan (south of Harlem) where the poor and working-class lived, and was thus available for further development as real estate values began to rise in the early 1980s. The East Village area of the Lower East Side has become a major center of recreational activity over the last 20 years and bars, cafes, dance and rock clubs line the streets and avenues.

The area also continues[9] to be a center of extralegal recreation. The entire spectrum of illegal drugs are to be found in this area: marijuana, heroin, cocaine, amphetamines, prescription drugs, psychedelics and the newer, so-called designer drugs, such as Ecstasy (MDMA) and Special K (ketamine) are all available. In addition to a wide variety of illicit substances being available, many different styles of drug distribution flourish in this heterogeneous environment: "house connections" (dealers operating out of apartments), long-term, street-dealing enterprises, freelance street dealers, businesses that operate via electronic pagers and delivery services are all to be found within a few blocks of each other.

Marijuana distribution on the Lower East Side in the early 1980s occurred in a wide variety of styles of distribution. The chart below outlines the range and approximate number of marijuana distributors that existed in 1983.

Table 1: Marijuana Markets on the Lower East Side — 1983 v. 1998

	Social Organization of Distribution					
Technical Organization of Distribution	Freelance Distributors		Bonded Businesses		Corporations	
	1983	1998	1983	1998	1983	1998
Street-level	>25	>10	>5	None	None	None
Indoor Sales	>10	>5	>5	None	>5	None
Delivery Services	None	>10	2	>2	2	>10

Street sales (primarily by freelancers) were common, most often made using small manila envelopes containing $5 and $10 quantities ("nickels" and "dimes," respectively). Most street dealers were African American and sales were concentrated in a small area (primarily East Ninth Street between First Avenue and Avenue A). Many of these distributors also sold marijuana in Washington Square Park in nearby Greenwich Village. Marijuana was also available in a number of off-street venues. The most notable (and probably the most popular among consumers) were the "doors." "We would always buy weed at these two places on my block, the 'Blue Door' and the 'Black Door.' Anyone could walk in, buy weed, it was like it was legal. We'd go there and buy a nickel during a commercial" (interview, "Dick"). The "doors" were storefront operations that made no pretense of selling legal commodities. They consisted of an empty storefront containing a teller window where consumers could purchase nickels, dimes and quarters (which purported to be quarter-ounce quantities and sold for about $35 to $40). Bodegas were another type of indoor locale that sold marijuana. They differed from the "doors" in that they appeared to be legitimate businesses (and indeed, to varying degrees, often were), offering various grocery items for sale, as well marijuana (and, often, other illegal drugs as well). Both the "doors" and bodegas were often run by Latinos and were generally characterized by socially bonded and corporate forms of organization.

These public and quasi-public distribution operations were far from being the only marijuana distribution venues in the Lower East Side in the early 1980s. "House connections" and early forms of marijuana delivery also flourished at this time. "House connections" were distributors operating from indoor locations (apartments or office spaces). They generally sold only to known customers, often sold "weight" (semiwholesale and wholesale quantities, such as ounces, quarter-pounds and pounds). Many were freelancers, although several socially bonded businesses (partnership and semipartnership operations) existed. Whites and African Americans dominated this portion of the marijuana market during this period. Finally, the earliest marijuana delivery services began at this time, notably a service run by "the Pope," who at one time advertised in the *Village Voice*. Another early service would deliver marijuana to any lower Manhattan address if the caller knew that the password was "What's on the menu?" The person answering the phone would respond with a list of the day's selections and prices and would then dispatch a delivery person on a bicycle to deliver whatever was requested.

Marijuana prices and quantities available for retail sale varied by the type of distributor. Marijuana sold on the street and in the "doors" and bodegas was sold in $5 "nickels," containing about 1-1.5 grams of marijuana or $10 "dimes," containing about twice as much. The price per ounce price was thus about $90 to $140. Marijuana purchased from house dealers or by delivery varied more widely in price, from approximately $50 per ounce (for average quality known as "mersh" or "schwag") to a high of $200 (for extremely high quality such as "Thai stick" or "skunkweed").

Marijuana markets have changed a great deal since the early 1980s. Population change, gentrification and the war on drugs are three prominent factors that have played major roles in propelling marijuana delivery services to the dominant market position that they have enjoyed since the mid-1990s. Street-level markets continue to exist, albeit smaller and slightly shifted in location (now primarily on First Avenue between St. Mark's Place and East Ninth Street). Since the "nickel" bag is obsolete on the Lower East Side, street markets now deal exclusively in "dimes," reflecting the inflation in marijuana prices since the early 1980s. The "doors" and bodega operations are long gone, casualties of more intensive policing, beginning with Operation Pressure Point in 1983 (Zimmer, 1985), and the ongoing gentrification of the neighborhood (Marcuse, 1986). House dealers continue to operate, but they are far fewer, almost totally devoted to wholesale deals, and very reluctant to take on new customers. The remaining former house dealers (those who did not make the transition to quantity sales to a strictly limited clientele) tend to operate on a quasi-delivery basis.

The Lower East Side marijuana market is currently dominated by large corporate-style delivery services, that deliver throughout Manhattan. At least 20 such operations exist today, typically offering to deliver, generally within a two-hour wait, $50 quantities of different types of marijuana,. Prices have also increased greatly. Delivery services charge their customers for service and insulation from the risks of street purchases. Per-ounce prices from one delivery service were $200 ("low"), $350 ("mid") and $560 ("high"). The current "high" is not nearly as good as $200 weed" in the early 1980s.

CONCLUSION:
The Developmental Cycle of Communities/Neighborhoods and the Embeddedness of Drug Markets within Them

The typology outlined in this paper provides a framework for systematically describing drug distribution activities, which allows and facilitates comparative analysis. One important lesson that emerged from the comparison of data from different neighborhoods was that the developmental trajectories of drug distribution and consumption varied considerably from neighborhood to neighborhood. Neighborhoods are complex, multidimensional entities where structural constraints and microfactors intersect to form culturally diverse social fabrics, and their study is a strength of ethnographic research. As the crucible where orientations, outlooks, behaviors, and lifestyles are forged and refined, neighborhoods and communities are critical to examine (Arensberg and Kimball, 1965). There are several excellent examples of how ethnographic methods and techniques can be employed to generate and integrate multiple sources of data to provide a comparative framework for understanding the similarities and differences between neighborhoods (Sullivan, 1989; Moore, 1978).

The substantial variation in our data suggests that changes in the manner in which drugs are sold and consumed are not an outcome of a "natural" progression of distribution styles or a "developmental cycle of drug use," but rather, highly dependent on their interaction with a complex array of factors, with each neighborhood having a unique configuration. To understand how drug distribution and consumption vary, it is first necessary to understand how they are integrated (or not) into a specific setting. In adopting such a perspective, the apparent mystery of why, for example, law enforcement interventions are not more uniformly successful, can be more easily understood.

By employing a typology that distinguishes between different forms of drug distribution and how they are embedded in a community, policy makers and law enforcement officials can devise interventions that are more responsive to local conditions and may earn community support rather than antagonism. For example, street-level corporate distributors who use neighborhoods simply as locales to "get money" are likely to be less integrated into those communities and are thereby more susceptible to traditional "buy and bust" tactics and more recent place-management strategies (Edmunds et al., 1996; Rengert, 1996; Eck, 1994). The notable success of the New York City Police Department in dismantling large street-level drug markets stands as testimony to this approach (Cunneen, 1999; Greene, 1999; Sviridoff et al., 1992). By continuing to employ aggressive tactics that emphasized large numbers of arrests in a market place that evolved partly in response to these tactics, police found that they had reached the point of diminishing returns. Furthermore, the very communities that had been freed from the oppressive rule of corporate-style distributors are now bearing the brunt of mass arrests that far surpass those made at the height of the crack epidemic (Fessenden and Rohde, 1999; NYPD Crime Analysis Unit, 1997).

Changes in the character of drug markets as well as shifts in the modus operandi of distributors and/or consumer preferences may well have more to do with community-level factors than it does with larger social forces (e.g., the influence of mass media) or the actions of law enforcement interventions that aim to eliminate them. While each site will undoubtedly have a different constellation of factors that exert influence on the configuration of local drug distribution and consumption, we are not suggesting that researchers return to a form of "historical particularism" (Harris, 1968:250-289) that makes it impossible to systematically compare and contrast different sites.

Clearly, drug markets are embedded in wider social environments — neighborhoods and communities — and are responsive to many noneconomic forces (see e.g., Sullivan, 1989; Arensberg and Kimball, 1965; Polanyi, 1957). This realization simply underscores that drug markets must also be understood as more than simply flows of capital or the exchange of goods and services for money. To appreciate the roles that drugs play in neighborhoods and communities, it is necessary to have a much more comprehensive view of them as commodities, symbols and tools. Drug markets also provide arenas where other social forces and dramas may manifest themselves and be played out (Bohannon and Dalton, 1965). Defined as such, markets are complex arenas of social interaction that may affect, and be affected by, a wide variety of noneconomic factors, and a "thick description" (Geertz, 1973) of them requires a multilayered rendering, sensitive to changes over time, that combines social, institutional, neighborhood and individual level factors into an intelligible whole.

Markets not only reflect the supply and demand for particular drugs, they help shape them. Besides being places where commodities were bought and sold, the market places observed in this research were also arenas where the socialization of neighborhood youth took place, often superseding in importance such places as playgrounds, parks, gymnasiums, and clubs. They were also places where trends were set: in the process of buying and selling drugs, styles in clothing and music were established. Being a drug distributor was not entirely about making money, it also provided distributors with a very public forum where a persona could be molded to help achieve noneconomic ends. Drug markets were not only venues where fads and trends in clothing, music and jewelry were started, they were also arenas where interethnic rivalries were most visibly acted out.

The typology also begs the question of why distinct forms of distribution arise and flourish at specific times in particular places. To unlock this mystery, we must look beyond limiting confines of drug research and realize that illegal substances are not simply about altering consciousness or making money, but ultimately, they are rooted in, and tell us much, about political economy. For example, it is no coincidence that street-level drug supermarkets operated by corporate-style distributors have been located in blighted minority neighborhoods. These urban backwaters had long been neglected by governmental agencies (except, perhaps, law enforcement), and the vacuum created by their malign neglect allowed drug organizations to fill the void. While such organizations are certainly about making money, they are often equally concerned with building and exercising power and authority. Such developments are not unlike situations found in other places and times when governments abdicated their responsibility or ceded authority to local power brokers (Hess, 1998).

Seen through the lens of political economy, the study of drug markets may progress from being an evaluative yardstick for law enforcement officials and policymakers to making significant contributions to theory development and the wider analysis of topics like power, authority, the state and other factors that more fruitfully occupy the time of social scientists. Through the typology of drug distribution that we offer we hope to bring structure and a common taxonomic vocabulary to a field that has been characterized by a great deal of description but relatively little analysis that can be used for comparative study.

Address correspondence to: Ric Curtis, Associate Professor, Department of Anthropology, John Jay College of Criminal Justice, New York, N.Y. 10019. E-mail: rcurtis@faculty.jjay.cuny.edu

Acknowledgments: The authors would like to acknowledge their debt to the sharp editorial eyes and insightful comments of Dr. Kate McCoy, and to Dr. Barry Spunt, Alix Conde, Stephanie Herrman and Judy McGuire of the Heroin in the 21st Century Project. This research was supported in part by National Institute of Drug Abuse Grant No. RO1 DA 10105-02 ("Heroin in the 21st Century") and in part by Grant No.11 999-IJ-CX-0100 ("Lower East Side Trafficking" Study), National Institute of Justice, Office of Justice Programs, U.S. Department of Justice. Points of view in this document are those of the authors and do not necessarily represent the official position or policies of the U.S. Department of Justice or of the National Institute of Drug Abuse.

REFERENCES

Agar, M.H. (1973). *Ripping and Running: A Formal Ethnography of Urban Heroin Addicts.* New York, NY: Seminar Press.

Appadurai, A. (1986). *The Social Life of Things: Commodities in Cultural Perspective.* Cambridge, UK: Cambridge University Press.

Arensberg, C. and S.T. Kimball (1965). *Culture and Community.* Gloucester, MA: Peter Smith.

Bernard, H.R. (1994). *Research Methods in Anthropology: Qualitative and Quantitative Approaches* (2nd ed.). Thousand Oaks, CA: Sage Publications.

Biernacki, P. and D. Waldorf (1981). "Snowball Sampling: Problems and Techniques of Chain Referral Sampling." *Sociological Methods and Research* 10(2):141-163.

Bohannon, P. and G. Dalton (1965). *Markets in Africa: Eight Subsistence Economies in Transition.* Garden City, NY: Doubleday and Company.

Bourgois, P. (1989). "In Search of Horatio Alger: Culture and Ideology in the Crack Economy." *Contemporary Drug Problems* 16(Winter):619-649.

Buerger, M.E. (1991). "Cops and Dealers: Enforcement Strategies Against the Street-Level Drug Trade." Paper presented at the annual meeting of the Academy of Criminal Justice Sciences, March 8.

Chitwood, D., J. Rivers and J. Inciardi (1996). *The American Pipe Dream: Crack Cocaine and the Inner City.* New York, NY: Harcourt Brace College Publishers.

Courtwright, D. (1982). *Dark Paradise: Opiate Addiction in America Before 1940.* Cambridge, MA: Harvard University Press.

—— H. Joseph and D. Des Jarlais. (1989*). Addicts Who Survived: An Oral History of Narcotic Use in America, 1923-1965.* Knoxville, TN: University of Tennessee Press.

Cunneen, C. (1999). "Zero Tolerance Policing and the Experience of New York City." *Current Issues in Criminal Justice* 10(3):299-313.

Curtis, R. (1996). "The War On Drugs in Brooklyn, New York: Street-Level Drug Markets and the Tactical Narcotics Team." Doctoral dissertation, Teachers College, Columbia University, New York, NY.

—— S.R. Friedman, A. Neaigus, B. Jose, M. Goldstein and G. Ildefonso (1995). "Street-level Drug Markets: Network Structure and HIV Risk." *Social Networks* 17:229-249.

—— and M. Sviridoff (1994). "The Social Organization of Street Level Drug Markets and Its Impact on the Displacement Effect." In: R. MacNamara (ed.), *Crime Displacement: The Other Side of Prevention.* East Rockaway, NY: Cummings and Hathaway.

—— and L. Maher (1992). "Highly Structured Drug Markets on Williamsburg's Southside." Report produced under contract with Social Science Research Council Working Group on the Social Ecology of Drugs and Crime.

Dorn, N., K. Murji and N. South (1992). *Traffickers: Drug Markets and Law Enforcement.* New York, NY: Routledge.

Douglas, M. and B. Isherwood (1981). *The World of Goods.* New York, NY: Basic Books.

Drug Enforcement Administration, Intelligence Division (1995*). Drug Intelligence Report: LSD in the United States.* Washington, DC: Drug Enforcement Administration, United States Department of Justice.

Eck, J. (1994). "Drug Markets and Drug Places: A Case-Control Study of the Spatial Structure of Illicit Drug Dealing." Doctoral dissertation, Department of Criminology and Criminal Justice, University of Maryland, College Park, MD.

Edmunds, M., M. Hough, and N. Urquia (1996). *Tackling Local Drug Markets.* (Crime Detection and Prevention Series Paper #80.) London, UK: Home Office, Police Research Group.

Fagan, J. (1989). "The Social Organization of Drug Use and Drug Dealing Among Urban Gangs." *Criminology* 27(4):633-670.

Fessenden, F. and D. Rohde (1999). "Dismissed before Reaching Court, Flawed Arrests Rise in New York." *New York Times*, August 23, p. A1.

Fleisher, M. (1998). "Ethnographers, Pimps and the Company Store." In: J. Ferrell and M. Hamm (eds.), *Ethnography at the Edge: Crime, Deviance and Field Research.* Boston, MA: Northeastern University Press.

Geertz, C. (1973). *The Interpretation of Cultures.* New York, NY: Basic Books.

Goldstein, P., D. Lipton, E. Preble, I. Sobel, T. Miller, W. Abbott, W. Paige and F. Soto (1984). "The Marketing of Street Heroin in New York City." *Journal of Drug Issues* 14(3):553-566.

Greene, J. (1999). "Zero Tolerance: A Case of Police Policies and Practices in New York City." *Crime & Delinquency* 45(2):171-187.

Hagedorn, J. (1994). "Neighborhoods, Markets, and Gang Drug Organization." *Journal of Research in Crime and Delinquency* 31(4):264-294.

Hamid, A. (1992). "The Developmental Cycle of a Drug Epidemic: The Cocaine Smoking Epidemic of 1981-1991." *Journal of Psychoactive Drugs* 24(4):337-348.

—— R. Curtis, K. McCoy, J. McGuire, A. Conde, W. Bushell, R. Lindenmayer, K. Brimberg, S. Maia, S. Abdur-Rashid and J. Settembrino (1997). "The Heroin Epidemic in New York City: Current Status and Prognoses." *The Journal of Psychoactive Drugs* 29(4):375-391.

Harris, M. (1968). *The Rise of Anthropological Theory.* New York, NY: Thomas Y. Crowell Company.

Hayeslip, D. (1989). *Local-level Drug Enforcement: New Strategies.* (Report No. 213.) Washington, DC: U.S. Department of Justice, National Institute of Justice.

Hess, H. (1998). *Mafia and Mafiosi: Origin, Power and Myth.* New York, NY: New York University Press.

Johnson, B., A. Hamid and H. Sanabria (1992). "Emerging Models of Crack Distribution." In: T. Mieczkowski (ed.), *Drugs, Crime, and Social Policy: Research, Issues, and Concerns.* Boston, MA: Allyn and Bacon.

Kleiman, M. (1988). "Crackdowns: The Effects of Intensive Enforcement on Retail Heroin Dealing." In: M.R. Chaiken (ed.), *Street-Level Drug Enforcement: Examining the Issues.* Washington, DC: National Institute of Justice, United States Department of Justice.

—— and K. Smith. (1990). "State and Local Drug Enforcement: In Search of a Strategy." In: M. Tonry and N. Morris (eds.), *Crime and Justice: A Review of Research,* vol. 12. Chicago, IL.: University of Chicago Press.

Lambert , E. (1990). *The Collection and Interpretation of Data from Hidden Populations.* (NIDA Research Monograph 98.) Rockville, MD: National Institute on Drug Abuse.

Maher, L. (1995). "Dope Girls: Gender, Race and Class in the Drug Economy." Doctoral dissertation, Graduate School of Criminal Justice, Rutgers University, Newark, NJ.

Marcuse, P. (1986). "Abandonment, Gentrification, and Displacement, The Linkages in New York City." In: N. Smith and P. Williams (eds.), *Gentrification of The City.* Boston, MA: Allan & Unwin.

Mieczkowski, T. (1990). "The Operational Styles of Crack Houses in Detroit." In: M. De La Rosa, E. Lambert and B. Gropper (eds.), *Drugs and Violence: Causes, Correlates, and Consequences.* (NIDA Research Monograph 103.) Rockville, MD: National Institute on Drug Abuse.

Moore, M. (1977). *Buy and Bust.* Lexington, MA: Lexington Books.

New York City Police Department, Crime Analysis Unit (1997). *Statistical Report, Complaints and Arrests.* New York, NY: New York Police Department.

Ouellet, L., A. Jiminez and W. Wiebel (1993). "Heroin Again: New Users of Heroin in Chicago." Paper presented at the annual meeting of the Society for the Study of Social Problems. Miami Beach, FL, August 11-13.

Polanyi, K. (1957). "The Economy as Instituted Process." In: K. Polanyi, C. Arensberg and H. Pearson (eds.), *Trade and Market in Early Empires.* Glencoe, IL: Free Press.

Preble, E. and J. Casey (1969). "Taking Care of Business: The Heroin User's Life on the Street." *International Journal of the Addictions* 4(1):1-24.

Rengert, G. (1996). *The Geography of Illegal Drugs.* Boulder, CO: Westview Press.

Reuter, P. (1985). *The Organization of Illegal Markets: An Economic Analysis.* Washington, DC: National Institute of Justice.

Riley, K. (1997). *Crack, Powder Cocaine, and Heroin: Drug Purchase and Use Patterns in Six U.S. Cities.* Washington, DC: National Institute of Justice/Office of National Drug Control Policy.

Spradley, J. (1979). *The Ethnographic Interview.* New York, NY: Holt, Rinehart and Winston.

Stephens, R. (1991). *The Street Addict Role: A Theory of Heroin Addiction.* Albany, NY: State University of New York Press.

Sullivan, M. (1989). *Getting Paid: Youth Crime and Work in the Inner City.* Ithaca, NY: Cornell University Press.

Sviridoff, M., S. Sadd, R. Curtis and R. Grinc (1992). *The Neighborhood Effects of New York City's Tactical Narcotics Team on Three Brooklyn Precincts.* New York, NY: Vera Institute of Justice.

Terry, C. and M. Pellens. (1928). *The Opium Problem.* New York, NY: Bureau of Social Hygiene.

Waterston, A. (1993). *Street Addicts in the Political Economy.* Philadelphia, PA: Temple University Press.

Weisburd, D., L. Green, F. Gajewski and C. Bellucci. (1994). "Defining the Street-Level Drug Market." In: D. MacKenzie and C. Uchida (eds.), *Drugs and Crime: Evaluating Public Policy Initiatives.* Thousand Oaks, CA: Sage.

Weisheit, R. (1998). "Marijuana Subcultures: Studying Crime in Rural America." In: J. Ferrell and M. Hamm (eds.), *Ethnography at the Edge: Crime, Deviance and Field Research.* Boston, MA: Northeastern University Press.

Weppner, R. (ed.) (1977). *Street Ethnography: Selected Studies of Crime and Drug Use in Natural Settings.* Thousand Oaks, CA: Sage.

Williams, T. (1989). *The Cocaine Kids.* Reading, MA: Addison-Wesley.

Zimmer, L. (1985). *Operation Pressure Point: The Disruption of Street-Level Drug Trade on New York's Lower East Side.* New York, NY: NYU School of Law.

Zinberg, N. (1984). *Drug, Set and Setting.* New Haven, CT: Yale University Press.

NOTES

1. Our typology is primarily concerned with urban drug markets, because it was generated by our experiences doing ethnographic fieldwork in New York City. However, it should be applicable to drug markets in suburban and rural settings. Such markets have been little studied (see Weisheit, 1998); ethnographic research into these markets do much to broaden our understanding of the role of drugs and drug markets in American society.

2. As we discuss below, the actions of law enforcement and the community at large are also important in configuring particular drug markets.

3. While the comparatively small number of African Americans may not comport with media-derived images of heroin markets, despite vigorous efforts to locate additional African-American heroin users and distributors, we were unable to find them. For more discussion of this see Hamid et al., (1997).

4. It may also be possible to develop useful typologies of drug consumers (see Curtis et al., 1995; Hamid et al., 1997), but that, too, is beyond the scope of this paper. However, just as distribution has been poorly understood by social scientists, so too has consumption. Consumer tastes wax and wane in ways that mystify many researchers and they have only recently begun to attract their interest (see e.g., Appadurai, 1986; Douglas and Isherwood, 1981). Rather than examining the conditions and circumstances by which consumers may be differentiated, many researchers have focused on the more sensational characteristics associated with the use of particular substances (Chitwood et al., 1996; Williams, 1989.). It is necessary to begin to develop a systematic framework to describe consumers instead of examining the most visually striking characteristics shared by some users or those that violate middle class norms. Of course, there are many ways to begin differentiating between consumers. In addition to the type and amount of drug that they buy and the frequency of their purchases, they may also be distinguished by their method of consumption and the social context in which they consume drugs. An exhaustive compilation of the various types of consumers and the development of a taxonomy of drug users requires fieldwork among the many different types of drug markets that exist in a neighborhood or city. In preliminary research, we discovered that our sample of users could be subdivided into distinct groups, and that for each, there were distinct patterns of use and modes of administration. "For each of these groups, [drug use] serves as a different charter for action, and promotes a unique way of looking at the world, associating with others, or assessing one's life and one's future. ...Embedded in larger, more encompassing lifestyles, the different patterns and conventions of [drug use] are intelligible only when viewed in their context" (Hamid et al., 1997:380).

5. Perhaps because of the need for accurate intelligence in wartime, law enforcement agencies have been more attentive to the social organization of distribution than have many drug researchers. Of course, like ethnographers, undercover law enforcement agents actually experience the lived reality of drug-markets, unlike many academic criminologists (Fleisher 1998).

6. "Rave" drugs refers to newly emergent drugs (e.g., Ecstasy (MDMA) and "Special K" (ketamine)) popular among young people who frequent "raves" (dance parties featuring "techno" and "jungle" music).

7. This need for trust is, of course, precisely why the socially-bonded businesses discussed above evolve in this direction.

8 The "doors" and "herb-gates" were storefront public marijuana sellers.

9. The Lower East Side was well established as a heroin selling area by the 1930s (Terry and Pellens, 1928; Courtwright, 1982; Courtwright et al., 1989).

"HIDDEN FROM HEROIN'S HISTORY": HEROIN USE AND DEALING WITHIN AN ENGLISH ASIAN COMMUNITY — A CASE STUDY

by

Shakeel Akhtar

and

Nigel South
Health and Social Services Institute
University of Essex, UK

Abstract: Heroin use and dealing within the English Asian community have received little research attention although involvement of Asian entrepreneurs in trafficking chains has been documented. This preliminary report arises from a qualitative case study of a locality in one South-Asian community in northwest England. The paper discusses methodological and background issues but primarily provides a picture of how a heroin distribution network developed. We focus on a key individual who sponsored dealing enterprises in an attempt to ensure they operated within terms and boundaries negotiated with him, rather than see them emerge as independent competitors. Friendships and kinship facilitated such sponsorship and negotiation. Subsequent suspicion, competition and conflict led to fragmentation of networks. The consequence of inter-personal conflict and break-down of trust was increased vulnerability to enforcement attention. The study also suggests there has been a "hidden history" of heroin use and dealing within, at least some, ethnic minority communities in England and that lack of recognition of this has implications for prevention and services.

Crime Prevention Studies, volume 11, pp. 153-177

INTRODUCTION

We report on a study conducted in a medium-sized town situated in northwest England. Our emphasis here centres upon the construction and decline of a localised heroin dealing network.[1] We explore reasons why, as well as how, such activity was conducted by lower-working-class Asian youth[2] in an area of multiple socio-economic deprivation, and how it provided one of a limited number of routes by which they empowered themselves, improved on legitimate low-income opportunities and secured a desired lifestyle (Bourgois, 1995; Collison, 1994; Cloward and Ohlin, 1960). The paper is about young Asian males and assertions of identity, status and masculinity (e.g., via "male bonding," business competition, risk-taking, the threat of violence, etc.) (Messerschmidt, 1993; Collison, 1996). We are acutely aware of the absence of young women in this picture but this reflects the focus of the study on the key dealers who were male. We hope to report elsewhere on the role of women in the wider social dynamics surrounding this local heroin scene (cf., Maher, 1997; Taylor, 1993).

Census figures since the early 1980s have indicated that ethnic minorities remain disproportionately concentrated in the deprived areas in which they first settled, and in terms of socioeconomic position and unemployment levels, persons of Bangladeshi and Pakistani origin fare worst. At the end of the 1980s and the beginning of the 1990s, the community studied faced levels of male unemployment of around 25.9% compared to 14.9% for the regional male population as a whole.[3] Much research suggests that a combination of youthful aspiration, social deprivation and/or structural barriers to opportunity, encourages a disposition toward criminal activity (Fitzgerald, 1990; Duster, 1987; Cloward, 1959). This study supports such a proposition.

Ethnicity, "Otherness" and Discourses of Control

Issues concerning the social construction of perceptions and realities of Asian criminality (Murji, 1999) fall beyond our scope here. However, such issues have been examined and explained with much success by Webster (1997, 1996) who argues that since the late 1980s "...we can observe the construction of a popular and public discourse about young 'Asian' masculine criminality said to reside in British localities" (1997:65). Webster notes that an important element in the manufacturing of a public discourse concerning Asian criminality can be found in local and national press or television reports about Asian communities. The main feature of this discourse is the transformation of Asian youth from "...primarily law abiding and/or victims of crime, especially racial violence, to being associated with criminality, drugs, violence and disorder …[According to Webster] the roots of this alleged criminality lay in generational tensions brought by the breakdown of Asian family controls on young people" (Webster, 1997:65).

The foundations of these "racialising" and "criminalising" discourses are evident not only in what Webster terms the "control culture" (media and the criminal justice system) but also among white and Asian youth on the streets as well as sections of the Asian parent culture.[4]

Just as there are popular stereotypes concerning "Asians and corner shops," new stereotypes are emerging concerning unruly Asian youth who reject not only their traditional culture but also reject "respect" for their elders (viewed as the means via which the community regulates itself). The reality is more complex. While the Asian youth engaged in street culture in our study retained a strong sense of Muslim identity, they apparently experienced no tension between strict religious codes and their conflicting lifestyle patterns, which included use of drugs and alcohol and engagement in casual sexual encounters. Arguably, the assertion of a strong sense of religious identity could partly reflect continuity of cultural tradition, especially given the continued significance of kinship, but more likely it reflects individual and collective perceptions of ethnicity and racism held by Asian youth. Such perceptions reinforce a feeling of the need for a strong identity and culture, while forming a response to the experience of "otherness" (Murji, 1999; Said, 1991).[5]

THE STUDY

Very little is currently known about the relationships between ethnicity and drug-user/dealing networks in the U.K. (see Murji, 1999; Pearson and Patel, 1998). This study focuses on how such social formations may function, how personnel operate, and how networks have the ability to mutate in order to accommodate market trends (Hobbs, 1995), especially in the face of increasing law-enforcement attention and penalties (Dorn et al., 1992).

Methodological Issues

At the outset, we must draw attention to the fact that the research would have been difficult, if not impossible, to carry out if the field-worker had not grown up in the town where our research took place. Some members of the local scene were well known from the past, and, significantly, some were known intimately through friendship and kinship networks. The study, therefore, has a distinctly "personal flavour." On the one hand are the advantages of authenticity and "insider knowledge," and on the other are potential problems of bias and the maintenance of analytical distance. We think the "briefing/debriefing" relationship between the authors has provided a balance between ethnographic empathy and critical neutrality, and we seriously doubt that the research would have been possible without some kind of personal route into the everyday life of the individuals and groups studied.[6] We believe that any methodological compromise has been more than outweighed by the value of embarking on what may well be a unique research focus on Asian young men and drug dealing in the U.K.[7]

The research so far has been carried out in two phases related to the availability of both funding and of the fieldworker. It is hoped that a third and final phase will be carried out in 2000, making the project the only longitudinal, qualitative study of an ethnic-minority drugs market in the U.K. of which we are aware. The first phase was carried out between 1994 and 1996 and included emphasis on retrospective data collection. Since then a second phase of several visits back to the site of field observations has been completed (1997-98). At the beginning of the first phase, research began covertly with a view to formulating a research proposal for funding; subsequently key informants were told about the research project and, knowing and trusting the fieldworker, agreed to let him "hang around."

Methods of data collection are principally field ethnography (Pearson, 1993) in the form of contemporaneous or subsequent memory-based note-taking about general conversations and observations. Where data and personal knowledge have permitted, we have begun to compile short life stories of the key participants. Of course such a methodology draws upon many sources and predictably recollections, accounts and justifications, conflict with each other. These contradictions represent an inevitable problem in this kind of research and, given the obvious absence of other validating sources, all we can do for purposes of analysis and reporting is cross-check accounts, producing the report that seems most coherent and reliable. We acknowledge however that we are only able to "tell a story" (Plummer, 1995).

Historical and Economic Background of the Locality

The town is in northwest England and its history of expansion and decline was bound up with the fortunes of the textile and manufacturing industries that were at the heart of the Industrial Revolution. The socioeconomic experience of the research town parallels that of Bradford, just across the Pennine mountain-range, which is the site of Pearson and Patel's (1998) study of outreach work with Asian drug users:

> Having survived the economic slump of the 1930s, [Bradford] shared the fate of other towns and cities dependent on the British textile industry, which has suffered a deep and sustained decline since the 1950s.

> In the case of Lancashire cotton and Yorkshire wool, the prolonged post-war decline coincided with the period of substantial immigration of people of Asian origin [Pearson and Patel, 1998: 205; and see note 2]

In the area of the research town, as manufacturing industry was slowly dismantled (Williams and Farne, 1992), the local economy shifted to reliance on textile production. The new South-Asian communities were a source of cheap labour, but in the face of overseas competition, this industry also declined and these communities suffered disproportionately.

HEROIN, LOCAL STREET CULTURE AND SOCIOECONOMIC LIFE: THE EARLY 1980S AND BEYOND

From the late 1970s and into the mid-1980s, the U.K. experienced an unprecedented growth in the availability and use of heroin, alongside the related expansion of drug dealing and trafficking (Dorn et al., 1992; Dorn and South, 1987). The epidemiological, policy and practice issues of the time have been discussed extensively elsewhere (South, 1997; Pearson, 1991). However, one significant conclusion drawn from the available research evidence, the experience of drug services and criminal justice statistics, was that the new heroin problem was "white" (Pearson and Patel, 1998:202). This conclusion seemed reasonable given the absence of contrary indicators. Even when researchers or services sought data on minority drug use to support challenges to "racist assumptions" or complacency (e.g., the argument that minorities "look after their own, that's why they don't present at services") little evidence of heroin use among ethnic minority groups emerged. As Pearson and Patel (1998) observe:

> It is surprising...that, on all the available evidence, Britain's black communities were relatively untouched by the 1980s heroin epidemic. Because of the paucity of ethnically sensitive research in this field, much of the evidence remains anecdotal

— and it is a matter of controversy as to whether drug use in minority ethnic communities is lower than in the majority community, or whether it simply goes unreported and unknown to public agencies. A late 1980s outreach project...clearly identified the way in which drug services were often seen by minority groups as remote and inaccessible – "run by white people for white people" – and this certainly reflects the historical legacy whereby drug services in Britain had traditionally catered to white, male opiate users (Awiah et al., 1990). [Pearson and Patel, 1998:202]

As our study shows, all of this does not mean that heroin use was absent, simply that research did not reveal it. Furthermore, services would indeed be a poor source of indicators, being seen as "white" and representative of a hostile "officialdom" (see below).

A Contrary Story: Heroin in the Case-study Community

During the early to mid-1980s, heroin use began to filter down to street level in the Asian community. Prior to this period, if there was any association between heroin trafficking and this Asian community (as was rumoured), it was confined to the upper levels of the drug trade, discreet and far removed from the daily life of the community.[8] Yet this study has found that around this time, a few Asian youths (referred to here as the "preliminary core group"), were using heroin on a recreational basis. Although numerically insignificant (n < 7) and also discreet, this heroin-using social group continued until at least 1985. Its very existence implies that the availability of heroin had been established in the community, even though the source had limited distribution impact and use was confined to a few individuals.

Nonetheless, the formation of this embryonic network was of profound significance. From this point onward, the seeds had been sown for the cultivation of a heroin-using and dealing subculture by a small group of local entrepreneurs, some of whom emerged from this preliminary core group. In the late-1980s a few decided to turn to dealing in order to finance their own habits, or to simply make money.[9] By the early 1990s heroin, both in terms of its sale and use, had become established within the community. Heroin became a source of economic occupation and social preoccupation for a small number of Asian young men in the town, who initially engaged in recreational use. Some eventually moved on to acute, chaotic or addictive states. However, this study concentrates on the development of the careers of the dealers rather than on the users.

Setting the Scene: A Mount with a View

A common point of convergence in the locality was a parking lot on a small hill or "mount" that overlooked the local Asian pub and parade of shops. From the hill one could note how often and by whom the shops and pub were frequented. The parade of shops included: an Asian clothes shop; pharmacy; two newsagents; car-repair shop; launderette; take-away kebab shop; and betting shop. Particularly referring to the pharmacy, the knowing observer could distinguish between ordinary patrons and those visiting to either exchange their prescription for methadone or to exchange their syringes under the "old for new" scheme.[10]

From the view the mount afforded, one could examine many of the intricacies and intimacies of daily life around the parade. A closer inspection could identify which prostitutes were "punting" for business and those who were the punters. One could detect other illicit market activity taking place that the disinterested observer would miss, e.g., buying and selling stolen goods. Much research time was spent on the mount observing and listening to an endless flow of gossip.

The mount became an established place where Asian youth would regularly meet for aid, trade and conversation.[11] Aid comprised of helping one another, usually only as long as both sides benefited. Aid and trade were part and parcel of "doing the business" (Hobbs, 1988). Conversation generally centred on some incident such as: who was doing what (usually with the view of procuring a stake for oneself), who was seeing whom (business or sexual relationships), and where one was going for "a night out." However, despite the significance of gossip as a currency for friendship and to oil the wheels of business, individuals were nonetheless careful not to expose too much about themselves or their activities.

The mount became central to the fieldwork since it was *the* place to hang out. Apparently, (1) it was a place where, knowing that friends and associates would pass by, one could park a car, relax and smoke cannabis; and (2) since the mount was situated directly opposite the local pub and shops, one could see the patrons and if anything interesting was happening.

Types of Heroin Dealers

Lewis et al. (1985:284) define a dealer as: "an individual who supplies drugs for a cash return, operating below the import level and distinct from a solely 'social' supplier, who provides drugs in friendship or for a share of the purchase." Dorn et al. (1992) describe dealers and their motivations within a typology of several categories:

Trading Charities; Mutual Societies; Sideliners; Criminal Diversifiers; Opportunistic Irregulars; Retail Specialists; and State-sponsored Traders. In analysing the material produced by this study, we adapted two existing categories familiar in the British literature and created one new one.

(1) *User-dealers* — A prime motive is to support and regulate one's own habit. Dealing was generally chosen as an alternative to shoplifting or burglary.

(2) *Bread-heads*[12] — Dealing is a business engaged in solely for profit. It provides the support for a desired lifestyle and the means to make substantial sums of money. Most dealers observed had no formal qualifications or employment skills. Instead, they opted for what they saw as the rational choice of making money by selling heroin. The vocabulary of motives (Mills, 1940; Sykes and Matza, 1957) employed construed this as a "survival strategy" since other economic options were perceived as limited or nonexistent.

(3) *Fashion and life-stylers* — These dealers tended to be younger and far more image-conscious than the bread-heads. Although making money was a primary goal, this aim ran parallel to having a good time — "for all junkies to see," as one dealer quoted from a song.[13] Their lifestyle was conspicuous and flamboyant. Life was all about "being flash" and drawing attention to how well you were doing in business by driving around in expensive sports cars. Little attempt was made to conceal the fact that one was dealing heroin. All that mattered was to act in a way that emphasised "you are a somebody!" These dealers did not hang around the same dealing locations all the time. Since their self-publicising obviously drew attention and suspicion from members of the local community and the police, it was prudent to move around the town.

From the 1980s to the early 1990s, we can identify a process of transition. From the preliminary core group of users emerged the user-dealers, some of whom "mutated" (Hobbs, 1995) into bread-heads and fashion-lifestylers, who subsequently developed into organised distributors, the Crews. The development of the latter is the focus of the next section.

HAKIM'S STORY[14]

One of the dealers had been engaged in the drug culture from the age of 16 (using cannabis from 1983; heroin from 1985). After leaving school he attended college to study for a vocational qualification but found himself edging into the drugs scene and eventually drifted into the use of heroin. The latter started in the mid-1980s when he became the driver for a group of older Asian young men (7 to 10 years his senior) to locations where they bought drugs. This group was the "preliminary core group" introduced earlier. At this time Hakim confined himself to cannabis and alcohol but after a while, once the group had scored, they would offer him heroin as payment for his driving services and discretion. Hakim was quite naive and was unaware of what was being bought or offered. He had heard of heroin but had never seen it before and did not know how to use it. When introduced to smoking the drug by chasing it off the foil ("chasing the dragon"),[15] he claims that he did not realise he was smoking heroin. This account echoes the experience of other new heroin users in the early-to-mid 1980s in the U.K. as reported by Pearson (1987). This was Hakim's initiation into heroin culture.

Around this period other friends began to experiment with heroin use, which rapidly became a recreational pastime for a small, but now visibly significant, number of Asian young men (the "first core group"). For some, recreational use quickly gave way to being a preoccupation.[16] From the early 1990s onward, heroin use in the community grew, which led to the "second core group." The first core group were generally a few years older and were evidently fully addicted. The new entrants were younger and more aware of heroin and its effects. This awareness was partly related to national drug-information campaigns and also because the problems of the "first core group" provided clear illustrations of the downside of heroin, its effects and associated life-style.

Hakim's Entry into Serious Heroin Dealing

In the late 1980s to early 1990s, Hakim had a severe heroin addiction and had been sentenced to prison for his user-dealer activities. On release in the early 1990s, his attempts to establish himself in legitimate forms of self employment, as well as working for others, were all unsuccessful. He found self employment problematic in the absence of funds for investment. Employed by others, he quickly became disenchanted with the opportunities available, described great difficulty in finding a job with financial prospects, and attributed this (rightly or wrongly) to his criminal record and lack of marketable employment skills. "It's hard getting a good job. Whose gonna wanna employ an ex-junkie and ex-con? — no one."

After approximately a year of such disenchantment he decided to again turn to drug dealing. This time he wasn't an addict and he convinced himself he knew the strategies to employ to avoid police attention. He established himself with a credit purchase of 1/4 of an ounce of heroin and began to build his local network into what became the first dealer business.

Around this time, Hakim gave a cousin, Safraz, a ride to college. Safraz knew little of the detail of Hakim's business but was well aware of rumours that he was dealing in heroin. One day, while dropping Safraz off at college and apparently without any prompting, Hakim began to explain and justify what he was doing. He stated that he had "nothing going for him" and that dealing was the only way he could make some decent money quickly. He also wanted "to make up for what he had lost" during his period in prison. He presented Safraz with this rationale and with one of the most familiar statements found in the research literature that he wanted to "get out of the business" when he had reached a set financial target. Not long after, he purchased a new sports car and increased his target.

For the first three months Hakim operated as a one-man enterprise, purchasing merchandise from his established supplier. Within a short space of time he had acquired a sizeable amount of cash and increased the volume of his purchasing. He had started at the 1/4 ounce level, quickly moved to buying a single 1/2 ounce, then a whole ounce. When business was brisk, purchasing of ounce quantities would be frequent. Prices of heroin varied, depending on quality and source, from as low as £700 to as much as £1,100 per single ounce. Although price was often a good indicator of quality, it did not necessarily follow that the more expensive the heroin the greater the purity-content. The average price paid by Hakim for an ounce of heroin was £800 to £900, and the quality was described as good. Nonetheless, Hakim next located a better source of supply in a neighbouring small town and began to capitalise on his "better deal."

It is worth reemphasising here that we are describing a network and market based almost exclusively on heroin. The exception was the occasional availability and sale of crack-cocaine (not cocaine powder), which we assume came from the nearby major city. Availability of cannabis was widespread but not the business of Hakim or associated dealers. This availability came from other sources and buying a great deal of cannabis and smoking it were activities that saw an overlapping of Asian and white friends in the area.

THE CREATION OF THE CREWS [17]

Shortly after Hakim began dealing, Maqsood (Hakim's brother), Safraz, Shaukat (Hakim's neighbour), and Anwar (very close friend of both Hakim and Maqsood), began to socialise in the evenings, enjoying a "champagne lifestyle" at Hakim's expense.[18] Both Maqsood and Shaukat were heroin addicts.

Shaukat's Entry and Exit

Taking advantage of Hakim's hospitality, Shaukat made considerable efforts to associate closely with him and before long found employment with Hakim. However, Shaukat was soon supplying his own habit by skimming the individual sales units for personal consumption.[19] This lasted for seven months. Although Hakim suspected Shaukat was still using heroin despite denials, since there was no discrepancy with the money he received, Hakim felt he had no reason to seriously interrogate him.

Throughout the period that Shaukat was working for Hakim, Maqsood was also using heroin. Hakim knew full well that his brother was still using heroin and instructed Shaukat not to serve him. However, Maqsood threatened Shaukat with violence unless he diverted some of the heroin he was dealing. By telling Hakim that he was selling £25 sales units (1 unit = .4 g) but actually selling 2 x £15 units (1 unit = .2g) instead, Shaukat managed to "sort" Maqsood for free. Then, for every 6 x £15 units sold, Shaukat would tell Hakim that he had sold 3 x £25 units, the £15 profit would purchase a £15 sales unit of heroin for Maqsood or accumulate as profit for Shaukat. Since Hakim placed a great amount of trust in Shaukat at this time, he brushed aside the infrequent complaints aired by customers about "short–weight," as Hakim knew the buyers were always "coming up short" with money and seeking cheap deals wherever possible. Besides, reasoned Hakim, the money Shaukat was giving him was correct.

In the course of the next few months, Hakim was to drastically question his trust in Shaukat. The turning point was marked by the disappearance of his "stash," the location of which only Shaukat knew, leading to threats of violence and the termination of Shaukat's employment.

Safraz and Heroin Dealing

Safraz was introduced to dealing by Hakim during sales preparation when Hakim and Shaukat were "bagging up" heroin.[20] Only when customers placed larger orders for heroin would Hakim be personally involved in face-to-face deals. He preferred to distance himself from even these deals and he was always hoping to find reliable "lieutenants" or "under-managers" he could trust. At a time when numerous large orders were being placed, Hakim felt under pressure and invited Safraz into the top-level of his operation. Using latex gloves, a McDonalds tea/coffee spoon and small plastic bags with sealable tops, Hakim showed him how to 'bag up' the individual sales units. Intriguingly, Safraz did not seem to derive any fixed financial benefits from such participation other than those Hakim chose to provide. Having grown up together, the relationship seemed to be based on a set of personal obligations arising out of kinship and friendship between the two. Encouraged by Hakim, Safraz had soon acquired knowledge of all Hakim's business practices. Throughout this period Shaukat was still dealing for Hakim and engaged in his "double deceit," supplying Maqsood for free and skimming units to create additional profit for himself. At this point, such embezzlement must have been lucrative. At the height of the business, in the period of transition involving Shaukat and Safraz, indications were that crew members were making up to 60 to 70 unit deals per day, serving customers who were occasional £15 unit users up to those with £100-per-day habits. An income of £1,500 per day was routinely reported. This scale of business gives some indication of the size and value of the market, though demand could fall just as significantly.

In this crew, the first of several subsequent and inter-linked groupings, Hakim saw his role as "chief executive." Shaukat, before his removal, had constructed a position as day-to-day managing director by overseeing the overall pattern of street-trade; and Safraz now joined the team as a kind of "management-trainee," and coordinated street-trade after Shaukat's fall. Hakim's small inner-circle also included a few other close friends and relations who were advisors and hangers-on. At the level beneath Shaukat and Safraz, a small number of street-level distributors were trusted with several sales units at a time. In turn, these personnel distributed units to small-scale user-dealers for use and sale (Johnson et al., 1985). Generally speaking, as far as we could ascertain, the street-level dealers with no management responsibility were not recruited on the basis of friendship or kin connections but in terms of reliability on the street.

The Organisation of Business

The selection criteria for street-level distribution employees in Hakim's business (and for those who followed in other crews), emphasised, (1) trustworthiness; (2) willingness and ability to execute operations in an effective and successful manner; and (3) physical ability to defend business interests. On the latter point, it is interesting to note that all the personnel recruited into dealing operations were physically weaker than their bosses and that control was a criterion in assessing suitability for recruitment. Selection of personnel would not take place if potential recruits were perceived to be physically stronger than their prospective employers and, hence, a potential threat. Physical power was emphasised as central to management control techniques.

At the same time, physical weakness had no value. Being part of a crew implied having the strength to at least display a show of force if the need arose to protect the enterprise. The crew bosses were unquestionably willing and able to fend off a physical assault on their commercial interests (whether from desperate and potentially violent heroin addicts or any predator out to steal drug profits). But only by acting organisationally as "a crew" could groups successfully regulate and enforce their business interests.

The Beginning of the End

The collapse of the heroin-distribution crews and their networks was not a result of the attentions of the police but from what was described as "the dishonouring of friendships" and business arrangements resulting in disagreements between Hakim, his employees, supplier and rivals.

Fall-out

A dishonoured agreement about the division of the market lay at the root of the fall-out. Hakim had helped establish his close friend Anwar in the £15 street market business on the understanding that, even if he built a successful crew of his own, he would not encroach on the £25 and £50 unit market. Anwar had barely been operating for two months when allegations that he was overstepping the agreed boundary began to surface. As a result, animosity developed between Hakim and Anwar. Although initially there was no face-to-face confrontation, all were aware of the new tension. As Hakim began to see his trade falling, and angered by rumours that Anwar was selling £25 and £50 sales units, he eventually confronted Anwar in person. Anwar strenuously denied the allegations but Hakim remained unconvinced and made it clear to Anwar that he would begin to sell £15 street units. Anwar responded by stating that this would force him to sell £25 and £50 bags. (See note 19 on value of units.) This was to become the turning point in their friendship. Money, greed and market-share had become the central issues.

Hakim: "I fucking set him up and that's how he pays me back." By now Hakim considered Anwar a direct threat to his operation by encroaching on his territory and poaching his business. On the other hand, Anwar was making good money and felt unable to turn away trade, especially when Hakim stated that he would begin to sell £15 bags. Anwar: "It's hard turning away money, if they're coming to me why shouldn't I sort 'em out?"

Although there was considerable animosity between Hakim and Anwar, they remained in contact. Disagreement, however, was firmly established. Dishonour and mistrust now characterised relationships. Among employees of Hakim, themselves part of the friendship network involving Hakim and Anwar, disagreement and split loyalties followed. The resulting fragmentation and dispute within the local drugs market was highly disruptive. Thereafter, vulnerability to the attentions of the police and their use of informants was greatly enhanced.

ANALYSIS AND DISCUSSION

We cannot present here a full picture of the activities and intrigues, complementarity and competition among rival crews in the study locality. We have only been able to provide an introductory picture. Nonetheless various themes for discussion emerge.

(i) Cultures of the Oppressed

Honour and Friendship

Many of the key participants in the new, heroin-dealing businesses had grown up and gone to school together, they were "friends from way back" and while kinship was important, so, too, was the honouring of friendship. Within the group, close friendship was equated with "having a good time" — and now having the money to pay for this! — as well as "knowing who you could trust," or that was the theory. Friendship was also important, of course, for external reasons: to present a united front and assert an identity when confronting dominant society, which was largely seen as racist and exclusionary.

The "Establishment" and "Officialdom" — The Enemy

The groups distrusted and had no respect for official law and authority, particularly the police. All were perceived as racist and part of a "white establishment." Perceptions were shaped by a mix of sociocultural street-level folklore (Keith, 1993) and the individual subjective experiences of police racism and racism of other public/official institutions.[21] Racism was *the* central issue. Without exception, all those observed were conscious of their ethnicity and identity and of their attribution of a secondary status by mainstream society. Mistrust among young Asian males in the drugs scene was abundant at times, related to business and territory. This was quite different to mistrust of the white "establishment" and "officialdom":

> You know so'mat, Pakis can't do shit in this town without being busted. How many Goray [whites] do you know who have been sellin' all kinds of shit for life and they haven't got busted? Tell me so'mat, why is it whenever a Paki tries to do so'mat, they get busted straight away? I'll tell you why, cause racist redneck pigs are always try'in to keep Pakis in their place, that's why...it's well on top for Pakis [Anwar].

Police were viewed as "pigs" and as racist, trying to "keep Pakis in their place." Asian youths reported that they were treated unfairly compared to white youths. This opinion, reported in local press stories on "police-community" liaison meetings, was supported by views of nondeviant, young Asian males.

Mirza and Karim: "Gangsta Rap" Aspirations — "Keeping it Real, Know How I Feel"

Some others engaged in the drug dealing culture, such as Mirza and Karim (members of a different business), had lifestyle aspirations borrowed from American gangsta rappers: "living life in the fast lane," portraying themselves as "coming from the ghetto." Their conversation focused on: (1) which local figures were successes in their eyes and which ones were not; (2) "machismo stuff" concerning how "tuff" [sic] a person is; and (3) conversations focused on their own material ambitions. Although they "dissed" (cursed) people who did not fit their description of a "street-wise, superfly guy," they did not take kindly to reciprocal verbal banter that they could not counter. This inability tarnished their street-smart, public image so essential to their sense of status. Mirza and Karim saw those in everyday legal employment as "suckers" and instead respected "gangstas, thugs and smugglers."[22] Since they perceived society to be oppressive, particularly toward ethnic minorities, those who defied laws and conventions for their own ends were "respected."

Younger than the other heroin dealers, and heavily influenced by Afro-American rap, gangsta and hip-hop music, film and fashion, Mirza and Karim consciously constructed identities based upon a fusion of these sources and their own ethnic background (Hebdige, 1979). In the absence of an Asian "cool cat" role model (Finestone, 1957) other than Bollywood (South Asian) movie stars, they tried to emulate in every manner possible, Afro-American urban/ghetto/ street youth culture.

(ii) Drug Markets and Dealers

"Playaz": Being a Player — Style and Form

The perception of being a "player" meant that one was able to look after oneself. A player was a "handy lad" and "game" (i.e., one who would be "ready and willing" to fight if trouble came along). Hence, in order to be a player, one had to be able to take care of oneself, successfully "take care of business," and also fend off potential predators.

For some, "image" was also thought to be a vital component in the role of being a player. Appropriate dress and "presentation of self" (Goffman, 1971) were essential elements in constructing street credibility, and as important for some as street knowledge. If one did not have the necessary street credentials, such as identification as a "hard man" who "knows the score" and was willing to employ violence, one could at least attempt to fake the image through style and dress codes.

Entrepreneuriality and Illicit Markets: "Who Says it's Easy Money? Those Who Deal or Those Who Don't?"

All involved in the businesses at an organisational level argued that the money they were making was good and was more than they would be making in lawful work. However, most, though not all, qualified the observation by saying that the notion that this was "easy money" was certainly not the case. Although street talk would often refer to: "easy money," "good money" and "a nice little earner," discussion and observation revealed these were bravado statements implying how well the speaker was doing. In fact such talk ironically covered-up the considerable work that went into running a dealing enterprise:

> You know so'mat, everyone [other than heroin dealers] thinks it's easy money but it isn't. I'm running around sweating, honestly, watching out for the junkies and pigs. Sometimes I'm so fucking paranoid that my minds working overtime. Too much going on in mi head, hard to control, that's paranoia for ya. Or is it cautiousness? I can't tell the difference anymore. The only time I'm relaxing is when I've clocked off and I've got nowt on mi. Even when I go to bed, sometimes I can't fucking sleep.

People think it's easy money, saying so an so's making good money, but you know so'mat, it ain't like that. I'd like to see them doin it, see how much balls they've got, then tell us it's easy money. It might be quick money, but I wouldn't say it's easy, I can tell you that. Well for me anyway [Karim].

Most of the organisers and distributors concerned suffered from episodes of paranoia. Given the illegal nature of the trade and that many of their clients were — sooner or later — likely to encounter the police, the majority suspected that some of their clients were "grasses" (informers; Dorn et al., 1992; Greer and South, 1998). Consequently they would often err on the side of caution when dealing with some individuals. However, care was taken not to identify someone as a "grass" unless one could prove the accusation. Suspicion was often provoked by an arrest followed by a surprisingly speedy release on police bail or the dropping or reduction of the severity of the charge. Most of the organisers felt they had a good idea which heroin addicts were "grassers" and those whom they thought were "all right" and "safe." Those who were seen to be "shady" were kept at arm's length. Paranoia is part and parcel of the drugs trade.

POLICY IMPLICATIONS

Fragmenting Drug Markets

The outcome of the events described above was the fragmentation of the local market. Significantly, this was not in the manner described by Dorn et al. (1992), which can render market operatives elusive, security conscious and difficult targets for police intelligence gathering. Rather, in this case, fragmentation meant the breakdown of relationships and trust, resulting in interpersonal conflict that greatly enhanced vulnerability to enforcement attention. The already recognized implication for law-enforcement, is that market disruptions may be achieved by use of undercover agents and informers, but degrees of effectiveness are dependent upon the vulnerabilities of the dealer organisations. To identify and possibly exacerbate such vulnerabilities, strategies may involve generating intelligence and distributing disinformation with the aim of stimulating new or emerging mistrust and erosion of mutual support within networks. The significant point here is that, if the nature and scope of a market is largely an "unknown," then neither enforcement — nor aid services for drug users — will have much chance of successful intervention. Of course, as the eventual success of police operations showed, there is another "hidden story" here, one which given the nature of our study, we have not been privy to. This is the history of police intelligence gathering, targeting and eventual action against the crews. Even so, the chronology of events suggests that prior to "fall-out" in the networks, police enforcement intervention was difficult to operationalize.

Social Capital and Institutional Racism

Recent work in the sociological and political science literatures has drawn attention to the notion of "social capital" as a source of community resources and strength:

> The premise is that the social networks generated by...patterns of sociability constitute an important form of "social capital" in the sense that they increase the trust that individuals feel towards others and enhance their capacity to join together in collective action to resolve common problems or to ensure that governments address such problems....Social capital is said to facilitate effective participation in politics, the implementation of many kinds of public policy, and generalized support for the political system [Hall, 1999:418].

However, in deprived communities facing various forms of social exclusion and institutional racism (Macpherson, 1999; Younge, 1999) such social capital is hard to identify, and lack of confidence in the political and policing processes is palpable. Resources and initiatives provided by families, the community, and by statutory or non-statutory services, face particularly difficult challenges where drug dealing and misuse, generational tensions, and distrust of police and the political establishment, are combined. Clearly, there are major questions of social policy and social justice that might be raised here but space precludes such discussion. For now, it seems clear from the case study presented that in an area where distrust of the police seems so strong, at least among young people, strategies aimed at policing drug — or other illicit — markets will meet with little assistance from the community. Since such strategies are usually information-dependent, police operations will be seriously hampered. In this study, police success was only made possible by the supply of information, which followed internal dispute and distrust in the dealing networks.

CONCLUSION

This study suggests there has been a "hidden history" of heroin use and dealing in England. Members of the community studied here have kinship and social links with other young men in other parts of the country, (e.g., a Thames Valley city and parts of West London). Field visits by the fieldworker for this and other projects (Akhtar et al., 1997), confirmed parallel, modest-to-heavy heroin user and dealer careers among South Asian young men in these areas. Yet the "official" history has been unable to record and reflect such developments. Perhaps problems arose because of difficulties of access, because of lack of funding (a problem this project has faced), or because of "political correctness" and sensitivity about research that associates minorities with criminal activities and social problems (Ruggiero and South, 1995;1997).

In the past, data from U.K. survey-based research has consistently suggested that self-reported drug use among Asians of Bangladeshi, Indian and Pakistani descent is low. However, more recent data derived from the 1994 British Crime Survey, show interesting variations regarding the results for young Asians. As Pearson and Patel (1998:203-4) note:

> Although their reported levels remain lower than average on some measures, the gap appears to be closing between them and other groups. Moreover, where self-reported heroin use is concerned, the rate for Pakistani and Bangladeshi respondents is four times higher than that for whites (Ramsay and Percy, 1996:57-60). This finding is so much out of line with the consistent trends identified by earlier research that it must be treated with caution. If further exploration should confirm that heroin use is much more prevalent among young Asians, however, this would suggest that there might be substantial numbers of Asian opiate users unknown to service agencies.

Quite so! This study cannot quantify a hidden population of Asian heroin and/or other drug users. However, it most certainly provides some qualitative evidence about the erroneous assumptions concerning the limited experience, use and dealing of heroin within Asian communities and that there is a "hidden history" of heroin use and dealing in the U.K., which is yet to be fully documented.

Address correspondence to: Nigel South, Professor of Sociology and Director, Health and Social Services Institute, University of Essex, Wivenhoe Park, Colchester, Essex CO4 3SQ, England. E-mail: soutn@essex.ac.uk

REFERENCES

Akhtar, S., R. Nightingale and N. South (1997). *Drugs, Unemployment and Unemployability.* (Project Report). Colchester, UK: Health and Social Services Institute, University of Essex.

Awiah, J., S. Butt and N. Dorn (1990). "'The Last Place I Would Go': Black People and Drug Services In Britain." *Druglink* 5(5):14-15.

Benzeval, M., K. Judge and C. Smaje (1995). "Beyond Class, Race and Ethnicity: Deprivation and Health in Britain." *Health Service Research: The Role of Race and Ethnicity in Health Service Research* 30, (1): part 2.

Bourgois, P. (1995). *In Search of Respect: Selling Crack in El Barrio.* Cambridge, UK: Cambridge University Press.

Cloward, R. (1959). "Illegitimate Means, Anomie, and Deviant Behavior." *American Sociological Review* 24(2):164-76.

—— and L. Ohlin (1960). *Delinquency and Opportunity: A Theory of Delinquent Gangs.* New York, NY: Free Press.

Collison, M. (1996). "In Search of the High Life: Drugs, Crime, Masculinities and Consumption." *British Journal of Criminology* 36(3):428-44.

—— (1994). "Drug Offenders and Criminal Justice: Careers, Compulsion, Commitment and Penalty." *Crime, Law and Social Change* 24(2):49-71.

Dorn, N., K. Murji and N. South (1992). *Traffickers: Drug Markets and Law Enforcement.* London, UK: Routledge.

—— and N. South (eds.) (1987). *A Land Fit for Heroin? Drug Policies, Prevention and Practice.* London, UK: Macmillan.

Duster, T. (1987). "Crime, Youth Unemployment and the Black Urban Underclass." *Crime & Delinquency* 33(2):300-316.

Finestone, H. (1957). "Cats, Kicks and Color." *Social Problems* 5(1):3-13.

Fitzgerald, M. (1990). "Crime: An Ethnic Question?" *Research Bulletin* 28: 33-37. London, UK: Home Office, Research and Statistics Department.

Greer, S. and N. South (1998). "The Criminal Informant: Police Management, Supervision and Control." In: S. Field and C. Pelser (eds.), *Invading the Private: State Accountability and New Investigative Methods in Europe.* Aldershot, UK: Ashgate.

Goffman, E. (1971). *The Presentation of Self in Everyday Life.* Harmonsdworth, UK: Penguin.

Hall, P. (1999). "Social Capital in Britain." *British Journal of Political Science* 29:417-461.

Hebdige, D. (1979). *Subculture: The Meaning of Style.* London, UK: Methuen.

Hobbs, D. (1995). *Bad Business.* Oxford, UK: Oxford University Press.

—— (1988). *Doing the Business: Entrepreneurship, the Working Class and Detectives in East London.* Oxford, UK: Clarendon Press.

Hough, M. (1996). *Drugs Misuse and the Criminal Justice System: A Review of the Literature.* London, UK: Home Office, Drugs Prevention Initiative.

Johnson, B., P. Goldstein, E. Preble, J. Schmeidler, D. Lipton, B. Spunt and T. Miller (1985). *Taking Care of Business: The Economics of Crime by Heroin Abusers.* Lexington, MA: Lexington Books.

Keith, M. (1993). *Race, Riots and Policing: Lore and Disorder in a Multiracist Society.* London, UK: UCL Press.

Lewis, R., R. Hartnoll, S. Bryer, E. Daviaud and M. Mitcheson (1985). "Scoring Smack: The Illicit Heroin Market in London, 1980-1983." *British Journal of Addiction* 80(3):281-290.

Maher, L. (1997). *Sexed Work: Gender, Race and Resistance in a Brooklyn Drug Market.* Oxford, UK: Clarendon Press.

Messerschmidt, J. (1993). *Masculinities and Crime.* Lanham, MD: Rowman and Littlefield.

Macpherson, W. (1999). *The Stephen Lawrence Inquiry: Report of an Inquiry by Sir William Macpherson of Cluny.* London, UK: The Stationery Office, CM 4262.

Miles, R. (1989). *Racism.* London, UK: Routledge.

Mills, C.W. (1940). "Situated Actions and Vocabularies of Motive." *American Sociological Review* 5(6):904-913.

Murji, K. (1999). "White Lines: Culture, Race and Drugs." In: N. South (ed.), *Drugs: Cultures, Controls and Everyday Life.* Thousand Oaks, CA: Sage.

Pearson, G. (1993). "Varieties of Ethnography: Limits and Possibilities in the Field of Illegal Drug Use." In: H.F.L. Garretson et al. (eds.), *Illegal Drug Use: Research Methods for Hidden Populations.* Rotterdam, NETH: Netherlands Institute on Alcohol and Drugs.

—— (1991). "Drug Control Policies in Britain." In: M. Tonry and N. Morris (eds.) *Crime and Justice: A Review of Research,* vol.14. Chicago, IL: University of Chicago Press.

—— (1987). *The New Heroin Users.* Oxford, UK: Blackwell.

—— and K. Patel (1998). "Drugs, Deprivation and Ethnicity: Outreach among Asian Drug Users in a Northern English City." *Journal of Drug Issues* 28(1):199-224.

Plummer, K. (1995). *Telling Sexual* Stories. London, UK: Routledge.

Ramsay, M. and A. Percy (1996). *Drug Misuse Declared: Results of the 1994 British Crime Survey.* (Home Office Research Study #151.) London, UK: Home Office.

Ruggiero, V. and N. South (1995). *Eurodrugs: Drug Use, Markets and Trafficking in Europe.* London, UK: UCL Press.

—— (1997). "The Late-modern City as a Bazaar: Drug Markets, Illegal Enterprise and 'The Barricades.'" *British Journal of Sociology* 48(1):55-71.

Said, E. (1991). *Orientalism.* Harmondsworth, UK: Penguin.

South, N. (1997). "Drugs: Use, Crime and Control." In: M. Maguire, R. Morgan and R. Reiner (eds.), *The Oxford Handbook of Criminology* (2nd ed.). Oxford, UK: Oxford University Press.

Sykes, G. and D. Matza (1957). "Techniques of Neutralization: A Theory of Delinquency." *American Sociological Review* 22(6):664-670.

Taylor, A. (1993). *Women Drug Users.* Oxford, UK: Clarendon Press.

Webster, C. (1997). "The Construction of British 'Asian' Criminality." *International Journal of the Sociology of the Law* 25(1):65-86.

—— (1996). "Asian Young People and Drug Use." *Criminal Justice Matters* 24(Summer):11-12.

Williams, M. and D. Farne (1992). *Cotton Mills in Greater Manchester.* Preston, UK: Carnegie Publishing.

Younge, G. (1999). "The Death of Stephen Lawrence: The Macpherson Report." *Political Quarterly* 70(3):329-334.

NOTES

1. This paper reports early work arising from the project. Further field-work is planned and analysis of other material is ongoing.

2. The terms Asian(s) and Asian youth refer to British residents whose ancestry lies in the Indian sub-continent, (especially Pakistani Muslims from the state of Punjab and province of Mirpur), including those, as well as their descendants, who came from the Indian sub-continent directly or via other countries. We are aware of controversy regarding the broad use of the term "Asian" to categorise people. Benzeval et al., (1995) con-

tend that the inevitable tendency of ethnic taxonomies to aggregate heterogeneous groups of people into single categories obscures significant variation. See Benzeval et al., (1995).

3. Source: *1991 Census - Local Base Statistics*, London, UK: Her Majesty's Stationery Office.

4. For definitions of "racialisation" and "criminalising" see: Miles, 1989; see also Webster, 1996. More recently, the Macpherson Report (1999) has drawn attention to the institutional nature of racism within the British police service, an analysis quickly extended by many commentators to other key institutions of society (Younge, 1999).

5. For an understanding of the social constructions and defining of the Orient, hence "otherness," see Said (1991).

6. We emphasise that the researcher was as close to "the action" and operation as one could get without actually being actively involved in the enterprise. However, the researcher established a firm line to avoid participation. This does mean that, while we have a great deal of background information, some more sensitive details were not revealed.

7. Pearson and Patel [1998] discuss the issue of "the missing minorities" in drug-related research in the U.K.

8. The anonymous reviewer of this article observed that in a study of heroin dealing in Bradford, the importers from the Asian community usually dealt the drug away from their own community. The heroin, however, was then sold back into the Asian community by white dealers from outside.

9. Other illicit means employed to support heroin use included: car crimes (theft of car stereo equipment and/or the car itself for the purpose of selling spare parts or "ringing"); house burglaries; shoplifting; and the occasional "armed blag" (armed robbery).

10. The prescribing of methadone and the operation of a needle-exchange scheme must have generated some statistics for the Health Authority and other agencies. What seems strange is that no specific research or public health attention seems to have followed submission of data indicating intravenous drug injection in a predominantly Asian area. One explanation seems to be that, given suspicion of white establishment systems of authority and surveillance, only a relative few chronic Asian users employed the syringe exchange (in any case an anonymized system). In-

stead, most users apparently obtained their works from other users, including white users.

11. Although the mount was described as "the" symbolic meeting location for Asian street youth, this had not always been the case. Previously, a local community centre served this purpose. However since its closure by a local authority as a cost-cutting measure, little was left by way of locally accessible recreational facilities for Asian youth or a place to sit, relax and pass time conversing with friends and acquaintances.

12 "Bread-head" is a street term in common use in Manchester, Liverpool and elsewhere. It describes preoccupation with the sale of heroin for profit rather than to sustain personal consumption ("bread" denotes money, and "head" refers to person.)

13. From: "Pusherman." This is a reference to a song from the film *Superfly* (Curtis Mayfield, Curtom Records 1972).

14. Hakim was one of the main subjects in the study and a key "broker" for the research.

15. In this environment, heroin was mainly used by "chasing," although some subsequently turned to intravenous use. The local culture did not embrace smoking heroin in a spliff (cigarette mixing tobacco and drug) as is reportedly common in the Asian drug scene in parts of west London. This process of heroin administration is conducted by placing a quantity of heroin on a piece of foil. The heroin is then cooked by placing a flame directly beneath the heroin powder in order to heat it until it turns into a liquid, care being taken not to burn it. With the aid of a pipe instrument (usually another piece of foil rolled into a cylindrical tube) the heroin liquid is chased from one end of the foil to the other, aided by running a flame underneath the foil in order to help chase the heroin. The fumes resulting from the burning of heroin are then inhaled. The inhalation of fumes deep into the lungs would get one high. Often a "puff" of a cigarette would accompany the inhalation of heroin fumes. This would be undertaken directly after, and between every inhalation of lines, in order to ensure the precious heroin fumes went into the lungs. Another name for this mode of ingestion is "tooting."

16. Most of these users were either on unemployment benefit, had low-paid, menial jobs in textile and clothing factories or were minicab drivers. Hakim held jobs as a minicab driver and textile worker in between periods of unemployment after dropping out of college.

17. The dealers did not use any particular term for their business operation. Crew is used here as a term familiar on the streets at the time and is still used. It also conveys the image of individual friends coming together to "take care of business" (Johnson et al., 1985).

18. From the moment Hakim engaged in the heroin-dealing culture, the money earned afforded him a lifestyle he craved and an ability to entertain. Cocaine and ecstasy were occasionally used as celebratory drugs by Hakim and associates. They always ate at restaurants and Hakim paid for those around him. This ability to entertain attracted free riders. Throughout the course of his dealing career, those who knew Hakim (and even those who didn't) endeavoured to socialise with him.

19. Of course, "units" had already been skimmed to create a profit, so customers were being given "short-weight" twice over. In the mid-1990s, a £15 unit should have been .25g but was skimmed to .2g; a £25 unit should have been .5g but was skimmed to between .4 and .45g; a £50 unit should have been 1g but was skimmed to .8g. These prices and weights obviously fluctuated but they roughly correspond to Hough's (1996:12) assessment of street pricing at this time: "Dependent heroin use generally ranges from a third of a gram to a gram a day. Street prices of £80 per gram are often quoted, although anecdotal evidence suggests a sharp fall in price in the north-west of England at least, with current prices [in 1995-96] of £10 a bag (putatively a quarter of a gram). Thus a dependent user might have to lay hands upon a minimum of £70 per week, rising to £300 or more for heavy users paying top prices."

20. At this point the sales preparation took place in Hakim's attic. Occasionally Safraz, Anwar and Razaq would also be present.

21. Such streetlore and subjective knowledge were shaped by a long accumulation of experiences of racist victimization, inadequate police protection, and perceptions of the police as more sympathetic to racists than minorities. The confrontation of National Front racists by the Asian residents of Southall on 23rd April 1979 was an early expression of resistance to these experiences. More recently, the outcome of the Inquiry into the Death of Stephen Lawrence (a young black man murdered by a gang of white youths) has concluded that racism is institutionalised in parts of the police and other public services in Britain (Macpherson, 1999).

22. Taken from the song "White Lines" by Grandmaster Flash, Melle Mel and the Furious Five, 1984.

SWEDISH DRUG MARKETS AND DRUGS POLICY

by

Johannes Knutsson
National Police Academy, Norway

Abstract: *This chapter offers an analysis of the consequences of the introduction of a Swedish drug policy in which police actively started targeting street markets in the beginning of the 1980s. The experience in Stockholm is used as an example, and two studies of the intervention against street markets have been examined. Additonal survey information is used to consider possible long-range preventive effects of the changed policy.*

INTRODUCTION

This chapter presents an analysis of the impact of a change in Swedish drug policy made in the early 1980s. Previously, enforcement efforts had concentrated on disruption of supply; the new policy involved demand-reduction brought about by the active disruption by the police of retail drug markets. The chapter focuses on experience in Stockholm. Availability of data and other factors limit the analysis to the period running from the beginning of the 1970s to the early 1990s. The chapter uses two evaluations of operations against street markets as cornerstones in its argument. It draws on additional data from the police and from surveys to consider possible long-range preventive effects of the changed policy. The ultimate question is whether the shift has decreased the level of abuse.

Crime Prevention Studies, volume 11, pp. 179-201

THE EVOLUTION OF DRUG MISUSE IN SWEDEN

Misuse of drugs emerged as a significant social problem in Sweden in the late 1950s. Initially amphetamine was the primary substance misused — a drug still playing a central role in the Swedish drug problem. At that time misuse was regarded as a medical-treatment problem (Olsson, 1984). Efforts were made to make doctors more restrictive when prescribing drugs. For a short period during the 1960s, a program of legal drug prescription was tried. In the wake of the program, use rapidly increased, especially among persons with a criminal background, and the program was soon suspended (Bejerot, 1977; Olsson, 1995). Cannabis was first used by jazz musicians during the 1950s and became popular among young people in the late 60s (Bejerot, 1968). Misuse of opiates was restricted to few drug addicts until the 1970s, when heroin use became more widespread. Cocaine has so far not been considered a significant problem in Sweden. During the last few years use of ecstasy and similar drugs has become established in some youth subcultures. There are clear indications that use of cannabis has increased among school pupils from the mid 1990s (Andersson et al., 1998). The same trend can also be seen among armed forces conscripts (Guttormsson, 1998).

Ever since the rapid spread of drug misuse in the early 1960s, criminality and drugs have been intertwined. In a study of the remand prison of Stockholm (Bejerot, 1975), the proportion of remand prisoners with physical signs of injecting drugs increased from about 20% in 1965 to about 50% in 1972 (Bejerot, 1979). Two studies on persistent offenders in Stockholm — one on household burglars and the other on cheque forgers — showed that about half were drug injectors (Knutsson and Kühlhorn, 1980; Persson, 1976).

CRIMINAL POLICY ON DRUGS

Sweden saw several changes in drug legislation in the 1960s and 1970s. Swedish legislators regard the stated maximum penalty as an important declaratory signal. In 1965, with the introduction of a new Penal Code, the maximum penalty for drugs offences was reduced from two to one year's imprisonment. However, when a new Narcotic Drugs Acts was enacted in 1968, the maximum penalty for aggravated cases was increased to four years. A year later the maximum penalty was increased again, this time to six years, and only three years later, in 1972, it was increased yet again to ten years. The last two reforms were designed to harmonize Swedish legislation with international standards for drug trafficking penalties.

A period of legislative calm followed until 1981. Then the maximum penalty for aggravated offences committed by repeat offenders was increased to 16 years. In 1985 a further amendment to the legislation was designed to signal the gravity of drugs offences in general. The least serious offence category was upgraded to Petty Offence from Misdemeanor and imprisonment was added to the list of sentencing options. For more serious offences, fines were removed from the sentencing options.

A controversial question has been whether misuse in itself should be considered a crime. Until 1988 it was illegal to produce, distribute, sell and posses drugs, but not to use drugs. In 1988 consumption became a punishable act. The offense was punishable only by fine, and this Swedish legislation severely limited the means by which the police could gather evidence of consumption. The legislation was intended to have a declaratory function, signalling the gravity of illegal drug use. This message was implicitly directed towards young people who might consider experimental use. Finally, in 1993, imprisonment was included as a sentencing option for consumption of drugs, making it possible for the police to collect evidence of use.

Instructions to Prosecutors

In the sphere of drugs, the instructions issued to prosecutors by the Prosecutor General have been very important in shaping prosecutorial — and thus police — practice. The Prosecutor General issued four Letters of Instructions between 1968 and 1972 directing prosecutors to waive prosecution for possession of drugs that were reckoned to be for personal use. The four letters progressively raised the threshold below which quantities should be regarded as for personal use. The 1971 letter included an explicit reference to "Labeling Theory," which was very influential at that time (Knutsson, 1977). It was assumed that novice or experimental users who were diverted from punishment would be spared the fate of being labeled as drug addicts, and that this would reduce the chances that they would be driven into careers as drug misusers.

During the 1970s there was a fierce and highly polarised debate over drugs policy. On the one side were those who looked upon drug addiction primarily as a social problem and favored treatment as the cure. On the other were those who favored a restrictive policy, aiming at reducing demand and availability by strict enforcement. Those favouring treatment dominated in the early 1970s. Their arguments shaped the practice of prosecutors, which in turn discouraged the police from focussing on drug dealing at street level. Towards the end of the 1970s, the second group got the upper hand. This is evident from instructions given to prosecutors. The Chief Prosecutor in Stockholm, where the problem was most serious, decided in 1977 that waiver of prosecution should not be used for the possession of heroin and cocaine, even for small amounts that were for personal use. Finally in 1980 the Prosecutor General reversed his position, deciding that waiver of prosecution for the possession of drugs should be the exception and not the rule. He issued an instruction that prosecution should be waived only in cases that were obviously minor, such as possession by first offenders of very small amounts. He argued that this would have the effect of decreasing availability of drugs, which would encourage drug addicts to get treatment and, crucially, would decrease the spread of illegal substances. He concluded that only actions targeting the distribution of drugs at retail level would have a significant impact on availability.

The Police

When the police were reorganised in 1965 from a local to a national system, a central drugs unit was created at the National Swedish Police Board. Previously, the main drug-related problems facing the police were burglaries of pharmacies and the forging of prescriptions. With the growth of drug misuse the National Police Board organized a countrywide operation against drug-related crime in 1969. About 750 police took part in the operation. This amounted to a short-term, fivefold increase in numbers of officers engaged in drug policing. However, probably reflecting the prevailing drug policy, the resources allocated to drug work steadily decreased between 1970 and 1975.

The downward trend was reversed in 1976 when county-level drugs units were set up, with a consequent increase in manpower assigned to drug work. This marked the start of a new era with a new preventive strategy. Previously the strategy had been to reduce supply by targeting traffickers and large-scale suppliers. Consumption was defined as a treatment problem, and not a real police issue. Towards the end of the 1970s and at the start of the 1980s the police started to target retail drug markets at street level with the aim of reducing availability and demand for drugs. The change in prosecutorial policy was critical in triggering this shift. Between 1980 and 1983, several centrally planned police operations took place. The drugs units were given even more resources and drug squads were created in some of the larger police forces specifically to target street markets.

DEVELOPMENT OF CONTROL POLICY — A SUMMARY

The development of Swedish drug-control policy can be summarized as falling into in five phases, described in Table 1 (Kühlhorn et al., 1996; but see Kassman, 1998).

Table 1: Characteristics of Control Policy

Period	Characteristics
Phase 1 to 1967	Efforts to decrease supply by control of medical prescription.
Phase 2 1968-1972	Stricter penal control. Increased maximum penalty from 1 year of imprisonment to 10 years. Generous use of waiver of prosecution for possession of illegal substance. Increase in police resources.
Phase 3 1973-1975	Decrease in police resources.
Phase 4 1976-1979	Tougher prosecution policy introduced by the Chief Prosecutor in Stockholm. Renewed increase in police resources.
Phase 5 1980-1992	More serious view on drug offences. Misuse criminalized. Letter from Prosecutor General restricting waiver of prosecution. Large increase in police resources. Police operations targeting street markets.

During the four first phases, with a possible exception for the police offensive in 1969, the strategy that dominated policing was supply reduction. It was only during Phase Five that demand reduction predominated. Subsequent developments are in accordance with the strict policy. In 1993 the police bought equipment to test suspects for drug misuse, and in 1996 a special "Rave Squad" was formed to tackle retail drug dealing in that environment.

It is beyond the scope of this work to explain the reasons for this shift in policy. However, it ought to be mentioned that in the late 1970s, there was pressure to change the principles that guided penal policy in general. It was argued that the previously ascendant treatment ideology had failed and that policy would be better guided by principles of general deterrence. The argument was not that treatment was ineffective at an individual level, but that it had the wrong declaratory effect. It was thought that strategies of general deterrence would serve more clearly to emphasize issues of values (National Council for Crime Prevention, 1979).

Figure 1 shows the impact of these legislative and policy changes on the criminal process. The figure presents statistics from 1973 to 1992 for the whole country. When interpreting the trends, it must be kept in mind that the police have a proactive relationship towards drug offences. To simplify, the number of cases detected and processed through the criminal process is a function primarily of levels of police activity (but see below).

Figure 1: Court Sentences and Waiver of Prosecution for Drug Offences, 1972-1992, Countrywide

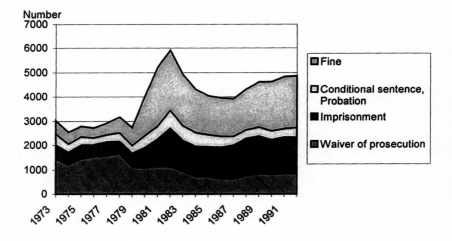

The number of cases dealt with more than doubled after the change in policy and the targeting of street markets in the early 1980s. After an initial surge, numbers declined in the mid 1980s, but remained at a considerably higher level than in the 1970s. With respect to variations in type of disposal, waivers of prosecution have decreased both in absolute and relative terms. Before the shift they accounted for about 50% of all cases; by 1992 they had fallen to around 18%. To a large extent fines seem to have replaced waivers of prosecution. Fines increased from just under 20% to about 40% of all disposals. The harshest punishment — imprisonment — grew from almost a fifth to almost a third of all disposals. The overall growth in numbers of cases processed ultimately reflected the changes in prosecutorial practice, which had a "knock on" effect on policing.[i]

THEORETICAL CONSIDERATIONS

The focus in this section is upon the long-term effects of the changes in the drug policy. The "preventive hypothesis" formulated by Kühlhorn et al. (1996) provides us with a useful starting point. The hypothesis is derived from a synthesis of the conventional theory of individual prevention and the theory of general deterrence.

According to the hypothesis, increased resources resulting in higher risks and stiffer penalties is presumed to limit the spread of the drug trade and the recruitment of new participants, and to reduce the attractiveness of drug use to existing users. Similarly, a decrease in the risks of discovery and punishment is assumed to stimulate the drug market by allowing it greater freedom of operation. Formulated in a more stringent form the hypothesis may be expressed in four propositions:

(1) Greater police enforcement raises the probability that a larger portion of drug offenders will be detected and identified.

(2) High risk of detection and threat of serious penalties means that engagement in drug trafficking begins when the individual has much to win and little to lose, i.e. when engagement in criminal activity has gone on for a long time and when the individual's experience of lost quality of life on detection and punishment weighs lightly in relation to the profits of dealing in drugs...

(3) Sales of drugs becomes concentrated to a network of older persons.

(4) Use of drugs begins at a later age, only a small number of new addicts are recruited [Kühlhorn et al., 1998:107].

The situational approach provides us with an alternative theoretical framework. The basic premise is that by manipulating different situational circumstances, people can be induced to abstain from committing illegal acts. One feature of the situational approach is its openness toward ideas of the causal processes leading to criminal acts. A distinction is made between what causes some persons to become more prone to commit crime — involvement — and circumstances that are related to situations in which the acts occur — the event (Cornish and Clarke, 1985). But there is an assumption within the situational perspective that thinking about crime has traditionally overemphasized the importance of more distant "dispositional" factors. If true this implies that the scope for effective preventive measures may have been underestimated. In the case of disrupting drug markets there are three potential preventive mechanisms (Clarke, 1997:18):

- *Increasing perceived effort*: Decreased availability will make it harder to get the sought-after drugs, which means that fewer will engage in the process of trying to get drugs.

- *Increasing perceived risks*: One of the primary goals with the changed policy is to increase both the risk of being apprehended and punished.

- *Removing excuses*: By making it clear that even the consumption of drug is a crime, it will be harder to neutralize the behavior.

From both perspectives it may be expected that the new policy would make drug markets more fragmented, less visible and more secluded, and that it will have its greatest impact on young persons. The vulnerability of juveniles is clearly stated in the preventive hypothesis, and it is implicit in the situational perspective that, because of their social situation, young persons are more amenable to situational measures.

THE INTERVENTIONS

This section draws on two evaluation studies: *Deprivation of Freedom and the Police — An Evaluation of the Temporary Custody Act —* (Kühlhorn, 1976) and "Restoring Public Order in a City Park" (Knutsson, 1997). The first evaluation includes a study of a police operation against drug misusers in Humlegården — a centrally situated park in Stockholm — in the beginning of the 70s. The second study consists of a focused study of an intervention against drug users in another of Stockholm's parks — Vasaparken — about 20 years later. Both studies are concerned with police operations towards street-level drug dealing. As will be clear from the preceding discussion, the operations took place in two very different policy contexts. During the first the "permissive" policy still prevailed; during the second the "restrictive" policy involving systematic police action against retail drug dealing had been in operation for a decade. Both operations can be regarded as "crackdowns." According to Sherman (1990), a crackdown consists of a temporary increase of police activities in a designated area for specific crimes considered to have been previously underenforced. The two studies consist of natural experiments, with all problems of making conclusions from evaluations with that type of design, which has occurred within a larger natural experiment.

The 1973 Humlegården Operation

The situation in Humlegården that led up to the operation was described by a contemporary observer:

> During July in 1972 the uniformed police noticed that in a short period of time, a considerable increase in Humlegården in the number of juveniles who were drunk or high on drugs. Youths gathered in gangs, smoked cannabis and drank beer. A lively market in drugs went on in the area....In the summer of 1973 the groups increased considerably. In the afternoons and evenings, as a rule, hundreds of youth gathered in Humlegården.... There was a serious problem of littering; the park amenities deteriorated, and the general public did not dare or did not want to visit the park, which, according to the police command, had become the center of the illegal drugs trade in Stockholm" [Bejerot et al., 1974:9-10].

According to police and social workers who had contact with drug users in the park, the main drug involved was cannabis, but amphetamine was also sold, with transactions often occurring quite openly.

As the situation in Humlegården failed to improve and complaints from local business and legitimate park users increased, the authorities decided to take action. The police assigned special uniformed patrols to the park. To restore public order, the police command decided to carry through an operation during the summer of 1973. All uniformed personnel from the local precinct took part. On a daily basis, as long as the campaign lasted, a detachment of about 20-30 officers patrolled the park intensively and arrested anyone who committed crimes or behaved in a disorderly way (including an attorney at law and some social workers). The Temporary Custody Act was extensively used. In short, the Act states that: "He who through his activities disturbs the public order or constitutes immediate threat to order, shall be detained by a police officer, if it is necessary for the maintenance of order. Such detention shall occur even when it is needed to ward off a prosecutable offense."

From June to August 1973, at the height of the operation, 1,467 persons were arrested in the park: 63% of these cases involved public-order offences, and 21% drug offences. However, even where arrests were for public order offences, the vast majority of those arrested were drug users — more than 80% according to one study (Bejerot et al., 1974).

During the operation the police used the powers that were then available. The way the Narcotic Drugs Act was practiced at that time, with waiver of prosecution for the possession of illegal drugs as the normal disposal, made it a somewhat unsuitable tool for the police. The typical outcome following arrest was detention in police custody for about two hours, followed by release. Drugs were always confiscated, regardless of the disposal of the case.

The police stopped the operation when they thought that the problem had been resolved, i.e., when the drug users left the park, the drug market had been dismantled and social order reestablished. The drug market, although fragmented, moved to other parts of the inner city. In the light of the data, I would argue that that the more a market becomes a well-established market, it will compound the problem by attracting both new buyers and new retail dealers. It is, therefore, wise to use a policy that disrupts and fragments markets.

The police operation gave rise to strong negative reactions from a pressure group representing the interests of drug addicts. It was claimed that the Temporary Custody Act was used in an arbitrary fashion and that the act restricted citizens' liberty. Some newspaper coverage followed in which the evaluation was criticized for being too uncritical towards the act.

The 1990 Vasaparken Operation

The Stockholm Police Force did not get a dedicated street-market unit until 1983. In 1991 the Stockholm County Police Force established a street-market unit covering the whole county. In practice, much of their work was carried out in the city of Stockholm. At the time of the intervention in Vasaparken, the drugs trade at street level was, according to the commander of the street-market unit, concentrated to two places in Stockholm. One was in the Center City Area (mainly Sergels Square) and the other in the park. In the Center City Area, on a daily basis, about 10-30 persons were engaged in drug dealing, mainly amphetamine and heroin.

Systematic observation was part of the evaluation of the police action in Vasaparken. From spring and until autumn of 1990, observers spent about 250 hours in the park. It is not as centrally situated as Humlegården, but is fairly easy to get to by subway. The situation in the park was described in the following way:

> Observers noted that the group of drug users was unusually hardy, congregating even in cold and inclement weather.... Their behaviors, such as loud, boisterous talking and public

urination, often intimidated legitimate users, who took pains to avoid passing the group.... The size of the group grew to an average of 15 to 20; sometimes as many as 30 gathered to smoke hashish.... Members engaged in drug sales discretely, with individuals leaving the group temporarily to conduct a transaction with a buyer [Knutsson, 1997:136].

The Swedish version of the report observed that: "Presumptive buyers were not always easy to identify. There were many remarks as to whether a person was a social worker looking for a client, a worried relative or a buyer" (Knutsson, 1995:6). Dealing centred on cannabis. In comparison with Humlegården, transactions were much less open.

At the time of the intervention in Vasaparken, reforms of the Narcotic Drugs Act and the way it was practiced made the act a suitable instrument for the police. To take care of the problem the street-peddling unit was temporarily increased by seven officers, bringing total strength to 18 officers during the spring of 1990. A "stationary method" tactic was employed. This involved covert observation in the park; the observers radioed descriptions of offenders to patrol officers outside the park, who then made arrests. During the operation 154 people were arrested for drug offences in or around the park. The park authorities also embarked on a program of work to assist in the restoration of order, redesigning parts of the park to make it less attractive for drug dealing.

Disposals differed according to the offence for which the person was arrested. The most common punishment was a fine for buyers and for the fewer sellers a short term in jail. Of course, the illegal substances were always confiscated — a consequence intensely disliked by the drug users.

Once the drug users had left the park and the drug market had been dismantled, the crackdown was discontinued. The general public appreciated the restoration of the public order, felt safer more secure, used the park more often and were more satisfied with the police.

The crackdown in Vasaparken seems to have displaced offenders to the inner-city and to other parts of Stockholm. Some offenders were arrested in another park on the outskirts of the city, where they tried to set up a new drug market (Ekenwall and Siipo, 1994). The location of the park, as well as the fact that it was used little by legitimate park users, made this author conclude that a spatial displacement had occurred but that the net effects of this were benign (cf., Eck, 1993; Barr and Pease, 1990).

According to the commander of the street market unit, the attempt to set up a new street market failed. In his opinion, the pressure by the Stockholm police force was so intense that it was a doomed enterprise from the outset.

The evaluation of the Vasaparken operation included an assessment of its perceived legitimacy. Strong support from the public was voiced for the activities of the police. The results of the evaluation were published in two major newspapers and caused no debate.

The Interventions — A Summing Up

It is evident that the street markets were quite different, and, if one accepts the opinion of the police, that retail drug markets had undergone a radical change. In the 1970s the Humlegården one was large scale, geographically focussed and located in the heart of Stockholm. In the 1990s the main street markets were the one in the city center and the Vasaparken one, which was small scale and situated away from the city center. The street market had transformed from a large-scale open market with hundreds of participants to a small and secluded setting. If this is not a result of the activities of the police, it must be argued that there is another reason: for example, the market imploded because of lack of interested customers, and this lack of interest had arisen independent of activities of law enforcement agencies.

In the theoretical section it was hypothesized that increased efforts to curb street dealing would affect mainly young persons, by limiting their involvement. This notion is supported by data on persons arrested during the actions (Ekenwall and Siipo, 1994; Bejerot et al., 1974). There is a considerable change in age structure, as Figure 2 shows.

More than half of those arrested in Humlegården were under 25. The corresponding figure for Vasaparken was 23%. The average age of those arrested during the crackdown in Humlegården was 26, while in Vasaparken it was 30.

LONG-TERM CHANGES REFLECTED BY POLICE DATA

The discussion so far has been limited to the situation at two points in time. In this section police data will be used to shed light on the long-term development. The data to be examined comprise statistics on police resources, on reported crimes and on suspects.

Figure 2: Age-Structure of Arrested Persons During Crackdown in Humlegärden 1974 and Vasaparken 1990

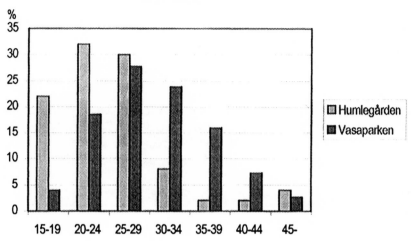

First we need to consider the relationship between police enforcement activity and crime statistics. In a situation with low rates of enforcement there will be relatively few reported crimes. When the police start targeting street markets and enforcement gets more intense, there will initially be an increase in the number of detected offenders and reported crimes. However, the market is likely to adapt to the increased risks, and dealing will be done more discretely, and in less public sites (see Edmunds et al., 1996). This means that it will be harder for the police to detect crimes, and, more to the point, the availability of drugs will decrease for those who do not have any connections with the drug scene. According to the hypotheses, the most vulnerable groups are youths, who will be exposed to a situation with more limited access to drugs. However, those who already have access to the market will continue to buy drugs.

Figure 3 shows trends in police resources allocated to drug work in the County of Stockholm. Increases in police resources reflect the police campaigns: the offensive in 1969 and the street-level operations at the start of the 1980s. The setting up of the street-market units in 1983 and 1991 is also noticeable. Figure 3 also displays the number of reported drug offences and number of suspects. Statistics on offences and suspects refer to the City of Stockholm alone.

There are three periods with sharp increases in police resources; each of these were accompanied by a growth in recorded drug offences, and, at least from 1975 when data were available, in numbers of suspects. The pattern is in accordance with what might be expected. The curves can be seen as an indication that risk of detection has increased, due to the new policy implemented in the 1980s. To engage in drug trafficking in an open setting in the 1990s was thus a far more risky enterprise than in the 1970s.

Figure 3: Number of Police Officers Assigned to Work with Drug Offences in the County of Stockholm, and Number of Recorded Drug Offences and Suspects in Stockholm, 1965 to 1992 (Suspects 1975-1992)

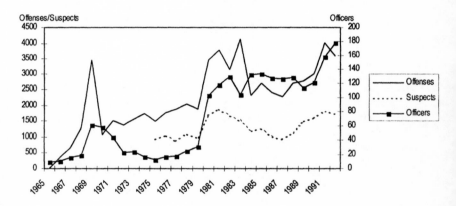

According to the hypotheses, younger persons should become less involved in drug markets as a consequence of the policy shifts. Information on trends in the age structure of suspects supports this notion. Figure 4 shows the annual number of drug offences, broken down by the age of the suspect. Information is available from the mid 1970s onward. There is some double-counting of offenders, since, during an interrogation suspects may have admitted to more than one crime, or may have been arrested more than once a year.

There is a sharp increase following the targeting of street markets in the beginning of the 1980s, followed by a new increase in 1983, when the street market units were formed. The background to the peak in 1987 for age group 25-29 is unclear. A possible explanation is that an exhaustive investigation of one ore more drug dealers resulted in a large number of recorded crimes. This upward trend beginning in the late 1980s may have been due to renewed efforts by the police. Age composition reveals a growth both in absolute and relative terms of persons older than 24 years of age. A similar reduction is apparent for younger persons.

Figure 4: Number of Crimes Committed by Suspects According to Age: Drug Offences, Stockholm, 1975-1992

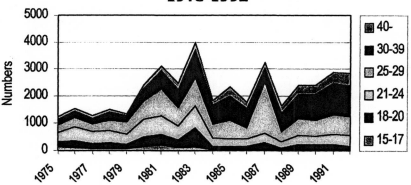

The three-year averages of numbers and proportions of crimes for drug offences for four age categories are displayed in Table 2. The data cover three periods: the mid 1970s, the early 1980s and the early 1990s. The periods have been selected to represent:

- A time when the police did not put much effort on street markets.
- The time when the police *started* targeting them.
- A time when the police had been targeting street markets for about a decade.

In the first period, those aged under 25 accounted for a considerable proportion of all crimes; altogether about 55%. During the offensive in the beginning of the 1980s, there was a marked increase in absolute numbers. This increase in all likelihood can be attributed to a larger risk of detection and not an increased level of dealing. But the proportion of crimes decreased for those under 25 to 40%. In the first years of the 1990s, despite even more marked activity by the police, there was a striking reduction both in absolute and relative numbers of younger persons involved in crimes. Together, in the last period, they account for about one fifth of all drug offenses among suspects. The decline is especially notable for those 15 to 17 years of age.

Table 2: Average Number and Proportion (%) of Drug Offences According to Age of Suspects, Stockholm, 1975-1977, 1981-1983 and 1990-1992

	15-17		18-20		21-24		25 and older		Total	
	n	(%)	n	(%)	n	(%)	n	(%)	n	(%)
1975-77	102	7.6	218	16.2	429	31.8	598	44.4	1,347	100.0
1981-83	145	4.5	456	14.3	660	20.7	1,926	60.4	3,187	100.0
1990-92	43	1.6	163	6.1	357	13.2	2,132	79.1	2,695	100.0

The pattern is what one would expect if there was a preventive effect. During the first period there were relatively few reported juveniles (and adults) when the risk of detection was low. Increases for all categories of age occurred during the second period as a result of a higher risk of detection, followed by a decrease of juveniles during the third period. In this chain of events, the reduction is an assumed result of the preventive effect.

SURVEY DATA ON LONG-TERM CHANGES

It has been noted that police data indicate as much about police activity as they do about drug dealing and thus they must be interpreted with caution. However, there are independent indicators supporting the view that there is a preventive effect.

In Stockholm, every third year since 1975, all pupils in 9th grade (14 to 15 year olds) are asked about their experience of drugs (for sources, see appendix). Figure 5 shows that in 1981 the proportion who had been offered cannabis for sale peaked at 44%; by 1987 the figure had fallen to 25%. The decline was most marked among those who had been offered drugs three or more times: from 22% in 1981 to 7% in 1987. A similar trend is shown for the use of cannabis in

Figure 6. The proportion using fell from above 20% in 1981 to less than 10% in 1993.

Figure 5: Percentage of 9th Grade Pupils Who Have Been Offered Cannabis or Other Drugs for Sale, by Frequency of Offer, Stockholm, 1975-1993

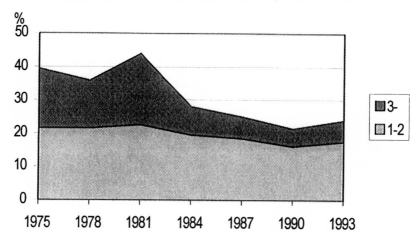

It is evident from Figure 6 that the decline is most apparent among frequent users. Of those who have used cannabis more than ten times, the proportion has decreased from 9% in 1981 to 2% in 1987. Thus, both exposure to and use of drugs among 9th graders in Stockholm have dramatically diminished after the onset of the policy.

Since the end of the 1960s, conscripts have been surveyed about their drug experience. (In Sweden military service is compulsory, and most people are 18 years old when they are conscripted.) The most commonly used drug is cannabis, and most of these users report first use in the year of enlistment or in the preceding year. The proportion of conscripts in the County of Stockholm with experience of drugs grew from about 20% in 1967 to a little less than 40% percent in 1973. After a decrease to 30% in 1976, there was a further increase to just below 40% in 1980. From that year on, there was a continual and very steep decline to about 14% in the mid-1980s. In 1992, the figure was just above 10% (Guttormsson, 1998).

If fewer young persons are exposed to drugs, it could mean that the basis for recruitment into careers as habitual drug misusers has diminished (Olsson, 1995). Two surveys investigating the prevalence of drug use have been conducted in the County of Stockholm; in each case the police and different authorities and organizations in the health- and social-care sectors were asked to give information about drug users known to them. The purpose of the surveys, carried out in 1979 and 1992, was to estimate number of drug addicts with heavy drug use. The results are shown in Table 3. Heavy use is defined as at least weekly use and/or injecting use.

Figure 6: Percentage of Pupils in 9th Grade Using Cannabis, By Frequency of Use, Stockholm, 1975-1993

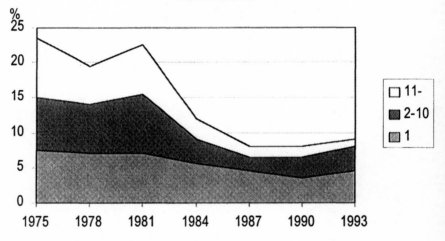

There is an increase in prevalence. However, this is not an unexpected finding since the drug epidemic is a fairly recent phenomenon. More interesting is the increase in age. This will occur if those who entered their drug careers earlier continue with their habit, in combination with a slowing down of new recruitment. That this is the case is indicated by the estimated lower value on incidence during the second nine-year period, which on the whole, entails the period when the new policy was introduced.

DEVELOPMENT

During the last few years a worrying development has taken place. Both in school- and conscript-surveys covering the whole country, far more young persons admit to having tried drugs, mainly cannabis. The levels are, however, much lower than in the beginning of the 70s (Guttormsson et al., 1999).

As yet, there is no firm information about the background to this development, except that it seems to be part of an international trend. Similar increases have also occurred in other countries. But Sweden differs in one important aspect. In an international survey conducted in 1995 comparing experience of drug use among juveniles in several countries, Sweden had conspicuous, lower levels than most other countries (Hibell et al., 1997). For example, the proportion who had used cannabis during the last 30 days was 1% in Sweden compared to 24% in the U.K. and 16% in the U.S. An interesting question is the extent to which the low Swedish level can be attributed to the proactive drugs policy. Comparisons between countries, and even cities, with different policies could be one way to get further information on this.

Table 3: Estimated Prevalence of Heavy Drug Misusers in the County of Stockholm, Age and Estimated Incidence (9th Grade) in 1979 and 1992

	1979	1992
Prevalence	3,424	4,727
Age		
Mean	28.6	34.3
Median	27	34
Incidence		
(9 years)	2,600	2,000

Source: Table 1, Kühlhorn et al., 1998:103.

DISCUSSION

In a situation like this, with a natural experiment occurring over a period of three decades, it is extremely difficult to isolate the impact of criminal policy measures and to assess their relative importance. Other factors have, of course, also been influential.

Over the last few decades Sweden has been transformed to a more open society where international influences have become far more salient. Partly it is a consequence of direct contacts in trade, tourism and immigration, etc., but also indirectly through cultural influences. These factors tend to increase the problem. New drugs have also been introduced, some of which have been aimed at younger persons.

The younger generations have, in contrast to the older ones, had the opportunity to witness the consequences of sustained drug misuse. The experiences of drug addicts are usually not very tempting, which could make it easier to abstain from drug use. The preventive efforts of schools and the social-care system must also be considered.

It is apparent that the liberal Swedish ideology about drugs dating from the 1970s developed into a far more restrictive one in the 1980s. Especially for juveniles, this change is probably an important factor. However, in the last few years, there seems to have been a shift towards a more permissive attitude again.

Still, there has been a marked turnaround in policy and police practice since the 1970s. The data presented here are consistent with the view that the new, tougher policies had preventive effects. It is impossible to make more far-reaching conclusions, but on the present evidence it would be unreasonable to accuse our politicians, who are ultimately responsible for the policies, of making unwise decisions.

Address correspondence to: Johannes Knutsson, National Police Academy, Norway, P.B. 5027 Mj., 0301 OSLO, Norway. E-mail: johannes.knutsson@politihs.no

REFERENCES

Andersson, B., K. Grönberg and B. Hibell (1998). *Skolelevers drogvanor 1997.* (Centralförbundet för alkohol-och narkotikaupplysning. Rapport #53.) Stockholm, SWE: Modintryck.

Barr, R. and K. Pease (1990). "Crime Placement, Displacement and Deflection." In: M. Tonry and N. Morris (eds.), *Crime and Justice: An*

Annual Review of Research, vol. 4. Chicago, IL: University of Chicago Press.

Bejerot, N. (1979). *Missbruk av alkohol, narkotika och frihet*. Stockholm, SWE: Ordfront.

—— (1977). *Narkotika och narkomani. 3:e upplagan*. Stockholm, SWE: Bonniers.

—— (1975). *Drug Abuse and Drug Policy. An Epidemiological and Methodological Study of Drug Abuse of Intravenous Type in the Stockholm Police Arrest Population 1965-1970 in Relation to Changes in Drug Policy*. Copenhagen, DK: Munksgaard.

—— (1968). *Narkotikafrågan och samhället*. Stockholm, SWE: Aldus/Bonniers.

—— I-L. Candefjord and J-Å. Candefjord (1974). *Omhändertagen i Humlegården*. Mölnlycke, SWE: Sober förlag.

Clarke, R.V. (1997). *Situational Crime Prevention — Successful Case Studies*. Albany, NY: Harrow and Heston.

Cornish, D. and R. V. Clarke (1985). "Modeling Offenders' Decisions: a Framework for Research and Policy." In: M. Tonry and N. Morris (eds.), *Crime and Justice: An Annual Review of Research*, vol. 6. Chicago, IL: University of Chicago Press.

Eck, J. (1993). "The Threat of Crime Displacement." *Criminal Justice Abstracts* 25:527-546.

Edmunds, M., M. Hough and S.N. Urquia (1996). *Tackling Local Drug Markets*. (Police Research Group, Crime Detection and Prevention Series Paper #80.) London, UK: Home Office.

Ekenwall, B. and R. Siipo (1994). "Omfördelning av brott." Mimeograph. University of Stockholm: Department of Criminology.

Guttormsson, U. (1998). *Mönstrades drogvanor 1997*. (Centralförbundet för alkohol- och narkotikaupplysning. Rapport #54.) Stockholm, SWE: Elanders Gotab.

—— S. Helling and B. Olsson (1999). *Vad händer på narkotikaområdet?* (Centralförbundet för alkohol- och narkotikaupplysning. Rapport #55.) Stockholm, SWE: Modintryck.

Hibell, B., B. Andersson, T. Bjarnarson, A. Kokkevi, M. Morgan and A. Narusk (1997). *The 1995 ESPAD report. Alcohol and Other Drug Use Among Students in 26 European Countries*. (The Swedish Council for Information on Alcohol and Other Drugs and The Pompidou Group at the Council of Europe.) Stockholm, SWE: Modintryck.

Kassman, A. (1998). *Polisen och narkotikaproblemet*. Acta Universitatis Stockholmiensis. (Stockholm Studies in Sociology, N.S.6.) Stockholm, SWE: Almqvist & Wiksell International.

Knutsson, J. (1997). "Restoring Public Order in a Park." In: R. Homel (ed.), *Crime Prevention Studies*, vol. 4. Monsey, NY: Criminal Justice Press.

—— (1995). *Polisen i parken — en studie i konsten att upprätthålla ordning.* (Rps forskning 1995:3.) Stockholm, SWE: Rikspolisstyrelsen.

(1977). *Labeling Theory — A Critical Examination.* (The National Council for Crime Prevention, Report #3.) Stockholm, SWE: Liber förlag.

—— and E. Kühlhorn (1980). *När checkbedrägerierna försvann.* Brottsförebyggande rådet. (Rapport 1980:4.) Stockholm, SWE: Liber förlag.

Kühlhorn, E. (1978). *Deprivation of Freedom and the Police - An Evaluation of the Temporary Custody Act.* (The National Council for Crime Prevention, Sweden, Report #4.) Stockholm, SWE: Liber förlag.

—— A. Kassman and M. Ramstedt (1998). "Prevalence Findings and Methodology in Drug Policy Evaluations." In: H. Waal (ed.), *Patterns on the European Drug Scene. An Exploration of Differences.* Oslo, NOR: National Institute for Alcohol and Drug Research.

National Council for Crime Prevention. (1979). *A New Penal System – Ideas and Proposals.* (The National Council for Crime Prevention, Sweden, Report #5.) Stockholm, SWE: Liber förlag.

Olsson, B. (1984). *Narkotikaproblemets bakgrund. användning av och uppfattningar om narkotika inom svensk medicin.* (Centralförbundet för alkohol- och narkotikaupplysning. Rapport #39.) Stockholm, SWE: CAN.

Olsson, O. (1995). *Liberalisering av narkotikapolitiken. En översikt av forskning och undersökningar om en restriktiv narkotikapolitik.* (Folkhälsoinstitutet. Centralförbundet för alkohol- och narkotikaupplysning.) Stockholm, SWE: Gotab.

Persson, L.G.W. (1976). "Inbrottstjuvar i Stockholm — en studie av individuell brottsbelastning, samhällelig brottsnivå och brottsutveckling." *Svensk Juristtidning* 66(Sept):527-541.

Rikspolisstyrelsen (1995). *Sållningsinstrument för analys av narkotika i urin.* Redovisning av en försöksverksamhet med vissa kommentarer. (Rps rapport 1995:9.) Stockholm, SWE: Gotab.

Sherman, L. (1990). "Police Crackdowns: Initial and Residual Deterrence." In: M. Tonry and N. Morris (eds.), *Crime and Justice: An Annual Review of Research*, vol. 12. Chicago, IL: University of Chicago Press.

APPENDIX - SOURCES FOR THE SCHOOL SURVEYS

1975-84: Fridenäs, R.; L. Hejdenberg and G. Olsson. 1984-års ANT-vaneundersökning i Stockholms skolor. Stockholms skolförvaltning Elevvårdsbyrån. ANT-informationen.

1987: Olsson, G. Erfarenheter av droger och våld i årskurs 9, vt-87. Stockholms skolförvaltning, Elevvårdsbyrån. ANT-informationen.

1990: Erhardt, J. Drogvanor och våldserfarenheter bland åk 9 elever i Stockholms skolor 1990. Stockholms skolförvaltning. Elevvårdsbyrån.

1993: Qvarnström, G. Drogvanor och våldserfarenheter bland åk 9 elever i Stockholms skolor 1993. Stockholms Skolor. Central Förvaltning 1994:1.

NOTES

1. The knock-on effect meant that it had an increasing effect on the efforts by the police.

CRIMINAL FRANCHISING: ALBANIANS AND ILLICIT DRUGS IN ITALY

by

Vincenzo Ruggiero
Middlesex University, London

Abstract: *This paper considers how trafficking of marijuana from Albania to Italy interlocks with other forms of illicit trafficking. While Albanians have tended to occupy only marginal roles in other forms of illicit drug trafficking, they are centrally involved in the production, importation and distribution of marijuana. The paper identifies a number of — probably unintended — benefits that this may bring. It has probably served to disentangle the marijuana market from the distribution of more harmful drugs of dependence such as heroin and cocaine. In providing a relatively cheap and plentiful supply of marijuana, it may have diverted Italian users from the more expensive heroin and cocaine. It may have provided a supply of jobs, although they are in the black economy. Thus against harm-reduction principles the near-monopoly held by Albanian traffickers has much to recommend it. The paper considers the implications of this for drug policy.*

INTRODUCTION

In Italy the number of people charged with drug offences between 1991 and 1997 has shown the following trends. Arrests for trafficking and supply of heroin have increased by around 20%, while for cocaine the increase has been around 50%. The number of individuals charged with trafficking and supply of hashish has slightly declined. Finally, the variation regarding marijuana offences has been outstanding. In 1991, 36 people were charged with international trafficking and 490 for supply, while in 1997, respectively, 1,246 and 5,078 were charged (Ministero dell'Interno, 1998). Trends regarding seizures indicate that the quantities of heroin and cocaine intercepted by the Italian police have declined, that quantities of hashish have remained stable, while quantities of marijuana have increased tenfold (European Monitoring Centre on Drugs and Drug Addiction [EMCDDA], 1998).

These trends provide the backdrop for this paper. It focuses in particular on Albanian migrants in Italy and the nature of their involvement in illicit economies, including the drugs economy. In part one an overview of the economic relationships between Italy and Albania is provided. In part two, the role of Albanian criminal groups is analysed, with particular attention given to their involvement in the illicit drugs business. Part three briefly relates the activities conducted by Albanian immigrants in Italy to the debate around ethnic minorities and crime. In the conclusion, policies are sketched with a view to minimising the social harm related to drug trafficking, supply and use in Italy. In this respect the notion of criminal franchising, of the production and marketing of marijuana, is discussed.

THE ALBANIAN DREAM

Before the collapse of the financial pyramids in the early months of 1996, there were more than 600 Italian companies operating in Albania.[1] These were middle-range or small firms involved in the building industry and in the manufacture of shoes, clothes and furniture. A large timber industry had established itself in Albania, and the country provided both the raw materials and a lively market for the final products. Overall, these companies employed some 30,000 people.

Italian financial institutions were involved in the largest private bank arrangement in Albania, the Italo-Shqiptare Bank, affiliated to the Bank of Rome. Oil derivatives produced by API (Agenzia Italiana Petroli) were also sold in Albania, supplying both state agencies and private entrepreneurs. Public works contracted to Italian firms included the building of the water-supply system of Tirana and Duress, while the restructuring of the electricity network and telephone lines were also entrusted to Italian firms. Finally, Albania imported from Italy around 40% of the goods purchased abroad.

This flurry of economic entrepreneurship prompted the major newspaper published in southern Italy, *La Gazzetta del Mezzogiorno* (6 March 1997, which also published an Albanian daily edition), to describe the thriving activities as the "Albanian dream" (Parise, 1997). Moreover, the "Switzerland of the Balkans," as enthusiasts also described Albania, was just 50 miles away from the Italian coast, and offered entrepreneurs very advantageous conditions in terms of taxation and business licensing (Carnimeo, 1997).

Italian business was also engaged in the development of tourism. Work was well on the way in Orikum, in the bay of Valona, and summer 1996 was fully booked up by VIPs from Bari and other towns of southern Italy. When news reports started alerting the world to the social turmoil caused by the collapse of some Albanian financial institutions, Italian entrepreneurs were told "not to panic" and would-be holiday makers advised "not to cancel their bookings": "order will soon be restored" (Mero, 1996).

THE ITALIAN DREAM

While Italian entrepreneurs were pursuing the "Albanian dream," Albanians had already been blinded by the "Italian dream." In 1994, no fewer than 5,000 individuals per month were estimated to cross the Adriatic Sea in small boats directed to Italy. There is a narrow strait separating Albania from the coast of the Italian region of Puglia, and crossing the strait in small boats became the new strategy adopted by migrants after the previous biblical exodus failed. This exodus started immediately after the collapse of the Communist regime, in 1991 and took the form of thousands of Albanians arriving in Italy in dangerously overloaded ships. In their expectation, which was to be disappointed, their departure from Communism deserved to be met with generous hospitality by capitalist countries.

Some data may explain the reasons why Albanians were, and still are, so determined to migrate. In 1995, governmental figures indicated that 80% of Albanians lived below the minimum standards established by the United Nations. More than 70,000 individuals received benefits totalling $31 per month. Pensioners experienced a 50% reduction in their purchasing power between 1991 and 1995 (*Albanian Daily News*, 3 June 1995). The transition from the Communist regime, which replaced state property with private property, "led to a huge increase in unemployment, and within a year 25-30 per cent of the total work force became unemployed" (Hysi, 1998:4). According to a survey conducted in 1996, crime victimisation rates in Tirana were the highest in transitional countries: nearly 60% of the respondents had been victims of one or more crimes in the previous year, half of them of violent crimes (Hysi, 1998:19).

While it is difficult, particularly after the 1997 crisis, to estimate the number of Albanians who escape such social conditions, changes in the social composition of those who arrived in Italy were noticeable. The new arrivals include, not only destitute families and unemployed individuals, but also ministers, army, navy and police officers, troop soldiers, and sentenced offenders who escaped from custody during the recent civil war.[2] Nearly 90% of these immigrants arrived, and still arrive, without valid identification, and most, shortly after being accommodated in camps or empty schools, disappeared. While some seek to enter Germany and other European countries, others remain as irregular immigrants on Italian territory.

The Italian authorities expel a higher percentage of Albanians than any other groups of migrants, a circumstance which officials justify with their "irregular status." Around 30% of the Albanians, about 26,000 individuals, who arrived in Italy between 1991 and 1995 were deported. As the rate of deportation shows no sign of abating, rejected migrants may try to re-enter Italy by other means. In other words, migrants may be encouraged to turn to the services of traffickers (Ruggiero, 1997; Salt, 1997). Trafficking in irregular and undocumented migrants is one of the activities in which Albanians are engaged, an activity which is intertwined with a number of other organised illicit activities, including drug production and trafficking.

CRIMINAL BUSINESS

Customs police seized 109 inflatable boats in 1998, claiming that half the fleet of the Albanian traffickers based in the town of Valona had been "taken off business." The cost of each such boat is equivalent to about £35,000, and the police claim that the average profits for each trip amount to around £8,000. Between 30 and 40 trips between Albania and Italy are made each night, with traffickers charging about £400 per passenger. Discounts are said to be applicable to families. Some 36,000 irregular migrants were intercepted in 1998, and in January 1999 the figure was already 2,000. On many occasions boats avoid coming too near the Italian coast, and traffickers force migrants to swim to Italy when a few hundred metres separate them from the shore (Mastrogiacomo, 1999).

Interviews with officials of the Italian Ministry of the Interior suggested that traffickers take extra care for the humans they take across the Adriatic only when these are young women destined for prostitution. One such official reported the following incident:

> We intercepted telephone conversations between one trafficker who was having problems in reaching the coast and his accomplices in Italy. As the little boat began to sink, the trafficker said that the "girls" would be taken care of, and when a second boat came to rescue them the girls had priority in boarding it. Five people drowned, and once ashore, the trafficker rang his

partner again saying that, fortunately, the "valuables" were all safe. [interview]

Trafficking in migrants is therefore only one of the activities carried out by Albanian criminal entrepreneurs. This activity is intertwined with supplying prostitutes to Italy and other European countries. Some young women are forced to become prostitutes when they reach the country of destination and are initially unaware of what and who awaits them there (Géry, 1999).

Research conducted by Lewis (1998) illustrates the complex nature of the illegal businesses carried out by Albanian groups. Activities are diversified but concomitant, with groups shifting from contraband in oil to illicit arms sale, and from drugs trafficking to the trafficking in humans or stolen cars. For example, many Mercedes stolen in Germany are marketed in Albania. The number of cars in Albania has soared since the collapse of communism, growing from 5,000 in the early 1990s to 50,000 in 1998. Yet, in the previous year only three new cars were officially registered (*The Independent*, 18 December 1998).

Albanian large-scale drug dealers have been identified in Germany as well as in Croatia and Slovenia. "The collapse of Albania, and its conversion to market economy have provided ideal conditions for two-way trading in weapons, oil, drugs, tobacco, stolen vehicles and migrant smuggling" (Lewis, 1998:224).

It is important to note that such activities are interwoven and that criminal entrepreneurs are extremely versatile. This circumstance, as we shall see later, should guide policy makers and legislators. In a final account of the entrepreneurial versatility of Albanian groups, it has been suggested that dealing in arms goes hand in hand with smuggling vehicles from Germany, smuggling of humans (including the establishment of prostitution networks), and finally "drugs trafficking with the middle East and with Colombia is accompanied by money laundering with Russia" (Mattera, 1997:98). Let us now focus on the illicit drugs business.

THE COLOMBIA OF EUROPE?

Albanian and Macedonian networks have fully exploited their access to suppliers in Turkey and the republics of the Caucasus, their simultaneous access to the Adriatic, and their established presence in Switzerland, Italy and Germany. Drugs refineries have been discovered in Macedonia, Kosovo and Albania (EMCDDA, 1998). The Albanian port of Durres is said to be the destination of hundreds of vehicles for the transportation and bartering of heroin and other products through the Balkans and via the ferry to Italy. Protected warehousing is provided in Albania itself, with consignments earmarked for Italy, Switzerland and Germany (Lewis, 1998).

Investigators suggest that Albania could become the Colombia of Europe. In the testimony of an officer of the Servizio Antidroga of the Ministero dell'Interno:

> Turkish heroin passes through Albania, and is destined for western European markets. Marijuana is cropped in Albania, particularly on the hills surrounding Saranda. The large plantations are well visible in that area. Marijuana cropping was the result of conversion, in the sense that it is grown in the same greenhouses set up by skilled floriculturists from Terlizzi, in the southern region of Puglia. The new plantations, of course, are more remunerative. In 1996, more than 7 tons of Albanian marijuana were seized by Italian customs police. [interview]

Interviews with marijuana suppliers in Rome revealed that drugs may be transported to Italy as a form of service due to migrant traffickers. Each migrant may be given between four and five kilograms. Large bags containing around 30 kilograms may be entrusted to families leaving Albania together. In the testimony of one informant: "Sometimes, the Albanians do not bring the drugs all the way to the Italian coasts, as other boats from Italy meet them a few miles from shore and take the consignments" (interview).

Regarded as physically "rough" but mentally sophisticated by investigators, Albanian drugs entrepreneurs are also thought to be engaged in a permanent search for autonomy. For example, after an initial phase in which drugs were purchased from Turkish intermediaries, Albanian groups are now said to access larger suppliers and producers directly. In this way, key business links with Afghanistan and other heroin producing countries, and also with Colombian cocaine producers, have been established. Large distributors residing in Italy take the consignments and feed middle range suppliers scattered in large cities. Groups that established themselves in the Emilia Romagna region are said to be in charge of the laundering of drugs proceeds by investing them in the tourist industry of Rimini and the surrounding area.

In cities such as Rome and Milan, the Albanian groups are said to have upset the old geography of criminal activity. An investigator reported that:

In the largest Italian cities, Albanians have networks of rented flats. In Milan, the police found that most of the flats were rented by one person, Peschepia Ritvan. He was an Albanian politician, the son of a diplomat and member of the democratic alliance in his country, who had escaped soon after the collapse of the financial pyramids. He used his regular passport for renting the flats, and was in business with traffickers, who nicknamed him "the falcon." [interview]

The high degree of organisation achieved by Albanian drugs entrepreneurs prompts the hypothesis that they have acquired independence from the more established Italian criminal groups. Do Albanians manage to conduct business without causing the resentment of mafia-type organisations? The little evidence available on this issue is contradictory.

While traffickers from Albania have established themselves in Italy, Italian criminal groups have set up entrepreneurial outposts in Albania. Partnerships have been formed, particularly in the recruitment of illegal migrants, who constitute cheap labour for farmers and other employers in the hidden economy. Albanians, in this area, seem to have acquired the standing to negotiate with Italian Mafia-type organisations on an equal footing. However, anecdotal evidence would indicate that in other areas Italian criminal entrepreneurs are unwilling to establish joint ventures with Albanians and are determined to retain their higher hierarchical position.

On the Romagna coast, two Albanians (Arben Kurani and Agim Lala) were killed on 20 May 1997. After arresting a group of suspects, detectives suggested that the two victims had tried to set up their own business in the heroin trade, and that they had been consequently punished by local members of organised crime. Albanians were said to be confined to the importation of the substance, due to their access to producing countries and their ability to move goods and people into Italy. They were, however, expected to refrain from wholesale and middle-range distribution, let alone independent distribution. The Italian groups were unprepared to share the profits of the heroin economy with the newcomers. Only at the lowest level of retailing, when "running" for Italian distributors who thought it wise to keep away from the street drug scene, was their presence tolerated.

Other episodes illustrate the problematic cohabitation of Albanian criminal groups with their Italian counterparts. The channel separating Albania from the region of Puglia is not only the conduit for migrants and drugs traffickers, but also a crucial conduit for long-established cigarette smuggling controlled by Italian groups. Clashes between these groups and the new traffickers are frequent. The Italians claim that the Albanians, by contributing to the militarization of the coasts, have made the traditional business of cigarette smuggling too dangerous. In January 1999 a number of blockades were organised by Italian smugglers against migrant traffickers in Puglia. One of leaders of this anti-Albanian protest spoke to a journalist in the following terms: "We have never seen so much control on this coast. The Albanians don't know what they are doing, they don't respect any rule, and they are in our way while we are working" [Buonavolgia, 1999].

However, some local investigators believe that an agreement between Italian and Albanian groups is possible, particularly in Puglia, where cigarette smugglers are endowed with radar for the interception of the customs boats patrolling the coast. If this service is rendered to Albanian traffickers, it is suggested, the two parties may find an easier co-habitation.

There is only one sector in the drugs business that does not show any sign of competition between Italian and Albanian organisations. This is the sector of marijuana, which traditionally has never been of interest to mafia-type groups in Italy. Marijuana is grown in Albania and transferred to Italy in large quantities. In 1995 Albanian marijuana was sold at the equivalent of £700 per kilogram, while after the financial crisis its cost dropped to little more than £70 per kilogram. Very cheap and of good quality, marijuana is widely, and increasingly, available in Italian cities. Due to its low cost at source, marijuana is particularly attractive to small dealers, who can access the market and make a living without causing price increases that would discourage purchasers. In sum, the low market price of marijuana makes for good employment opportunities in its distribution. The involvement of large numbers of intermediaries, each making a profit, is unlikely to produce an increase in retail prices that might keep consumers away.

The peculiarity of the marijuana market in Italy deserves further examination, as it is part of the traditional debate around immigration and criminal activity.

IMMIGRANTS AS JOB PROVIDERS

In Italy, like elsewhere, analyses of the relationship between immigration and crime offer a variety of explanatory tools ranging from "relative deprivation" to "stereotyping," and from "differential law enforcement" to "cultural difference." Advocates of relative deprivation, for example, posit that the image of Italy in developing countries, an image associated with nice cars and elegant clothes, engenders disappointment among new settlers. They end up pursuing the official goals of consumption and success by illegal means, the legal means being unavailable to most of them (Colombo, 1998). Explanations revolving around stereotyping, instead, focus on the reaction of victims, who are said to be more likely to report crimes committed by immigrants than those committed by their compatriots, which contributes to the statistical anomaly regarding the prevalence of immigrant offenders (Gatti et al., 1997). In their turn, commentators resorting to explanations based on differential law enforcement pinpoint the visibility of immigrants and, consequently, the more intense police activity to which they are subjected in addition to the harsher responses they receive from the judiciary (Melossi, 1998; Palidda, 1997). Finally, cultural adaptation and "ladder step" hypotheses are mobilised by authors claiming that crime committed by immigrants is the result of their marginalisation in the host country and that social improvement will resolve their initial cultural disorientation (Marotta, 1995).

With respect to illicit drugs, contemporary accounts in Italy echo similar accounts prevailing in other countries, where drugs are associated with immigrants and "alien invasion" (Murji, 1998). Research also suggests that drugs economies display a division of labour based on ethnicity so that, for example, import operations are often performed by non-Italians. These poorly paid "expendable mules" provide a service to indigenous wholesalers who are part of established distribution networks and usually are not directly involved in importation (Ruggiero, 1996, 1992; Ruggiero and South, 1995). On the other hand, the presence of ethnic minorities is very visible at street-level distribution, where risks of apprehension are higher and profits lower. Frequently, for example, immigrants are employed by indigenous distributors to deliver doses and to keep street contact with customers. In brief, the illicit drugs economy would appear to broadly mirror the division of roles characterising the official economy, the lower stages of both being mainly occupied by immigrants and ethnic minorities.

The case of the Albanian marijuana business seems to constitute a significant anomaly vis-a-vis this pattern. Albanian groups are involved in the production, importation and finally the distribution of the illicit substance (Barbagli, 1998). In an unusual role reversal, Albanian distributors sell quantities of marijuana to Italian street suppliers who are in closer contact with enclaves of users. In this sense, Albanians create job opportunities for young Italians, which partly resolves the problem of youth unemployment in Italy (Ruggiero, 2000). Moreover, as remarked by one of the police investigators I interviewed: "Albanian marijuana is a blessing for the Italian younger generation, as it has diverted users from crack, ecstasy, and even from heroin, whose consumption has declined" (interview). The "anomaly" of the Albanian marijuana business is worthy of further analysis aimed at the identification of a specific harm-reduction policy.

FRANCHISING AS HARM REDUCTION

The set of social policies that can be grouped under the rubric "harm reduction" prioritises the aim of decreasing the negative effects of drug use (Newcombe, 1992). These include individual as well as social effects. The most obvious individual effects pertain to the health of users, while the most relevant of the social impacts consists of acquisitive crime. Harm reduction tries to replace interventions inspired by moralism with more pragmatic interventions aimed at minimising both the individual and the social effects of drug use. Advocates of this strategy also stress that the concept of harm reduction should be expanded to include harm produced by law enforcement, criminal justice and the penal system. In other words, harm reduction entails the belief that the damage caused by drug use results, in large measure, from its illegality.

Although its main roots are in the public-health model, harm reduction may impact substantially on law enforcement by releasing police resources. Police attention, in other words, may be diverted from users and street dealers to large traffickers and distributors. In this respect, policies adopted in the Netherlands may be illuminating. Marijuana smokers and small-scale distributors have been removed from the criminal justice system (Jansen, 1991). Informal tolerance has been accompanied by the designation of controlled places where distribution and use may occur, while the police are "free to focus attention on drug traffickers, instead of tracing minor drug users. From an economic point of view, we have to conclude that this is more cost-effective" (Zaal, 1992:92). From the users' perspective, this policy is beneficial because they can obtain "good-quality products for reasonable prices, so they do not need to resort to criminality to be able to buy them" (Zaal, 1992:92).

These benefits relate to a policy I would like to suggest: namely the franchising of the marijuana business to Albanians. Such a policy, of course, cannot be translated into legislation that would "reserve" this specific market solely for Albanian nationals. Instead, it should be understood as a form of harm reduction implemented through a variety of enforcement policies. For example, informal tolerance towards use, possession and supply of marijuana would bring de facto decriminalisation of the business. More formal legislative intervention, in turn, would aim at legalisation and the consequent control of the market through taxation. It would also consider increasing the divergence in penalties between marijuana-related offences and offences related to other drugs.

Informal tolerance and formal legislation would be accompanied by precise spatial divisions between marijuana and hard drugs at the retail level. Retailers, for example, would be involved in making such divisions clear by displaying agreed "rules" to be observed by clients at designated places where marijuana is sold, and by participating in health campaigns concerning the effects of hard drugs. The beneficial effects of both these informal and formal types of intervention emerge when the analysis moves to the minimisation of harm caused by criminal organisations.

CONTRACTING OUT

This analysis focuses on economic categories such as monopoly and competition. Monopolies, it is argued, allow for the rise of prices at which goods and services can be sold. They also result in the overall reduction of output due to the absence of competing firms. This perspective has led some authors to emphasise the "preferability" of structured, large-scale illicit activities as opposed to dispersed disorganised ones. With the former, it is suggested, external costs become internalised (Schelling, 1967). External costs are those falling on competitors, customers and others outside the firm itself. Violence is one such external cost. If some illicit goods and services were provided by a monopoly, we would witness a reduction of these goods and services (Rubin, 1980). In competitive situations, instead, external costs, such as violence, fall on society at large. This is exemplified by an individual hijacker who might kill a bystander to eliminate a potential witness, even though criminals as an occupational group would suffer from public outrage and increased police activity. In contrast, monopolies in illicit businesses may create a collective interest in restricting violence so as to avoid the disapproval of the public and attention from the police. Society, therefore, might "contract out" some of the regulatory functions to criminals themselves, "encouraging them to stick to less damaging kinds of crime" (Reynolds, 1980:43).

Let us formulate some hypotheses around the beneficial effects of "contracting out" the marijuana business to Albanians. First, the marijuana economy would be disentangled from the other illicit businesses conducted by Albanians that have been described above. It should be reiterated that heroin and marijuana are smuggled into Italy alongside migrants, weapons, and young women destined for prostitution. Figures provided by the police indicate that almost 19,000 Albanian migrants have been charged with an offence during 1998.[3] Among the complaints voiced by the police is that such figures obscure the fact that ideally most offenders (around 6,000) would limit themselves to violations of the immigration law if precise distinctions were made between the different types of offences and respective legislations. Other migrants would limit themselves to the smuggling of marijuana if legislative distinctions were made between heroin, cocaine and marijuana offences. Attributing an illegal status to all illicit goods and services provided by Albanians may have encouraged the conflation of the respective businesses and markets and produced the multi-entrepreneurial efforts described above. Seizures of heroin and marijuana imported by Albanians have increased. Albanians make up the largest contingent of Europeans charged with drug offences (Maritati, 1998; Colussi, 1998). Isolating marijuana from other illicit goods would establish selective barriers between criminal entrepreneurs and persuade some to devote themselves to less harmful initiatives.

Second, franchising the production and marketing of marijuana to Albanians would, of course, entail forms of decriminalisation or legalisation of marijuana use. However, as remarked by advocates of drug legalisation in other contexts, legalisation would produce benefits in terms of employment and profits (Ruggiero, 1998; Karel, 1991). Marijuana crops in Albania would provide job opportunities for farmers and unskilled labourers, as well as pharmacists, chemists and retailers. Italian young people, some of whom are already employed in the business, would also benefit from the consequent expansion of job opportunities in retail distribution. Legalisation would also be consistent with the views of the majority of Italian people, particularly youth, most of whom regard cannabis consumption as a "right" (Pizzo, 1999; Gruppo Abele, 1997).

Third, in response to objections that franchising would create a monopolistic condition and consequently an increase in prices one could argue that the marijuana business is already virtually monopolised by Albanian producers and distributors. This monopoly has not caused a substantial increase in prices due to low production costs. Franchising the marijuana business to Albanian entrepreneurs would in fact produce benefits in terms of decline of violence. This is because monopolies tend to make external costs such as violence internalised in the very groups holding monopolistic positions. Frictions with Italian organised groups would also decrease as a consequence of Albanians being diverted from activities traditionally performed by the indigenous groups.

Finally, franchising would be an ideal policy considering the recent evolution of criminal enterprises in Italy. It should be noted the recent success of the Italian judiciary against organised crime caused an unpredictable situation that could be described as follows. The possibilities for organised crime to enter the legitimate arena of business were reduced dramatically. Rules regulating public contracts were redrawn in every sector of the national and local economy. As a consequence, the most successful "families" who had accumulated large amounts of finances, shifted into some licit sector of the official economy. Their crime, now, falls in the domain of white collar or corporate crime. The unsuccessful families were pushed into conventional criminal activity, particularly the cocaine and heroin business and protection rackets. It is in these sectors of the criminal economy that most homicides take place. The criminal markets, as a result of legal options being increasingly inaccessible to organised crime, are now extremely crowded. Devising strategies that confine the activities of Albanian drug entrepreneurs to the marijuana market would partly avoid adding to such overcrowding and the consequent degree of violence associated with it.

Address correspondence to: Vincenzo Ruggiero, Professor of Sociology, School of Social Sciences, Middlesex University, Queensway, Enfield, Middlesex EN3 4SF, U.K.

REFERENCES

Albanian Daily News (1995). "Albanians Still Poor." 3 June:3-7.

Barbagli, M. (1998). *Immigrazione e criminalità in Italia.* Bologna, IT: Il Mulino.

Buonavoglia, R. (1999). "Guerra contrabbandieri-scafisti, diminuiscono gli sbarchi in Puglia." *Il Corriere della Sera* 11 January:15.

Carnimeo, N. (1997). "Svizzera dei Balcani o Colombia d'Europa?" *Limes* 3(1):67-72.

Colombo, A. (1998). *Etnografia di un'economia clandestina*. Bologna, IT: Il Mulino.

Colussi, G. (1998). "Lamerica." *Narcomafie* VI(7/8):4-7.

European Monitoring Centre for Drugs and Drug Addiction [EMCDDA] (1998). *Annual Report on the State of the Drugs Problem in the European Union*. Lisbon, PORT.

Gatti, U., D. Malfatti and A. Verde (1997). "Minorities, Crime and Criminal Justice in Italy." In: I.H. Marshall (ed.), *Minorities, Migrants, and Crime*. London, UK: Sage.

Géry, Y. (1999). "Les filières bulgare et albanaise." *Le Monde Diplomatique* 10 February.

Gruppo Abele (1997). *Annuario Sociale*. Turin, IT: EGA.

Hysi, V. (1998). "The International Crime Victim Survey in Tirana (Albania)." In: O. Hatalak, A. Alvazzi del Frate and U. Zvekic (eds.), *The International Crime Victim Survey in Countries in Transition*. Rome, IT: United Nations Interregional Crime and Justice Research Institute (UNICRI).

The Independent (1998). "Albania: More Mercs than Germany." 18 December:12.

Jansen, A.C.M. (1991). *Cannabis in Amsterdam. A Geography of Hashish and Marijuana*. Amsterdam, NETH: Coutinho.

Karel, R.B. (1991). "A Model Legalisation Proposal." In: J. Inciardi (ed.), *The Drug Legalisation Debate*. Newbury Park, CA: Sage.

Lewis, R. (1998). "Drugs, War and Crime in the Post-Soviet Balkans." In: V. Ruggiero, N. South and I. Taylor (eds.), *The New European Criminology*. London, UK: Routledge.

Maritati, A. (1998). "Piccoli pusher crescono." *Narcomafie* VI(2/3):31-32.

Marotta, G. (1995). *Immigrati: devianza e controllo sociale*. Padua, IT: Cedam.

Mastrogiacomo, D. (1999). "Un clan degli scafisti nel parlamento albanese." *La Repubblica* 25 January:26.

Mattera, O. (1997). "Adriatico, il mare delle mafie." *Limes* 3(1):95-100.

Melossi, D. (1998). *Multiculturalismo e sicurezza*. Bologna, IT: Regione Emilia Romagna.

Mero, A. (1996). "In Albania la Vefa non farà crac." *La Gazzetta del Mezzogiorno* 16 February:8.

Ministero dell'Interno (1998). *Numero di persone indagate in Italia per produzione, traffico e spaccio di stupefacenti, dal 1991 al 1997*. Rome, IT: Direzione Centrale Servizi Antidroga.

Murji, K. (1998). *Policing Drugs*. Aldershot, UK: Avebury.

Newcombe, R. (1992). "The Reduction of Drug-Related Harm. A Conceptual Framework of Theory, Practice and Research." In: P. O'Hare, R. Newcombe, A. Matthews and E. Bunin (eds.), *The Reduction of Drug-Related Harm.* London, UK: Routledge.

Palidda, S. (1997). *Immigrant Delinquency.* Brussels, BEL: European Commission.

Parise, L. (1997). "Affari d'oro per quei boss prima della truffa." *La Gazzetta del Mezzogiorno* 6 March:13.

Pizzo, A. (1999). "Lo spinello della giustizia." *Il Manifesto* 5 March:7.

Reynolds, M.O. (1980). "The Economics of Criminal Activity." In: R. Andreano and J. Siegfried (eds.), *The Economics of Crime.* New York, NY: John Wiley.

Rubin, P.H. (1980). "The Economics of Crime." In: R. Andreano and J. Siegfried (eds.), *The Economics of Crime.* New York, NY: John Wiley.

Ruggiero, V. (2000). *Crime and Markets: Essays in Anti-Criminology.* Oxford, UK: Oxford University Press.

——— (1998). "Drugs as a Password and the Law as a Drug: Discussing the Legalisation of Illegal Substances." In: N. South (ed.), *Drugs: Cultures, Controls & Everyday Life.* London, UK: Sage.

——— (1997). "Trafficking in Human Beings: Slaves in Contemporary Europe." *International Journal of the Sociology of Law* 25(3):231-244.

——— (1996). *Organised and Corporate Crime in Europe.* Aldershot, UK: Dartmouth.

——— (1992). *La Roba. Economie e culture dell'eroina.* Parma, IT: Pratiche.

——— and N. South (1995). *Eurodrugs.* London, UK: UCL Press.

Salt, J. (1997). *Current Trends in International Migration in Europe.* Strasbourg, FR: Council of Europe.

Schelling, T.C. (1967). "Economic Analysis of Organised Crime." In: *Task Force Report: Organized Crime.* The President's Commission on Law Enforcement and the Administration of Justice. Washington, DC: Government Printing Office.

Zaal, L. (1992). "Police Policy in Amsterdam." In: P. O'Hare, R. Newcombe, A. Matthews and E. Buning (eds.), *The Reduction of Drug-Related Harm.* London, UK: Routledge.

NOTES

1. The pyramid schemes, which promised high returns to masses of Albanian savers, are forms of financial investments in which new liabilities are issued to finance existing liabilities. In other words, money is borrowed for the single purpose of paying interests on previous loans. In this way, an increasing number of new lenders is required to pay the high return promised to the old lenders. The inherent fragility of these schemes manifested itself most dramatically in Albania, triggering violent protest by savers.

2. The civil war was caused by the collapse of the financial institutions known as "pyramids" in 1996. Adventurous financiers, including large foreign investors, who had committed themselves to the payment of interest rates as high as 40%, were suddenly forced to declare bankruptcy. Smaller investors rose against the government to claim their money back.

3. Figures were provided by the Servizio Centrale Operativo della Polizia di Stato in Rome.

A GEOGRAPHIC ANALYSIS OF ILLEGAL DRUG MARKETS

by

George Rengert
Sanjoy Chakravorty
Tom Bole
Kristin Henderson

Temple University
Philadelphia, USA

Abstract: *Past research has established two important geographic principles concerning the retail sales of illegal drugs: (1) illegal drug markets tend to be spatially concentrated, and (2) the location and marketing characteristics of these markets will vary depending on whether the customers are local or regional. The present research will build on these principles and determine whether the location of illegal drug markets in Wilmington, Delaware can be predicted using variables that measure the relative size of the local demand combined with variables that measure accessibility to regional customers. The data include arrest records from the Wilmington police department for the years 1989, 1990 and 1991 in order to be comparable with the 1990 census data.*

INTRODUCTION

The sale of illegal drugs in the United States is a multibillion-dollar enterprise. Like any other large-scale enterprise, there are areas where raw materials are produced, locations where these raw materials are processed into a finished product, and sites where the finished product is sold or distributed to the consumer. It is the quantity demanded by the final consumers and the price they are willing to pay that determines the level of profit at each stage of the enterprise. One criterion for determining the quantity demanded at a given price is the location of the illegal markets. In other words, the quality of the sales location is directly related to the quantity of profit for the illegal drug dealers.

We are not sure how illegal drug dealers choose their market locations. If it is by trial and error, the most profitable sites will attract competition and the unprofitable locations will soon go out of business. If it is chosen through some sense about which location is most profitable, this knowledge would be valuable information for public policy planners whose objective is to remove as much profit as possible from this illegal enterprise. Proceeding from this latter perspective, this analysis seeks to identify (from a retail marketing perspective) the advantageous locations. Then, using data from Wilmington, Delaware, in the United States, we test whether or not such locations have been chosen as sites for illegal drug markets. In this manner, we determine whether marketing principles are useful for predicting where illegal drug markets are likely to locate and where they are likely to be displaced spatially if they are successfully closed in one location. We can also identify factors associated with successful market locations that can be altered to create a less-profitable location for illegal drug dealers. We begin by determining the spatial structure of demand for illegal drugs much as a marketing consultant would determine relative demand in a sales area for any legal product.

SPATIAL ASPECTS OF ILLEGAL DRUG MARKETS

The National Institute of Justice funding of the Drug Market Analysis Program led to the most important findings concerning the siting of illegal retail drug markets (Maltz, 1993). This research was housed in five cities: San Diego, Jersey City, Pittsburgh, Kansas City, and Hartford. Three of these five sites produced important findings concerning the spatial characteristics of illegal retail drug markets.

Eck's (1994) analysis focused on San Diego. He determined that there was not just one type of drug market. In fact, four types of drug markets were identified using contrasting concerns for security on the part of drug dealers and their customers: neighborhood, open regional, semi-open regional, and closed regional markets. These categories result from the interaction of two variables. The first is whether the customers are local or regional. The second is whether the location of the drug market attracts customers or whether customers determine the location of the drug market through a social network. The first variable is closely related to Reuter and McCoun's

(1992) variable, which categorized drug markets based on whether customers were residents of the transaction neighborhood, or whether they were generally outsiders who brought money into the neighborhoods where the drug transactions occurred. If the customers were largely outsiders, the markets tended to be open and located near major thoroughfares that funnel customers into the region. If the customers were local, markets would tend to be closed and located at sites most accessible to the local demand. Locations catering to nonresidents can be very different from those serving a local clientele.

Weisburd and Green (1995) focused their analysis on Jersey City, New Jersey. They determined that illegal drug market places could be spatially concentrated, and mapped "intersection areas" that were hot spots of illegal drug sales. They discovered that these drug hot spots made up only 4.4% of the street sections of Jersey City. However, they accounted for approximately 46% of narcotics sales arrests. These results illustrate the degree to which illegal drug markets are spatially concentrated in Jersey City, New Jersey.

Olligschlaeger (1997) examined illegal drug sales in Pittsburgh. His analysis moves beyond describing where illegal drug markets are located by attempting to predict where they will be sited in the future. He developed a new spatio-temporal forecasting method (chaotic cellular forecasting, based on neural networks) for use as an early warning system for police and public policy analysts concerned with the location of emerging illegal drug markets. He was successful in tracking displacement in time and space, identifying new hot spots before street officers were aware of their existence. He also found that the illegal drug markets were concentrated in space.

These studies used various types of police data to identify drug markets. In San Diego, Eck (1994) used police records of arrests, calls for service, and patrol information. He also collected information from agencies other than the police on the type of structure of the dealing location. In Jersey City, Weisburd and Green (1995) used police arrest data for drug offenses and for crimes assumed to covary with the location of illegal drug markets. In Pittsburgh, Olligschlaeger (1997) supplemented police data on drug-related calls for service and arrests with data from the revenue office on property ownership, tax evaluation, and property characteristics.

We built on the San Diego, Jersey City and Pittsburgh studies to analyze drug markets in Wilmington, Delaware. Wilmington is an excellent environmental laboratory in which to examine illegal drug markets. It is a small city (population of 72,000), which is also part of a large agglomeration (Philadelphia metropolitan area), and which manifests many of the features considered typical of older U.S. cities.

Wilmington is a central city, with large proportions of minority and lower middle class populations living in largely segregated conditions. The downtown is dominated by high-rise buildings, and is also typically accessible by a major highway (I-95). Transportation and movements in the city are overwhelmingly based on automobiles (as our analysis will repeatedly point out), much more so than in mass-transit based cities in Europe and developing nations. This special feature of American cities makes spatial comparisons with cities elsewhere difficult; therefore, we hesitate to claim international generalization of our analysis. Indeed, the different policy and cultural environments in countries around the world would allow for few generalizations. Our spatial analysis is further circumscribed in that its lessons are likely to be true only of automobile based cities in the United States.

Wilmington also contains a surprisingly wide variety of environments for a city of its size. Housing types range from the very expensive in the northwest to the very modest in the center and southeast. It contains an active port, financial institutions, and corporate headquarters — notably the Du Pont Chemical Corporation. Finally, it contains a small tourist and entertainment industry.

There are a variety of locations that theoretically should attract illegal drug dealers. We used police arrest data for illegal drug sales to identify spatial concentrations of illegal drug sales. One problem with police arrest data is that police may stop making arrests while an illegal market is still operating. This policy is termed "containment" (Rengert, 1996) and occurs when police write-off an area while concentrating on keeping the sale of drugs from spreading to surrounding communities. Therefore, we tested for the temporal consistency of the spatial arrangement of arrests for illegal drug sales.

We used data from the years 1989, 1990, and 1991 (at the census tract level) so as to be close to the 1990 census data used later in this analysis. The census tract is an enumeration unit that on average contains about 4000 people. The problems inherent at this aggregation — over-inclusiveness and error-prone border effects — are well known. We are, however, in good company since the census tract is the most widely used intra-urban analytical unit in the U.S. The broad outlines of the scale of arrests over time are suggested in Figure 1. Figure 2 illustrates the spatial arrangement of drug arrests in Wilmington. Notice in Figure 1 that there is temporal consistency in the spatial arrangement of arrests for illegal drug sales. Figure 2 demonstrates the spatial concentration of drug arrests in a few census tracts located in central and eastern Wilmington.

In the following analysis, we determine whether we can identify the high-ranked census tracts using models of retail marketing developed in geography. To begin, we focused on the demand of local addicts. If an illegal drug dealer wished to serve the needs of local addicts, he or she would first need to identify their individual characteristics. In marketing geography, we use demographic profiling to determine the characteristics of a hypothetical person who would have the greatest demand for illegal drugs.

Figure 1: Number of Drug Sales Arrests, Wilmington DE 1989-1991

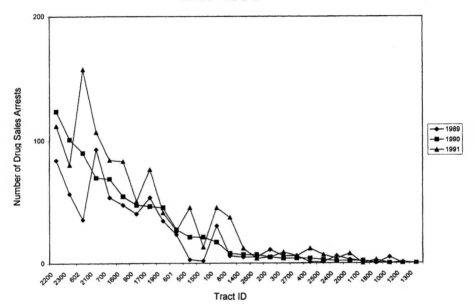

DEMOGRAPHIC PROFILE OF DEMAND FOR ILLEGAL DRUGS

There have been many studies that identify the characteristics of addicts. These studies generally agree with the findings of The National Household Survey on Drug Abuse (U.S. Department of Health and Human Services, 1993). Addicts tend to be young (18 to 30 years of age), have less than a high school education, and are unemployed in the formal economy. These variables formed the basis of our demographic profile of the local spatial demand for illegal drugs.

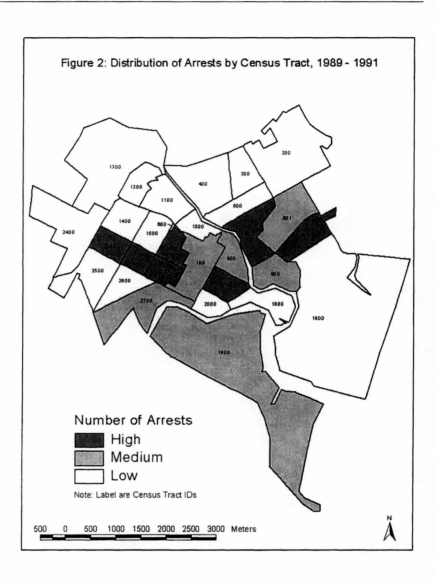

Figure 2: Distribution of Arrests by Census Tract, 1989 - 1991

Other studies also have identified and used these variables in the analysis of illegal drug use. Olligschlaeger (1997) used a younger age profile of 12 to 24 years to identify the population at risk for drug use in Pittsburgh. However, in Inciardi's (1995) sample of heroin users, he found the median age of first use to be over 18 years. Only alcohol had a median age of first use below 15 years. The median age of first drug use excluding alcohol identified in Inciardi's (1995) study was 15.2 years.

In their study of crack users in Miami, Florida, Indiardi and Pottieger (1995) determined that school attendance was not a high priority among the school age crack users. Twenty-two percent of the subjects had dropped out of school. More telling, 89.4% had been expelled or suspended from school. Since the entire sample of 254 youths was below 17 years of age (some as young as 12), school dropout rates will undoubtedly be higher as the sample approaches and exceeds 18 years of age. Concerning the informal economy to obtain money for crack use, these 254 youths were responsible for over 220,000 criminal offenses during the twelve months prior to the interview. The main source of income was from drug sales. Over 61% of the offenses were for illegal drug sales, 11.4% were vice offenses including prostitution, 23.3% were property offenses, and 4.2% were major felonies such as robbery and burglary. It would be difficult to maintain a serious educational career while simultaneously concentrating on a career of crime and drug abuse (Rengert and Wasilchick, 1985).

McCoy, Miles and Inciardi (1995) determined that female crack cocaine users over the age of 18 also were not likely to be high school graduates. Of the sample of 235 female crack users, 59.7% did not have a high school diploma, 64.5% exchanged sex for money and 24.2% exchanged sex for drugs. Again, these activities are not conducive to a serious formal career (Rengert and Wasilchick, 1985).

When we focus directly on employment, Fagan (1993) identified unemployment as an important factor leading many youths to choose to sell illegal drugs in postindustrial cities. As industries close or move from these cities, high-wage low-skill fabrication and assembly jobs also disappear leaving few, if any, legitimate alternative employment opportunities of the same caliber. John Ball (1991) determined that drug addicts are typically not legally employed. He describes how they support their drug habits in the informal economy. He found that addicts in New York, Philadelphia, and Baltimore committed an average of 603, 631, and 567 offenses respectively each year in those cities. These rates compute to well over one offense per day. In other words, crime is a routine activity in the daily lives of these drug addicts. Finally, Pettiway (1994), in his ethnographic study of addicts in the Philadelphia inner city, found the vast majority to be unemployed in the formal economy.

These studies illustrate that not only local demand, but also the local availability of labor to sell illegal drugs may be closely related to the unemployment and school-dropout status of an area. Therefore, if one were an illegal drug dealer concerned with maximizing profits from sales to a local clientele, a major consideration would be accessibility of the site to the young, the unemployed, and the post-teens with less than a high school education. This leads to methods of identifying such sites, methods developed in marketing geography.

MARKETING GEOGRAPHY

The retail sale of illegal drugs has principles in common with the sale of legal products. For both the goal is to make a profit. Illegal operations also have the additional goal of avoiding apprehension. The location of the sales enterprise is a strong factor in the attainment of both goals (Rengert, 1996). Ghosh and McLafferty (1987:2) highlight the importance of spatial location:

A well-designed location strategy is an integral and important part of corporate strategy for retail firms. Whether selling goods or services, the choice of outlet locations is perhaps the most important decision a retailer has to make. It is through the location that goods and services are made available to potential customers. *Good locations allow ready access, attract large numbers of customers, and increase the potential sales of retail outlets.* [Emphasis added]

Seldom have the locations of illegal enterprises been evaluated from this marketing perspective (Eck, 1994). More commonly, the locations are related to the social and economic status of neighborhoods (Davis et al., 1993), and the deterioration of the built environment (Skogan, 1990).

Marketing geographers have identified several strategies for determining optimal locations for retail firms (Davies, 1984). One such strategy is a location-allocation model (Ghosh and McLafferty, 1987). Location-allocation models of retail geography consist of five basic elements: (1) the objective function; (2) demand points; (3) feasible sites; (4) a distance matrix; and (5) an allocation rule.

In the present study, we used the objective function of maximizing sales volume by minimizing distance to potential customers. The demand points are assumed to be the centroids of census tracts in Wilmington, Delaware. In this initial analysis, we used a "planar model" that assumes feasible sites for illegal drug markets exist everywhere in Wilmington. This assumption was relaxed later in the analysis to mask wealthy housing areas where drug markets are not likely to be established. Computing the distance between the centroids of census tracts in Wilmington formed a distance matrix. The allocation rule is that potential customers are assigned to the census tract that minimizes total distance traveled by potential customers of illegal drugs.

THE ANALYSIS

We began the analysis by determining which census tract is the most centrally located in Wilmington. This was determined by summing the distances between each census tract and all the others in Wilmington (the columns in the distance matrix). The census tract with the smallest sum, tract # 1600, is the most centrally located in Wilmington (Figure 2).

This tract is the most accessible to the total area if we ignore transportation infrastructure and the distribution of potential customers. Secondly, we determined which census tracts contain the most arrests for illegal drug sales per square kilometer during the years 1989-91. This turned out to be census tract 2200 (see Table 1). In other words, if police arrests for drug sales are an indicator of the location of illegal drug sales, then they were more concentrated in census tract 2200 than any other. There also were high concentrations in census tracts 2100, 2300, and 1600.

We next turned to the spatial arrangement of local demand for illegal drugs in Wilmington. We considered each variable in turn and then combined them into a profile of spatial demand for illegal drugs. The first factor was age; the number of people between the ages of 15 and 29 who resided in each census tract in Wilmington. The objective was to determine the census tract to which these people would have to travel the least distance if they all purchased illegal drugs within the same tract. This can be computed by weighting the distance matrix by the number of people aged 15 to 29 in each census tract. This weight gives us the total number of person-miles that would have to be traveled if all illegal drugs were purchased in a single census tract. From the perspective of each specific census tract, when we sum each column, we have the number of person miles all persons aged 15 to 29 in Wilmington would have to travel if all of them traveled to a given census tract to purchase illegal drugs. Given this factor, the most accessible census tract to 15- to 29-year-old residents of Wilmington was tract # 600 (Figure 2). This is a very small tract near the Central Business District of Wilmington. It contained no arrests for the sale of illegal drugs.

The next factor considered was educational attainment. The census listed the number of individuals over 18 years of age who have not graduated from high school for each census tract in Wilmington. If we weight the distance matrix by this factor and sum the columns to determine the census tract that is most centrally located for those over 18 without a high school diploma, it is tract # 1600. This also is the most centrally located tract in Wilmington. It also was a major center of arrests for drug sales, although it was not the highest in the city.

Table 1: Drug Arrests per Square Kilometer

Census Tract #	Area (sq KM)	Drug Arrest Total	Drug Arrest % by Tract	Arrests (sq KM)
2200	0.26	320	13.3%	1230.8
2100	0.30	270	11.2%	900.0
2300	0.35	239	9.9%	682.9
1600	0.32	186	7.7%	581.3
1700	0.38	174	7.2%	457.9
602	0.64	284	11.8%	443.8
700	0.55	205	8.5%	372.7
900	0.40	132	5.5%	330.0
500	0.49	69	2.9%	140.8
100	0.79	91	3.8%	115.2
800	0.54	51	2.1%	94.4
601	0.85	77	3.2%	90.6
1500	0.41	36	1.5%	87.8
1400	0.49	24	1.0%	49.0
2000	0.28	13	0.5%	46.4
300	0.47	19	0.8%	40.4
2600	0.45	16	0.7%	35.6
1900	4.44	114	4.7%	25.7
1000	0.28	5	0.2%	17.9
2500	0.76	13	0.5%	17.1
400	1.02	17	0.7%	16.7
2700	0.91	15	0.6%	16.5
200	1.79	21	0.9%	11.7
2400	1.29	12	0.5%	9.3
1100	0.60	4	0.2%	6.7
1200	0.41	1	0.0%	2.4
1800	6.07	4	0.2%	0.7
600	0.01	0	0.0%	0.0
1300	2.25	0	0.0%	0.0
TOTALS	27.80	2412	100%	

Finally, we considered the unemployment factor. When we weight the distance matrix by the number of unemployed persons living in each census tract and sum the columns, we determined which census tract is most centrally located to unemployed persons in Wilmington. This again was tract # 1600.

Our next step was to combine the three factors into a single weight for the distance matrix to create a composite geo-demographic profile of locations for illegal drug sales. Since we did not have data on the individual characteristics of those arrested for illegal drugs in Wilmington, we used data from the National Household Survey on Drug Abuse (U.S. Department of Health and Human Services, 1993). We determined the proportion of each category in this national sample that used drugs in the past year. For the age category used in our analysis, the proportion using drugs ranges from 14% to 29%. Therefore, we weighted the age factor by .20. About 30% of the people with less than a high school education used drugs in the past year. Therefore, we weighted our educational attainment factor by .30. Finally, 37% to 41% of the unemployed used drugs in the past year. Therefore, we weighted our unemployment factor by .39. These weighted scores were summed for each census tract and applied as a composite weight to the distance matrix. When the three demographic factors were combined, census tract # 1600 again turned out to be the most accessible.

LIMITATIONS OF THE INITIAL LOCATION-ALLOCATION MODEL

There are two important limitations of the simple form of the location-allocation model. The first is the assumption of a "planar model" in which any location in the city of Wilmington is a potential site for an illegal drug market. Clearly residents of stable neighborhoods with expensive homes are not likely to tolerate open-air drug markets in their midst. In fact, even indoor drug sales locations have been sites of confrontations in stable neighborhoods (Lacayo, 1989). Therefore, we relaxed this assumption to mask out residential areas in which the median value of housing was above average for the city.

The second limitation is the assumption that local addicts will travel anywhere in Wilmington to purchase illegal drugs. Pettiway (1994) determined that most addicts do not travel beyond a mile in their journey to purchase illegal drugs. Therefore, we modified our model with a dummy variable of zero if a census tract center was beyond a mile of another and a value of one if it was equal to or less than a mile.

We combined these two revisions of the original model by first excluding from the analysis combinations of census tracts that are more than a mile from each other. Following this, we used the composite factor model, which did not consider census tracts containing residential units valued above the median for the city, and did consider the next most optimal census tract. In this case we no longer used the distance matrix. In its place we used a matrix containing zeros and ones and identified those tracts that were within a mile of the largest number of people who fit our composite profile of potential illegal drug users.

This analysis produced more realistic spatial arrangements than the previous analysis. Figure 3 illustrates there are two clusters of census tracts that are within one mile of the most potential customers who were identified by the composite demographic profile and are below the median value of housing for the city of Wilmington. The most advantageous location is the area including the contiguous census tracts 2200, 2300, and 1400. These three tracts ranked first, second, and third on our composite profile of potential customers while still containing homes below the median for the city. Using these same criteria, the census tracts that ranked fourth and fifth form a second cluster to the east along state highway 13. They are the contiguous census tracts 900 and 602.

These census tracts identified in our final analysis rank near the top in terms of arrests for the sale of illegal drugs. In fact, each forms the heart of a major spatial cluster of arrests for illegal drug sales in Wilmington. Tract 2200 is also the location of a major interchange from interstate highway I-95. Therefore, it also is expected to serve the nonlocal commuter traffic funneled into the city.

To this point, we had not considered these nonlocal customers commuting into the city; we only considered the spatial arrangement of local demand for illegal drugs. However, Eck (1994) determined that local markets may be the most difficult for police to identify and therefore may not be identified by police arrest records. They may be indoors and require a social network to determine their exact location. They are less likely to be open-air markets that focus on the demand for illegal drugs by commuters. The best locations for selling drugs to commuters are more likely to be open markets near or along major transportation arteries funneling automobile traffic into the city (Eck, 1994).

THE ILLEGAL MARKET FOR NONRESIDENT DRUG USERS

The major transportation artery funneling drivers into Wilmington is I-95 — an interstate highway connecting East Coast cities. There are three interchanges leading off of I-95 in Wilmington. We assumed that the closer an area is to one of these interchanges in Wilmington, the more advantageous it is to establish an open-air drug marketplace to serve some of these commuters. In Figure 4 we developed a spatial model of the location of sales areas relative to these interchanges.

In this spatial model of demand for illegal drugs by those who do not reside in Wilmington, we created distance bands of 500 meters in width from each intersection from highway I-95 in Wilmington. Twelve distance bands were required to encompass the entire city (see Figure 4). However, the outer bands contained large areas that were not within the municipal boundary of Wilmington. In this analysis we only considered areas within a distance band that also were within the city. The area within each distance band that also was within Wilmington was then divided by the number of arrests for sale of illegal drugs that have occurred within this same area. The result is the number of arrests for illegal drug sales per square kilometer in each distance band in Wilmington.

We expected that the inner distance band that contains the interchanges from interstate I-95 will contain the most drug sales arrests per square kilometer. We also expected that each succeeding distance band outward from this inner band would contain fewer illegal drug sales arrests per square kilometer. We expected this to decrease monotonically with distance from the I-95 interchanges. Note, that the analysis here is likely to be applicable only to automobile-based cities. Cities based on public transportation, such as New York City, and cities in developing countries may have drug sales concentrated about public transportation stations rather than highway interchanges (Block and Davis, 1996).

Table 2 illustrates the results from this analysis of the spatial arrangement of commuter demand for illegal drugs. Our expectations are largely substantiated by actual data on illegal drug-sale arrests per square kilometer. In fact, the inner band that contains the interchanges from interstate highway I-95 contains nearly 2.6 times the arrests per square kilometer than the next highest band. Especially high is census tract 2200, which is largely within this distance band and is predicted to have both high local and commuter demand.

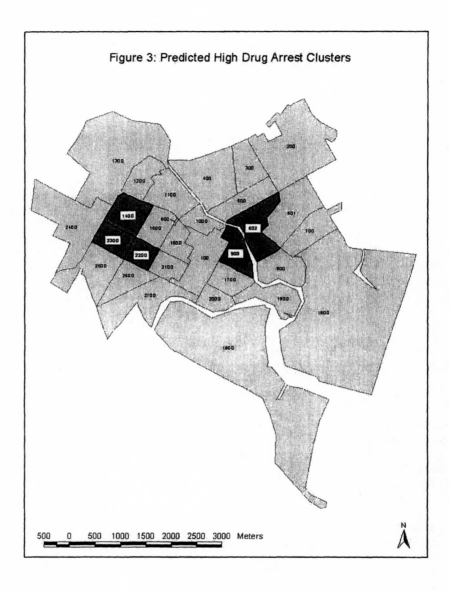

Figure 3: Predicted High Drug Arrest Clusters

The prediction of advantageous locations for the sale of illegal drugs from an economic and geographic marketing perspective is valuable information for both the police and public policy planners. The key issues are what policies one can derive from this information in order to make the sale of illegal drugs less profitable and, therefore, less likely to be established in each location. In the final section of this paper, we identify potential policies designed to take some of the profit out of illegal drug sales by making the market places less spatially accessible and by decreasing the local demand for illegal drugs.

Table 2: Drug Arrests by Distance Band

Distance Band (m)	Area (sq KM)	Drug Arrest Total	Drug Arrest % by Band	Arrests (sq KM)
500	2.001	711	29.5%	355.3
1000	3.369	460	19.1%	136.5
1500	4.046	244	10.1%	60.3
2000	4.134	562	23.3%	135.9
2500	3.625	232	9.6%	64.0
3000	2.675	195	8.1%	72.9
3500	2.454	6	0.2%	2.4
4000	1.9	2	0.1%	1.1
4001 +	3.571	0	0.0%	0.0
TOTALS	27.775	2412	100.0%	

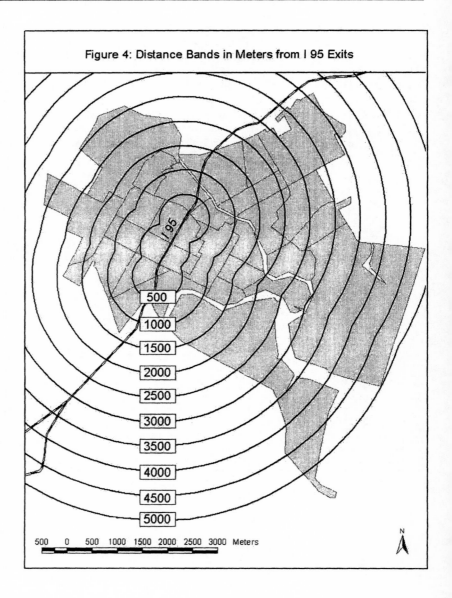

Figure 4: Distance Bands in Meters from I 95 Exits

POLICY IMPLICATIONS OF THE MARKET ANALYSIS

Tactics Focusing on Customers From Outside the City

There are several tactics designed to make open-air drug markets less accessible to people who do not reside in the community. Since it is not feasible to eliminate the exits from a major interstate highway in a city, one tactic is to rearrange street patterns so that illegal drug markets are less accessible from the exits. Commuters prefer easy in-and-out routes much like drive-through restaurants. A tactic to make access more difficult is to establish or change the pattern of one-way streets. This can be accomplished by designating a series of three or more streets as one way onto the feeder route off the exit rather than toward a drug market place. If the commuter is required to drive four or more blocks before being able to exit a feeder route, she or he will spend more time and feel less secure traveling through an often strange and potentially hostile neighborhood (Rengert and Wasilchick, 1989).

A related tactic is to establish a series of dead end streets leading from the feeder highway. Again, nonresidents will feel less comfortable buying illegal drugs in an area where they are required to spend time attempting to turn around to get back on the feeder road and the interstate. This tactic is termed the "St. Louis Private Street Plan" (Newman, 1973). It is essentially the same as creating cul-de-sacs (of the type that suburban residents enjoy in their neighborhoods) in the city. It has been determined that this type of street is less crime-prone than one that has many avenues of egress (Bevis and Nutter, 1977).

Another tactic that focuses on the nonresident who purchases drugs in the city is to arrest the buyer and require him to forfeit the vehicle used during the purchase. This practice was termed "operation fishnet" in Philadelphia. It was designed to discourage commuters from entering urban neighborhoods to purchase drugs.

There are many problems associated with this tactic including the possible confiscation of borrowed vehicles or vehicles belonging to a company rather than to the individual purchasing the drugs. Also, the past practice of the police is to keep the operation a secret from the public so that more cars can be confiscated before the public is aware of this possibility. A better tactic to discourage the commuters from visiting drug market places is to advertise beforehand that cars will be confiscated from those who drive into a community to purchase drugs and then carry out the tactic, perhaps on a random time basis. Then, when the public is notified of the confiscated cars, they are more likely to take this possibility seriously than if it is accomplished secretly. Secrecy can be punitive but cannot simultaneously be a deterrent.

The best-known tactic focused on open-air drug markets is the "weed and seed" program (Rengert, 1996). This tactic is to plan a police sweep through a community to rid it of illegal drug dealers combined with training of residents to assist the police in resisting their return. Effective cooperation is essential between the police and residents of the community who may not trust the police. If successful, there is a multiplier effect, since a given amount of police resources can be more effective than when there is no community cooperation.

Tactics Focusing on Local Demand

Public policy should not ignore local demand. Rengert (1996) illustrates that even less noxious indoor dealing can have an adverse effect on a community since the dealer can not control the activities of drug users once they leave the establishment. By spatially aggregating the drug dependent property offenders at a dealing location, the market also aggregates the related property and violent crime that tend to focus on the immediate environment. Therefore, even seemingly unobtrusive drug dealers, because of the crime they attract, can destroy the social fabric of a community. Localized demand for illegal drugs should not be ignored, since it determines where a local market place will be profitable.

There are many tactics that focus on the local demand for illegal drugs. The most obvious is to establish effective treatment programs so that those who wish to kick the habit have a means of doing so.

Public policy should also focus on the temporal dimension of addiction. A common feature of drug addiction is that it requires time to afford and to enjoy illegal drugs (Rengert and Wasilchick, 1985). One means of curtailing the time available to experimental drug users is to enact an effective school-attendance policy. There are benefits to taking school truancy seriously and providing meaningful education for urban as well as suburban and rural youth. This may require a more effective means of funding public education other than local property taxes, where low-income housing areas invariably have under-funded schools. It also may entail transfers of resources from more wealthy districts to inner-city schools. Note, again, the importance of national and local policy environments — the specific contexts of both truancy and funding sources for public education vary widely worldwide, and any generalization beyond the U.S. could only be misleading and uninformed.

An effective jobs program that requires time on the job means time that cannot be spent on illegal drug procurement and use. This is related to an effective educational program but goes further. While employment training should be for jobs that are available in the postindustrial city, they will not be effective if they are make work-jobs programs. The current welfare-to-work programs that are sweeping the United States seek to remove people from public assistance and to move them into gainful employment. However, if the available jobs are unattractive compared with those available in the informal economy (such as illegal drug sales), it is likely that many will not accept them (Fagan, 1993).

Finally, the antidrug campaigns reported by the local and national media need to be focused on potential users better than they have been in the past. Many of these radio and television spots have been written without research on what concerns potential drug users, especially young people. They have tended to focus on health issues that have little meaning for youth, as compared to the middle-aged ad writers who create these media campaigns. Recently, these ads have changed their focus to a major concern of many youth: social acceptance. Using popular sports figures is also more likely to maintain the attention of potential users than ads that use a person from the streets who tells of the dangers of drug abuse.

The importance of targeting these potential users can not be over emphasized. They create the market and therefore the profits from illegal drug sales. If addicted, many form a symbiotic relationship with illegal drug dealers by softening the social fabric of a neighborhood through their crime. This in turn allows drug dealers to operate more openly. Through geographic market analysis, we attempted to predict where it is most profitable to locate these local markets, although not all may have attracted the attention of the police. If these local markets have locational advantages, they may be the forerunners of more noxious open-air drug market places.

Address correspondence to: George Rengert, Temple University, Department of Criminal Justice, 1115 W. Berks Street, 5th Floor, Philadelphia, PA 19122.

Acknowledgments: Supported under Award #1999-IJ-CXK-005 from the National Institute of Justice, U.S. Department of Justice. Points of view in this document are those of the authors and do not necessarily represent the official position of the U.S. Department of Justice.

REFERENCES

Ball, J.C. (1991). "The Similarity of Crime Rates Among Male Heroin Addicts in New York City, Philadelphia, and Baltimore." *The Journal of Drug Issues* 21:413-427.

Bevis, C. and J. Nutter (1977). "Changing Street Layouts to Reduce Residential Burglary." Paper presented to the American Society of Criminology, Atlanta, November.

Block, R. and S. Davis (1996). "The Environs of Rapid Transit Stations: A Focus for Street Crime or Just another Risky Place?" In: R.V. Clarke (ed.), *Preventing Mass Transit Crime.* (Crime Prevention Studies, vol.6.) Monsey, NY: Criminal Justice Press.

Davies, R.L. (1984). *Store Location and Store Assessment Research.* New York, NY: John Wiley.

Davis, R.C., A.J. Lurigio and D. Rosenbaum (eds.) (1993). *Drugs and the Community: Involving Community Residents in Combatting the Sale of Illegal Drugs.* Springfield, IL: Charles Thomas.

Eck, J.E. (1994). "Drug Markets and Drug Places: A Case-Control Study of the Spatial Structure of Illegal Drug Dealing." Doctoral dissertation, Graduate School of the University of Maryland, College Park, MD.

Fagan, J. (1993). "The Political Economy of Drug Dealing Among Urban Gangs." In: R.C. Davis, A.J. Lurigio and D.P. Rosenbaum (eds.), *Drugs and the Community.* Springfield, IL: Charles Thomas.

Ghosh, A. and S.L. McLafferty (1987). *Location Strategies for Retail and Service Firms.* Lexington, MA: Lexington Books.

Inciardi, J.A. (1995). "Heroin Use and Street Crime." In: J.A. Inciardi and K. McElrath (eds.), *The American Drug Scene: An Anthology.* Los Angeles, CA: Roxbury.

—— and A.E. Pottieger (1995). "Kids, Crack, and Crime." In: J.A. Inciardi and K. McElrath (eds.), *The American Drug Scene: An Anthology.* Los Angeles, CA: Roxbury.

Lacoya, R. (1989). "On the Front Lines." *Time* September 11:14-18.

Maltz, M.D. (1993). "Crime Mapping and the Drug Market Analysis Program (DMAP)." In: C.R. Block and M. Dabdoub (eds.), *Workshop of*

Crime Analysis Through Computer Mapping, Proceedings: 1993. Chicago, IL: Illinois Criminal Justice Information Authority.

McCoy, H.V., C. Miles, and J.A. Inciardi (1995). "Survival Sex: Inner-City Women and Crack-Cocaine." In: J.A. Inciardi and K. McElrath (eds.), *The American Drug Scene: An Anthology.* Los Angeles, CA: Roxbury.

Newman, O. (1973). *Defensible Space.* New York, NY: Collier Books.

Olligschlaeger, A.M. (1997). "Spatial Analysis of Crime Using GIS-Based Data: Weighted Spatial Adaptive Filtering and Chaotic Cellular Forecasting with Applications to Street Level Drug Markets." Doctoral dissertation, H. John Heinz III School of Public Policy and Management, Carnegie Mellon University, Pittsburgh, PA.

Pettiway, L.E. (1994). "Copping Crack: The Travel Behavior of Crack Users." Mimeo.

Rengert, G.F. (1996). *The Geography of Illegal Drugs.* Boulder, CO: Westview Press.

—— and J. Wasilchick (1989). *Space, Time, and Crime: Ethnographic Insights into Residential Burglary Final Report.* Washington, DC: National Institute of Justice.

—— and J. Wasilchick (1985). *Suburban Burglary: A Time and A Place for Everything.* Springfield, IL: Charles Thomas.

Reuter, P. and R. MacCoun (1992). "Street Drug Markets in Inner-City Neighborhoods: Matching Policy to Reality." In: J. Steinberg, D. Lyon and M. Vaiana (eds.), *Urban America: Policy Choices for Los Angeles and the Nation.* Santa Monica, CA: RAND.

Skogan, W.G. (1990). *Disorder and Decline: Crime and the Spiral of Decay in American Neighborhoods.* New York, NY: Free Press.

U.S. Department of Health and Human Services (1993). *National Household Survey of Drug Abuse: Main Findings 1991.* Rockville, MD.

Weisburd, D. and L. Green (1995). "Policing Drug Hot Spots: The Jersey City Drug Market Analysis Experiment." *Justice Quarterly* 12:711-736.

DRUG TRAFFICKING AS A COTTAGE INDUSTRY

by

John E. Eck
University of Cincinnati

and

Jeffrey S. Gersh
W/B HIDTA and University of Maryland, USA

Abstract: *The structure of illicit drug markets is not well defined. This is particularly true of illicit markets that operate, at least in part, above the retail level. In this paper we contrast two hypotheses concerning how such markets are structured. The first posits an oligopolistic market composed of a relatively small set of large, hierarchically organized distribution networks. The second hypothesis posits a cottage industry of drug trafficking composed of many small groups of traffickers that form and break-up easily. Using data collected from federal, state and local drug investigators in the Washington-Baltimore area, we examine the behaviors of traffickers investigated in 1995, 1996 and 1997. These data suggest that the cottage-industry hypothesis is a better characterization of drug trafficking in the Washington-Baltimore area than the concentrated-industry hypothesis. We conclude by drawing some implications for the control of wholesale drug markets.*

MODELS OF CRIME ORGANIZATIONS

How can we prevent drug trafficking? Answering this question requires us to know a great deal about the behaviors of traffickers. In particular, we need to know how illegal drugs get from their source to their points of retail sale. Despite increasing research on retail drug dealing, much less is known about the illicit transactions that precede sales to final consumers. This is not surprising: these transactions are better hidden and the drug enforcement agencies that operate at this level have received less scrutiny from outside researchers. Since little is known about middle-level drug distribution, domestic policies to address this problem rest exclusively on enforcement. Yet the same lack of information stifles policy makers' ability to evaluate the effectiveness of enforcement and to find alternative means for interrupting the flow of drugs through the United States.

Middle-level drug trafficking is a form of organized crime, but the question is, how organized is it? In a recent article, Liddick (1999) contrasts two models of organized crime. The enterprise model asserts that the primary forces governing organized crime are the same forces that govern legitimate business and that organized crime groups (like legitimate business organizations) cannot grow unless there are economies of scale in their illegitimate industry. Reuter's (1983) analysis of gambling and loan sharking found that most illegal enterprises were small, largely because the economic conditions of their markets did not lend themselves to large oligopolies. Alternatively, the "conspiracy/bureaucratic" model of organized crime suggests that criminal organizations can grow to large sizes due to the ability of ethnic networks to dominate illicit markets through intimidation and corruption (Liddick, 1999). Based on an analysis of 51 New York City Police investigations conducted in the 1960s, Liddick (1999) suggests that the conspiracy/bureaucratic model may be superior to the enterprise model. Jacobs' and Gouldin's (1999) recent description of the Cosa Nostra also is more consistent with the conspiracy/bureaucratic model than the enterprise model.

These two models have major implications for law enforcement. The enterprise model implies that criminal enterprises are small, common, and difficult for law enforcement to suppress. In contrast, the conspiracy/bureaucratic model suggests that a concerted and persistent attack by law enforcement can significantly curb the power of such an organization (Jacobs and Gouldin, 1999). Since these models and their supporting research are based largely on illicit markets other than drugs (for an exception, see Reuter and Haaga, 1989), on criminal enterprises in New York City, and rely on small samples of cases over twenty years old, it is not clear how well they describe current drug trafficking in other parts of the United States.

In this paper we will examine the behavior of drug traffickers in one part of the United States — the Washington/Baltimore region — using a unique data set containing information about drug traffickers obtained from systematic interviews of federal, state, and local investigators targeting mid-level drug traffickers. We begin by describing two contrasting hypotheses about the structure of drug traffickers operating within the borders of the United States. As we will see, these hypotheses form the basis of drug-control policy decisions. We use these hypotheses to organize our data and descriptions of drug trafficking.

The largest part of this paper describes drug-trafficking behaviors related to six core activities: (1) *communication* among traffickers; (2) the traffickers' *organizational* structures; (3) the methods of *moving* drugs from place to place; (4) the physical and social *environment* that the traffickers use; (5) the packaging of drugs for *transactions*; and (6) the *security* traffickers use to protect themselves. We will use information about these six behaviors to draw inferences about the nature of drug trafficking in the Washington/Baltimore region, and, by inference, throughout the United States.

Our paper concludes with suggestions for prevention and research. Because the data set we use is unique, additional research is required before definitive conclusions can be drawn.

TWO VIEWS OF DOMESTIC DRUG TRAFFICKING

Domestic drug trafficking has not received extensive empirical scrutiny by social scientists (see Karchmer, 1992; Adler, 1985; and Natarajan, this volume for counter examples). There are two reasons for this. First, it is the least visible part of the drug-distribution process. Retail markets have to be somewhat visible so that buyers and sellers can meet and transact business. This makes them vulnerable to police actions. Social scientists can study these markets by examining police data and talking with police officials, or by directly interviewing or observing the buyers and sellers involved (Olligschlaeger, 1997; Edmunds et al., 1996; Green 1996; Weisburd and Green, 1995; Eck, 1994; Williams, 1989). Though the growth and smuggling of drugs is far less visible than retail markets, both the production and smuggling of drugs requires activities that increase the risk of detection from law enforcement. Data resulting from law enforcement can be used to construct models of drug flows and prices (see, for example, Reuter and Kleiman, 1986). Between these two extremes, the movement of drugs becomes virtually invisible.

The second reason we have so little research into the nature of drug trafficking has to do with the nature of drug enforcement. Domestic drug-trafficking investigations are conducted by a collection of federal, state and local police agencies, sometimes organized into multiagency, multijurisdictional task forces. Researchers have difficulty getting access to these law-enforcement groups because they are less open than local police organizations. Further, domestic drug intelligence appears to focus on case-making — supporting complex investigations — rather than learning about the overall structure of drug trafficking in a region. Though strategic information could be made public, tactical information is seldom released and then only for adjudicated cases. Though an important source of information, prosecutorial case records have two important limitations. First, they are unlikely to contain case information not revealed in court. Second, they exclude cases not prosecuted and cases plea-bargained so as to avoid evidentiary disclosure to defendants' attorneys.

The consequences of secrecy on the part of the offenders and the police is that we have little systematic information on this important part of drug trafficking. This can lead to reduced policy options and misdirected antidrug strategies when policies are based on unverified assumptions about the drug trafficking industry.

As a framework for examining domestic drug trafficking, we will contrast two polar hypotheses describing this industry. The first is the "concentrated industry" hypothesis. It has a strong resemblance to organized crime as depicted in movies, in television and in popular fiction. The concentrated industry hypothesis is consistent with the conspiracy/bureaucratic model. The second is the "cottage industry" hypothesis. This hypothesis is the antithesis of the first and is more consistent with the enterprise model.

Concentrated Industry

The concentrated industry hypothesis asserts that the movement of drugs from importation (or domestic production, as in the case of some marijuana or methamphetamine) to retail sales is controlled by a few highly organized groups. These highly structured groups have abundant resources so they use sophisticated technology to remain hidden from law enforcement and to dominate their markets. They distribute most of the drugs in a region, and they can move large volumes of drugs in a short time. These few groups are well entrenched, but if they could be eliminated it would take a long time for these organizations to be replaced. In the interim, the volume of drugs in the region would be less. Their elimination would create at least a short-term disruption in retail drug markets.

The concentrated industry hypothesis implies that trafficking organizations, though well hidden and entrenched, are somehow separate from normal society. Though this hypothesis is seldom stated so bluntly, it appears to be commonly accepted by some policy makers, particularly at the federal level of enforcement. In 1996, for example, the Office of National Drug Control Policy (ONDCP) issued a program guidance to the High Intensity Drug Trafficking Areas (HIDTA) funded by ONDCP. The HIDTAs are federally funded, multiagency, drug-enforcement projects in particularly troublesome drug importation, manufacturing, growing, or distribution regions. The program guidance stated that the "[f]unding levels for each HIDTA will be adjusted on the basis of...[t]he impact of dismantling or severely disrupting the most significant national, regional and local drug trafficking organizations (particularly those having a harmful impact in other areas of the Country)" (ONDCP, 1995:1).

The 1999 National Drug Control Strategy set goals, objectives, and measures for various efforts to control drug problems in the United States. Under the Objective to "Improve the ability of High Intensity Drug Trafficking Areas to counter drug trafficking," this document set as a target, "By 2002, increase the proportion of drug trafficking organizations disrupted or dismantled as identified in HIDTA threat assessments by 15 percent above the proportion in the 1997 base year. By 2007, increase the proportion disrupted or dismantled to 30 percent above the base year ratio" (ONDCP, 1999:109). The proportion of trafficking organizations disrupted or dismantled by or within HIDTAs is to be used as the measure of compliance with this target.

These objectives only make sense if a relatively few drug organizations control a given market and if they cannot be easily replaced. If the industry is not concentrated in this way, then dismantling and disrupting will have little impact on drug trafficking.

Cottage Industry

In contrast to the concentrated industry hypothesis, the cottage industry hypothesis asserts that domestic drug trafficking, from importation to retail, is handled by a large number of small groups and individuals. Entry and exit from this industry is relatively easy and common, and no group or individual controls a large proportion of the drugs brought into an area. Many of these groups have weak organizational structures; firmly established leaders may be absent; there is likely to be an absence of specialization; and group membership may be fluid. Their access to the resources needed to use sophisticated technology is limited, so they use common, everyday, off-the-shelf technology that is easy to learn and not particularly expensive. Their access to transportation is highly variable. Some have vehicles, but others may not. Consequently, they will use private automobiles and public transportation. No trafficker will move a great volume of drugs at one time, though over time and collectively they will move large quantities of drugs. The consequence is that even the removal of the largest of these organizations will have little detectable impact, even in the short run, on regional availability of drugs.

Like the concentrated industry hypothesis, the cottage industry hypothesis is seldom stated explicitly. Nevertheless, there seems to be at least tacit acceptance of it by some law enforcement officials, particularly at the local level. Which hypothesis is the better description of drug trafficking? After we describe the source of our data, we will use the data to address this question.

DATA COLLECTION

The Washington/Baltimore HIDTA

The Washington/Baltimore High Intensity Drug Trafficking Area (W/B HIDTA) is a drug enforcement, treatment and prevention program funded by the Office of National Drug Control Policy in the urban and suburban cities and counties of Maryland and Virginia, including the District of Columbia and the City of Baltimore. The two biggest drug problems in the area are cocaine (including crack) and heroin, although marijuana is widely used. While methamphetamine is not a major problem, there have been some seizures of it within the region (W/B HIDTA, 1998).

Drug enforcement operations are carried out by 23 squads, known within HIDTA as "initiatives," comprised of investigators from federal, state, and local jurisdictions. Investigators come from the Drug Enforcement Administration, U.S. Customs Service, Secret Service, Federal Bureau of Investigations, Bureau of Alcohol, Tobacco and Firearms, the Virginia State Police, the Maryland State Police, Metropolitan (DC) Police Department, Baltimore Police Department, and other city, county, state and federal agencies. These initiatives focus on a variety of drug related problems: (1) interdicting drug shipments at airports (there is one national and two international airport in the region), bus terminals, and train stations; (2) investigating money laundering; (3) disrupting drug trafficking networks; and (4) breaking up illegal firearms-trafficking operations. On occasion, W/B HIDTA-funded investigators have addressed concentrated retail markets, but this is not their primary focus.

The initiatives are located in any of four W/B HIDTA offices around the region. These initiatives are assisted by four support systems. First, a computer network connects all 23 groups and allows quick and secure information exchange. An intelligence section provides advanced case support on complex investigations. The Watch Center permits quick access to federal, state, and local police data bases, as well as private proprietary data bases. The Watch Center also serves as a "firewall" to prevent unauthorized use of these data. Finally, the W/B HIDTA has an administrative component that provides strategic direction, fiscal oversight, software development and evaluation. The information used in this paper comes from the Law Enforcement Evaluation Section, a part of the administrative component.

The W/B HIDTA is the only HIDTA with a full time evaluation staff. The evaluation section was created with the formation of the W/B HIDTA in 1994. As a unique entity, it had to develop a new approach to evaluating HIDTA performance. The authors have in the past or currently head the evaluation section.

C.O.M.E.T.S.

To develop an evaluation strategy, we had to confront several issues. First, experimental manipulation of law enforcement tactics was not possible. The W/B HIDTA was established to facilitate coordination among law enforcement agencies across the region, including local, state and federal agencies. No provisions were made for scientifically testing tactics and strategies. Second, available data on drug-trafficker enforcement were inadequate. They consisted of information describing law enforcement activities, including arrests for drug trafficking and related offenses, drugs seized, money and goods confiscated, and offenders prosecuted. Third, there was no body of evidence or theory that suggested the law enforcement practices envisioned for the W/B HIDTA would create substantial reduction in drug trafficking.

It seemed reasonable, however, that effective law enforcement might change the nature of drug trafficking, even if it could not eliminate it. Law enforcement might displace trafficking behaviors so that traffickers became more efficient at avoiding law enforcement, and as a consequence, less efficient at distributing drugs. That is, for the same level of effort, traffickers who spent more energy avoiding being caught would be able to distribute fewer drugs. In the long run, this would reduce their drug trafficking capacity, even as it improved their effectiveness at thwarting legal intervention. If this occurred, law enforcement agencies would have the choice of either living with decreasing returns for their efforts, or changing enforcement tactics to improve their effectiveness. When explaining this theory to law enforcement practitioners, we often used the analogy of predator-prey coevolution.

This theory of enforcement-trafficker coevolution provided a structure for organizing the evaluation. First, we had to measure the behavior of drug traffickers. Second, we had to measure this behavior repeatedly, over many years, to detect changes. This meant we needed to develop a procedure for accomplishing these two objectives. There are several ways of doing this: interviewing offenders on the street, interviewing arrested offenders, or interviewing people knowledgeable about offenders, such as police officials. We chose to interview law enforcement officials for purely pragmatic reasons. We had access to them. We could ask them detailed questions. We could bound the questions by focusing on recent investigations, rather than offenders in general. We could do this repeatedly, year after year. And these respondents would have credibility in the eyes of the primary users of the evaluation reports: law enforcement executives.

Discussions with law enforcement officials and intelligence analysts suggested that we could divide trafficking behavior into six categories, and the name for the data collection process took its name, COMETS, from the acronym formed from the names of these categories. Questions about communications focused on how traffickers signaled their suppliers, customers, and each other. Organizational questions delved into the structure of the group trafficking in drugs. In the movement category we addressed the way drugs were transported from one location to another. The physical and social settings of trafficking were examined in the environment section of the questionnaire. The transactions section dealt with the way traffickers packaged, priced and disguised their goods. Finally, we examined the ways traffickers protected themselves from other offenders and the police in the security part of the data collection instrument. Several drafts of the questionnaire were developed, discussed and field tested.

We then took the questionnaire to the W/B HIDTA Executive Committee. They were concerned with two issues. First, we had originally proposed having the questionnaire completed by the lead investigator for every case investigated. Since the board felt this would impose a large burden on investigators, we adopted a sampling strategy. Second, the questionnaire, which was very long, was shortened to about 15 pages. We also switched from having the instrument self-administered to having the evaluation staff conduct interviews. With minor modifications, the questionnaire approved by the Executive Committee is the questionnaire the W/B HIDTA has used for its annual survey.

Collection Methods

At the beginning of each calendar year, the evaluation section receives a list of case numbers for investigations begun in the previous year. For the 1995 cases, a minimum of 10 cases was randomly selected from each group (all were selected if a group had fewer than 10 cases). In subsequent years the minimum number of cases was increased from 10 to 20. A member of the evaluation section then contacted the supervisor of each investigative group, told them of the cases selected and arranged times to interview the lead investigator for each sampled case. If the lead investigator was not available, then the supervisor of the group was interviewed.

It was not always possible to gather information about a sampled case. The case may have been closed and adjudicated, the case file may have been shipped to the agency's headquarters for storage, or the investigator transferred or retired. In such circumstances there would be no information about the case available, nor would anyone familiar with the case be available to answer the survey questionnaire. When this occurred, no interview was conducted for the case and the case was treated as missing. About 9% of the target sample was missing, yielding a 91% completion rate for interviews. Though these missing cases reduce the representativeness of the overall sample, for this analysis they are less troublesome. They were far more likely to involve quick investigations of small trafficking groups than long term investigations of large organizations.

The COMETS data we will use comes from 445 sampled cases (representing 620 cases) from drug trafficking investigations begun in 1995, 1996, and 1997. Some of these cases had been adjudicated when the data was collected, but many were not, and some cases may never be prosecuted. Table 1 shows, for each year, the number of new cases begun by W/B HIDTA initiatives, the number of cases sampled for which interviews were completed, and the number of sampled cases that were treated as missing. The weighted total of 620 cases for all three years is used in the following tables and figures unless otherwise specified.

Table 1: Cases Investigated and Sampled

	1995	1996	1997	Total
Cases initiated	203	216	201	620
Completed sample	120	163	162	445
Missing cases	6	25	14	45

Notes:
    Cases initiated = investigations (population)
    Completed sample = sampled cases with interviews
    Missing = sampled cases without interviews

Though these data were drawn from a probability sample of investigations, it cannot be construed as a probability sample of drug-trafficking organizations operating in the Washington/Baltimore region. That population is unknown and unknowable. There are other law enforcement operations looking into drug trafficking within the region that are not part of the W/B HIDTA. Further, it is highly likely that some drug trafficking groups escape law enforcement detection, perhaps for extended periods of time. Nevertheless, the W/B HIDTA has broad mandate, receives many referral cases from law enforcement agencies throughout the region, and applies a diverse set of investigative strategies. Thus, W/B HIDTA cases probably come closer to depicting the nature of drug trafficking in the region than any other single agency's cases.

Beginning with the 1996 cases, we asked investigators what circumstances prompted the initiation of the investigation. We see in Table 2 that in both years — 1996 and 1997 — involved citizens (i.e., informants) launched the largest proportion of cases. Referrals from another law enforcement group or agency started the second largest proportion of cases. We do not know what prompted these referred investigations, although involved citizens probably are the source.

As noted earlier, the primary drug problems in the Washington/Baltimore region involve crack and powder cocaine, and heroin. Table 3 shows investigators primarily targeted crack and cocaine.

COMPARING THE TWO HYPOTHESES

The COMETS data set is useful for comparing the two hypotheses describing domestic drug trafficking. What would the COMETS data show if one or the other of the hypotheses is reasonably correct? If a

Table 2: Reasons For Initiation of Drug Investigations

	1996	1997
Involved Citizen	48.4	43.2
Referral	38.8	35.3
Observation	4.9	10.4
Uninvolved Citizen	2.5	7.7
Confidential Sources	5.4	3.5
Total	100% (216)	100% (201)

Types of Sources of Information

Uninvolved citizens – Citizens who have no relationship with offenders reporting information to investigators.

Involved citizens – People involved with offenders providing information to investigators, often for payments (i.e. informant, cooperating defendant).

Confidential sources – Unnamed involved citizens.

Referral – An investigative group passing on information.

Observation – Investigators watching a location.

Table 3: Types of Drugs That Traffickers Move, 1995 to 1997 (percent)

	1995 (203)	1996 (216)	1997 (201)	1995-1997 (620)
Crack	45.1	58.3	41.4	48.5
Cocaine	31.7	32.6	36.8	33.7
Marijuana	16.1	15.8	22.7	18.2
Heroin	15.4	16.4	20.9	17.5
Other	9.9	6.9	9.0	8.4

concentrated industry is operating in the Washington/Baltimore area, then we would expect the investigated traffickers to be using technology that could block law enforcement access to their communications – secured fax and telephones, computers and clone phones. We would expect them to be involved with large groups with designated leaders and a hierarchical organization. Traffickers in concentrated industries should be able to move large quantities of drugs. If they move large quantities, we might see some use of large vehicles. It is not clear what types of physical or social environment concentrated industry traffickers should operate in. Drugs in a concentrated industry should be carefully hidden from law enforcement to avoid detection. Finally, traffickers in a concentrated industry should show evidence of threatening or using force to protect their assets.

In contrast, cottage industry traffickers would have a somewhat different set of characteristics. We would expect them to use everyday technology and not use encryption or other sophisticated technology. Their groups should be small and unstructured. Cottage industry trafficking should be characterized by the movement of small amounts of drugs that can be hidden on a person or in a private automobile. It is not clear what type of environment cottage industry traffickers would prefer or whether their preferences would be different from concentrated industry traffickers. These traffickers, however, would probably not engage in elaborate deceptions to hide their drugs, rather they would use common subterfuges available to virtually anyone. Finally, we would expect cottage industry traffickers to use threats and actual force to protect themselves.

Table 4 summarizes the differences between these two hypotheses with regard to each of the six types of behaviors.

THE BEHAVIORS OF DRUG TRAFFICKERS

Communications

Drug traffickers investigated in the Washington/Baltimore region use standard technologies available to most people. We see in Figure 1 that the most frequently used communication methods do not require much sophistication. Nor are these methods secure from law enforcement. They are, in fact, communication methods commonly used by many people for transacting normal, legitimate business. At the other extreme, secured telecommunications are rarely used. Investigators found very few traffickers used computers to communicate.

Table 4: Expected Behaviors of Traffickers by Hypothesis

	Concentrated Industry	Cottage Industry
Communications	Use of sophisticated technology to block law enforcement	Use of common everyday technology
Organization	Large stable groups, hierarchically structured	Small temporary groups, with little structure
Movement	Large quantities	Small quantities
Environment	No prediction	No prediction
Transactions	Carefully hidden and disguised from law enforcement	Barely hidden
Security	Use of threats and force	Use of threats and force

Natarajan, Clarke and Johnson (1995) drew attention to a new development in illicit, drug trafficking communications technology: clone phones[1] (see also Natarajan et al., 1996). We did not ask about clone phones during the first year of data collection, so we have information about their use for only 1996 and 1997. For those two years, cloned phones are the only common communication mechanism used by traffickers that are not used by the general public: 13% of the traffickers investigated used cloned phones. We do not know the degree to which the production of cloned phones is highly organized. If it is a relatively decentralized form of criminal activity, then the use of cloned phones does not support the concentrated industry hypothesis. If phone cloning is a highly concentrated criminal enterprise, then this finding could be construed as weak evidence for the concentrated industry hypothesis. But even in this case, it is possible to have a highly concentrated phone cloning enterprise supporting a very fragmented drug trafficking industry.

Figure 1: Communication Methods

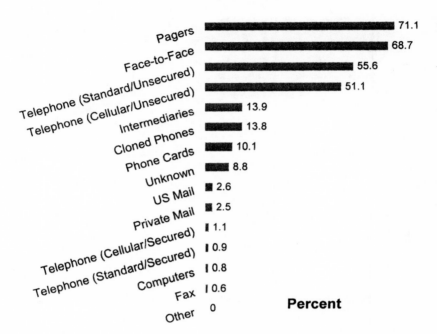

Organization

We asked investigators to describe the organizational structure of the trafficking groups they were investigating. Roughly a third (35%) were individuals without any obvious organizational affiliation. Another one-quarter (25%) were part of loose knit groups. That is, the trafficking was handled by friends and acquaintances without any formal organizational structure. Almost 40% (39.1%) were involved in some form of criminal organization. This is shown in Figure 2.

Table 5 shows the distribution of sizes of these groups. First, over a third of the traffickers are individuals, seemingly operating alone. When traffickers are involved in networks, these networks do not seem to involve many people. Among organized groups, we see that most are small, although there are a few that have more than 20 members. If the region is dominated by a few large criminal organizations, then it is among these organizations we are most likely to find the traffickers.

Figure 2: Organization Type

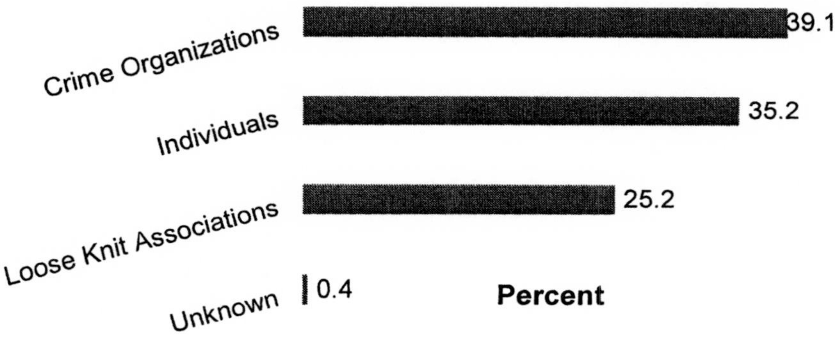

Crime Organizations — 39.1

Individuals — 35.2

Loose Knit Associations — 25.2

Unknown — 0.4

Percent

Movement

There are two questions we can ask about movement patterns. The first is how far (or from where) the drugs are being moved. The second is how are the drugs being moved. Table 6 addresses the first question. Most of the drugs the groups are moving have their source within the region, indicating that traffickers are purchasing drugs locally for sales locally. Since cocaine, heroin, and the vast majority of marijuana are not produced in the region, they have to come from somewhere outside the region. Investigators we have interviewed indicate that New York City is the single biggest source. This seems reasonable since it is a five-hour car ride at legal speeds from Washington DC, and even less from Baltimore. Buses, trains, and planes provide easy connections to New York from Washington and Baltimore.

Table 5: Size of Trafficking Groups (in percent)

Number of Members	Individuals	Loose Knit	Organized	Total %	n
1	100.0	0	0	36.5	(222)
2-5	0	62.1	17.1	22.2	(135)
6-10	0	15.7	23.9	13.1	(80)
11-15	0	7.2	15.0	7.6	(46)
16-20	0	3.9	10.7	5.1	(31)
21+	0	2.0	17.1	7.1	(43)
unknown	0	9.2	16.2	8.5	(52)
Total	100%	100%	100%	100%	(609)
n	(222)	(153)	(234)		
missing cases		3	8		11

How drugs are moved is shown in Figure 3. The most common methods of transport are the least sophisticated and cannot be distinguished from the activities of other people engaged in everyday legal activities. Large volume vehicles, and some. everyday transportation methods are seldom used by traffickers. Commercial aircraft is not a common method of transporting drugs, though one would expect it to come up frequently given the attention to airports by W/B HIDTA interdiction investigators. There are two explanations for this. First, commercial flights are expensive relative to cars, buses, and even trains. Second, airport security designed to thwart terrorism may also curb drug trafficking. In 1996, when airport security was heightened, investigators reported fewer drug traffickers using airports.

Environment

Where do drug traffickers do their business? The traffickers investigated by the W/B HIDTA typically conducted their business in residences or in public places. Almost 10% of the trafficking groups used entertainment spots — such as nightclubs, restaurants and bars — as sites for their activities. They were seldom found in public housing (the stereotypical location of retail drug dealers).

Table 6: Drug Source (Origin Of Goods)

Within W/B HIDTA Region*	22.8
Eastern Seaboard*	36.9
Other Parts of the US*	8.7
Other Countries*	5.6
Unknown	16.6
Not applicable**	9.5
Total	100.0%
(n)	(613)
(missing)	(7)

* Does not contain groups from rows above.
**For example, drug possession

Transactions

The COMETS data set contains a variety of information about the packaging of drugs. The packages are not carefully concealed or marked with a brand name (Table 7). Traffickers do not seem to take major precautions in disguising their drugs. Neither do they use distinctive markings or packaging to capitalize on "brand name recognition."

Investigators also revealed that most of the drug parcels were small to moderate in size (Table 8). Crack cocaine parcels are generally very small — usually under 30 grams. The size distribution of cocaine and heroin parcels is bimodal — many below 30 grams and another large group in the one-to-10 kilogram range. In comparison, the distribution of marijuana parcels is quite even. Except for some of the marijuana shipments, the drug parcels can be carried either by hand or in small vehicles. In short, the size range of parcels is well within the capabilities of small trafficking organizations to handle on a sporadic or regular basis.

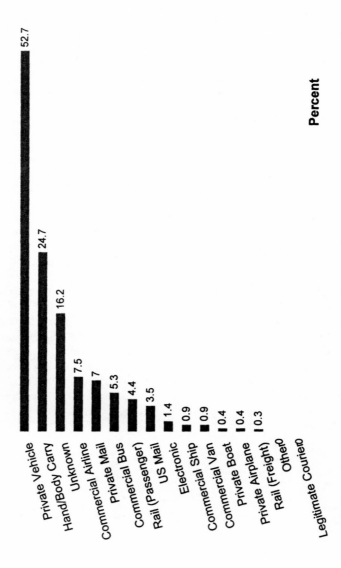

Figure 3: Methods of Moving Drugs

Private Vehicle — 52.7
Hand/Body Carry — 24.7
Unknown — 16.2
Commercial Airline — 7.5
Private Mail — 7
Commercial Bus — 5.3
Rail (Passenger) — 4.4
US Mail — 3.5
Electronic — 1.4
Commercial Ship — 0.9
Commercial Van — 0.9
Commercial Boat — 0.4
Private Airplane — 0.4
Rail (Freight) — 0.3
Other — 0
Legitimate Courier — 0

Percent

Figure 4: Drug Trafficking Locations

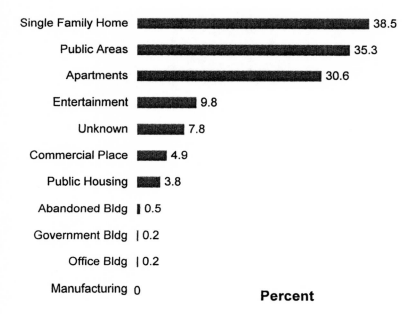

Percent

Table 7: Packaging of Drugs (percent)

Packaging unknown	10.2
Distinctive packaging	4.6
Distinctive markings	3.2
Camouflaged/disguised	2.6

Table 8: Size of Parcels (grams)

	Cocaine	Crack	Heroin	Marijuana
< 30	25.2	36.9	24.8	15.7
31 - 62	3.0	11.0	2.6	1.7
63 - 999	8.9	11.3	13.7	13.9
1,000 - 10,000	20.8	6.6	11.1	13.0
> 10,000	4.0	0.4	0.9	13.9
Unknown	30.7	24.1	32.5	27.0
Other	7.4	9.9	14.5	14.8
TOTAL	100% (202)	100% (274)	100% (117)	100% (115)

Security

Drug traffickers are concerned about two types of security: protection against other offenders (including robbery of drugs or money), and protection from law enforcement. In the COMETS data base, we have information about each. Although these are distinct forms of security, it is difficult to separate them. The same measures that might protect traffickers from being robbed, can also protect them from law enforcement. The use of threats, for example, can deter other offenders and police informants. This distinction may become blurred because the investigators we interviewed are probably more conscious of security measures designed to thwart them than security measures designed to thwart other offenders and may, therefore, assume that most forms of security are directed against law enforcement. For these reasons, we will examine security in general and will refrain from distinguishing the security targets.

Figure 5 shows the types of security used by traffickers. A large proportion of the traffickers did not use physical security. The dominant type of security was the threat of force, followed closely by surveillance of approaches to their location.

Figure 5: Security Types

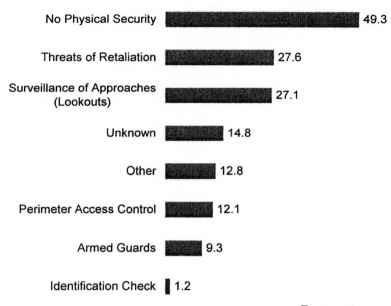

No Physical Security — 49.3

Threats of Retaliation — 27.6

Surveillance of Approaches (Lookouts) — 27.1

Unknown — 14.8

Other — 12.8

Perimeter Access Control — 12.1

Armed Guards — 9.3

Identification Check — 1.2

Percent

DISCUSSION

Analysis of the COMETS data suggests that the traffickers investigated by the W/B HIDTA law enforcement teams do not fit the concentrated industry description. They do not use particularly sophisticated communication technology. With the notable exception of clone
phones, they rely on readily available common technology many legitimate business people use. Most of the trafficking groups investigated were fragmented and small, and have limited connections to
other traffickers outside the Washington/Baltimore area. Instead of
moving large quantities of drugs at any one time, they seem to move

small amounts repeatedly. In addition, they do not seem to use extraordinary measures to conceal their packages; they simply stash their packages out of plain view. All of this information suggests that the cottage industry hypothesis has more support than the concentrated industry hypothesis.

This conclusion is further supported when we examine investigators' estimates of the "market share" of the trafficking groups. When investigators were asked to identify the geographic area that the trafficking group served, they usually gave general boundaries (e.g., the west side of city X, or Z county). On occasion, however, they described the territory of a highly localized trafficker and in this case they could provide the streets and block numbers within which the trafficker operated. Based on the reports of investigators, the traffickers do not appear to be major regional traffickers. Many trafficking groups might be characterized as large, drug-retailing groups that also engage in midlevel trafficking.

Once investigators estimated the market area served by a trafficking group, investigators were asked to estimate the proportion of the drugs consumed in that area. Here again, investigators gave very imprecise estimates that may overestimate the proportion of the market a group supplied. For example, two investigators estimated that the two groups they investigated had each supplied 25% or more of the drugs to the same high-volume drug-dealing area of a city. If we use the lower bound on these two estimates, then half of the drugs in this part of a city were supplied by these two groups. There was no apparent diminution of drug dealing in this area following the arrests of these traffickers, as one would expect if 50 percent or more of the supply was disrupted. Consequently, we must view these data as providing an extreme upper bound on the scale of operations of these groups.

Table 9 shows, reported in two ways, the estimated proportion of drugs supplied by investigated trafficking organizations. Originally, the categories for the proportion of the drug market supplied had a lower bound of under 10% (columns one and two). Two years later we found that most of the cases still fell into this category, so in 1997 we changed the question to get a more information on the lower end of the distribution of the data (columns three and four). Based on investigators' estimates, it is clear that the overwhelming majority of trafficking organizations have very small market shares for the areas they serve.

To learn more about the very few trafficking groups that served more than 10% of their market area, we examined the narrative portion of the data collection instrument. Only seven sampled cases that fit this criteria. A description of the trafficking groups involved is shown in the appendix. No group served the entire W/B HIDTA region, though group 4, with around 50 people, operated throughout the United States and has contacts abroad. Interestingly, group 4 moves types of drugs that are not the highest level of priority for law enforcement. Thus, it may have grown so large not because of intimidation and corruption, but because law enforcement has not placed a high priority on the drugs is moves. Only group 7 served an entire city. This is the largest organization and it appears to use sophisticated communication technology as well as technology to thwart investigations. This comes closest to the kind of organization predicted by the concentrated industry hypothesis.

Table 9: Investigators' Estimates of Percent of Drugs Supplied to Traffickers' Supply Areas

1995 – 1996 % of Drugs Supplied	Proportion of Investigated Groups Supplying this %	1997 % of Drugs Supplied	Proportion of Investigated Groups Supplying this %
		<2%	66.2
<10%	96.2	2-9%	8.6
10-39%	1.7	10-24%	2.6
40-59%	0.5	25-49%	.7
60-90%	0	>50%	.7
90+%	0		
Unknown	1.7	Unknown	16.4
Not Applicable	0	Not Applicable	5.1
	n=419		n=201

CONCLUSIONS AND IMPLICATIONS

These data suggest that the Washington/Baltimore region is supplied by a large number of free-lance traffickers, rather than by a few, large scale organizations. This fragmented trafficking industry is consistent with the limited empirical research on drug trafficking (Karchmer 1992; Reuter and Haaga, 1989; and Kleiman, 1987).

These findings also are consistent with those of Natarajan and Belanger (1998). Based on a much smaller sample (n=39) of federally prosecuted trafficking cases in New York, they conclude that trafficking organizations ranged in size but "(t)he small freelance groups were a little more likely to be involved in tasks higher up the distribution chain, whereas the larger organizations were somewhat more involved lower down. The largest "corporate" organizations were also generally involved in dealing at the retail level" (Natarajan and Belanger 1998, page 1019). Finally, our findings are also consistent with a wider body of criminological theory that suggests that most crime is easy to commit and does not require extensive learning or technology (Felson, 1998; Gottfredson and Hirschi, 1990).

When we look at the trafficking groups that are the most likely to be large-scale movers of drugs, we found only one (about 0.2% of the population of cases investigated in the three year period). Rather than having a few, large, well-hidden drug organizations supplying the Washington/Baltimore area, it seems more plausible that at any given time there could be drug organizations of a wide variety of sizes, although the vast majority of them are small. The large organizations do not dominate the market, but grow out of it. The larger they grow the more vulnerable to law enforcement they become, so they never get the opportunity to exert a dominate influence on the market.[2] The implication is that while one will occasionally find large, sophisticated, drug trafficking organization, eliminating it will do little to curb drug trafficking.

We must note that we have never heard a claim by law enforcement officials that they uncovered one or more organizations that supplied the bulk of the drugs to the region. In fact, when results like those shown here were presented to law enforcement officials, they neither suggested the trafficking industry had a few dominant players that we had overlooked, nor that such entities exist but had not been uncovered yet.

We must be careful with these conclusions. The data came from law enforcement officials and it might be that they were unable to detect and identify large trafficking organizations during the three years for which we have data. The large trafficking organizations predicted by the concentrated industry hypothesis may have successfully avoided detection by law enforcement, or the investigators of such groups failed to note the scale of their operations. These are possibilities which we cannot refute.

We do not believe that these explanations are valid, however. The law enforcement teams we examined were directed at large-scale trafficking. The investigators and their supervisors appeared to enjoy talking about the seriousness of their targets. And given the opportunity, investigators and their supervisors would describe the largest and most serious traffickers with whom they had recent contact. Given the formal and informal pressure to find such groups, it would be rather surprising that, if large-scale trafficking existed, it could go undetected for long. If results like these continue to be forthcoming from annual surveys, the chances of failing to uncover large, drug-trafficking organizations will diminish.

A single study based on a sample with unknown representativeness of an unknown population is a thin reed upon which to hang policy recommendations. Our only defense is that policy in the area of drug-trafficking enforcement is generally supported by even less information collected in less rigorous ways. Clearly, efforts should be undertaken to examine other wholesale drug markets in other parts of the United States. We hypothesize that if evidence contradictory to the cottage industry hypothesis is to be found anywhere within the United States, it will be in areas with a great deal of drug importation. Further, any large organization found in importation areas will be either a part of an off-shore trafficking organization, or a domestic trafficking organization with close business links to off-shore organizations. We also hypothesize that the cottage industry hypothesis will find its greatest support in areas where importation is uncommon.

If the cottage industry hypothesis is consistently supported and the concentrated industry hypothesis is consistently rejected then continued investment in federally sponsored, covert drug investigations to suppress drug trafficking must be questioned. Some law enforcement pressure is probably required to keep large trafficking organizations from forming and becoming established. This would put a cap on the size of drug trafficking organizations. In fact, the fragmented nature of drug trafficking may be due to earlier law enforcement against larger organizations. As Moore (1977) has noted, the larger the illicit organization, the greater its vulnerability to penetration by law enforcement. If true, this would suggest an adaptive response by the drug trade to past law enforcement. But if the cottage industry hypothesis is valid, the current trafficking industry is too fragmented for this approach to drug control to make additional progress. Drug trafficking on the small scale may be too easy and too lucrative.

Once an individual has established contacts with people engaged in drug sales, it may not be difficult to find partners for trafficking. This small group will find few barriers to getting the technology necessary for trafficking. Virtually all the technology required can be found in legitimate stores. Nor will these new entrepreneurs find it difficult to learn how to traffic drugs. The major barriers to entry into this market may be developing the contacts needed to acquire drugs in quantity and the necessary customers to buy the drugs. If law enforcement activities place a cap on the size and power of rival drug organizations, the field is left open to small groups.[3] Dramatically reducing the flow of drugs brought into a region by such groups will be extremely difficult, and the cost will be extremely high.

Should large-scale, covert investigations of traffickers be abandoned? Some drug-trafficking enforcement will be required to keep large trafficking organizations from forming and dominating a market. It is not obvious what else can be done, however. The principal reason we have no obvious alternatives for controlling trafficking is that drug trafficking has been defined by law enforcement as a crime that can be addressed by enforcement. The combination of a settled strategy and some legitimate need for operational secrecy has meant that information on drug traffickers has been severely restricted. With little information available, it is difficult to find alternatives to an enforcement strategy.

If we had more information and details about how traffickers behaved, it is possible we could craft situational crime prevention measures that would be more effective. These measures will require far more information than we have presented here, and this information would have to come from a variety of sources, not just investigators.

We are led to our final implication. It appears that the limited information on drug trafficking available to criminologists also limits the effectiveness of drug-control strategies. Until antidrug units of local, state, and federal agencies open themselves up to research on this topic, they are unlikely to make much progress. If our conjectures are reasonable, however, once they do create more research opportunities, the most effective ways of preventing drug trafficking may turn out to have little to do with law enforcement.

Address correspondence to: John E. Eck, Division of Criminal Justice, University of Cincinnati PO Box 210389, 600 Dyer Hall, Cincinnati, OH 45220-0389. E-mail: john.eck@uc.edu

Acknowledgments: We would like to thank Mangai Natarajan, Mike Hough and participants at the International Workshop on Drug Markets held on April 8 and 9, 1999, at the John Jay College of Criminal Justice for their helpful comments. We would also like to thank Thomas H. Carr, Executive Director of the W/B HIDTA, and the W/B HIDTA executive committee for their support of this study and other research to improve the effectiveness of drug control and prevention efforts. Nevertheless, we are responsible for any errors in this paper.

REFERENCES

Adler, P. (1985). *Wheeling and Dealing: An Ethnography of an Upper-level Drug Dealing and Smuggling Community.* New York, NY: Columbia University Press.

Bak, P. (1996). *How Nature Works.* New York, NY: Springer-Verlag

Eck, J.E. (1994). "Drug Markets and Drug Places: A Case-Control Study of the Spatial Structure of Illicit Drug Dealing." Doctoral dissertation, Department of Criminology and Criminal Justice, University of Maryland College Park, MD.

Edmunds, M., M. Hough and N. Urquia (1996). *Tackling Local Drug Markets.* (Crime Detection and Prevention Series Paper #80.) London, UK: Home Office, Police Research Group.

Felson, M. (1998). *Crime and Everyday Life* (2nd ed.) Thousand Oaks, CA: Pine Forge Press.

Gottfredson, M. and T. Hirschi (1990). *A General Theory of Crime.* Stanford, CA: Stanford University Press.

Green, L. (1996). *Policing Places with Drug Problems.* Thousand Oaks, CA: Sage.

Edmunds, M., M. Hough, and N. Urquia. (1996). *Tackling Local Drug Markets.* (Crime Detection and Prevention Series Paper #80.). London, UK: Home Office, Police Research Group.

Jacobs, J.B. and L.P. Gouldin (1999). "Cosa Nostra: The Final Chapter?" In: M. Tonry (ed.), *Crime And Justice: A Review of Research,* vol. 25. Chicago, IL: University of Chicago Press.

Karchmer, C. (1992). *Strategies for Combating Narcotics Wholesalers.* Washington, DC: Police Executive Research Forum.

Kleiman, M. (1987). "Organized Crime and Drug Abuse Control. " In: H. Edelhertze (ed.), *Major Issues in Organized Crime Control.* Washington, DC: National Institute of Justice.

Liddick, D. (1999). "The Enterprise 'Model' of Organized Crime: Assessing Theoretical Propositions." *Justice Quarterly* 16(2):403-30.

Moore, M. (1977). *Buy and Bust.* Lexington, MA: Lexington Books.

Natarajan, M. and M. Belanger (1998). "Varieties of Drug Trafficking Organizations: A Typology of Cases Prosecuted in New York City." *Journal of Drug Issues* 28(4):1005-1026.

—— R.V. Clarke and M. Belanger (1996). "Drug Dealing and Pay Phones: The Scope for Intervention." *Security Journal* 7(4):245-251.

—— R.V. Clarke and B.D. Johnson (1995). "Telephones as Facilitators of Drug Dealing: A Research Agenda." *European Journal on Crime Policy and Research* 3(3):137-153.

Office of National Drug Control Policy [ONDCP] (1995). *HIDTA Program Fiscal Year 1996 Program Guidance.* Washington, DC: Executive Office of the President.

—— (1999). *National Drug Control Strategy — Performance Measures of Effectiveness: Implementation and Findings.* Washington, DC: Executive Office of the President.

Olligschlaeger, A. (1997). "Spatial Analysis of Crime Using GIS-Based Data: Weighted Spatial Adaptive Filtering and Chaotic Cellular Forecasting with Applications to Street Level Drug Markets." Doctoral dissertation, H. John Heinz III School of Public Policy and Management, Carnegie Mellon University, Pittsburgh, PA.

Reuter, P. (1983). *Disorganized Crime: The Economics of the Visible Hand.* Cambridge, MA: MIT Press.

—— and J. Haaga (1989). *The Organization of High-Level Drug Markets: An Exploratory Study.* Washington, DC: RAND.

—— and M. Kleiman (1986). "Risks and Prices: An Economic Analysis of Drug Enforcement." In: M. Tonry and N. Morris (eds.), *Crime and Justice,* vol. 7. Chicago, IL: University of Chicago Press.

Washington/Baltimore HIDTA (1998). "Threat Assessment 1998." Greenbelt, MD: Washington/Baltimore High Intensity Drug Trafficking Area.

Weisburd, D. and L. Green (1995). "Policing Drug Hot Spots: The Jersey City Drug Market Analysis Experiment." *Justice Quarterly* 12(4):711-736.

Williams, T. (1989). *The Cocaine Kids: The Inside Story of a Teenage Drug Ring.* Reading, MA: Addison-Wesley.

APPENDIX

Characteristics of Groups Most Likely To Be Part of a Concentrated Industry

Group	1	2	3	4	5	6	7
Area	sections of City X	suburban county	suburban town	all over US	part of City Z (streets)	section of City X	city X
Drugs served	heroin	marijuana & crack	cocaine	marijuana & MDMA	crack	crack	heroin & firearms
Communications	cione phones		cione phones		secured cellular phone		secure cellular phones
Organization	size unknown, shared leadership	50-60 people (generalists) with a designated leader	20 people (specialists) with a designated leader	50 people (specialists) with a designated leader	12 people (generalists) with a designated leader	20 people (generalists) with a shared leadership	100 people (specialized) with a designated leader

Group	1	2	3	4	5	6	7
Movement	transports Colombia via airlines & from NY via passenger rail	transport via car from California	transport via private mail	transport from Mexico & Netherlands via bus, train, car & commercial airlines	transported via car from NY	transport via car (hidden compartments), bus & train	transport via car (hidden compartments), bus & train
Environment	Sell drugs out of single family home	sell their drugs on the street corner	sell their drugs out of an apartment	sell drugs out of a single family home	unknown	sell drugs out of a bar/ nightclub	sell drugs out of a single-family home
Transactions	heroin is of an above average purity (90%+)	sell marijuana in pounds and crack in ounces	kilograms	Marijuana in 20 lb. bricks	sell the crack by the ounce		sell drugs by the kilogram (purity 90%+)
Security	restricted access with security cameras, scanners to pick up DEA communications	threats and firearms	varying communication methods, use an alarm	security cameras, use of threats	threats of retaliation	armed guards	known to carry out threats of murder, use scanners & equipment to detect body wires
Percent served	about 50%	10% - 24%	10% - 24%	10% - 24%	about 50%	10% - 24%	25% - 49%

NOTES

1. A clone phone is created when a person electronically intercepts the Electronic Serial Number (ESN) of a legitimate cellular telephone, and then reprograms a new or stolen cellular telephone with the intercepted ESN. The legitimate phone customer then gets billed for the calls made on the clone phone. This not only provides free phone calls to the user of the clone phones, but if the clone phone is used for trafficking, law enforcement agents have trouble identifying the fraudulent user. Further, clone phones make the analysis of phone records from wire taps and dial number recorders much more difficult.

2. This raises an interesting possibility that cannot be developed in this paper. It may be that the size of drug organizations follows a power-law function over a large range of sizes. This would imply that the process that generates small trafficking organizations is the same process that generates large organizations, and that one could gain as much information studying abundant small trafficking organizations as rare large ones (Bak, 1996).

3. Karchmer (1992) describes heroin trafficking in Baltimore in the late 1980s. Based on interviews of investigators and the examination of cases, he states that the city had been divided among a few kingpins who kept out competition and kept violence to a minimum. Successful law enforcement operations had decreased their control on the market with the result that new traffickers started moving into the city. In response, the remaining established traffickers hired "freelance assassins to kill them." (p. 12) This increased the vulnerability of these groups, and they eventually succumbed to further law enforcement effort. So law enforcement may have not only created an environment that makes small time trafficking possible; in the process it might also create situations that can increase the violence associated with drug trafficking.

UNDERSTANDING THE STRUCTURE OF A DRUG TRAFFICKING ORGANIZATION: A CONVERSATIONAL ANALYSIS

by

Mangai Natarajan

John Jay College of Criminal Justice
The City University of New York

Abstract: *Wiretap records and other prosecution materials were used to uncover the structure of a large drug trafficking organization in New York City. Using a variety of techniques, including network analysis, wiretap conversations were analyzed in detail to determine the roles and status of individuals in the organization. The analysis confirmed that the organization was of the "corporate" type, involving a large number of individuals, clear division of labor and a recognizable hierarchy. The field workers had few contacts with others in the organization. This fact means they would be unable to provide information about those at higher levels in the organization to law enforcement officers. The analysis also revealed that those running the organization placed a heavy reliance on telephone contacts. This reinforces the value of wiretap data, not just for law enforcement, but also for social scientists studying these organizations. The methods developed in the course of this research may, therefore, have more general value in studying the operations of large criminal organizations.*

INTRODUCTION

Social scientists have experienced considerable difficulty in penetrating the secret world of drug trafficking (Moore, 1977). The ethnographic methods they have used successfully in studying street-level dealers (Williams, 1998; Knowles, 1996; Bourgois, 1995; Johnson and Natarajan, 1995; Miller, 1995; Dunlap et al., 1994; Johnson et al., 1994; Mieczkowski, 1994, 1992, 1988; Altschuler and Brownstein, 1991; Hamid, 1991; Williams, 1989) cannot readily be adapted to study the upper-level traffickers who play a vital part in creating and maintaining street markets. This situation is a result of the small monetary inducements available to researchers to pay informants, that will not be sufficient to gain access to, or achieve cooperation from traffickers. In addition, direct contact with these dealers may involve significant risks for the researcher as well as for third parties who help to locate the dealers for interview. According to Adler (1993:27), one of the few researchers to conduct ethnographic research on trafficking, ethnographers will be "confronted with secrecy, danger, hidden alliances, misrepresentations, and unpredictable changes of intent" in dealing with traffickers and smugglers. She describes many of these individuals as being particularly volatile and capable of becoming malicious toward each other or other people with little warning.

Because of the difficulties of ethnographic work with active traffickers, attempts have been made to use alternative data collection methods. For example, Reuter and Haaga (1989) conducted retrospective interviews with traffickers confined to prison. However, as noted by these authors, such interviews have their own drawbacks. It is difficult to evaluate the accounts given by the dealers who may either downplay or exaggerate their roles. In addition, imprisoned dealers, especially those who agree to be interviewed, are unlikely to be representative of the broader population of traffickers.

The records of cases prosecuted in the criminal courts constitute a third source of data about trafficking. After the case is closed, these records have little further value to the court and law enforcement agents, but they are publicly available and can be used for research. Natarajan and Belanger (1998) used these records to test the idea, widely held but with little empirical basis, that drug trafficking enterprises fall into two main types — structured and loosely structured. In fact, they found that their sample of 39 trafficking cases prosecuted in New York City could not readily be classified into these two groups. Instead, they fell into four main organizational types: (1) "corporations" (similar to the structured type identified in the previous literature); (2) "communal businesses"; (3) "family businesses" (approximating to the loosely structured organizations); and (4) "freelance."

These four types of trafficking organizations are also found among street level dealing enterprises and they have parallels among legitimate business organizations. Natarajan and Belanger, therefore, argued that the typology they developed might have general validity, despite the limitations of their exploratory study. Much more information about the organizations exists in the court records, especially in the wiretap records (Reuter, 1994). They recommended that this information be used to undertake detailed analyses of individual enterprises, drawn systematically from the four main types. In this way a more complete understanding might be obtained of the structure and functioning of the full range of drug trafficking organizations.

Their suggestion would require a considerable investment of research, beyond the resources available to most social researchers. However, individual researchers can make a contribution by undertaking case studies of particular organizations, particularly if the organizations are located within the framework provided by Natarajan and Belanger's typology.

The present paper reports one such case study of a cocaine trafficking organization that was successfully prosecuted in a New York City court in 1996. The prosecution charged that the organization was responsible for transporting approximately two to 10 million dollars worth of narcotics per week and for receiving and selling hundreds of kilograms of cocaine monthly. Most of the individuals prosecuted were of Colombian origin and the organization was linked to a prominent drug cartel. In terms of Natarajan and Belanger's typology, this was a "corporate" organization.

Wiretap data relating to the case were analyzed using a hypertext software program, which allowed qualitative data to be converted to a quantitative format. A series of linked analyses were performed to clarify the organizational structure and the roles played by particular individuals. Inferences from earlier stages were subject to sometimes quite important modifications in the light of findings from the subsequent stages. As a result, a much more detailed picture of the organization, and of the roles played by individual members, was obtained than would have been found in the court documents. As will be argued, this result has considerable implications for further research into drug trafficking.

OVERVIEW OF THE METHODOLOGY

The wiretap surveillance conducted in the course of investigating the case yielded nearly 600 pages of transcripts of 151 telephone conversations, ranging in length from two to 10 minutes.[1] (The conversations were recorded in Spanish and subsequently translated into English.) These 600 pages represent less than 10% of all the wiretap records made by agents of the prosecution in this case, i.e., only conversations relevant to the prosecution were transcribed. They came from just 12 of the 34 phones (most of which were cell phones) tapped during a two-month period in the early part of 1993. Seven of these 12 phones were owned by the central figure in the organization who appears to have operated several phones at any one time. It seems that he changed these regularly, perhaps to evade detection.

Before conducting the analysis, the transcripts had to be electronically scanned[2] and imported into a "Folio Views" database. Folio Views is a hypertext software program developed to store, sort, retrieve and analyze textual data. It meets many of the requirements of qualitative research in terms of ease of use, retrieval speed, access to very large textual data files and compatibility with standard word processing programs (Natarajan and Belanger, 1996). It is particularly helpful in quantifying some aspects of essentially qualitative data and materially assists in developing theoretical understanding of large and complex textual files.

In order to obtain a comprehensive picture of the organization and of the place of particular people within it, an analysis was undertaken comprised of five sequential stages:

- **Stage I**: *Conversational count by individuals.* Counts were made of the number of conversations in which each individual was involved and the numbers of other people with whom he or she had telephone contact.

- **Stage II**: *The status analysis.* Using a coding guide developed for this study, the relative status of individuals in the organization was determined through an analysis of the conversations in which each was involved.

- **Stage III**: *The task analysis.* The major tasks performed by each individual were identified by inspecting the content of conversations in which he or she was involved.

- **Stage IV**: *The network analysis.* Links between individuals were analyzed using a software program.

- **Stage V**: *The organizational chart.* An organizational chart for the organization was developed by combining the information yielded by stages I-IV. This was compared with the chart constructed from the prosecution documents.

STAGE I: CONVERSATIONAL COUNT BY INDIVIDUALS

Using court listings of the individuals talking in each conversation, 28 people were identified in the database.[3] The query option of FolioViews enabled the number of conversations in which each person was involved to be counted (see Table 1). One individual, Kay, participated in 125 conversations, 83% of the total. Nine people were involved in 7 to 24 conversations, while 19 people talked in three or fewer conversations. This pattern shows that most individuals were involved in a relatively small number of calls. Moreover, most people talked to only a few individuals. Twenty people talked to only one or two other individuals.

Members of this organization, probably due to the need for security, were very limited in their contacts with others. While informative, this analysis does not identify the position occupied by each individual within the organization. Kay is an important figure because he talks to a disproportionally large number of individuals (24). However, no further definitive statements can be made about the hierarchical structure of the organization based on this analysis.

STAGE II: THE "STATUS" ANALYSIS

A content analysis of conversations was undertaken to gain information about the relative positions of individuals within the organization. This analysis was designed to yield information about conversational tone, which would help to clarify the relative status of different individuals. A coding guide was constructed to use in quantifying these aspects of tone. The first step was to identify an appropriate unit of analysis, the "segment," which was defined as a continuous, uninterrupted utterance by an individual. This definition can be clarified by the following example:

Person X:	Hello! How are you?
Person Y:	All right. And you?
Person X:	Can't complain!

This fictitious excerpt has three segments.

Table 1: Individuals Involved in the 151 Wiretapped Conversations

#	Individuals Involved	Gender	Number of Conversations	%	Number of People Individual Talks To
1	Kay	M	125	83	24
2	Menna	M	24	16	5
3	Steve	M	20	13	4
4	Dante	M	20	13	3
5	Tommy	M	19	13	7
6	Blacky	M	15	10	5
7	Ross	M	15	10	2
8	Fabio	M	10	7	3
9	Frank	M	9	6	3
10	David	M	7	5	2
11	Donald	M	3	2	2
12	Peter	M	3	2	2
13	Doug	M	3	2	1
14	Louis	M	3	2	1
15	Charles	M	3	2	1
16	Marzio	M	2	1	2
17	Perretta	F	2	1	2
18	Lara	F	2	1	1
19	Gabriel	M	2	1	1
20	Bill	M	2	1	1
21	Lorena	F	2	1	1
22	Rosa	F	1	1	1
23	Shawn	M	1	1	1
24	Bruce	M	1	1	1
25	Howard	M	1	1	1
26	Jenny	F	1	1	1
27	Marky	M	1	1	1
28	Robert	M	1	1	1

The Coding Guide

The next step was to construct a coding guide that would distinguish between people of higher and lower status. The following six items were selected to serve this purpose:

(1) *Requesting information*: People of lower status are generally accountable for their actions and have to report to their superiors. Superiors will, therefore, tend to request information from subordinates about their ongoing, past or future activities and about the operation as a whole. Requests for information are stated mainly in the form of a question. Examples: "What's up?" "How did the round go?" "How are you going to arrange that?"

(2) *Expressing satisfaction*: Higher-status individuals will tend to express their satisfaction with reports of past, ongoing or planned activities. A segment of conversation includes an expression of satisfaction whenever someone is content and approves the actions of others, or is simply happy about the development of some issue. People normally express satisfaction only after being provided with information. The following words or expressions are examples of those indicative of satisfaction: "good job," "well done," "great," "good," "perfect."

(3) *Providing information*: Lower-status people will tend to provide information about their activities, not just when asked. The nature of the information provided is not important. It can relate to the development of some issue, the activities of particular individuals, the time or place of a meeting, the way the drugs are packaged, etc.

(4) *Giving orders*: Superiors will tend to give orders for action on the part of others; for example, "do this," "do that," "call him and tell him...."

(5) *Clarifying orders*: Lower status individuals will tend to clarify orders given to them by superiors. This includes clarifying some elements of the order, or simply repeating the order.

(6) *Use of "sir"*: People tend to use the word "sir" when they are talking to someone they respect or someone of higher status.[4]

The coding guide, consisting of these six items, enabled a detailed analysis to be made of the conversation segments. For the individuals in each conversation, the number of segments were counted that contained instances of each of the six items above.

Reliability of the Coding Guide

Before coding the conversations, the reliability of the guide had to be determined. For this purpose, a random sample of 20 conversations was selected. Two coders then independently coded each segment of the 20 conversations. Correlation coefficients were calculated between the ratings made by each rater for both individuals involved in the 20 conversations. Each conversation thus had two correlation coefficients, one for each of the individuals involved.

Example: Conversation # 1, Involving Steve and Kay

	STEVE		KAY	
	Coder 1	Coder 2	Coder 1	Coder 2
Requesting Information	5	3	2	1
Expressing Satisfaction	0	1	0	1
Providing Information	2	1	8	10
Giving Orders	0	0	24	12
Clarifying Orders	12	20	0	0
Use of "Sir"	0	0	0	0
	"Steve" coefficient: 0.96		"Kay" coefficient: 0.90	

The mean of all 40 correlation coefficients was 0.80 and it was concluded that the reliability of the coding guide was satisfactory.

Sampling Procedure

The sampling method had to permit the status of all members of the organization to be determined. Accordingly, one conversation was selected at random from each of the 40 combinations of telephone contacts between two people identified in the database (see Table 2). (Where only one conversation was recorded for a particular dyad, that conversation was included.)

Method for Determining the Status of Individuals

In determining the relative status of two individuals, it was assumed that higher-status individuals would generally express satisfaction, request information, and give orders; in addition, these individuals would generally not clarify orders, not use the word "sir" when talking to others and not provide information.

Table 2: Conversational Dyads (N=148*)

Dyad	Individuals	Number of Conversations
1	Kay and Menna	19
2	Kay and Dante	18
3	Kay and Ross	14
4	Kay and Tommy	11
5	Kay and Black	10
6	Kay and Steve	10
7	Kay and Frank	7
8	Kay and David	6
9	Steve and Fabio	4
10	Tommy and Fabio	3
11	Kay and Fabio	3
12	Kay and Doug	3
13	Kay and Louis	3
14	Steve and Peter	3
15	Kay and Charles	3
16	Kay and Lara	2
17	Kay and Donald	2
18	Kay and Gabriel	2
19	Kay and Bill	2
20	Menna and Blacky	2
21	Kay and Lorena	2
22	Kay and Peter	1
23	Kay and Peretta	1
24	Kay and Bruce	1
25	Kay and Marky	1
26	Kay and Marzio	1
27	Kay and Howard	1
28	Kay and Jenny	1
29	Menna and Tommy	1
30	Menna and Peretta	1
31	Menna and Frank	1
32	Tommy and David	1
33	Tommy and Marzio	1
34	Tommy and Donald	1
35	Tommy and Rosa	1
36	Blacky and Dante	1
37	Dante and Robert	1
38	Steve and Shawn	1
39	Blacky and Frank	1
40	Blacky and Ross	1

*This total excludes three conversations involving unidentified people.

To check these assumptions, correlation coefficients were calculated across the six items of the coding guide (see Table 3). The coefficients, of which five were significant, generally supported the assumptions. Thus, clarifying orders was correlated with the use of the word "sir" (0.34) and giving orders (-0.23). Giving orders (0.33), expressing satisfaction (0.28) and providing information (-0.26) were correlated with requesting information.

To illustrate the method of determining the higher-status person in a dyad, the conversation in the example above involving Kay and Steve is used. In this conversation, as scored by coder 1, Kay requests information in two segments, compared to five for Steve; he gives orders in 24 segments, while Steve gave none; he never clarifies orders, compared to Steve who does so in twelve segments. Up to this point Kay has, therefore, earned three "status" points and Steve has earned none. Since neither of them uses the word "sir," or expresses satisfaction, no points are given for these items. Steve, on the other hand, gets a point for providing information in only two segments, compared to eight for Kay. Because Kay obtains a total of three "status" points compared to one for Steve, he has, therefore, the higher status of the two.

Results of the "Status" Counts

The mean status scores for the dyads in which they appear, and the proportion of dyads in which they emerge as higher-status individuals is given in Table 4 for each of the 28 individuals in the organization. In many cases, this information is sufficient to establish an individual's status. For others, this information had to be combined with the conversational counts contained in Table 1 before their status could be determined. For a third group, the information in Tables 1 and 4 had to be supplemented by a close reading of the conversations in which they were involved.

Table 3: Correlations Between the Six Items of the Status Instrument (N=80)

Items	Requesting Information	Expressing Satisfaction	Providing Information	Giving Orders	Clarifying Orders	Use of "Sir"
Requesting Information	1.00					
Expressing Satisfaction	0.28*	1.00				
Providing Information	-0.26*	0.08	1.00			
Giving Orders	0.33*	0.01	0.10	1.00		
Clarifying Orders	-0.18	-0.09	-0.18	-0.23*	1.00	
Use of "Sir"	-0.17	-0.10	-0.17	-0.17	0.34*	1.00

*p<0.05

Table 4: Relative Status of the 28 Individuals in the Organization

#	Individual	Mean Status Scores	Appears in # of Dyads	Higher Status in # of Dyads
1	Ross	5	2	2
2	Frank	4	3	3
3	Dante	4	3	3
4	Lara	4	1	1
5	Gabriel	3	1	1
6	Kay	2.5	24	14
7	Tommy	2.1	7	1
8	David	2	2	0
9	Doug	2	1	0
10	Lorena	2	1	1
11	Rosa	2	1	0
12	Steve	1.8	4	1
13	Fabio	1.7	3	1
14	Menna	1.6	5	3
15	Peter	1.6	2	1
16	Blacky	1.2	5	0
17	Donald	1	2	1
18	Charles	1	1	0
19	Marzio	1	2	1
20	Howard	1	1	0
21	Jenny	1	1	0
22	Perretta	.5	2	0
23	Marky	0	1	0
24	Louis	0	1	0
25	Bill	0	1	0
26	Shawn	0	1	0
27	Bruce	0	1	0
28	Robert	0	1	0
	Total Average	**1.6**		

The analysis reported in Table 1 had shown that Kay talks to many more people in the database, and is involved in many more conversations (83% of all conversations) than anyone else in the database. Table 4 indicates that he is actually a figure of authority. Out of the 24 dyads in which he is involved, he is clearly the higher-status individual in 13 of the cases. These data indicate that that Kay is the key individual in the organization, and is in charge of its daily operations. In four other conversations involving Kay, it was unclear who was the higher-status person (see below), while in seven conversations, the other person obtained a higher status score. These were Dante, Frank, Ross, Lorena, Jenny, Peter and Gabriel. As it turns out Dante, Frank and Ross were all bosses in Columbia and Gabriel is directly associated with them. Lorena and Jenny, both women, are treated respectfully by Kay even though they do not hold important positions. By all the other evidence Peter is a low-level worker and his higher score in the conversation with *Kay* is an anomaly resulting from the nature of the scoring procedure.

STAGE III: THE TASK ANALYSIS

The two previous stages of the analysis provided insight into the structure of the organization and the relative status of individual members, but little information about the tasks performed by particular individuals (except that Kay was clearly managing the day-to-day operations for a group of bosses). This information could only be obtained by reading the conversations, sampled one at a time for each individual (starting with the conversations sampled for the status analysis), until it was clear what tasks he or she performed. As a result, individuals could be classified into four main groups: bosses in Colombia, assistant managers reporting to Kay, lower-level field operatives working under the assistant mangers and field workers working directly for Kay.

(1) *Bosses in Columbia*: Dante, Ross and Frank oversee the operations through Kay. They make sure that meetings with customers are well prepared and that the operation is running smoothly. Lara acts as Frank's secretary. She takes messages from Kay whenever Frank is not around. Gabriel is not a boss, but works directly with them. His principal role appears to be a courier. He was involved in at least one trip carrying drugs from Columbia or taking money to Colombia.

(2) *Assistant managers*: Menna takes care of the technical aspects of the operation. He buys and sells cars for employees, and is in charge of getting license plates and the proper documentation from the Department of Motor Vehicles. He

also is in charge of buying and replacing beepers and cellular phones. He constantly changes the numbers for both in order to elude surveillance. He also obtains useable credit cards for Kay. Blacky is in charge not only of interrogating suspect employees but also of planning to kill them. He was hired, relatively recently, to carry out a few specific tasks and so enjoys a certain degree of autonomy. Tommy is in charge of delivering narcotics and money. An active worker, he is trusted by Kay. Steve, also an active and apparently trusted worker, takes care of important narcotics and/or money tasks, such as delivery and storage.

(3) *Field workers reporting to the assistant managers*: David runs errands and is in charge of making a delivery to Bill. Peter makes deliveries of money and runs other errands. Marzio assists Tommy. Perretta has most contact with Menna. She is in charge of a stash house, in which she lives, and does not play an important role in the organization. Shawn works with Steve. Donald and Rosa work principally for Tommy in transporting drugs.

(4) *Field workers reporting to the chief operator*: Louis meets with people (customers) on behalf of Kay. Charles is a delivery worker, who was suspected of having stolen some money. Blacky had planned to interrogate him and, depending on the outcome, kill him. Jenny may be in charge of a stash house. Marky, Doug and Bill are lower-level workers. While their tasks are unclear, they seem to be involved in transporting drugs. Howard is in charge of bringing a suspect employee for interrogation, along with Blacky and Gabriel. Fabio has a special position: he seems to be *Kay*'s special assistant with a somewhat higher status than the field workers. He acts as a link between Kay and Tommy and Steve, two of the assistant managers.

STAGE IV: THE NETWORK ANALYSIS

The three previous stages of the analysis provided information about the structure of the organization, about the relative status of individual members, and about the tasks they perform. It is clear that there is a considerable degree of specialization of roles and that individuals are loosely grouped into teams of workers headed by "managers" who take responsibility for particular areas of the organization's functioning. However, the degree to which there is contact among the various members of a "team" and among the various teams is unclear. A method of determining this is provided by network analysis, particularly varieties making use of the concept of centrality (Wasserman and Faust, 1994; Berkowitz, 1982). This provides a measure of the degree of interaction among the members of the organization.

According to Baron and Tindall (1993:258), "Degree centrality is measured by counting the number of others that are adjacent to an individual and with whom she/he is in direct contact." Sparrow (1991), who has used network analysis in studying criminal organizations, contends that there are different centrality notions of varying complexity. For the purposes of the present analysis, however, it was sufficient to produce a rudimentary graphic representation of the links between individuals and groups.

Accordingly, the "simulated annealing" features[5] of KrackPlot[6] were used to create an adjacency matrix (Krackhardt et al., 1995) that identified individuals playing important roles in the organization, measured by degree centrality. Figure 1 depicts Kay, Tommy, Menna, Blacky, Dante, Frank, Steve, Ross, Fabio, Perretta, Marzio, David and Peter as being important in the organization based on their direct contact with other individuals in the organization. However, Kay emerges, once again, as the central figure in the organization. In addition, Blacky, Tommy and Menna are the foci of three "teams." This fact is consistent with the task analysis revealing Menna as the center of technical operations, Tommy as the center of distribution tasks and Blacky as the center of security.

Figure 1 also suggests that there is limited contact between the groupings or teams in the organization and that many members of the organization are quite isolated. For example, Kay has links to many individuals (10) who are not directly linked to any of the clusters or any other individuals. A further example is provided by Blacky, who appears to be in charge of security issues for the organization. He has direct contact with the bosses in Columbia, but no direct contact with the distribution network managed by Tommy.

A measure of the degree of inter-relatedness or density of contacts between individuals or teams is provided by "set" analysis. Using Barnes's set-analysis formula recommended by Ianni and Ianni (1990), "percent-density" scores[7] (see Table 5) were calculated for the organization as a whole, with Kay as the focal point, and for the three principal teams (Menna, Blacky and Tommy). In all cases the percent-density scores are well below the critical value of 80%. These scores indicate that this is a loosely connected organization, with many relatively isolated individuals and relatively little contact between teams responsible for major organizational functions.

Figure 1: Network Structure of the Drug Trafficking Organization

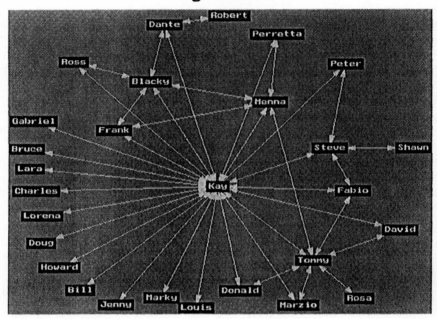

Table 5: Density Scores for the Organization and for the Three Teams

	Percent Density
1. Organization as a whole (Kay as central or focal point)	10
2. Drug Distribution Team (Tommy as central or focal point)	43
3. Menna as central or focal point	60
4. Blacky as central or focal point	66

STAGE V: THE ORGANIZATIONAL CHART

Based on the results of the analyses reported above, it is possible to produce an organizational chart for the trafficking enterprise (see Figure 2). This can be compared with the chart derived from the prosecution's case materials (see Figure 3). This comparison shows that the organizational chart derived from the analyses presented above (Figure 2) is the more complex of the two in that it:

- identifies the individuals in Colombia who were the bosses of the organization, and reveals their connections with the chief operator and other members of the organization;

- distinguishes among assistant managers on the basis of the tasks they perform;

- shows that the chief operator directly supervises many of the field workers;

- makes connections between individual field workers and particular assistant mangers.

The picture of the organization presented by the prosecutors is of course related to their goals, and some aspects of the organization are likely to have been of peripheral interest to them. This includes the identities and the roles of the bosses in Columbia because they were outside the reach of the prosecutors. Nor is the division of tasks within the organization of much importance to the prosecution — perhaps because they were more concerned with emphasizing the seriousness of the organization's activities (amounts of drugs and violence), coupled with the involvement of particular individuals.

DISCUSSION AND CONCLUSIONS

The sequential steps of the analysis reported above reveal a more complete picture of the structure of this "corporate" drug trafficking organization than presented in the prosecution case. In particular, it identifies the individuals in Colombia who were the bosses of the organization, and reveals their connections with the chief operator and other members of the organization. It distinguishes among assistant managers on the basis of the tasks they perform and shows that the chief operator directly supervises many of the field workers. It shows which field workers are linked to particular assistant managers. Finally, it suggests that many of the field workers have limited contacts with others in the organization.[8]

The prosecutors might not, in fact, have needed so much detail about the structure of the organization in order to achieve a successful result. On the other hand, Peterson (1994) has observed that many law enforcement agencies have not properly incorporated intelligence and analysis into their organized crime control function for two reasons. First, the benefits may be unclear to them and, second, they may be reluctant "to deviate from the traditional methods of investigation" (Peterson, 1994:360).

It is possible that more detailed information available to the prosecutors in this case might have resulted in their pursuing a somewhat different approach, focused more on other individuals in the trafficking organization. This is not to criticize the prosecutors or the quality of their analysis. Rather, it is to suggest that the kind of sociometric analyses undertaken above could be of practical value in helping the prosecution to develop an understanding of drug trafficking organizations that they must indict.

Law enforcement intelligence analysts already make some use of network analysis, such as Anacapa Charting System (Sparrow, 1991). Indeed, according to Ianni (1990:82), network analysis has been found to be "...an invaluable tool for amalgamating and translating the often disparate bits of information and observations into an understandable pattern of behaviors and social action, and determining the logic or 'rules of the game' which structure those relations." Such analyses might not be justified on a routine basis, but might become valuable when the organization is large and important, and when the case has aroused significant public disquiet.

By the same token, when using court records of prosecuted cases to study criminal organizations, social scientists must remember that prosecutors do not have to present a more detailed picture of the organization than is needed to achieve their goals. This means that they present only some of the information available to them. Accordingly social scientists must not rely completely on the prosecution's description of the case. Rather, they must always undertake their own analyses of court data if they are to obtain a thorough understanding of the structure of the organization, its constituent personnel and the roles played by these individuals in its functioning (Parsons, 1968). For example, an understanding of the network of relationships among field workers was important for the sociological analysis presented above, but this may not have been needed in prosecuting the case.

Figure 2*: Structure of the Drug Trafficking Organization According to Wiretap Database**

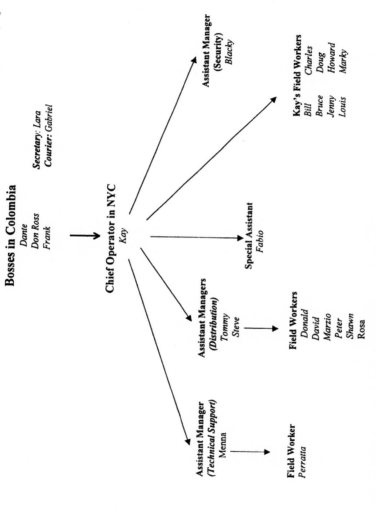

Bosses in Colombia
Dante
Don Ross
Frank

Secretary: Lara
Courier: Gabriel

Chief Operator in NYC
Kay

Assistant Manager (Security)
Blacky

Kay's Field Workers
Bill   *Charles*
Bruce   *Doug*
Jenny   *Howard*
Louis   *Marky*

Special Assistant
Fabio

Assistant Managers (Distribution)
Tommy
Steve

Field Workers
Donald
David
Marzio
Peter
Shawn
Rosa

Assistant Manager (Technical Support)
Menna

Field Worker
Perratta

*The roles of *Robert and Lorena* cannot be determined from the wiretap data
** *Bruce, Bill, Doug, Marky, Peter and Fabio* are not accused of crime in the prosecution records

Figure 3: Structure of the Drug Trafficking Organization According to the Prosecution Records*

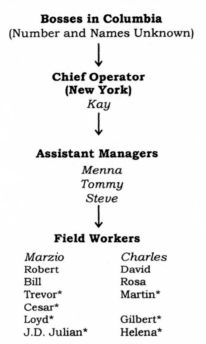

Bosses in Columbia
(Number and Names Unknown)

↓

**Chief Operator
(New York)**
Kay

↓

Assistant Managers
Menna
Tommy
Steve

↓

Field Workers

Marzio	*Charles*
Robert	David
Bill	Rosa
Trevor*	Martin*
Cesar*	
Loyd*	Gilbert*
J.D. Julian*	Helena*

*These seven individuals do not appear in the wiretap data. In addition, for six individuals who were mentioned in the prosecution case no information could be found concerning their roles in the organization.

One novel feature of the methodology employed above is that it has undertaken a quantitative analysis of essentially qualitative information. It has produced a detailed picture of one trafficking organization based upon what individuals in the organization said to each other in wiretapped conversations. These wiretap records are available for many trafficking cases prosecuted in the courts. The method seems to be robust and could be used to study not just "corporate" organizations of the type analyzed above, but also the three other kinds of trafficking organizations — "communal businesses," "freelance" and "family businesses" — identified by Natarajan and

Belanger (1998). Such studies would considerably enhance our knowledge of drug trafficking.

Wiretap records have their limitations as a source of data about criminal organizations. Thus, suspects targeted for wiretapping may not be representative of the organization as a whole. Their phones may be tapped for relatively brief and possibly unrepresentative periods. Since they often speak in a foreign language, translation may result in loss of important information. They also sometimes speak in code that may not be easy to decipher. Finally, the records of conversations are not always maintained in a complete form. Despite these problems, analysis of wiretapped conversations might also prove to be of more general value to social scientists in studying other kinds of illegal organizations. If so, this would be important in view of the difficulties mentioned above of studying these organizations through conventional ethnographic methods.

In addition to lessons for methodology, the results of the present study also have implications for policy. Because they reveal a loosely structured corporate organization with a lack of ties between individuals, they underline the difficulties of interdiction. No doubt this structure has been deliberately created with just this in mind. "Corporate" organizations of the kind studied here cannot rely on personal, communal or family loyalties to protect the organization when a lower-level employee is arrested. Instead, they must ensure that these employees do not know much about the organization, especially about the major players. In other words, arresting lower-level employees would achieve little in terms of interfering with the organization's operations and would produce little useful intelligence about the bosses.

Faced with these difficulties, law enforcement agents have pursued the alternative approach of conducting intensive wiretap surveillance focused at higher levels in the organization. This may be a lengthy and difficult process, but this surveillance exploits what may be the most vulnerable aspect of trafficking: the essential need for frequent telephone contacts between various members of the organization. Without this telephone contact, it would be impossible for bosses in Colombia to exercise such close control over the organization and impossible for the managers to direct and instruct the lower-level workers.

The cloning of cell phones has been a godsend to traffickers because this has not only reduced the costs and difficulties of using phones, but has also helped to protect them from arrest (Natarajan et al., 1996, 1995). Wiretap techniques have been improved with the result that cloned phones are no longer out of reach of surveillance. It may therefore not be long before traffickers begin communicating via the Internet. This will lead to yet another round of "catch-up" measures by law enforcement agencies and more despair about the difficulties of effectively intervening in trafficking.

One response to the difficulties of interfering with the supply of drugs might be to focus instead on reducing the demand. But demand for drugs is inextricably entwined with their supply, and reducing demand may depend on reducing supply (Smart, 1980; Huba et al., 1980). In any case, it seems premature to abandon interdiction at this stage when so little is known about how drugs reach this country, how they are distributed locally and how they get into the hands of users.

The key to the successful prevention of many other kinds of crime has been a detailed understanding of how these crimes are committed (Clarke, 1997, 1995). We must therefore broaden and deepen our knowledge of these matters for drug trafficking. The methodology developed in this paper usefully expands the techniques currently available for this purpose.

Address correspondence to: Dr. Mangai Natarajan, Department of Sociology, John Jay College of Criminal Justice, The City University of New York, 899 Tenth Avenue, New York, NY 10019. E-mail: mnjjj@cunyvm.cuny.edu

Acknowledgments: This research was primarily supported by a grant from the National Institute on Drug Abuse (1K21DA00242-04 & 05). Viewpoints in this paper do not necessarily represent the official positions of the U.S. Government, National Institute on Drug Abuse and John Jay College of Criminal Justice. The author acknowledges the assistance of Mathieu Belanger and Laura Parisi in data analysis and wishes to thank Ronald V. Clarke of Rutgers University for his advice and Ms. Mari Maloney of Special Narcotics Prosecutors' Office for her comments.

REFERENCES

Adler, P.A. (1993). *Wheeling and Dealing: An Ethnography of an Upper-level Drug Dealing and Smuggling Community.* New York, NY: Columbia University Press.

Altschuler, D.M. and P.J. Brownstein (1991). "Patterns of Drug Use, Drug Trafficking, and Other Delinquency Among Inner-city Adolescent Males in Washington, D.C." *Criminology* 29(4):589-622.

Berkowitz, S.D. (1982). *An Introduction to Structural Analysis: The Network Approach to Social Research.* Toronto, CAN: Butterworth.

Baron, S. and D.B. Tindall (1993). "Network Structure and Delinquent Attitudes Within a Juvenile Gang." *Social Networks* 15(3):255-273.

Bourgois, P. (1995). *In Search of Respect: Selling Crack in El Barrio.* New York, NY: Cambridge University Press.

Clarke, R. (1997). *Situational Crime Prevention: Successful Case Studies.* Albany, NY: Harrow and Heston.

—— (1995). "Situational Crime Prevention." In: M. Tonry and D. Farrington (eds.), *Building Safer Society: Strategic Approaches to Crime Prevention,* vol. 19. Chicago, IL: The University of Chicago Press.

Dunlap, E., B.D. Johnson and A. Manwar (1994). "A Successful Female Crack Dealer: Case Study of Deviant Careers." *Deviant Behavior* 15:1-25.

Hamid, A. (1991). "Differences Between the Marijuana Economy and the Cocaine/Crack Economy." *International Journal of the Addictions* 26(8):825-836.

Huba, J.G., A.J. Wingard and M.P. Bentler (1980). "Framework for an Integrative Theory of Drug Abuse." In: J.D. Lettieri, M. Sayers and W.H. Pearson (eds.), *Theories on Drug Abuse: Selected Contemporary Issues.* (NIDA Research Monograph #30.) Rockville, MD: National Institute of Drug Abuse.

Ianni, A.F. and R.E. Ianni (1990). "Network Analysis." In: P.P. Andrews and M.B. Peterson (eds.), *Criminal Intelligence Analysis.* Loomis, CA: Palmer Enterprises.

Johnson, B.D. and M. Natarajan (1995). "Strategies to Avoid Arrest: Crack Sellers' Response to Intensified Policing." *American Journal of Police* 14(3/4):49-69.

—— M. Natarajan, E. Dunlap and E. Elmoghazy (1994). "Crack Abusers and Noncrack Abusers: A Comparison of Drug Use, Drug Sales and Nondrug Criminality." *Journal of Drug Issues* 24(1):117-141.

Knowles, G.J. (1996). "Dealing Crack Cocaine: A View from the Streets of Honolulu." *FBI Law Enforcement Bulletin* 65(July):1-8.

Krackhardt, D., J. Blythe and C. McGrath (1995). *KrackPlot 3.0. User's Manual.*

Mieczkowski, T. (1994). "The Experiences of Women Who Sell Crack: Some Descriptive Data from the Detroit Crack Ethnography Project." *Journal of Drug Issues* 24(2):227-248.

—— (1992). "Dealing on the Street: The Crew System and the Crack House." *Justice Quarterly* 9(1):151-163.

—— (1988). "Studying Heroin Retailers: A Research Note." *Criminal Justice Review* 13(1):39-44.

—— (1986). "Geeking Up and Throwing Down: Heroin Street Life in Detroit." *Criminology* 24(4):645-666.

Miller, J. (1995). "Gender and Power on the Streets: Street Prostitution in the Era of Crack Cocaine." *Journal of Contemporary Ethnography* 23(4):427-452.

Moore, M.H. (1977). *Buy and Bust: Effective Regulation of an Illicit Market in Heroin.* Lexington, MA: Lexington Books.

Natarajan, M., R. Clarke and B. Johnson (1995). "Telephones as Facilitators of Drug Dealing: A Research Agenda." *European Journal of Criminal Policy* 3(3):137-154.

—— R. Clarke and M. Belanger (1996). "Drug Dealing and Payphones: The Scope for Intervention." *Security Journal* 7(1):245-251 (An earlier version of this paper was published in Japanese in the *Japanese Journal of Crime and Delinquency* 110:63-84.)

—— and M. Belanger (1998). "Varieties of Upper-level Drug Dealing Organizations: A Typology of Cases Prosecuted in New York City." *Journal of Drug Issues* 28(4):1005-1026.

—— (1996). "Use of Folio Views (Hyper Text Program) in Qualitative Research." Paper presented at the American Society of Criminology Meeting, Chicago.

Parsons, T. (1968). *The Structure of Social Action.* New York, NY: Free Press.

Peterson, M. (1994). "Telephone Record Analysis." In: P.P. Andrews and M.B. Peterson (eds.), *Criminal Intelligence Analysis.* Loomis, CA: Palmer Enterprises.

Reuter, P. (1994). "Research on American Organized Crime." In: R. Kell, K. Chin and R. Schatzberg (eds.), *Handbook of Organized Crime in the United States.* Westport, CT: Greenwood Press.

—— and J. Haaga (1989). *The Organization of High-Level Drug Markets: An Exploratory Study.* Santa Monica, CA: RAND.

Sparrow, M. (1991). "The Application of Network Analysis to Criminal Intelligence: An Assessment of the Prospects." *Social Networks* 13(3):251-274.

Smart, G.R. (1980). "An Availability-Proneness Theory Of Illicit Drug Abuse." In: J.D. Lettieri, M. Sayers and W.H. Pearson (eds.), *Theories on Drug Abuse: Selected Contemporary Issues.* (NIDA Research Monograph #30.) Rockville, MD: National Institute on Drug Abuse.

Wasserman, S. and K. Faust (1994). *Social Network Analysis: Methods and Applications.* Cambridge, MA: Cambridge University Press.

Williams, P. (1998). "The Nature of Drug-trafficking Networks." *Current History* 97(618): 54-159.

Williams, T.(1989). *The Cocaine Kids.* Reading, MA: Addison-Wesley.

NOTES

1. The wiretap data were organized in terms of separate conversations between suspected drug dealers. The database originally contained 131 conversations. When inspecting these, 27 were found to involve several individuals, resulting from the use of call waiting and because different people were taking turns on the phone. Such calls were treated in the original transcripts as single conversations, even though they might include one or more "sub-conversations." For the present analysis each "sub-conversation" was treated as a separate "dyadic" conversation with its own record. This yielded a total of 161 conversations of which 10 were very brief — only including greetings — and which were deleted from the database. When this cleaning process was complete, a total of 151 dyadic conversations were obtained for analysis.

2. Two steps were involved in transferring the data from the case records into an electronic format: scanning and character recognition to convert the images to textual form. Once the pages were scanned, several formatting modifications needed to be made before performing the character recognition. These included cleaning the page (getting rid of dark spots), straightening it, and getting a sharper image.

3. In this paper fictitious names have been used to identify the individuals involved.

4. It is assumed here that "sir" is a translation of the Spanish "Señor." Señor is, at times, used a little differently in Spanish than sir is in English.

5. "Simulated annealing" is an optimization routine that maximizes certain positive features (such as nodes that are not too close to each other, edges that are not too long, nodes that do not go through the edges) of graph layout defined by the annealing algorithm (Krackhardt et al., 1995).

6. KrackPlot is a graph layout software for social network analysis.

7. Percent Density = $\dfrac{100 \times na}{\frac{1}{2}n \times(n-1)}$

Where:

na = # of actual relations
n = # of person
½n x(n-1)= # of theoretically possible relations

8. This conclusion is especially subject to the limitation that only data from 12 of the 34 phones tapped were made available for this study. Conversations on the remaining 22 phones might have revealed more contacts among field workers.

PERFORMANCE MANAGEMENT, INDICATORS AND DRUG ENFORCEMENT: IN THE CROSSFIRE OR AT THE CROSSROADS?

by

Nicholas Dorn
DrugScope, London

Abstract: *The climate of public accountability impinges upon managers of enforcement agencies as it does upon managers of all public agencies. This paper explores the prospects for meaningful Performance Indicators (PIs) in relation to drug enforcement. Against those cynical of the desirability or possibility of meaningful PIs in drug enforcement, the author argues that the effort is justified not only in the interests of the manageability and accountability of enforcement agencies but more broadly as an aspect of transparency in policy making and of the balancing of competing claims in a democratic society. Drawing particularly upon U.K. sources, the author illustrates the urgency of the demand for PIs, explores some political, conceptual and technical difficulties in their development, proposes a broad framework within which they may be conceptualised, and advocates a vigorous research engagement with these issues. Challenges include improving the interpretability of established measures such as drug seizures and arrests, evaluating new orthodoxies such as disruption, and developing measures of impacts of interventions and policies in terms of market-related harms and enforcement-related harms. Practical issues include the development of independent, audit-type checks of those PIs that rely on an element of judgement by enforcement officers themselves. The author urges consideration of the merits of a move to multi-year reporting/accounting periods, in order to: (1) concentrate interpretative resources on larger and more robust data sets and, (2) reduce the presentational effort currently distracting senior enforcement managers, policy makers and indeed researchers from the focused and sustained work needed to improve interpretability.*

Crime Prevention Studies, volume 11, pp. 299-318

INTRODUCTION

It is clear even to the sheltered specialist that interest in performance management is by no means restricted to drug policies and their implementation. It represents a much broader, one might say global phenomenon — an aspect of *managerialism*. Developed in the competitive arena of the private sector from the 1960s onwards, sweeping as "value for money" auditing into the public sector in the 1970s and 1980s, and taking hold in seemingly intractable problem areas such as drug policy in the 1990s, performance management and auditing will not lightly be brushed aside. The consequences of their rise in enforcement generally, and in drug enforcement in particular, cannot be prejudged as being either conservative or liberal in terms of political complexion or practical impact (Dorn, 1995). Of course, if done cynically and without critical edge, then performance management may amount to no more than a rubber stamp, a rhetorical gloss on existing strategies and tactics, at best a justification for introduction of "new" measures that have already been politically decided upon. But, if pursued rigorously and with imagination, then the methods and measures adopted may lead to real surprises, open debate, reflection and innovation.

This chapter examines the prospects for meaningful Performance Indicators (PIs) in relation to drug policies at global, European and national levels, with special reference to PIs on drug markets and enforcement.[1] The vantage point from which this is written is that of someone working for an independent agency providing consultancy, research and commissioning advice to government, in the context of the U.K. drug strategy 1998-2008, which places special emphasis on PIs (Cabinet Office, 1999, especially page 19). However, it is not an objective of this chapter to describe existing national, European or international drugs strategies and associated PIs, nor programmes for development of the latter: that would be a worthwhile task but beyond the scope and resources deployed here.[2] Here, in ground-clearing mode, we identify some issues of principle, practice and research that cross boundaries.

The New Right to Know

> It is helpful to think of performance indicators as being used either as dials or tin-openers. Implicit in the use of performance indicators as dials is the assumption that standards of performance are unambiguous; implicit in the use of performance indicators as tin-openers is the assumption that performance is a contestable notion...the majority of indicators are tin-openers rather

than dials; by opening a can of worms, they do not give answers but prompt interrogation and inquiry, and by themselves provide an incomplete and inaccurate picture [Carter, 1994].

It is widely accepted that performance-management information is poorly developed in relation to drug enforcement, that is to say, not only poorly developed in relation to information on prevention and treatment programmes, but also in relation to the expectations of state auditing bodies. This is reflected in a report of the Comptroller and Auditor General (1988) whose conclusions regarding Her Majesty's Customs and Excise (HMC&E) were taken up and indeed amplified by the political process. In the U.K. in 1999 the House of Commons Committee of Public Accounts summarised the situation in the following terms.

> The C&AG's [Comptroller and Auditor General's] Report noted that the Department's [Customs'] key performance indicators do not show the extent to which the Department have any overall impact on the illegal drugs market in the United Kingdom, either in the short or the long run. Increases in drug seizures may indicate that Customs and Excise have seized a greater proportion of the drugs available on the illegal market, or they may reflect a growth in the volume of drugs smuggled. Increases in drugs prevented[3] or organisations dismantled indicators, whilst confirming that some organisations have been prevented from importing drugs into the UK, do not show whether there has been any overall reduction in supply, since other organisations may have stepped in to make up any shortfall... There is a need for better performance measures. [Committee of Public Accounts, 1999, paragraphs 37 and 45:xv-xvi]

This perception is widely held. If agencies cannot generate performance information, then they cannot perceive themselves, or be perceived by others, as professional or properly managed, they cannot demonstrate that they are deploying their resources rationally, and they risk political pillory and economic damage. Consider for example the following exchanges between, on the one hand, Members of Parliament sitting on the Committee of Public Accounts and, on the other hand, the Chairman of the Board of Her Majesty's Customs and Excise, on the question of disruption or dismantling of criminal organisations and its measurement.

Question   ...How many organisations smuggling drugs into this country are there, would you say?

Answer   Well I do not think I could give you an authoritative answer to that, not least because the organisations are constantly shifting. I would guess that the National Investigation Service [of HMC&E] has got some ideas about this because of the work that they are doing, some of which is very sensitive and confidential.

Question Without having some idea — and I understand the confidentiality — of how many there are, how meaningful is a target for performance which talks about organisations dismantling [sic]? Is it a drop in the ocean or is it most of what is out there?...

Answer   I am afraid this is the nature of the difficulty. What you are dealing with is a totally clandestine situation. There is nobody in this country who would be able to give you a total satisfactory answer to the question.

Question We might not have an entirely satisfactory answer but we might be able to grope our way towards one. Do you not think that it is important to try?

Answer   I do think it is important to try which is why we have been trying, and I am sorry that we have not succeeded but we are not backward in this area compared with other law enforcement agencies either here [U.K.] or anywhere else... [Committee Public Accounts, op cit., extracts from paragraphs 116-118:18]

The high-profile interaction from which this extract is taken was widely seen as a dreadful ordeal for HMC&E. In the widespread intake of breath in enforcement circles that followed, enforcement managers became more concerned about the state of play vis-à-vis PIs. It should be emphasised, however, that the pressure for such information comes from within the agencies as well as from the political system.

One of the things that struck me the most when starting to work on these issues has been the forcefulness of the demand from managers of enforcement agencies for more meaningful PIs on the activities that their agencies undertake. As one senior officer put it in conversation, "We *have a right* to know how we are doing." If ever there was a time

when enforcement agencies might have been afraid of informa-
tion/research that might establish cost-effectiveness not only of specific
form of interventions, but also of their activities as a whole vis-à-vis
drug trafficking and other forms of organised crime, then that time is
not now.

Even performance information showing low levels of effectiveness
and cost-effectiveness would be better than no information at all. At
least there would then be a basis for management action. In today's
organisations, seemingly endless effectiveness reviews, reorganisations,
downsizing and restructuring are everyday fare for senior managers:
change has been normalised. But a lack of the information needed to
formulate, direct and underpin such actions paralyses managers. Hence
the new mantra: the right to know, the right to have performance measures in drug enforcement as in many other spheres.

Three Obstacles to Anti-trafficking PIs

What, then, has been holding things up? To this observer, three factors seemed to be in play, one "technical," one "political" and one "conceptual."

The technical factor is largely historical, but none the less still rather
pressing. Due to the seemingly low interest of governments prior to the
mid-1990s in commissioning research on drug markets[4] and due to the
relative recency of evaluation in policing generally,[5] the concepts, in-
struments, systems and data have not been in place to support a rapid
deployment of PIs for drug enforcement.[6] Of course, there are some
private sector enforcement evaluations in the U.S. (as contributors to
this collection show) and some primarily qualitative work in parts of
Europe (see Fijnaut et al., 1998 for an audit from a national point of
view). But it is still early days in the effort to pull this together and to
build upon it the concepts, systems and data necessary to support
broad statements about the effectiveness of drug enforcement. The
demand for PIs has arisen fast and it will take some time for the state
of the art to catch up. While some researchers might say that we should
put most of the available research money into other areas because the
quality of work is more advanced there, such a response only reinforces
the problem. On the contrary, a period of disproportionately high "catch
up" funding to develop PIs on drug enforcement is what is needed.

The second factor that has impeded the development of drug enforcement PIs is a degree of ambivalence among many independent
researchers and, possibly for some, prejudice. It is possible to encounter
a degree of liberal sanguineness at the prospect that the outcomes of
drug enforcement might not be assessed for quite some time. If no

effectiveness data at all were to be forthcoming for enforcement, then resources could be switched to other sectors. No great urgency, from this point of view, for prioritising research and development of anti-trafficking PIs. This "freezing out" approach may be fine as political rough-housing and in-fighting for resources, but it is poor for democracy. Enforcement agencies, as well as citizens (concerning hospital treatment, food safety, etc.) have a right to know.

Allied to this liberal sanguineness is an objection that, if attempts are made to develop PIs for enforcement, then surely the agencies would manipulate the outcomes. Well, maybe they would if they could — but in any case exactly the same questions arise, for example, in relation to medical doctors, their pharmaceutical and IT suppliers, insurance providers, and the whole industry of social and health care. The answer will not be found in an abstract contest of moral virtues, but in full-hearted support for robust forms of PI and independent safeguards in all sectors. Those who suggest it cannot be done should perhaps be invited to rephrase their sentiments (perhaps on a five-point scale, running from "I very much would like it to be done well and soon," through to "I very much would not...").

But *can* it be done? In addressing this question, I move first to conceptual problems, presenting a broad model for contextualising the issues. A sufficiently inclusive model (in analytic terms) may help to provide a common framework of reference for geographically dispersed and professionally diverse teams working on different aspects of PIs and drug policy evaluation. It may also offer jumping-off points for critiques. The central sections of the chapter are concerned with some evident shortcomings facing anti-trafficking PIs. Some practical and methodological suggestions are made for improvement. Lastly I pick up the theme of the title of this chapter and point to some general limits to knowledge.

UNDERSTANDING ENFORCEMENT IN GLOBAL CONTEXTS

In his book *The Prince*, Machiavelli advises that, if the archer wishes to hit a target, then it is necessary to aim above and beyond it. To do this, one has to exert one's force beyond the target. One may not be able to see clearly beyond the target, but that is where one must project one's thoughts if one is not to fall short. With this in mind, the reader is asked to glance at Figure 1. This represents an attempt to analytically model the broad contours of the interaction of policies and outcomes (capable of being represented by PIs), in the context of broader, global[7] issues and the responses of social groups. It admits the potential significance of three facets — broader (global) policies, drug trafficking policies, and policies on drug use(rs) — at the levels of policy formulation, implementation/outputs and outcomes/impacts.

As far as the international picture is concerned, it is clear that trafficking (and hence consumption), anti-trafficking policies and broader policies on organised crime certainly have been much affected by broader, international, politico-economic events such as war, low intensity armed conflicts, crumbling state authority and the arms trade.[8] As far as national policies are concerned, not only drug policies but also wider policies — economic, social welfare, housing policies, etc. (cf. Lenke and Olsson, 1996) — I share with other commentators an emphasis on the implementation of policies, from which much (but not necessarily all) of the "impacts" of policies may be derived.[9] A feedback loop goes from outcomes, back to policies, in recognition of the possibility that, for those who like to think in one-directional causal terms, the statement "outcomes drive policies" sometimes may be as valid a proposition as "policies drive outcomes."[10] For the U.S., for example, and perhaps also in some respects for Europe, the trajectory of drug problems may have driven aspects of policy-making not only on drugs but also on wider aspects of policy. In general, it is a moot point whether some much-focused upon aspects of drug problems — the quantities consumed, for example — have been much impacted upon by drug policies per se. We now attempt to insert into the broad and sweeping framework represented by Figure 1 some specific considerations about the construction and interpretation of PIs.

Advancing Beyond the Fixation on Amounts of Drugs

Questions of quantities of illicit drugs produced, trafficked and consumed have dominated the debates on drug PIs. In the United States, until recently, policy has been assessed in these terms and, particularly, in terms of levels of consumption (Reuter, 1999). However, from the late 1990s onwards, in the U.S. and in many European countries, indicators have been developed in relation to other indicators. The U.S. has developed a set of "cross cutting" indicators that still centre on, but certainly go wider than, drug supply and drug consumption. In Europe, up into the late 1990s, monitoring by the European Union's body — the European Monitoring Centre on Drugs and Drug Addiction — focused on indicators on the consumption side: drugs prevalence, health status, infection rates, etc. (EMCDDA, 1999). Add to this a keen desire at national level in many E.U. Member States to reduce levels of acquisitive crime associated with some patterns of drug use, for which national PIs

Figure 1. Performance Indicators (PIs) in Global Context

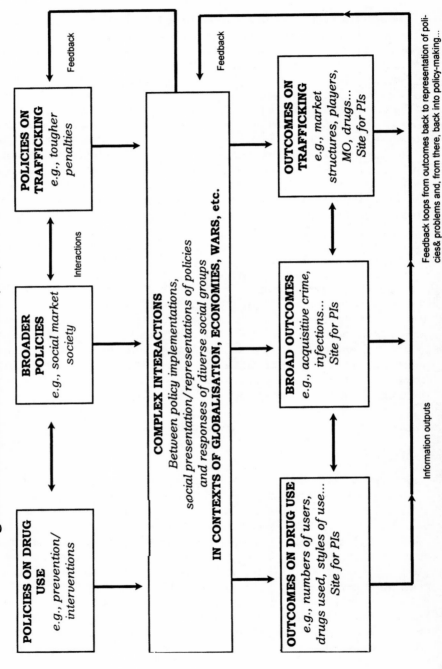

POLICIES ON DRUG USE
e.g., prevention/ interventions

BROADER POLICIES
e.g., social market society

POLICIES ON TRAFFICKING
e.g., tougher penalties

Interactions

Feedback

COMPLEX INTERACTIONS
Between policy implementations, social presentation/representations of policies and responses of diverse social groups
IN CONTEXTS OF GLOBALISATION, ECONOMIES, WARS, etc.

Feedback

OUTCOMES ON DRUG USE
e.g., numbers of users, drugs used, styles of use... Site for PIs

BROAD OUTCOMES
e.g., acquisitive crime, infections... Site for PIs

OUTCOMES ON TRAFFICKING
e.g., market structures, players, MO, drugs... Site for PIs

Information outputs

Feedback loops from outcomes back to representation of policies& problems and, from there, back into policy-making…

have been developed (see, for example, Cabinet Office, 1999:16-17). These "other" concerns and indicators correspond to policy goals of harm reduction at the levels of communities and individuals.

In relation to trafficking at national and international levels, forms of harm *other than* provision of drugs are reasonably well conceptualised by at least some senior enforcement practitioners, as are potential harms of enforcement actions. But these trafficking-related harms have been inadequately formulated by researchers and have not yet been reflected in the form of PIs. This needs to be done.

Reducing Market-related Harms: From Practice to Theory

It is possible to think of outcomes and PIs in relation to, for example, (1) levels of violence in and around trafficking organisations, (2) destabilisation of institutions and communities, and (3) the ability of trafficking organisations to neutralise and subvert enforcement agencies. The latter capacity is a very important consideration for national enforcement agencies in making decisions about which criminal organisation to give the highest priority for action. It seems strange that, at least as far as the U.K. in 1999 was concerned, such important targeting criteria are not reflected in a specific PI, either in relation to anti-trafficking work or anti-serious crime work generally. How can a management system be coherent when its targeting criteria do not correspond to its PIs?

The implication is that output/outcome measures, including, but not restricted to, amounts of drugs, need to be re-developed to reflect the harms that agencies seek to reduce. This would mean working out what aspects of trafficking are *least disliked* and constructing PIs capable of capturing these features. Such thinking is already implicit in many local policies for management of some retail-level drug markets. Here the objective may be to keep them from spilling into public or private areas containing members of social groups who, for one reason or another, are considered especially vulnerable (young children, as far as offers of drugs are concerned; older people and those living on their own, as far as disturbance and fear are concerned).

Police officers are generally sensitive to potential problems of geo-social displacement, and the best officers may (on a very good day) critically appraise alternative courses of action in the light of possible unintended consequences as well as intended consequences (see Hough, this volume). At higher levels, when facing crime organisations, it is normal for enforcement agencies to try to think through the consequences of taking out an important organisation: how will other crimi-

nals react, and in what terms can one evaluate the foreseeable reshuf-
fling? Yet, although such thinking exists in enforcement agencies, the
present set of output measures recognise results only in a much nar-
rower vein.

Disorganisation, Disruption, Dismantlement — and Disinformation

The language of disruption abounds in the U.S., as other contributions to this volume show. For the U.K., during 1999 dismantle-
ment/disruption became a shared or "corporate" PI to be contributed to
by all national enforcement agencies (Dorn and Lee, 1999; Cabinet
Office, 1999:19, eight bullet-point). The question is, what practices does
it describe? And can it be adequately quantified and meaningfully
reported?

The unfortunate impression sometimes gained is that disruption can
come to mean not much more than arrest. For example, at a local level
police may issue figures on numbers of traffickers disrupted in a manner indistinguishable in media reports from figures on arrests. Even
when the concept is deployed a little more selectively, the problems are
huge. For example, it is a commonplace but perplexing observation
among European enforcement people that some trafficking organisers,
once convicted and imprisoned, continue to direct activities from prison.
Where does that put any disruption measures? It would be salutary to
see enforcement agencies reviewing previous years' disruption data and
revising it downwards to take out an element corresponding to suspected trafficking from prison. It is a serious question, using a basis of
adjustment related to the original calculation of the disruption, whether
this should be considered.

Another, equally disturbing question about disruption measures
concerns attempts by more sophisticated criminal organisations to try
to steer enforcement agencies to false conclusions through informants
(who necessarily point both ways), feints and camouflages, bad information and sacrifices of non-essential parts of the organisation (Dorn
et al., 1999). There will be times when an enforcement agency acquires
certain shipments of drugs because the organiser allows that to happen
as a business expense. This concept is widely understood (Committee
on Public Account, op cit.). Likewise, there will be times when personnel
are handed over, in circumstances that are constructed to incriminate
an individual in both trafficking and the organisation. Even when a case
officer "smells a rat" and shares that feeling with supervising senior
officers or (in many parts of Europe) investigating magistrate or prose-

cutor, unless the case officer can quickly find another more rewarding basis for action, he or she will be under pressure to accept the sacrifice. Those captured of course protest their innocence, or quite often, not their innocence, but their indignation at finding themselves "in the frame" for a charge bigger than that they thought they were risking — but then such stories are routine. The overall point is that both the police and traffickers engage in case construction.

Such actions by organisers transfer evidence from themselves and the valuable parts of their organisations to others. This ability actually enhances the capability of organisers to continue in business and is the opposite of what is intended to be measured as disruption/ dismantlement.[11] In such cases, while it would be correct to record seizures, arrests and convictions,[12] the recording of a disruption (temporary), let alone a dismantlement (long term), would be positively misleading. In fact we should be asking ourselves whether a minus score might sometimes be merited. This and other considerations suggest that disruption indicators need careful thought.

How to Define, Count and Validate "Events"

From a methodological point of view, anti-trafficking PIs present three broad problems. There seem at least partial solutions to each of these problems.

The first problem has been illustrated in several ways by the preceding paragraphs. How does one construct criteria that can guide enforcement agencies in knowing how in principle to "count" (identify, verify, quantify) claims such as disruption when these do not have an externally/independently adjudicated basis in the way that a conviction has?[13] In practice, this question has led to the construction of scoring systems, which are negotiated between the various enforcement agencies so as to be "do-able," without incurring undue administrative burdens. Since it falls to the parties involved, there may not be very much that researchers from outside the agencies can do in relation to this process of negotiation. Nevertheless, it seems highly desirable that some independent research input be mandated for this process, so as to raise issues-in-principle about the concepts that may only be implicit in the criteria developed. This may involve, for example, raising issues about potential double-counting (e.g., is it allowable that arrest and disruption data refer to more or less the same, or only to different events?).

Once criteria have been set, the next problem is how to allocate particular cases to PIs. In some cases, this problem does not exist for the enforcement agency because they do not make the key decisions (e.g., convictions), while in other cases (e.g., disruption) the problem is acute. It seems hard to quarrel with the view that such PIs should be "open to fully independent validation" (Committee Public Accounts, op. cit., para 6(v), page vi). At present it seems that this is being done in the U.K. by Her Majesty's Inspectorate of Police. These officers follow up a sub-sample of PI records to confirm that the basis on which they were formulated seems reasonable. This is an understandable approach, but it is based on a rather limited understanding of "independent validation." A more radical approach, which would test the data more directly, would involve presenting case data "blind" to an officer (i.e., one who does not know the way in which it was rated by the original case officer) or to a panel. Of course, this "blind" approach would result in more discrepancies than the "seen" approach. Discrepancies would be investigated by a "data adjudicator" (including genuine outsiders) and data, with explanations, could be re-allocated. Then the PI data for the whole accounting period would be adjusted pro-rata the changes made to the sub-sample.

Multi-year Accounting Periods

The third problem is how to interpret PI data. As mentioned, agency outputs can best be interpreted against data on the total market: drugs not seized, persons not captured, and organizations not disrupted or dismantled, etc. Moreover, if the intention would be to make a year-by-year commentary on the performance of the agencies, which seems to implicit (if only for historical and accounting reasons), then the accuracy of the background data required would have to be consistently high on an annual basis. The reality, however, is that the background data are poorly developed. As a result, the interpretation of anti-trafficking PIs is a challenge that neither the U.S. nor European countries have sorted out. Much work remains to be done.[14]

One practical response is to consider whether three-, five- or even ten-year cycles could improve interpretability. Certainly, it would be easier to fit a trend line to data over five years than over two consecutive years. This interval would be applied to drug amounts (total/sized), organisations (active/disrupted) or persons (involved/removed). Although this would not solve the problems, it would mitigate them. There might be additional advantages in at least partially dispelling the annual anxiety-game of releasing key performance data, looking for the suggestions that it might or might not support, and producing rebuttal statements.

There would also be broader advantages in moving to multi-year cycle. Major policy decisions about strategies and resource allocation, rather than for one year, are usually taken over a three- or five-year cycle. Even if highly reliable and interpretable PI data could be obtained on an annual basis, it is doubtful if the policy system could make much of it, since policy volatility might rise to dysfunctional levels. The planning of the evidence base should be brought into line, in terms of time as well as content, with the requirements of policy making as process. A longer period for non-routine assessment — say five years of so — would result in more interpretable PIs, less argument and better input into policy and resource decisions. Not only enforcement managers, but also audit bodies and politicians, should welcome that.

DISCUSSION: BEYOND CYNICISM

It is clear that drug enforcement PIs have a long and hard road ahead of them. One might ask, will the effort be worthwhile? Before coming to a positive conclusion, we identify a position that goes beyond making a catalogue of the practical difficulties inherent in PIs, and proposes as *a matter of principle* that PIs are useless.

Indeed the danger does exist that the self-imposed and external pressures on governments and enforcement agencies could lead them and their research interlocutors to bluff their way though. A combination of technical virtuosity and public relations bluster could result in performance management in the field of organised crime taking the form of a millennium cult. By burying convenient but dubious assumptions deep within calculations, by using formulae that are abstruse, and by presenting results in forms that are intuitively understandable by few people, producers of PIs could perhaps find sanctuary of a sort.

This would be wrong because, at the end of the day, social auditing is never just a technical matter, since it involves assumptions and judgements that most people would call political. The important thing is make these assumptions and judgements apparent. Citizens in a democracy can then see the limits of expert knowledge and they can pick and mix to develop their own viewpoints and formulate their policy demands.

Some might regard these sentiments as touching but naive. They would point out that, like other signs or discourses that claim to be authoritative, anti-trafficking PIs have postmodern characteristics. They just are themselves, signifying not much else, and certainly not a set of "impacts" on "underlying" drug problems. Rather, performance management is a set of discourses and practices that generate PIs within a stream of other spectacular and mundane signs. The constructions we make and the meanings we grasp in order to move forward are our own:

a foundationalist alternative is not possible. From a postmodern perspective, PIs are never going to be more than "hocus-pocus," and the role of researchers should not be to speak as if they can be "grounded" but to show how tenuous such claims are.

Now it may be that some would think that such critiques could or do contribute to public debates on drugs, trafficking, organised crime, enforcement policies, etc. I hardly think so. On the contrary, such a view is paralysing in practical terms. It seems to me that both enforcement professionals and researchers need to be capable of both forms of professional action — critical and constructive — combining them to "design out" some of the problems in which PIs are currently mired and to make them as meaningful as they can be. This will take years and, along the way, many uncertainties will remain. In the short term, some forms of interpretation, made with the best of intentions and with the most earnest efforts, will no doubt continue to be at best dubious and possibly sometimes misleading. With increasing attention being paid, these problems will become more apparent. Of course this is embarrassing. But it is a necessary phase if conditions are to improve. From the point of view of our freedoms in the long term, what matters is not so much the outcome of specific discussions and decisions on strategies and policies, but rather the reproduction of the conditions — transparency, democracy and accountability — that make open and reasoned discussion, management and policy-making possible.

CONCLUSION: WAYS FORWARD

Performance management and anti-trafficking PIs will often find themselves at the centre of public debate and sometimes, at least, will be a basis for public action. Because of this, they have to be taken seriously, positively and critically. As well as continuing to measure amounts of drugs (drug flows) at various levels of drug markets, PIs should be re-developed to reflect aspects of concern, including:

- Internationally and nationally: ways of reflecting in PIs success in action against those trafficking organisations having the potential to neutralise enforcement agencies and/or to corrupt government and the private sector on a trans-national scale.

- Nationally and regionally: the ability to measure success (or the lack of it) in reducing trafficking-related harms. For example, reduction of violence within and around the trade; reduction in destabilisation of institutions; reduction in penetration of the private sector; and avoiding target-hardening.

- Locally: the measures that describe reduction of trafficking-related harms to communities, e.g., containment of trafficking within areas where it least impinges on vulnerable groups, moulding local drug markets into forms that have the lowest level of associated social harms, minimising negative displacements, and, possibly, describing the consequences of involvement of enforcement agencies in control strategies that run wider than the criminal law (see the Introduction to this volume and, more broadly, Dorn, 1999).

A number of technical improvements in anti-trafficking PIs have been identified. These include:

- In order to improve the interpretability of agency activity and output data, we should move to multi-year cycles instead of 12-month reporting/accounting cycles.
- In order to develop better criteria for "what counts" as an example of "disruption," we should involve independent researchers in the criteria-making process.
- In order to validate PIs more convincingly, we should introduce more rigorous audit techniques, taking sub-samples of disruption PI data, having them re-scored "blind" and then adjusting the whole set.

To these we could add some standard quality assurance processes:

- Review the integrity of the data used in performance management through exercises that involve mounting challenges by joint teams of enforcement officers, auditors and researchers who look for weaknesses and possible improvements.
- In order to come closer to reality and to enhance credibility, the concept of a negative score against at least some PIs should be accepted in principle. Practical procedures should be developed for recording those outcomes that can reasonable be assessed as having a counter-productive element.
- Be prepared to revise PI data for past years, just as economic and other important data are revised, in order to reflect better information as this comes available. Such revisions should be regarded as routine signs of quality assurance, not as problems.

Finally, on interpretability, there is a need to bring the PIs together with other social and economic data within the context of an overarching model of policies and problems. An aim should be to achieve coherence or, to put it in everyday language, to tell a story. What we need is not a variety of anti-trafficking PIs that are expressed (explicitly or implicitly) each in a different framework, but a set that is conceptually coherent. This means broad analytic and conceptual model-building as well as quite focused studies.

Most of these issues require cooperation at national, regional and international levels. So far, there is a limited amount of relevant work at international level. Work has been done on the interpretability of measures relating to drug markets, seizures, etc. (Office of National Drug Control Policy [ONDCP], 1999). For the European Union, the work of the European Police Office (EUROPOL) is understood to be at an "early stage," while up to 1999 that of the European Monitoring Centre on Drugs and Drug Addiction has focused on drug demand issues and indicators (EMCDDA, 1999). On the much broader canvas of "mutual evaluation" by EU Member States of their actions in the context of the fast developing arena of "freedom, security and justice" (European Union, 1997), EUROPOL, together with the national agencies, is becoming more involved in strategic work, with limited co-funding available through E.U. programmes such as *Falcone* or *Oisin*.

We conclude that tying together the opportunities for cooperation at international, European and national levels for research and development of enforcement PIs could be as challenging as doing the research.

Address correspondence to: Nicholas Dorn, DrugScope, 32 Loman Street, London SE1 0EE, United Kingdom. E-mail: nicholas@drugscope.org.uk; www.drugscope.org.uk

REFERENCES

Cabinet Office (1999). *Tackling Drugs to Build a Better Britain. United Kingdom's Anti-Drugs Co-Ordinator's Annual Report 1998/99; United Kingdom Performance Targets for 2008 and 2005; National Plan 1999/2000.* London, UK: Central Office of Information.

Caulkins, J., C. Rydell, S. Everingham, J. Chiesa and S. Bushway (1998). *An Ounce of Prevention, A Pound of Uncertainty: The Cost-Effectiveness of School-Based Drug Prevention Programs.* Santa Monica, CA: RAND Corporation.

Carter, N. (1994). "Performance Indicators: Backstreet Driving or Hands Off Control?" In: D. McKevitt and A. Lawton, (eds.), *Public Sector Management: Theory, Critique and Practice*. London, UK: Open University.

Committee of Public Accounts, House of Commons (1999). *Fifteen Report: H. M. Customs and Excise: The Prevention of Drug Smuggling (HC 35)*. London, UK: Her Majesty's Stationery Office.

Comptroller and Auditor General (1998). *HM Customs and Excise: The Prevention of Drug Smuggling*. (Ordered by the House of Commons to be printed on 13 July 1998, HC 854 of Session 1997-98.) London, UK: The Stationary Office.

Dorn, N. (ed.) (1999). *Regulating European Drug Problems: Administrative Measures and Civil Law in the Control of Drug Trafficking, Nuisance and Use*. The Hague, NETH: Kluwer Law International.

—— (1995). "A European Analysis of Drug Enforcement." In: G. Estievenart (ed.), *Policies and Strategies to Combat Drugs in Europe: Framework for a New European Strategy to Combat Drugs?* Dordrecht, NETH: Martinus Nijhoff.

—— and M. Lee (1999). "Drugs and Policing in Europe: From Low Streets to High Places." In: N. South (ed.), *Drugs: Cultures, Controls and Everyday Life*. London, UK: Sage.

—— L. Oette and S. White (1998). "Drugs Importation and the Bifurcation of Risk: Capitalization, Cut Outs and Organised Crime." *British Journal of Criminology* 38(4):537-560.

European Monitoring Centre on Drugs and Drug Addiction (EMCDDA) (1999). *Report on the State of the Drugs Problem in the European Union*. Lisbon, PORT. (EMCDDA outputs are accessible via www.emcdda.org)

European Union (1997). *Consolidated Versions of the Treaty on European Union and the Treaty Establishing the European Community*. Luxembourg, LUX: Office for Official Publications of the European Communities.

Farrell, M., A. Vesrter, M. Nilson, P. Metrino, M. Davol and S. Howes (1999). *Reviewing Current Practice in Drug Substitution Treatment in Europe*. Lisbon, PORT: EMCDDA (with National Addiction Centre London and Observatorio Epidemiologico Rome), pp. 38.

Fijnaut, C., F. Bovenkerk, G. Bruinsma and H. Van de Bunt (1998). *Organised Crime in the Netherlands*. The Hague, NETH: Kluwer Law International.

Lenke, L. and B. Olsson (1996). "Sweden: Zero Tolerance Wins the Argument?" In: S. Dorn, J. Jepsen and E. Savona (eds.), *European Drug Policies and Enforcement*. London, UK: Macmillan.

MacCoun, R. and P. Reuter (in press). *Alternatives to the Drug War: Learning from Other Vices, Times and Places.* New York, NY: Cambridge University Press.

Office of National Drug Control Policy (ONDCP) (1999). *Performance Measure of Effectiveness: Implementation and Findings.* Washington, DC: Executive Office of the President of the United States. (Accessible via www.whitehousedrugpolicy.gov/policy/99pme/contents.html).

Reiner, R. and S. Spencer (eds.) (1993). *Accountable Policing: Effectiveness, Empowerment and Equity.* London, UK: Institute for Public Policy Research.

Reuter, P. (1999). "What Have We Learnt and What Could We Know?" Presentation to ISDD Seminar on Research on Drug Policies, held at the United Kingdom Anti Drug Coordination Unit, Cabinet Office, London, 1 July 1999.

NOTES

1. A definitional point: in principle, the term "drug markets" is used throughout in the wider sense, meaning *all* levels of market from production, transit, distribution, retail, etc. None of these "levels" may match the national administrative level all that well. Most drug strategies have a strong national theme and anti-trafficking PIs are being developed at this level. But, for practical reasons the main focus here will be on the national level.

2. What can be said in summary is that, at national level, many developed countries are grappling with the range of problems identified in the present chapter. Their national drugs strategies are devoting small but increasing amounts of resources to focused research on PIs and vexed issues of their interpretability (ONDCP, 1999; EMCDDA, 1999; Cabinet Office, 1999).

3. In the parlance of Her Majesty's Customs and Excise, "Drugs prevented" is a hybrid measure consisting of two components, (1) amount seized in a particular operation and (2) the amount that an officer estimates would also have been trafficked by that organisation over the next year. It is expressed annually in aggregate form in money value (at retail level) of all drugs prevented. Since it is not used by other agencies it is likely to be phased out, partly in response to unease over its semi-subjective basis (Custom's Officers' judgements). However, currently fashionable disrupted/dismantled measures have a similar basis.

4. There seems to have been a quickening of international interest at that time. See, for example, UN International Drug Control Programme, 1994; present status of knowledge on the illicit drug industry, discussion paper for ACC Sub-Committee on Drug Control, Vienna, 5-7 September, pp 45. Savona et al. (eds.), 1994. Cocaine markets and law enforcement in Europe, Final Report, Rome: UNICRI, pp 410.

5. Not forgetting the linking of evaluation ("technical") questions of democracy ("political"): see Reiner and Spencer, 1993.

6. Actually, the situation is not that much better in relation to PIs on demand reduction activities, despite a the better level of evaluation in the fields of drug education (Caulkins et al., 1999 look at cost effectiveness of U.S. programmes) and treatment (for ways into this literature in Europe, see Farrell et al., 1999). The relationships between, on the one hand, evaluation results about demand reduction activities and, on the other hand, their contributions to broader drug problems (taking into account contexts, trends and factors generally left outside the design of the evaluation) are only loosely established (EMCDDA, 1999).

7. The term "global" is used here in the French sense, meaning a wide span of issues as well as geographical scope (global/local).

8. The Far East, Latin America, Afghanistan and, for the 1990s, the Balkans, at various times come to mind.

9. It is presumed that the symbolic aspects of policies may have significance for the actions of some actors, who may respond to the public representation of policies — or representations as mediated by others — as much as, or more than, to any direct experiences of policy as implemented. Obviously this may apply to the public at large, or particular socio-political groups, but it could also apply to drug traffickers and others involved in illegal markets. One hypothesis might be that it is in one sense the least "professional" or "organised" criminals who take the greatest account of symbolic aspects (for example, either seeking to evade enforcement that is presented as "tough," or seeking close encounters as a form of challenge or game). The more "organised" players (e.g., risk minimisers, in terms of the research of Dorn et al., 1998) may be less drawn into the symbolic aspects of policies.

10. The work of Reuter (1999) and MacCoun and Reuter (in press) is acknowledged.

11. Here the term "disruption" is used to refer to short term interruption of some activities of the criminal organisation, and long-term dismantlement or cessation of activities by removal of its central resources.

12. It seems that political sentiment favours attention to prison years as a potential indicator of apprehension of organisers (Fifteenth Report, op. cit.). The dangers of this are clear enough. If society wants prison years, then this is the gift that organisers will offer.

13. Here it is not being claimed that all jury decisions are correct, or that they are not influenced by the enforcement agencies that construct most evidence (traffickers, as noted above, construct some, in addition to judges and lawyers); only that the decision, having been fought for by all sides, is arrived at through the judicial process.

14. In the U.K., in the context of the drug strategy, a high-level, multi-agency Supply Side Research Board was formed in 1999 to agree to lines of research to be tendered in the U.K. and possibly in some cases carried out in cooperation with international and European partners. The main requirements (knowledge gaps) identified as of 1999 included sizing drug markets, understanding the middle market, charting higher drug flows, investigating cost effectiveness of specific types of interventions and, eventually, synthesising a model of markets in interaction with controls.

EPILOGUE:
CONNECTING DRUG POLICY AND
RESEARCH ON DRUG MARKETS

by

Peter Reuter
School of Public Affairs and
Department of Criminology
University of Maryland, USA

Over the last two decades a substantial body of field research has accumulated describing characteristics of various low-level markets for illicit drugs, primarily cocaine and heroin. At least for a few American cities, a good deal is known about who retails these drugs, the size and stability of the organizations in which they work, their careers, the prices they charge, and the incomes they earn. A much smaller body of research has examined various aspects of high-level trafficking.

A principal, perhaps dominant, motivation for this research is that it can inform policy and lead to reductions in the nation's drug problems. It is unclear that the existing work, summarized in the first half of this chapter, does so; the second half of the chapter describes how a more policy-relevant research agenda might be developed.

WHAT HAS BEEN LEARNED?

I focus on retail markets because for higher-level trafficking there exist so few studies that one could only list their findings individually rather than draw consistent conclusions. Only the major substantive results, with scarcely any reference to methods are presented. The review is limited to studies that have been interested in more than just prices.

The price literature is reviewed in Caulkins and Reuter (1998). The principal finding about prices is that they are not only high (with heroin more than 50 times the price of gold) but also remarkably variable across places such as cities and neighborhoods (see e.g., Caulkins, 1995); they even vary within a single market location in short periods of time (see e.g., Weatherburn and Lind, 1997). Intriguing as these findings are for those interested in market structure, no one has yet attempted to explain what kinds of markets would generate these patterns of variation, though Caulkins (1997) has presented a model of diffusion of cocaine across metropolitan markets that begins the research task.

Some of the principal findings about drug markets are:

Monopoly control is rare. Prior to 1980, it was widely believed that the Mafia had dominated the major illegal markets such as those for bookmaking, loansharking and even for heroin importation into New York City until the late 1960s (e.g., Cressey, 1969). Despite finding that some dealers within the U.S. have enormous incomes and traffic in large quantities, no researcher has found evidence, except on the most local basis (e.g., a few blocks), that a dealer organization has the ability to exclude others or to set prices,[1] the hallmarks of market power (Katz and Rosen, 1994; chapter 13).

Even at the trafficker level, market power seems elusive. Notwithstanding references to the Medellin and Cali "cartels," these seem to be only loose syndicates of independent entrepreneurs who sometimes collaborate but who also have to compete with other, smaller, Colombian smuggling enterprises (Clawson and Lee, 1998: Epilogue). The small share of the retail price accounted for by all activities up to import is strong, but not conclusive, evidence of competition at this level[2]. The continuing decline of prices over an almost twenty-year period at all levels of the market suggests that, if market power ever existed, it has now been dissipated. Thus, there is no level at which policy makers need be worried that tough enforcement will lead to price declines because a cartel is broken, a matter raised thirty years ago by Schelling in his classic paper on organized crime (Schelling, 1967). The explanation for the lack of market power may also be contained in Schelling's paper; the Mafia may have been collecting "rents" on behalf of corrupt police departments that had exclusive jurisdiction and little external scrutiny.[3] Those departments are now less systemically corrupt and face substantial oversight from federal investigative agencies, which was lacking until recently.

Retail employees now have very low earnings. In 1988 in Washington, D.C. low-level drug dealers were estimated to earn an average of $30 per hour, four times their legitimate wage rate (Reuter, et al., 1990). However, by the mid-1990s a number of research studies reported hourly earnings apparently well below the minimum wage (e.g., Caulkins et al., 1999; Bourgois, 1995). This is broadly consistent with the assumption that the markets are competitive. In the 1980s there were rents for being an early entrant into a cocaine market characterized by very high levels of violence; the returns may have also been merely the accounting returns to survival in that market. These rents have been eroded by the maturing of the market, while measured incomes may be lower because of the reduction in violence and what might be called "barriers to exit." That is, retail level workers, now mostly in their 30s with more than a decade of addiction and extensive careers of jail, have difficulty in finding alternative employment, legal or criminal.

That most low-level sellers are frequent users of the drugs they sell is a distinctive and overwhelmingly important feature of cocaine and heroin markets. Users have lower costs than non-users in markets in which a principal cost element is time of exposure to arrest. Whereas the drug-abstinent dealer must sell all of his bundles in order to realize his returns, the user obtains the same returns by selling a smaller number of bundles and retaining the remainder for own use. This strategy reduces the arrest risk associated with a given return. Users are also more likely to have already been convicted of drug offenses and thus lose fewer legitimate work opportunities as a consequence of an additional arrest.

Structure and conduct varies across space, time and drugs. Some markets have large, stable distribution organizations, while others are predominantly serviced by individual dealers with only opportunistic relationships to other participants. These different structures may be the result of: markets passing through phases (initiation, expansion, maturity); the level and form of enforcement; and characteristics of the drug or of the users. Johnson, Dunlap and Tourigny (this volume) assert that police targeting has led to the demise of "vertically integrated, relatively large crack distribution groups controlled by one or two dealers who benefit from the labor of 15 or more people." The difference between crack and powder cocaine markets in the 1980s may have been primarily a consequence of the fact that the crack market was initially dominated by very young males, who were more willing to engage in violence than those who serviced the powder cocaine and heroin markets, and less reliable as commission agents. Aging of sellers may lead to less violence and again to more stable, though small, organizations. The same result can follow simply from a selection effect: the more violent sellers have higher probability of exit over time because they are at greater risk of death and incarceration themselves.

Immigrants play an important role. The European literature is particularly rich and consistent on this issue. Immigrant groups are prominent among drug dealers in almost all wealthy nations in Western Europe. Killias (this volume) shows that the role of Albanians in the Swiss market extends well beyond drug importation. Ruggiero (this volume) supplements this finding through his study of the source-country population, revealing that drug dealing and importation are important activities for immigrants. In the U.S., despite the dominance of foreign nationals in the importation of cocaine and heroin, the evidence on immigrant participation in retailing is inconsistent. At least two of the most prominent groups in importation (Colombian and Chinese) play a much smaller role in street selling. In the U.S., minorities provide an alternative underclass cut out of mainstream of economic opportunity in the same way as immigrants in Europe.

Immigrants have advantages both in importing and retailing. In the source countries they have better knowledge of potential sellers and opportunities for corruption. In the U.S. their communities are less cooperative with the police. Even language can be a major asset. For example, few police departments are able to conduct effective wiretaps or other electronic surveillances of people speaking various Chinese languages. Immigrants have better opportunities for exit and weaker licit market opportunities than most of the native population. Continuing immigration is thus likely to serve as a source of new entrepreneurs and reduce the effectiveness of enforcement interventions. This situation may have been the case with organized crime and Italian immigration in the early part of the twentieth century.

Retailing is characterized by low trust. Whether it be from product impurities, violence, or police action instigated by informants, dealers and customers operate in an environment of extraordinary riskiness. Loyalty ought to be a highly valued quality, much cultivated and rewarded as it is in the diamond business, another market with few enforceable legal contracts. Quite the contrary, even within extended families, seems to be true for cocaine and heroin. Perhaps this reflects desperation of customer needs, the erratic behavior of people who use cocaine frequently and the incentives to inform created by intense enforcement and lengthy sentences. Loyalty is simply an implausible attribute in those circumstances.[4]

This lack of loyalty manifests itself in a number of ways. Akhtar and South (this volume) refer to how "lower price wins over loyalty," a finding that also puzzled me when I was interviewing mid-to-high-level cocaine and marijuana dealers in the mid-1980s (Reuter and Haaga, 1989). While every dealer we interviewed proudly emphasized the high quality of his product and service, each thought a customer would desert as soon as he found a lower-price source. Even kinship ties seem weak in face of these threats. The recent finding (e.g., Riley, 1997) that customers have multiple sources is yet another manifestation of this response to uncertainty. The high-level network analyzed by Natarajan (this volume), reflecting the very rapid turn-over in high level traffickers, at least in the United States, hints at this kind of avoidance of dependence on a single supplier at high levels.

These factors jointly help explain why cocaine and heroin markets are characterized by small, short-lived, vertically unintegrated and technologically unsophisticated sole proprietorships that generate great violence and disorder. This has an important strategic implication: investigations of high-level traffickers are not only likely to be challenging, because of the lack of many subordinates with access to the principal, but also have to be justified on grounds of condign punishment rather than any distinctive effect on the availability of drugs.

MOTIVATING RESEARCH ON MARKETS

I can identify three distinct motives for research on drug markets.

1. Prurient curiosity, a powerful motive for studying a phenomenon as large and subversive as drug distribution. That curiosity is served by more journalistic books such as Simon and Burns' *The Corner* (1996) and accessible ethnographies such as Bourgois (1995) and Williams (1989).

2. Scientific interest in the role of law in markets. Illicit drugs are, ultimately, consumer goods, and like other goods in modern societies they are provided primarily through markets. Illegal drug markets lack some of the principal mechanisms that facilitate modern commercial markets. Learning how markets work when the government and courts aim to suppress rather than support them may provide insights for those interested in law and economics. This is not likely to generate much funding and seems a stronger motivation for the National Science Foundation than for the National Institute of Justice or the National Institute on Drug Abuse, the principal funders in this field.[5]

3. Raising the effectiveness of enforcement, which aims not only to lower the availability of drugs but also to reduce the harms associated with these markets. The relevant harms include: violence, corruption, disorder around market places, illegal income, the size distribution of that income, and the cumulative number of participants, especially the number who end up with felony records. That is, enforcement should not only aim to reduce drug use but also to punish those who use violence as an element of their conduct; to make corruption risky enough for both dealers and officials so that few corrupt transactions are consummated; to prevent the accumulation of large fortunes; and to protect juveniles from the temptations of drug dealing as well as drug use.

Research might help policy in at least three ways:

(1) Developing measures of effectiveness. Eck and Gersh (this volume) tentatively propose as an indicator the number of organizations destroyed, which is similar to the measure in the latest *Performance Measurement Effectiveness* system developed by the Office of National Drug Control Policy (ONDCP) (1998). The value of that measure depends on the organization of the market as a whole. If dealing enterprises are truly ephemeral, this measure may capture little of consequence, though it is certainly no more myopic than maximizing the number of arrests or quantity of drugs seized.

(2) Reconceptualizing the problem. How do drug markets, both as places and as mechanisms for distribution, adversely affect society? The much cited Boston Youth Gun Project, concerned with suppressing homicide among young males in a poor section of Boston, came in part from an understanding of how they acquired guns and the transience of explicit markets for firearms (Kennedy et al., 1996). That project provides an exemplar of how detailed studies of markets may alter the way the problem is viewed by enforcement agencies.

(3) Choosing among methods of reducing drug markets. Discretion in policing surely reaches its extreme in drug enforcement; the doubling of marijuana-possession arrests between 1992 and 1997 (to 675,000) in the face of flat usage of the drug[6] is just the most recent manifestation of this power. Police in a major city can rapidly increase drug arrests if they choose. What is important is where and when they focus their activity, their choice between buyer and seller, and how aggressively they pursue low-visibility selling, etc. Market studies focused on dealer conduct can help inform these decisions.

A RESEARCH AGENDA

A characteristic of the research in this area, as in many others, is that policy implications are drawn from studies, which were simply not designed for that purpose. For example, Rengert et al., (this volume), conclude that "local" demand should be reduced through increased treatment, better employment opportunities, etc. No doubt these are reasonable propositions, but they are not implications of the research reported in the paper, which shows only that there are limits to what can be accomplished through enforcement, not that other programs can do more. Policy questions have to be built into the research design, not grafted on at the end.

The starting point for a policy-research agenda should be identification of the decisions that are to be informed. One line of writing, particularly associated with Kleiman (1992; chapter 6), considers what highly rational enforcement agencies would need to know in order to reduce drug use, drug selling and associated harms. These writings should be treated as prescriptive rather than positive analyses, since there is no way to show that enforcement agencies have such clear strategic aims.

Research on policing generally can provide a model here. It has only been through an understanding of the dynamics of policing itself, such as the high discretion inherent in the individual officer, the reliance on community for information and the norms of police, that it has been possible to identify the central issues and capacities of police departments and thus what will be useful research.

The same has not yet been accomplished for drug enforcement. Is it likely that policy will be influenced by the development of a taxonomy of dealing organizations, the subject of many articles in this area? Perhaps whether to use "buy and bust" to work "up the chain" in a particular market should reflect whether the organizations in this market are "corporate" or "freelance," to use a common terminology (e.g., Johnson et al., this volume) but no research has described decision-making by enforcement agencies in order to determine how these decisions are made.

Indeed, for a host of reasons (the glamour of large seizures, condign punishment of those who apparently profit most from the trade, etc.), agencies will attempt to apprehend those who deal in larger quantities and to seize drugs in larger bundles. In an immature market it is possible that the removal of a few dealers will substantially reduce the efficiency of the market, as measured by price dispersion and search time. For mature markets such as those for cocaine, heroin and marijuana in large American cities in the late 1990s, it is implausible that the removal of any small number of dealers could have such an impact. Additional research on market structure is hardly needed to make this point, though Kleiman argues that neighborhood markets may indeed be quite fragile and thus affected by the elimination of a small number of dealers, as he found in the town of Lynn, Massachusetts in the mid-1980s (Kleiman, 1988).

It is useful to note here just how many persons are involved in the drug trade. Total revenues are estimated to be $50 billion (ONDCP, 1997). If average earnings of a full time participant is $50,000 per annum, well above recent estimates, then the market supports one million Full Time Equivalents (FTE). Many participants are only part-time; and, assuming that there are 1.5 participants for each FTE, that produces a total of 1.5 million people regularly involved in selling activities. It seems likely then that in any large city one would have to remove many hundreds of dealers to have an effect.

Enforcement agencies do seem to have accepted the value of making markets more discreet (e.g., by driving them indoors) —even if that makes further enforcement more difficult — and of reducing the violence associated with retailing. Studies of markets that allow the assessment of how well different enforcement strategies accomplish these goals may have considerable value.

Johnson et al., (this volume) claim that: "Extensive investment in crime control has not had — and probably never will have — important measurable impacts upon drug use patterns, drug selling patterns or prices of illicit drugs in the nation's inner cities." This is a strong policy conclusion that requires what we transparently do not have, namely an understanding of how enforcement interacts with price-and search-time determination. It cannot be established by observational research alone but requires analysis of the relationship across time and space between enforcement and prices. It is also contradicted by the Arrestee Drug Abuse Monitoring System (ADAM) finding that New York City arrestees were much more likely to report not having been able to score on at least one occasion in the past month than arrestees in cities with apparently less vigorous street-level enforcement. Moreover, even if we find that current enforcement has limited impacts, that doesn't say much about enforcement based on tipping models and using direct communication with offenders to shape behavior. But ethnographic studies such as those carried out by Johnson and colleagues (see references in Johnson et al., this volume), if focused on the process of price determination at the individual level, can help the development of models for this analysis.

CONCLUSION

If this field of study is to grow, researchers must establish the utility of their work with law enforcement agencies. This is not merely to generate more research funds but also because access to data for any but the lowest levels of the market requires assistance from the agencies. Adler (1985) was able to describe some of the characteristics of higher-level cocaine markets in their infancy through ethnographic work that had a largely accidental origin. Fuentes (1998) a mid-level police officer, was able to obtain interesting interviews with Colombian traffickers, for his doctoral dissertation, through the Drug Enforcement Administration, perhaps because of his credentials as an enforcement officer. An active research agenda will require more predictable modes of entry. The agencies are not simply expressing prejudice against academic researchers by screening so heavily. Providing researcher access is both time-consuming and risky in terms of loss of authority and privacy-protected information. They will need to be persuaded by a clearer articulation of the policy value of this work.

Address correspondence to: Peter Reuter, School of Public Affairs, University of Maryland, College Park, MD 20742.

Acknowledgments: I would like to acknowledge most helpful comments from Jonathan Caulkins, Mark Kleiman and Robert MacCoun.

REFERENCES

Adler, P. (1985). *Wheeling and Dealing: An Ethnography of an Upper Level Dealing and Smuggling Community.* New York, NY: Columbia University Press.

Bourgois, P. (1995). *In Search of Respect: Selling Crack in El Barrio.* New York, NY: Cambridge University Press.

Caulkins, J.P. (1997). "Modeling the Domestic Distribution Network for Illicit Drugs." *Management Science* 43(10):1364-1371.

—— (1995). "Domestic Geographic Variation in Illicit Drug Prices." *The Journal of Urban Economics* 37(1):38-56.

—— (1990). "The Distribution and Consumption of Illicit Drugs: Some Mathematical Models and Their Policy Implications." Doctoral dissertation in operations research, MIT, Cambridge, MA.

—— B.D. Johnson, A. Taylor and L. Taylor (1999). "What Drug Dealers Tell Us About Their Costs of Doing Business." *Journal of Drug Issues* 29(2):323-340.

—— and P. Reuter (1998) "What Can We Learn from Drug Prices?" *Journal of Drug Issues* 28(3):593-612.

Clawson, P. and R. Lee (1998). *The Andean Cocaine Industry.* New York, NY: St. Martin's Press.

Cressey, D. (1969). *Theft of a Nation.* New York, NY: Harper and Row.

Fuentes, R. (1998). "Life of a Cell: Managerial Practice and Strategy in Colombian Cocaine Distribution in the United States." Doctoral dissertation, City University of New York, New York, NY.

Katz, M. and H. Rosen (1994). *Microeconomics* [2nd ed.]. Burr Ridge, IL: Irwin.

Kennedy, D., A. Piehl and A. Brega (1996). "Youth Violence in Boston: Gun Markets, Serious Youth Offenders and a Use-Reduction Strategy." *Law and Contemporary Problems* 59(1):147-195.

Kleiman, M. (1992). *Against Excess: Drug Policy for Effects.* New York, NY: Basic Books.

—— (1988). "Crackdowns: The Effects of Intensive Enforcement on Retail Heroin Dealing." In: M. Chaiken (ed.), *Street Level Enforcement: Examining the Issues.* Washington, DC: National Institute of Justice.

Office of National Drug Control Policy (1998). *Performance Measures of Effectiveness System: A System for Assessing the Performance of the National Drug Control Strategy.* Washington, DC.

Reuter, P. and J. Haaga (1989). *The Organization of High-Level Drug Markets: An Exploratory Study.* Santa Monica, CA: RAND.

—— R. MacCoun and P. Murphy (1990). *Money from Crime: A Study of the Economics of Street Level Drug Dealing.* Santa Monica, CA: RAND.

Riley, K.J. (1997). *Crack, Powder Cocaine, and Heroin: Drug Purchase and Use Patterns in Six U.S. Cities.* Washington, DC: National Institute of Justice and Office of National Drug Control Policy.

Schelling, T. (1967). "Economic Analysis of Organized Crime." In: President's Commission on Law Enforcement and the Administration of Justice, *Task Force Report Organized Crime.* Washington, DC: US Government Printing Office

Simon, D. and E. Burns (1996). *The Corner.* New York, NY: Broadway Books.

Varian, H. (1993). *Intermediate Economics: A Modern Approach* (3rd ed.). New York, NY: W.W. Norton.

Weatherburn, D. and B. Lind (1997). "The Impact of Law Enforcement Activity on a Heroin Market." *Addiction* 92(5):555-570.

Williams, T. (1989). *The Cocaine Kids.* Reading, MA: Addison Wesley.

NOTES

1. The best evidence against control is simply the ease with which new sellers enter and the speed with which dealers depart. There may be rents for various capacities but certainly no power to exclude.

2. If demand is inelastic with respect to price, then a seller with market power can increase revenues and decrease costs by cutting production until reaching a level at which the demand is elastic. Though the demand for cocaine and heroin may have elasticity of greater than one with respect to final price at current levels, it is very likely that that elasticity is less than one with respect to high-level prices, though there are extreme models of price mark-up from import to trafficking that would yield a different result (see Caulkins, 1990).

3. "Economic rent is defined as those payments to a factor of production that are in excess of the minimum payments necessary to have that factor supplied" (Varian, 1993).

4. Caulkins (personal communication) suggests another, more technical factor. The instability of drug markets makes repeat transactions less likely; that encourages defection. In addition, because of drug use and other factors that lead to continued criminal involvement, this is a population with a high discount rate. That, in turn, encourages defection.

5. Perhaps illegal drug markets can inform other disciplines broadly; I am not well enough read to venture an opinion on this.

6. Use has increased among adolescents, as measured by either the National Household Survey on Drug Abuse (NHSDA), Monitoring the Future or Arrestee Drug Abuse Monitoring system. However, the NHSDA also provides data on adults; rates have declined for those over 24 years of age and the net effect is a flat total prevalence since 1990.

Printed in the United States
200879BV00003B/370-390/A